BURT FRANKLIN: RESEARCH AND SOURCE WORKS SERIES #233
Theater & Drama Series #6

THEATRICAL RECORDER

VOL. I.

Costume of Mrs Jordan, in
Matrimony.

THE

THEATRICAL RECORDER

BY

THOMAS HOLCROFT

VOL. I.

BURT FRANKLIN: RESEARCH AND SOURCE WORKS SERIES #233
Theater & Drama Series #6

BURT FRANKLIN
NEW YORK

Published By
BURT FRANKLIN
235 East 44th St.
New York, N.Y. 10017

ORIGINALLY PUBLISHED
LONDON: 1805
Reprinted 1968

Printed in U.S.A.

ADVERTISEMENT.

THE plan and conduct of The Theatrical Recorder appear thus far to have given satisfaction. No complaints have been made, except the following :

That more ought to be said, concerning the theatrical news of the day :

That, instead of the monthly plates of Costume, it would be more desirable to have a representation of striking scenes :

That the likenesses of performers were not given; of this however there has been but one complainant :

And that the Art of Acting would greatly facilitate the progress of students, were it a separate work.

The plan of The Theatrical Recorder is intended to be complete, with respect to every thing passing in the theatrical world, which is of a nature to be at all times interesting. To instruct, to preserve a vein of pleasantry, and in every department to afford either information or amusement, without descending to practise any of the means which have but too frequently degraded periodical publications, is the design in which the Editor began this work.

Trifles, that are forgotten almost before they are read, tales, that spread detraction, flippant remarks, and praise or blame, which can be supposed to originate in any wrong motives, have been continually and carefully avoided.

In the decorations, a particular attention has been paid to utility. Pretensions have frequently been made to exhibit striking scenes in plays, and to give the likenesses of performers in their favorite characters; but it has rarely happened that either of these has been done with effect. In the best resemblances of this kind, strong caricature has generally prevailed; and scenes from plays have seldom deserved a moment's attention, from the man of taste.

The plates of Costume, in this work, claim the merit of informing the theatrical student how his character ought to be dressed; and preserve, to those who philosophize on the variations of fashion, the dress of the times.

The heads of authors, that have hitherto been given, are taken from plates believed to be authentic, and accompanied with decorations, by which these authors are intended to be characterized, each according to his genius. An artist, H. Thomson, R. A. whose superior talents of this kind are well known, has given the designs; nor will they be passed with neglect, by the true connoisseur.

In the plates of theatrical dresses, it has not been pretended to give the likenesses of persons by whom they were worn; though such likenesses have frequently been at least as good as when such pretensions, in many cases, have been made.

To the Treatise on the Art of Acting, and to the Essay on Dramatic Composition, the author has bestowed peculiar attention, and is determined to persevere in his endeavors.

As the work increases, it will be his constant effort to make it the most complete body of dramatical knowledge, and delightful entertainment, that has hitherto appeared, on this subject.

THE
THEATRICAL RECORDER:

BY

THOMAS HOLCROFT.

London :
Printed by C. Mercier and Co. No. 6, Northumberland-court,
Where the Work may be procured;
And at all the Booksellers;
And published for the Author, by H. D. Symonds, Paternoster-row

1805.

THE

TENDER SISTERS:

A COMEDY,

IN THREE ACTS,

TRANSLATED FROM

THE GERMAN OF GELLERT.

DRAMATIS PERSONÆ.

CLEON.

MAGISTER, or Master of Arts, his Brother.

SIEGMUND, the Lover of CHARLOTTE.

DAVENPORT *, the Lover of JULIA.

Mr. SIMON, his Guardian.

CHARLOTTE, CLEON's eldest Daughter.

JULIA, her Sister.

SCENE, Germany; perhaps Leipsic, but no particular place is mentioned.

TIME, Twelve Hours.

---

* *The German name is* Damis, *which is altered for the sake of sound.* Magister *frequently designates a teacher, in or out of a University, but of a superior order. The names given to the daughters, by* GELLERT, *are* Lottchen *and* Julchen.

THE

TENDER SISTERS:

A COMEDY.

~~~~~

ACT I.

SCENE I.—CLEON, CHARLOTTE.

Charlotte.

MR. Davenport is here, my dear father, and breakfast is ready in the garden: pray come.

Cleon. Where is Mr. Davenport?

Charl. Conversing with Julia.

Cleon. Is it disagreeable to thee, child, that I have invited him to spend the day with us? Thou knowest why: does it affect thee? Dear child, I am grieved for thee: thou art the eldest sister, and shouldst have been married first; but——

Charl. Grieved, Sir! Why grieve? Why should I marry before Julia? I am a few years older, I grant, but she is much the handsomest. A husband so wealthy, kind, and virtuous as Mr. Davenport, may justly give the preference where it is due. I think his alliance an honour to myself, am rejoiced at my sister's good fortune, and justly satisfied with my own.

Cleon. If these are thy serious thoughts, child, thou art a sweet girl! With little pretensions to learning, thou speakest with more wisdom than my sententious scholastic brother.

Charl. I have your love, my dear father; and, so little have I to boast, that love is more perhaps than I deserve.

Cleon. Nay, but thou lookest grave, and I must know why? Virtue itself would not be ashamed of a heart like thine.

Charl. How you humble me! Praise which I cannot deserve is more bitter than merited reproach.

Cleon. I had no such meaning: my praise is not indiscriminate; and I always take pleasure in receiving praise myself, when it is deserved. Praise is the reward of virtue, and as such should be accepted. If Julia be the handsomest.

thou hast the most understanding. Persuade her to be less capricious, and accept the hand of Mr. Davenport, before I assume a father's authority. I cannot conceive why she entertains such whimsical thoughts, concerning her liberty.

Charl. I think she loves him, and hope her little caprice will easily be changed to lasting affection: my aid shall not be wanting.

Cleon. Thou art my treasure! Tell her I could not die in peace and leave her unsettled.

Charl. Nay, dear father, such a motive would be little less than constraint. Julia has sources enough of affection in her own heart, and the worth of her lover; these I will oppose to her phantastic whims, and leave them to gain the victory.

Cleon. Right; but do not delay. Praise Mr. Davenport; remind Julia he possesses great wealth, and—— Poor child! How painful to thee that thy sister will be so rich! Well, though not the most handsome, thou wilt not be left wholly unprovided. Do not be afflicted.

Charl. Afflicted! Yes, Sir, that you should think me so selfish. Shall I not wish prosperity to my own sister? Come to breakfast, dear Sir.

Cleon. Your feelings interrupt me. Courage, my child; I cannot portion thee well, but will do all I can. Suffer your language, drawing, and music masters to return: I will pay them, should it cost me fifty dollars a month. Siegmund, thy friend, or rather thy lover, has been impoverished by an unlucky lawsuit; but he has gained experience, and your happiness will be mutual.

Charl. Mr. Siegmund, my dear father, is now more estimable than ever. I know you approve our love: taking on myself the part of a housewife, I will cheerfully leave the rest to him. I think so highly of him, and of his honour, that I would patiently wait for his hand these ten years. Do me the favour to let him dine with us to-day.

Cleon. Knowing it would give thee pleasure, my dear girl, he is already invited, and will soon be here.

SCENE II.

(SIEGMUND *enters unperceived by* CHARLOTTE.)

Charl. The servant may have missed him. I will write him a line myself—I am sure it will please him: he will certainly come, and the part he will take in Julia's good fortune will be great. His heart is no less upright than tender! Forgive me for talking of him so much.

Cleon. Then thou lovest him dearly?

Charl. So dearly that, had I the choice of him with a poor pittance, and any other man with the greatest riches, he alone should be my husband.

Cleon. Indeed! I did not think thee so far gone in love.

Charl. Rather say affection: I should be unhappy were it less tender;

especially when he prefers me to every woman on earth. Without beauty, without wealth, I have no attraction, except my innocence : yet, were I the paragon of the world, he could not love me more.

Cleon. Dost thou tell him all this?

Charl. Not so plainly: he is so timid that he takes none of the usual methods to show his love, and I have a thousand times wished that he would make it necessary for me to discover what he so well deserves.

Cleon. Thy wish is accomplished, my dear girl; he is here.

Charl. How! Have you heard me?

Siegm. Forgive me, dearest Charlotte; never in my life did I listen with such rapture! My senses are intoxicated, and I can offer nothing but love as my excuse.

Charl. You cannot find a better. Well, you have heard, and I did not know that you heard ; therefore, my acknowledgment was the more open and just. If I have committed a fault, being prompted by my dear father, I will commit it again wilfully. Does this extravagance give you pleasure ?

Siegm. Dear, dear Charlotte ! My present confusion must show you the feelings of my heart. You love me! And tell me so in your dear father's presence ! You! My Charlotte! Do I deserve it? Can I answer? How?—Let me take a turn and recover myself.

Cleon. You are disturbed, Sir, and my company may lay you under constraint. Bless you, my children! Remember Julia: I will converse with Mr. Davenport. [*Exit.*

SCENE III.

Siegm. Will you repent, dear Charlotte, of what you have said?

Charl. Before I answer, tell me if it be what you would have wished to hear?

Siegm. Wished? How often have I wished! How have I deserved such tenderness!

Charl. Let my heart speak, and you deserve much more!

Siegm. No, I am not yet worthy of your heart ! But my life shall be devoted to prove I am not insensible to such affection. How dignified is your mind! While your lover, I lost my whole property ; yet, in my misfortune, your love is unshaken! Your affection has increased, and this renders the calamity supportable. Tenderness so fixed is your greatest honour, for such treasures are only to be found in a noble mind; and I should deserve the contempt of mankind, could I cease to love you.

Charl. I discover my weakness by listening to your praise; but it is so delightful that I could listen for ever. Two years experience must have taught you whether my heart be honest : what pleasure to recollect the days and hours I have passed in the sweet society of virtue, love, and you.

Siegm. Are you so satisfied with me? Why can I not make you happy? How great must be the joy to reward a heart like yours, when the mere imagination of such power thrills me with rapture! Ah, Charlotte, how much happier than yourself is your sister!

Charl. Such another word will offend me: nay, I am offended. Julia is not more happy than myself. Her obligations to her husband will be great, but mine to you still greater. From you, and your example, I have learned content, tenderness, and the enjoyment of true pleasure. Are these nothing? But let us devote this day to Julia, my dear friend: she is unconsciously in love. Her whole behaviour assures me that the proud thoughts, which she cherishes concerning her liberty, are nothing but love: unfortunately, her mind too is overclouded by the odious imaginary picture she has drawn of marriage; let us disperse such clouds.

Siegm. In what manner? But I willingly obey. He deserves her, and she will make a charming wife.

Charl. He is here.

SCENE IV.—*Enter* DAVENPORT.

Charl. You look melancholy, Sir.

Dav. I have cause. To-day I imagined I was to meet Julia as my bride, which pleasure I have waited for a whole year: but, the more I speak of love, the less she feels: the more she is a witness of my affection the more she is offended. Wretched man! Happy should I be could I love Julia less.

Charl. Rejoice in this appearance of obstinacy; it is nothing less than love. Feeling herself conquered, she is making a last effort to embitter the pleasure you will receive from victory. We need only show what passes in her heart, and she will comply.

Dav. Is she not wilfully blind?

Charl. We must take her by surprise, and unexpectedly make the disco-very necessary. You need not be married just at present: what would be happiness to-day, will be happiness to-morrow. (*to* Siegmund.) Will you agree to what I shall propose?

Siegm. With pleasure, if it can make Mr. Davenport happy.

Dav. I know your mutual kindness. For my part, I will agree to any thing that can make Julia mine.

Charl. Then you must change your language, when she is present. Begin gradually to speak in favour of freedom: this apparent sympathy will first please, and afterward make her secure. She will think she loves you for this cause, though she has long had a much better, and thus will discover her thoughts.

Dav. Should this prove true, dear Charlotte how happy shall I be!

Charl. (*to* Siegmund.) You must play an under part, and affect to love her:

this will disturb her; she will regard you with anger, and express her scorn of such love to Mr. Davenport. Make me responsible for success.

Siegm. I do not like my part.

SCENE V.—*Enter* JULIA.

Jul. So, so! There you all are! My papa was inquiring for you; I can now let him know. (*going.*)

Charl. Nay, dear sister, why so hasty? Can you find better society?

Jul. Oh, no! But, where you and Mr. Siegmund are, love is sure to be the subject, and I have no present inclination to be a listener.

Charl. Why are *our* names alone mentioned? Why is *Mr. Davenport* unworthy of the same honour?

Jul. Mr. Davenport has kindly promised not to tease me again on the subject, and he has too much honour to break his word.

Dav. Yes, Julia; which promise, before this good company, I repeat. I only hope you will permit affection to be changed to esteem: the first you may forbid, but it will be impossible for me not to esteem you. Do not shun me, now that I am no longer your lover; but permit me to be your friend.

Jul. Most willingly! *Much friendship, and no love,* is my very wish. Let me have the intercourse of a friend, but not be fettered and tormented by love. Talk no more of love, and I am yours all day.

Charl. Let us be gone, Mr. Siegmund; we can give no pleasure to such frozen people. Their platonic ice is too cold, unless a thaw should come.

[*Exeunt* Charlotte *and* Siegmund.

SCENE VI.

Jul. My sister is dear to me, but would be much more dear if she talked less of love. Love *may* sometimes have a pleasant face, but his lamentable looks have so often disgusted me that I can never see him smile. My sister gives me an example of his languishing life: my sister, who was once so cheerful and free——

Dav. Nay, my promise is past; and friendship indeed, if well considered, appears to have the preference.

Jul. Oh, it gives freedom and ease to the heart, which *love* would render sickly. If people are pleased with each other, forsooth, they must be *in love,* and then they are not pleased long. Am I not right?

Dav. Nay, if I talk of love, you may tell me I have broken my promise.

Jul. You may think me capricious, or I know not what, that I should fly from love; but, as I tell you, on that depends my peace. Sweet liberty is my delight. I hate to be pierced by flames and darts. I discover in myself that my sister is wrong. But why so silent? I have all the talk. You are not vexed? I am delighted to think you are no longer my lover. What a long face you make, when I expected you to be pleased.

Dav. Face!—Long!—Not longer than usual.

Jul. Oh, long or short, I care but little, if you will but tease me no more about love. I am sorry to see you so gloomy—but, *as your friend*, that does not alarm me; I am the same myself, sometimes: one is overcome one knows not how. Do not think I suspect you: no, I won't suspect, though I appear to be in the company of the deaf and dumb. Am I become quite indifferent to you?

Dav. My charming friend, do not take it ill if, for a moment, I appear to have lost all sensibility. I am maintaining a combat with myself, in obedience to you, to stifle the last agonies of love, and assume the true character of a friend. Reason prevails: love *was* my delight and would be still, were it yours; but now I find insensibility has its charms, which lesson you alone could have taught me. Be assured I will exert myself; only forgive me if, now and then, I inadvertently stumble on my former character. I no longer love you, but I wish you to know the strength of my esteem.

Jul. But why then those downcast eyes? Cannot friends look each other in the face?

Dav. Oh, I am combating *love*, and that is a part of the battle! Who can look at you and not love you?

Jul. Why, did not you just now say you loved me no longer? You are quite dismal. I am alarmed for you. One minute you are so much in love that you frighten me, and the next as indifferent as if you had never seen me before. Keep to your purpose; you are still wavering. Is this the intercourse of friendship? Why should people love, since liberty is so much more noble?

Dav. But it requires much greater strength of mind.

Jul. So I say. Then why accuse me for esteeming it so highly? Why pout because I would rather have ten friends than one lover? Who but must prefer the variety of friendship to the mawkishness of love? Are my reasons so bad that I ought to lose your esteem? Declare honestly whether this preference ought to be called obstinacy? (*a tender look from* Dav.) Lord, what a look! Do you pity me? I cannot understand what your eyes would say? I should take you for an inquisitor, not a friend! Why do you notice every thing I do, and nothing that I say? I wish, Sir, to see——

Dav. Me gone. Sweet or bitter, I must obey. You need not dislike me so very much; I will trouble you no more on the old subject. I am— your very humble servant. (*going.*)

Jul. Dislike! When did I tell you I disliked you? I understand——because you must not be my lover, you—you more than *dislike me*. Generous indeed! The fine fruit of all your fine love! Well, be liberty mine; though you should again, with all your unfeeling pride, repeat I am your very humble servant. A very courtly speech.

Dav. A speech of respect. [*Exit.*

SCENE VII.

Jul. How! Is he gone!—Why am I so—restless? I do not *love* him—I—I only *like* him. His pride is insupportable! Leave me! Perhaps I have offended him? He used to be so—easily managed—so—Oh no, he did not love me! It was all a pretence.—I—I am quite out of humour.

SCENE VIII.—*Enter* Charlotte *unseen.*

I wish I had my lute, I would——

Charl. (*advances*) I will bring it you. But why, child, do you talk to yourself? It is not your custom to converse much with that dull gentleman Mr. Solitude.

Jul. What harm in that? I don't know why, just to-day, I should be suspected!

Charl. Matter of fact, not *suspicion.* If you had not talked aloud of your lute, how should I have known it; since you did not see me?

Jul. You are in a league to contradict me.

Charl. How so? If Mr. Davenport should have done it, that is not my fault. He told me, passing, how cross you had been, because, by accident, he had forgotten himself, and had just slightly mentioned love.

Jul. It seems, sister, your errand is to cross-question me. I will not be forced to love.

Charl. Right, Julia, since you do not like Mr. Davenport.

Jul. What a wise speech is that! Do not *like!* Must people *hate* each other because they are not languishing in love? I never questioned you whether you *liked* your Mr. Siegmund.

Charl. No; but if you should ask, I would answer yes, dearly, from my heart; for I am never ashamed to tell the truth. There is more dignity of mind in *feeling* rational *love* than in *talking* about *liberty.*

Jul. You will drive me mad, among ye! Mr. Davenport maintains the reverse: who shall I believe? I know you have more penetration than myself; yet do not wonder, dear sister, if I prefer my own. And why indeed should not the opinion of Mr. Davenport be as good as yours? You have always called him a rational and a—a—an agreeable man.

Charl. Oh dear, we were not talking about the agreeables: though I do not wonder this should be your opinion. I own him to have more understanding than myself; but even *he*, being human, may be mistaken.

Jul. Oh, then, you are come to inform me that Mr. Davenport is a *man*,

and not an *angel*—in *understanding*. I think so too: but really, my dear Charlotte, your wit makes me very dull. I could easily retort that Mr. Siegmund is only mortal: but, no; pray think him a *saint*. Do not imagine I defend Mr. Davenport from obstinacy: oh no! He has neither the *understanding*,
the *gallantry*, nor the *high worth* of your *Mr. Siegmund.* I am therefore right
to maintain my freedom, and not to love him.

Charl. Why so warm, my dear sister? You chide me, and find fault with
my lover, yet I think as well of you as ever. Who could think otherwise?
Without intending it, your eyes and tongue betray the state of your heart.
You are and always will be my dear sister. Your little faults become you;
they belong only to an honest heart. Do you know I had a remarkable
dream, last night, of a young charming bride, who——

Jul. Pray leave me, sister. I am *vexed—tormented*—and the more I talk the
worse I am.

Charl. Vexed because, in disputing, I just said a word against Mr. Davenport.

Jul. Why mention *him* again? Have *I* not follies enough? Leave him
with his *weakness* of understanding, and me with my *captiousness*, and suffer
me to be alone a minute. Elder sisters always think they have a right to
lecture the younger.

Charl. I will go; but pray follow me, for I want to speak with you again.
[*Exit.*

SCENE IX.—*Enter* MAGISTER.

Jul. How teasing! Must I never be alone! What is your urgent business,
dear Sir? Pray tell me, briefly, which way I can oblige you.

Mag. I would converse with you a little, young niece; and considering my
years, studies, and experience, I *may be thought qualified* for such an office. I
love you, and you know that, in every affair of life, *understanding* is a thing of
great necessity.

Jul. Perhaps so; though to-day I could wish to be without it: I might
then be more at peace.

Mag. Too precipitate. I would help you to distinguish between truth
and falsehood; and to know the *seeming*, or the *shining*, from the *sure.* What
man shall wind the will, and bring it to just and fortunate distinctions and
decisions, if he have not himself *understanding?* Would you be so charming as
you are, if *you* had not *understanding?*

Jul. Dear uncle, put out your lamp; you are not in your study. Why
torment me with your logic? It is clear I must be less wise than yourself, unless I had all your profound penetration and learning.

Mag. Just now you wished to be without understanding, yet you prove
you have it by your modesty. I require no learning from *you:* when speaking

with you, I would even forget *my own*. On the step that you shall take to-day your future fate dependeth ; yet it doth not appear that you are thereto determined. Your father wisheth much that you were : I have promised him *my trifling interference*, and wish you to hear, answer, and offer your objections; I will *patiently* endure them. Love is one of the most *charming*, but the most *dangerous* of the passions : it revengeth itself upon us, if despised ; and doth take no less revenge when too slavishly obeyed.

Jul. Your *trifling interference* taketh scope enough to display itself. I have no objections to make ; only leave me in peace. My *understanding* cannot cope with your *philosophy*, but it serves my purpose : I understand my own heart.

Mag. Knowest thou not, child, our passions are often the most victorious when we appear to be the most at peace ? The heart of man is the worst of deceivers, and *the wisest knoweth not himself.* Some people are not aware how much they love, until they find their love is not returned. Take not this on my affirmation : those great inquirers into the human heart, *Socrates, Plato, Seneca,* confirmed by many *modern philosophers,* all have said the same.

Jul. I do not know one of them, and have no wish for their acquaintance. But, Sir, supposing them to be as wise as you say, you may add that a heart ill at ease must become more so by these *trifling interferences.* I only hope that, if Mr. Plato, Seneca, and the rest of them, were all here, they would have so much penetration and politeness as to leave me, when so requested. Should I ever be governed by my passions, and especially by love, I will beg the assistance of your philosophy.

Mag. Your *sincerity* pleaseth me, though it appeareth to me like *contradiction* ; but I should hold myself as no philosopher if I could not support contradiction. You have given—that is, I will take, no offence. No offence ! But you have said, your heart is ill at ease : now, be this granted, ought not reflection to make it well ? What disturbeth you ? Is it the effect of love, or of aversion ? Is it fear, or desire ? I should wish you to have a clear knowledge thereof : when we know the *cause* of moral evil, a moral *antidote* may be discovered. My intention is good ; I speak simply, and wish to be more simple, not less.

Jul. I make not the least question of your simplicity, your good intentions, or your learning ; but I am vexed : I cannot tell what ails me, and if you would leave me at peace you must leave me in ignorance. You are too profound for me.

Mag. Wherefore praise me for my profundity ? When you have studied truth the many years that I have, you may, perhaps, be no less lucid in thought. Dispel these melancholy clouds, and ruminate on the good fortune which this day waiteth your acceptance. Mr. Davenport wisheth for, and doth deserve, your love ; what answer doth your *understanding* give ? On the choice of love doth marriage happiness depend ; and no error vexeth us so sore as when we are mistaken in that choice; yet in what can man more easily mistake?

Jul. All this is very fine, but what is it to me?

Mag. Your eloquence is warm, but my tranquillity shall not be disturbed. You will not love; will not marry. Are you not in duty bound? Shall I recount the proofs in my behalf that nature hath in store? Shall the human race become extinct? That it shall not nature doth teach, and thereto love doth tend: now, he who would obtain this end, however wise the man, must take the means. Are you not then bound to marry? Tell me, do you not feel the force of arguments like these?

Jul. No indeed. If love be only duty, I wonder how so many hearts are thus enslaved. Give me love without this learning: I will wait in patience for its magic spells.

Mag. Niece, those persons are called stiff-necked who shut their eyes on arguments so luminous. If you grant you are bound to marry, which way can your will be *undetermined?* Is not conviction of the mind and decision of the will one and the same thing? Why will you not conclude to marry Mr. Davenport, being *convinced* it is your duty?

Jul. Pray forgive me, Sir, that, learned though you are, I am yet *unconvinced.* Poor girl! how can I help myself that I am not quite so discerning as Plato, Seneca, and the rest of them? You must ask them how it happens that I have no mind to marry; though, according to you, that is my duty. I am wanted in the kitchen, or the parlour, or somewhere or other.   [*Exit.*

SCENE X.—*Enter* CLEON.

Mag. I have discoursed with thy daughter, Julia, with most interrogatory and rational precaution; have spoken with marvellous patience and self-denial; have clearly stated incontrovertible truths: but——

Cleon. I wish you had rather given her a few examples of young women happily married.

Mag. More than once I have suffered contradiction from her; yet *never once* have I forgotten decorum. I gave her *demonstration* that it was her duty to marry.

Cleon. You have given yourself great trouble, brother; but a girl of eighteen pays little attention to this kind of demonstration.

Mag. I made every thing so plain that she was necessarily convinced: for if, when conversing with the unlearned, who are not accustomed to abstract, we do not sink beneath ourselves, and call ingenuity to our aid, we shall not be comprehensible.

Cleon. But what have you done? Will she have Mr. Davenport? Has she discovered what her inclinations are? I cannot trifle with that gentleman, he means so well and deserves so much.

Mag. She saith she is not at peace: now this was ill; for the elements of philosophy require a calm mind to actuate, or act upon. If the understanding doth suffer through a tempestuous inclination and perverse will, it then hath little power of remark; and without the power of remark, its keenest weapons are but as blunted arrows.

Cleon. Less logic, dear brother. Your skill would have appeared greater, to me, had she been less disturbed.

Mag. No mode was unemployed. I showed her the pleasing side of love. I began even with informing her that a happy marriage was a great blessing.

Cleon. A marvellous discovery! But you should have told her that, in her case, the probability of happiness was great indeed. That was my intention when I sent you here.

Mag. In brief, I well perceive she cannot be convinced by argument and proof. She perfectly understandeth a simple proposition; but when several propositions must be combined, and the *ergo*, the useful conclusion drawn, her understanding doth then begin to fail; till, being overburdened, it can contain no more.

Cleon. Then your persuasion has been of no effect?

Mag. There are yet certain acute modes of persuading: such as the *argumentum ad hominem:* and such as are to be found in the ancient authors, by whom they are called fables and allegories, or parables. To people who have not depth of thought, such circumlocutions of wit may be serviceable. I will try to obtain, by the stratagems of my ingenuity, that wherein my *understanding*, not being *understood*, hath failed: for I know not but that a *fable* may induce her to marry even sooner than a *demonstration*. I will invent one, and will read it to her as a treasure discovered in the book of a youthful student at Leipsic. I mean that student who, by his tales and fables, hath made himself so beloved by the scholars *.

Cleon. Pray do: let no means be neglected. Should the fable be a good one, you may publish it at my daughter's wedding: but do not let it be too long. A fable is not an oration: nor must it be too logical. My daughter will not think you the author. Only make her say yes, and my thanks, at least, shall not be fabulous. [*Exit* Magister.

SCENE XI.—*Enter* CHARLOTTE.

Charl. The guardian of Mr. Davenport has sent his servant with this note to you, Sir.

---

* GELLERT *here evidently alludes to his own tales and fables, which were written at Leipsic, and had become so highly popular.*

Cleon. (*reads*) " According to your desire, I will do myself the honour to take a dish of coffee with you. I am greatly pleased with the choice of my ward, Mr. Davenport; he could not have made a better. Briefly, I mean to spend a happy day with you and your daughters, for I have received pleasant news from court. I must further inform you that the will of your dead relation, Mrs. Stephen, will be opened to-day or to-morrow. I am well persuaded your name is in it, and I perhaps may bring you more information about four o'clock. I am, &c." Good! very good, my child! I feared Mr. Simon would have withheld his approbation; my daughter not having a fortune.

Charl. So did not I. Mr. Simon is as liberal as he is ready to serve; and will rejoice to make a young woman happy, whose greatest defect is the want of fortune.

Cleon. True, child; he is a good man. I thought, I own, he must have had faults; since he is nearly forty, and has no employment*. But what are we the better, if Julia will not have Mr. Davenport?

Charl. Fear nothing, my dear father. Julia is half conquered; and I think you could not make her more unhappy than by forcing her to accept her *beloved liberty* for life. I have certain proofs that she loves him.

Cleon. Indeed! I hardly dare believe it. Ah, you sly girls always pretend that men are your aversion; though secretly they are your hearts' delight. Well, well; in this world love is a first necessity.

Charl. Dear Sir, your satire on sly maidens does not reach me: I never made a secret of my love. I never supposed that rational love merited reproach more than rational friendship.

Cleon. If my dead relation should have remembered me, I shall be glad to affiance you directly, my dear child, and fix the wedding-day. Nothing at least on my part shall be wanting.

Charl. You are a dear good father! But, should that be so, it would be very wrong for you to leave yourself poor in order that we may be married. I can willingly wait; for Mr. Siegmund will not think of marrying till his income shall be sufficient.

Cleon. Exert thyself, that Julia may consent. A young girl may be coy, and prudish, but she must not carry such things too far.

Charl. Our dear mamma rather thought like Julia.

Cleon. Ah, rogue! A father may *think* too. I have been young, and have not to repent of my youth. I and thy dear mother lived like children, one year before and sixteen years after marriage! For the happy hours we have enjoyed she has my heart-felt thanks in her grave. Without vanity, children, she has given you both a good education. All will go well with thee;

---

* *At Court; or bestowed by the Elector.* GELLERT *appears here again to glance at himself.—See the Account of him which follows this Comedy.*

be at peace. Thou hast been my comfort, my housekeeper. After my death,
I will leave thee an honourable name, and a good education. Lay me by
thy mother's side : where she sleeps I would sleep.

Charl. Why, dear father, teach me to be weak? If *my* prayers are heard,
your life will be long; and you will know what delight I take in seeking to
make you happy. Oh, that I could so live these hundred years! I should then
only have paid a just debt. To-day ought to be a day of enjoyment: but,
perhaps, the soft melancholy in which you now indulge is the greatest charm
a dear and worthy father can feel. Do you know, Sir, there is no wine in
the cellar, except the cask which you laid in the year when I was born. What
shall we set before our guests to-day ?

Cleon. Tap that: were it nectar it were not too good for this happy season. It will soon be dinner-time—I will go to market for some fish. If I see
Julia, I will send her to you that you may speak with her again.

Charl. Do, Sir, and I will wait.   [*Exit* Cleon.

SCENE XII.—*Enter* SIEGMUND.

Siegm. I have had a short conversation with Julia : she is out of humour
about Mr. Davenport ; but her complaints all to me appear to be like a declaration of love in a foreign language. I did not think she was so affectionate.
Love and friendship reign both in her eyes and on her lips; and the more she
wishes to conceal her love the more it is visible.

Charl. Hey day, my dear friend ! If you proceed, I shall be jealous. My
sister is more charming than I am ; yet you love me.

Siegm. Who can love you once and not for ever ? Your sister has many
deserts, but you have many more. You know my heart; be that the pledge
of my fidelity.

Charl. Yes, I know it, and am proud. Ah, dear Siegmund! I must inform you that we have a prospect of a little good fortune. I shall be happy
to afford you some degree of pleasure! The guardian of Mr. Davenport has
informed my father, by a note, that the will of a female relation is to be read
to-day; and, as Mr. Simon believes, there is a legacy for our family. Oh,
how fortunate should I be could I help to improve your circumstances !

Siegm. Do not be uneasy : you love me more than I deserve. Take patience : all will be well, and——

Charl. *You* are uneasy! What is the matter, tell me ? Life is not dearer
to me than your peace.

Siegm. Ah, my dear girl, I want nothing but the good fortune to be
eternally yours ! I am a little absent in mind : I did not sleep well.

Charl. Be cheerful for my sake. Julia is in her chamber; we will go to
her : the dinner will soon be ready.   [*Exeunt.*

END OF THE FIRST ACT.

ACT II.

SCENE I.—Cleon *and* Julia.

Cleon. YOU must know whether you like him or not!

Jul. *How*, dear father, can I know it? I will willingly obey you, leave me only my dear liberty.

Cleon. " You will willingly obey, leave you only your dear liberty!" Little ape, do you know what you say? Can that be obedience? I forbear to force you; I am much too indulgent to you: only tell me this, does he please you?

Jul. Please me? Really—perhaps—I cannot positively say.

Cleon. Daughter, do not blush to open your heart to your father: you are now a young woman, and love is not forbidden. Do his form and person please?

Jul. I—I see nothing much amiss: perhaps—I am well enough satisfied.

Cleon. What do you mean, girl, by perhaps? We are not in the clouds: ask your heart.

Jul. My heart—oh, my heart deceives me: it will answer nothing precisely.

Cleon. Talk common sense: your heart is yourself, and you must know what you think. If a young, handsome, intelligent, virtuous and wealthy man desire your hand, you can easily tell whether you will have him for a husband.

Jul. Husband!—Ah, Sir, let me breathe: I am not myself to-day, and I may be too hasty in such a state of mind. I cannot indeed think I love him; for, if I did, I should be cheerful and happy. Beside, who can tell whether I—am to his satisfaction?

Cleon. A rational cause of doubt to be sure! Foolish girl! If you were not to his satisfaction, he would not trouble himself so much concerning you. Perhaps he knows you better than you know yourself. Imagine, when your mother was young, and I begged of her to have me, whether she did not please me. When Mr. Davenport speaks to you, does he call you dear Julia, or how?

Jul. Calls—calls—he calls me Miss.

Cleon. That is not truth, child. *He* call you Miss! No, no.

Jul. Miss, or dear Miss, or—I don't know what.

Cleon. Daughter, you are a hypocrite. I am your father. In truth and sincerity how does he call you?

Jul. ˙Dear—who can remember such nonsense? Calls—calls—sometimes he says *my dear Julia.*

Cleon. Why do you speak so mournfully, and sigh at your own name? It is not disagreeable. Well—*my dear Julia:* what beside?

Jul. Nay, papa—sometimes it's *my beautiful Julia.* But why all these questions?

Cleon. Little fool! You make me happy. A good father is always happy when his children behave properly. I have ever treated you like a friend. But to the point: Mr. Davenport says to you, " My dear Julia, my beautiful Julia, for *thee* I——"

Jul. Oh, no! He always says *you: thou* never escapes him; that would be too familiar; quite insufferable.

Cleon. No, no; the word *thou* would be no disgrace to you. I have taken that liberty before marriage, with your dear mother, more than once, and it thrilled me with pleasure. Well—once more he says " I like you!" and no doubt adds, " you please me ;" or perhaps he places that first.

Jul. Oh, he says no such things.

Cleon. How vexatious! I have heard it myself more than once.

Jul. That he said I *like* you?

Cleon. Yes.

Jul. With your permission, papa, Mr. Davenport never said so to me in all his life. He has often enough said I *love* you, *from my heart :* but never I like you.

Cleon. (*smiles*) You are very particular and accurate about your terms.

Jul. I *like you !* Poh! I love you *from my heart* has a better sound. Oh, there is no comparison!

Cleon. May be so. I said the same to your mother to the last, and it always gave her pleasure.—But no matter that phrases vary. Maidens now are as anxious about a word, more or less, as an arithmetician would be at a false cypher. And you are pleased with his mode of speaking? Then pray be pleased with himself too. Why delay? I am descending to the grave, and I tell thee, child, thy bridegroom would not disgrace a countess; he wishes now to know with certainty whether he——

Jul. Papa!

Cleon. Well, what next.—Be not so reserved: though I am your father, I would be as gentle to you as a sister.

Jul. Will you grant me one thing, papa?

Cleon. Most willingly. You are as dear to me as Charlotte, though she has more steadiness. Ask what you will.

Jul. Ask—was I going to ask ?—Lord, I am very nonsensical—undecided —disturbed.

Cleon. What would you ask? Speak.

Jul. Only—only my liberty.

Cleon. Eternally your liberty! I thought you wanted to bespeak your wedding-clothes. Take your liberty ! I will use no constraint, only bethink yourself: remain in this place an hour and reflect. I will disturb you no more. [*Exit.*

SCENE II.—*Enter Mr.* DAVENPORT.

Dav. May I speak with you, dear Julia?

Jul. Oh yes; you are just come in time. The health you drank at table, about love, made me unwell. My sister laughed at it ! So cannot I. She has been full of contradiction to-day, which she has extended even to yourself.

Dav. To me ! May I ask how ?

Jul. I told her you maintained the opinion that liberty, rather than love, denoted dignity of mind : on which she began to ridicule you; and boldly affirmed you were wrong. Take no notice, however, or she might think I wish to make you her enemy.

Dav. No, no ; she will not so misinterpret : she is innocence itself.

Jul. I cannot discover why she should contradict me so, except that I was induced to repeat your arguments. I own my sister is better than I am : she preaches in favour of love ; I cannot follow this good example.

Dav. Pray forgive her, though she may have spoken against me: I am not without failings, and perhaps should have pleased you better were they less visible.

Jul. What should this mean ? Perhaps, by the word *failings*, you have me in view.

Dav. Charming Julia! Will you never believe how kind my meaning always is to you ?

Jul. I have little doubt of that : you like my sister, and—no doubt—it will not be *very disagreeable* to you to bestow the same liking upon myself.

Dav. Yes, I assure you, did I not know Julia, I should think Charlotte the most charming girl on earth.

Jul. Very flattering indeed ! You are not afraid of making me too vain by a *compliment.*

Dav. My dear friend, why mistake this for a compliment ? Why not think me sincere ?

Jul. Think!—I—Oh, I have a very good opinion of you.

Dav. Why praise me in so melancholy a tone? Is it against your will ? Really I am very unfortunate; the longer I see you, and the more I speak to you, the more you are dissatisfied. What is it that disturbs you ? I make no attacks upon your dear liberty ; no, not the slightest attempt upon your heart shall escape me. I love you entirely, hopeless and unrewarded. Would you deprive me even of this pleasure ?

Jul. I confess you have more merit than I thought: this free, this unfettered love will give me great pleasure. I can say no more. Do not reproach me any more with my dissatisfaction; I will be just and rid you of
my company.

Dav. Why? What is the matter, my angel?

Jul. I—really—I don't know. Every thing is so irksome to me—nay, it
even appears as if I sought for vexation, and loved it. I request—I beg I
may not suffer in your esteem. I am very ill bred to you to-day, now that
you are our guest. I am—I don't know how—Something is come over me—
I will take a dish of coffee; perhaps that may dissipate the—the vapours.
Don't come with me; Charlotte would begin to jeer—Stay here; will you
be so good? [*Exit.*

SCENE III.—*Enter* CHARLOTTE.

Charl. Well! What say you now, Sir? Tears! Is it possible?

Dav. Let me enjoy myself! My whole soul is absorbed in gratitude.
Had you but heard the charming girl! Had you seen the struggles of her
heart! At last, she freely owned she was not herself. What delight did she
give, and how innocently was it said! Yes, I have won her heart without her
own knowledge. Let us contrive, my dear Charlotte, oh, let us contrive
how to——

Charl. To lose it. Why were you not more explicit?

Dav. Let me first calm my thoughts. She has told me every thing
was irksome to her, and sweetly requested she might not suffer in my esteem:
but she pronounced the word *esteem* in such a voice—oh, it was the voice of
love! At last, she innocently told me she would take a dish of coffee, to dissipate the vapours.

Charl. Dear girl! Could coffee cure the heart-ach, so many of us would
not be sick. Well, she will soon learn to distinguish between love and liberty:
her melancholy proves, in my opinion, how little she begins to value the
latter. You must now again gradually resume the character of the lover. I
do not think it will give her *much offence.*

Dav. The change will be very natural; only I fear, if too many
persons be present, her heart will again take the alarm. When she left me,
she requested I would not follow her, because she feared your jokes. This
proves her timidity.

Charl. It proves, well interpreted, that she spoke thus to you:—" Do not
go with me, for Charlotte must not see how dearly I love you." She does
not shrink from love itself, but from the word. If her habitual timidity were
less, her affections would be seen more openly; but not perhaps with so many
charms: and, perhaps, if we women would truly please, the thoughts like
the person should in part be concealed.

Dav. But what think you, sister, should—— Hey day! I am very familiar with the word *sister;* yet know not how to apologize——

Charl. You have committed no fault, dear brother of my heart, and deserve no reproof. Well, what have you to say?

Dav. Do not ask me; I have forgotten. My thoughts are not my own. Julia thinks, feels, and speaks in my bosom; and, since I have seen her melancholy, I have a strong inclination to be the same. Sympathy governs our hearts. I feel my happiness, and would enjoy it. I see my Julia loves and cherishes a sweet melancholy; in all things I would resemble her. My heart is making new discoveries.

Charl. Indulge the inclination, and be as melancholy as you please; for absence of mind is the thing I wish to both. She will soon be weary of herself, and make room in her heart for happiness.

Dav. I am full of fears. I doubt, when I see her again, I shall not be able to speak.

Charl. That may easily happen; and Julia perhaps may soon be as dumb as yourself. I should like to see you both without being seen! So full of thought, you will have nothing to say: when a word is endeavouring to find its road, it will not be able to escape for a sigh: this treacherous sigh you will swallow, and try to disguise by an air of indifference! "I pray you leave me," says she; and then some sly means will be taken to detain you. Your part will be just the same; and the probability is, that in the midst of this tragedy, the grand catastrophe will be kissing!—I hear her coming, and will not disturb you.

[Charlotte *retires to the side scene, and listens.*

SCENE IV.—*Enter* JULIA.

Jul. Where is my sister? Was not she here?

Dav. (*absorbed in thought*) She said something as she went about not disturbing us.

Jul. Disturbing! What does that mean?

Dav. Pardon me—I forget myself—Oh lovely Julia * !

Jul. Forgot yourself! Why? But—I—I will leave you—you are thoughtful.

Dav. Leave me! My lovely Julia! Me——

---

* Julchen *is the German name, which here the lover changes to* Juliana. *But the word* Julchen *could not have been elegantly preserved.*

Jul. " My lovely Julia !" You never called me so before. You say you forget yourself. I will be gone.

Dav. Oh, not yet ! I have a thousand things to say ! Much, much!

Jul. What then ? Would you keep me against my will ?—Has any thing happened to you ?—What have you to say ?—Speak.

Dav. (*mournfully*) My lovely Julia !

Jul. (*with a faltering voice*) You have said so to me now *three times*— Silent again ?—Well, I must go. (*going ; they mutually cast a mournful look*) I really fear something must have befallen you ; may I not be told ? (*he approaches her.*)

Dav. Would you but forgive me, I should then—Oh, no—I should forfeit your friendship, and—— (*kissing and keeping hold of her hand*) No, I have nothing to say. You seem sorrowful, my lovely Julia !

Jul. (*roused*) Am I ?—No, no, not I ; only I am frightened to see you unlike yourself ! I—no, I am not sorrowful. I am quite calm, and wish to see you so. Don't hold my hand—Well, I will leave you ; I will go to my sister and tell her——

Dav. Tell her what, dear girl ?

Jul. Tell her ——Tell her——that my father asked for her.

Dav. Your father, my angel ?

Jul. No, no ; it was Mr. Siegmund, who wishes to speak to her, and desired me—— (*looks at him*) You look so very melancholy that—— (*turning away her face*) I pity you!

Dav. My lovely Julia ! Pity me—I am overcome !

Jul. What ails me ?—Why do you keep me here ?—Why these tears ? (*endeavouring to conceal her own*) What is the matter ?—Let me beg of you to leave me.

Dav. (*sighs*) Yes.

Jul. (*aside*) He is going.

Dav. (*turning back*) But why may I not know what ails you ? You were not thus in the morning.

Jul. I do not know myself.—You are going : my present humour is irksome to you ; yet tell me why you—you do not speak ?

Dav. Speak ?

Jul. Speak.

Dav. How beauteous do you look through your tears ! Oh lovely Julia !

Jul. Why do you sigh ? You forget—— Suppose Charlotte were to come ! Only think should she see you so sad, and me so—— What would she say ?

SCENE V.—*Enter* CHARLOTTE.

Charl. I should say that people, by their dismal questions and tears, make the strongest declaration of love, without uttering a word on the subject: *that* is what *I* should say.

Jul. (*aside*) Oh, how malicious!—I must be gone.

Charl. Yes, I have seen you going often enough; yet here you are.

Jul. Seen me?—Spiteful!   [*Exit.*

SCENE VI.

Charl. I am almost sorry to have disturbed you! But I could contain myself no longer! What can be more delightful than to see two poor innocents sighing and dying for love, but not daring to own it! What do you think *now* of my little plot? Could I but have withheld myself for half a minute, I should have seen you sink into each other's arms.

Dav. I fear not. I was greatly affected, and am so still.

Charl. I see your *condition*, and know how it teases you to stay here, prattling with me. Entice your mistress back: I will make all right.

Dav. A thousand thousand thanks!   [*Exit.*

SCENE VII.—*Enter Mr.* SIMON.

Mr. S. I ask pardon, Miss, for thus breaking in upon you; but joy makes me impolite. Are *you* not the charming young lady who is affianced to my ward?

Charl. Supposing me so, what then?

Mr. S. I have the pleasure to inform you that your deceased aunt has left you her sole heiress. This day you will receive information of it from the town-hall. The will has been opened, and your godfather, the court counsellor, being present, has commissioned me to bring this pleasing news to your father, before he could receive it in due form.

Charl. Is it possible! My aunt has tenfold performed her promise. How fortunate is my sister! But she deserves it, however extraordinary. Sir, you have given me the most heartfelt pleasure! I am not affianced to your ward, but I could scarcely have felt so much delight had I been the heiress!

Mr. S. I do not know, Miss, which of you is affianced to my fortunate ward; but it is the youngest sister who inherits the estate, and likewise personalities worth more than fifty thousand dollars.

Charl. I am the eldest sister. Oh what happiness!

Mr. S. I am grieved I could not bring the same intelligence to yourself, that your happiness might have been equal. Where is your good father?

Charl. Be kind enough to follow me—only grant me this request. Give me the satisfaction of being the first to convey the joyful news to my sister and Mr. Davenport. I know no pleasure equal to that of being a witness of the enjoyment of others; and, had I as much myself, I really think I could give it all for this high gratification! Let me have this happiness!

Mr. S. Most willingly. To find two other sisters with an equally noble and disinterested affection would be no easy task. It quite surprises me! I knew you were not affianced to my ward, and only wished to soften the painful task I had to perform. I did not imagine I should have given you so much joy; but I see the contrary, and (*tenderly*) *almost* * begin to wish you had yourself been promised to my ward, and the fortunate heiress of your aunt.

Charl. If a love for others and being free from envy can gain your esteem, I hope to enjoy it during life. Then you will suffer me to inform my sister and Mr. Davenport of this bequest? Will you be so good?

Mr. S. And your father, likewise; though I was deputed to him. Here he comes.

SCENE VIII.—*Enter* Cleon *and* Siegmund.

Cleon. I have been seeking you, dear Sir, with Mr. Siegmund in the garden. I saw you come in, and thought you would have taken your coffee there. Your company does me honour, and gives me the greatest pleasure.

Mr. S. I am rejoiced to see you so well; and to be a witness of your happiness.

Charl. Oh, my dear father! Oh, Siegmund! Shall I speak, Mr. Simon?

Mr. S. Oh yes; it will delight me almost as much as if I had been still ignorant of the event.

Cleon. What dost thou mean, child? Wilt thou speak to me, or to Mr. Siegmund? Which is the dearest to thee, darling?

Charl. In my dear respect, you are the first; but in affection——

Cleon. Ay, ay, I understand.

Charl. Then I will repeat to you both the good news of Mr. Simon. My deceased aunt has left her whole estate to Julia. The will has been opened, and my godfather has sent us the news by Mr. Simon.

Cleon. Imagine a father's feeling! The estate too is freehold †. Joy

---

* *A deviation from the author is here made, to give a stronger shade of probability to the plot.*

† Weiberlehen : *an estate that can descend to females, according to the German law.*

makes me shudder. I never suspected this: yet she was always kind to the girl! The whole estate?

Siegm. Most excellent! A right worthy woman!

Mr. S. In your name, I desired a copy of the will to be made, and hope you will have it this evening. You will likewise soon have legal documents.

Cleon. This is so extraordinary! The poor shall have their part! And yet, poor girl, you are cut short.

Charl. Oh, no, dear father! Who knows whether I should properly support such good fortune? Beside, who is so happy as I am? What say you, Mr. Siegmund? Tell me your opinion.

Siegm. It is that *you* are quite as *estimable* as your *sister.*

Cleon. You told me, Sir, in your note, you had yourself received good news: walk with me into the garden, and let me hear. (*ironically*) These wrangling lovers can support our absence; if not, they will follow.

[*Exeunt* Cleon *and Mr.* Simon.

SCENE IX.

Charl. Had I not known you so well, I should have trembled while relating my sister's good fortune before you; but I am convinced I shall not for a moment appear less worthy in your eyes. We are at the disposal of Providence, and Providence is just and wise: it is watchful over us, though it should not appear at the moment when we wish.

Siegm. My dear Charlotte, how easy is it, remembering you, to forget ill fortune. Let us continue to hope: pardon me if I still seem absent; I have been talking to your father, and really I know not about what.

Charl. If you love like me, I do not wonder that, on such a day, when all these preparations are making, you should wish and be uneasy. Once more, trust in Providence. This very day it is a year since, by an unlucky lawsuit, you lost your inheritance. Perhaps the thought troubles you? Who can say but that, in another year, it may again be restored? Have you spoken with Julia, and affected love for her, to serve Mr. Davenport?

Siegm. No; I have been too absent, too——

Charl. No matter; the trouble is scarcely necessary: her heart will do its office. But do not say a word of the inheritance! I will seek her, and relate the happy event to herself and her lover.   [*Exit.*

SCENE X.—Siegmund *alone.*

What a cursed event!—Julia!—The whole estate! Julia—already possessed of such beauty, such charming graces! Were I ignorant of Charlotte's worth, perhaps Julia—— But is Julia less worthy, less generous, prudent, innocent? Is she not propriety itself?—Has Charlotte her winning timidity? or—— Cursed love, how thou tormentest me! Must I be faithless against my will?—Why should not Charlotte have had the estate? Did the aunt discover greater merit in her sister?—Wretched man! How great is my loss, without any fault of mine! Yet—am I less agreeable than Davenport? Julia refuses his love—Would it be a crime to—— Should she win my heart, how can I help it? Would my desires be unjust, should they agree with those of Julia? Here she is, and by herself!

SCENE XI.—*Enter* JULIA.

Jul. My sister desired me to wait here in your company. She is in search of Mr. Davenport, and will bring him to relate something agreeable to both.

Siegm. Will you not find *my company* dull?

Jul. *Your company!* Certainly not. You have been quite kind to me to-day; and it can be no secret that you are agreeable to *me*, though less to me than to my sister.

Siegm. (*kissing her hand*) You are flattering, charming bride!

Jul. Am I to be a bride? No body has yet told me so. No, you must not call me by that name. Though I should happen to please Mr. Davenport, must I therefore be his bride? No, he is so very good that—that—he scarcely now mentions love.

Siegm. And were I to mention love, would you be angry? You little know how highly I——You——

Jul. In your company, I am safe; while the world contains *a Charlotte*, I need not fear a declaration of love from *you*. Should you wish to discover my private thoughts, you will be deceived.

Siegm. Sweet girl! I could wish I were dissembling, but *am not*. Recollect, man cannot——

Jul. Cannot what?

Siegm. *Look at you* and remain unmoved.

Jul. I perceive you are playing the part of Mr. Davenport.

Siegm. I should then be very unfortunate, since you dislike the part he plays.

Jul. How can it affect you and my sister, though I should not yield to his wishes?

Siegm. I, perhaps, should be *a gainer*; you, perhaps, would discover the *intentions of a faithful heart*. I honour you, and how shall I tell you what I feel?

Jul. Upon my word, you are an excellent actor: but I do not like love, even in sport. I wonder where is my sister, and what she has to tell me. She kissed me with such joy! It must be something serious—I will go and find her; excuse me a moment.   [*Exit.*

SCENE XII.

Siegm. (*alone*) Monster! What have I done? Would I betray a faithful heart, that loves me with rapture! I!—Yet, how beautiful, how charming is Julia! She does not love *him*—but is she inclined to *me*? Then reason—it must be silent—my affections may—may change. —Should I fail in the attempt, Charlotte will still certainly be mine. Did she not herself request I would make love to Julia?—I shall not therefore appear faithless.—How! Julia again! Does she seek me?

SCENE XIII.—*Enter* JULIA *and* MAGISTER.

Jul. (*to* Siegmund) Charlotte will not tell me till Mr. Davenport returns, who is gone home for half an hour. You will be kind enough to go to my papa?

Siegm. When you command—But dare I hope?—

Jul. (*a little suspicious*) Nay, if you play the lover, I will act the coquet: ask my papa what he says.

Mag. True, Mr. Siegmund; my brother waiteth in expectation of you, and my desire is to speak a word in private with this young maiden.

[*Exit* Siegmund.

SCENE XIV.—JULIA, MAGISTER.

Jul. Pray, Sir, can you tell me what news my sister Charlotte brings?

Mag. No; I have not encountered her: I come from my library, where I have been amusing myself with reading a book of German fables. If you will grant attentive ear, I will audibly read one which, in my poor opinion, has great merit. You are a lover of wit and genius.

Jul.⁺ Yes, but not to-day: my mind is not at ease. But how happens this? You were not used to read me fables. Nay, you used even to make comical wry faces if you saw me reading those of La Fontaine, or Hagedorn *.

Mag. I grant it; I being more the friend of serious argument, which is gold, while wit is little better than dross: but the bow of the understanding, if kept always bent, will lose its elasticity; therefore, light reading may at times be admissible. Will you hear the fable; the title whereof is THE SUN.

---

* HAGEDORN *is a celebrated German poet, who wrote toward the middle of the last century.*

Jul. Dear! I have read many fables about the Sun. I'll take your word for it, and believe it charming; only spare me the trouble of hearing it.

Mag. Niece, my powers of divination cannot discover why you, to-day, are in this moody mood. For your advantage, I have wasted some valuable hours—have laboured in your behalf, and for your tranquillity: yet you are so ungrateful as to give me continual offence. Am I so insignificant? And doth my good-will not even deserve your notice? Are not your duties toward me, your uncle, accurately delineated, as it were in a map? Wherefore then contradict me thus? Am I to blame that you should be by reason bound to marry? Have I passed the limits of that obedience in which you are indebted to your father and myself? Are those limits not defined by reason?

Jul. You complain of me, uncle, but you complain so learnedly that I have nothing to say. Well, pray read me the fable, that I may run to my sister. You do not know, uncle, how highly I esteem you.

Mag. Why not know? Though your understanding is not of the highest *genus*, your heart is of a most excellent *species*. If, instead of reading the *Beyträge* of Bremen *, and such-like trifles, you would seriously pursue a system of moral philosophy, I augur well you soon would learn to think. Did you understand the powers of the will, and their nature, philosophically, you then would also understand how the powers of love do form a power which——

Jul. Always on the subject of love! Did you ever while young act the lover, that your knowledge of it is so accurate? If so, what is it? Who can solve that riddle?

Mag. All those who have sufficient understanding to understand the nature of things. Love is the concord, the agreement, or the harmony of two wills to produce one effect. This methinks is demonstration; or, shall I invent another figure?

Jul. No, no; one is quite enough. I would rather hear your fable and go.

Mag. I own, a fable is not so difficult to comprehend as a definition of cause and effect. It is short, and in my opinion is rather an allegory than a fable. Listen and hear. (*reads*)

" The Sun, as we are told, formerly fell in love with the Moon, and dis-
" covered his passion in the most soft and tender manner; but the Moon, as
" was her nature, continued cold and insensible. She ridiculed every reason,
" which the neighbouring planets could offer, in favour of the passion of
the Sun. Her pride made her preserve the air of a prude, though the
" love of the Sun gave her secret pleasure. She confided in her clear and

---

* *See an account of* GELLERT, *which follows this Comedy,*

" beautiful face, till a Deity, at the request of the Sun, darkened it with
" spots; and these are the spots which at this time may be seen in the face
" the Moon."

This is the fable: now, what is the moral, think you?

Jul. I think—that it does not please me so much as it pleased the author
who made it. I hope you do not think this an agreeable tale?

Mag. I do freely grant the powers of understanding cannot display their
strength in witty trifles. But suppose I were myself the author?

Jul. If you were, I should suppose myself blind, for not seeing its beauties.

Mag. There is cunning in that excuse. I will inform you, the work is
mine; though I would not be vain thereof; since we find it possible for the
unlearned to have wit. But reflect upon it well, and tell me the moral.

Jul. You had better tell it to me.

Mag. Be attentive. A handsome maiden, who long had ridiculed her
lover, became in danger that age should injure her beauty.

Jul. Your invention, Sir, is rich to-day; and your moral *very new*. So I
am the moon, Mr. Davenport is the sun, and you and my sister are among
the planets?

Mag. I do discover that when, by figure and allegory, I have presented
my thoughts, the impression made by them is great. Niece, think intensely
upon the fable, and no longer withstand the love of the Sun. What answer
shall I return with to my brother?

Jul. Why—tell him that—though I was dull enough when I heard your
fable—I could not help laughing. Uncle, your most obedient. [*Exit.*

SCENE XV.—*Enter* CLEON *and* SIEGMUND.

Cleon. Well, dear brother, what says Julia? I fancy you might have prevailed without your fable.

Mag. She remaineth stedfast. I know not wherefore, for an obstinate
girl, a person of high respect should give himself so much trouble. When
neither philosophy nor ingenuity can prevail, a relation hath no other choice
but force. Henceforth I am silent. Ay, thus it is when parents neglect early
to give the solid foundation of knowledge, and make morality the superstruc-
ture. Often have I requested that I might instruct thy daughter, and teach
her the principle of things: but, no; she would be fanciful, and not reasonable.

Siegm. This, Sir, is a bold assertion. Is not Julia rational enough?

Mag. Indeed! So warm! I understand you. Another time I will do
myself the honour of a reply: my pupils now are waiting. [*Exit.*

SCENE XVI.

Cleon. I know not which to believe, my brother or Charlotte: their accounts are contradictory. How can my brother be mistaken? What is your opinion, Sir?

Siegm. Why, Sir, in my opinion, Mr. Davenport is rather disagreeable to Julia.

Cleon. How can that be inferred? Did she know of the inheritance, I might think it had made her proud. The worthy intentions of Mr. Davenport are visible: he wished to marry her while she was poor; gratitude should now induce her to accept his hand; so I am persuaded she will act.

Siegm. You are well aware, Sir, of the evil consequences of constraint in marriage?

Cleon. We shall see: I depend on time. And I now could wish, Mr. Siegmund, if you are so inclined, to affiance my daughter Charlotte to-day, and thus double my pleasures.

Siegm. Yes—only my circumstances—I am several hundred dollars in debt.

Cleon. These debts shall be paid out of Julia's inheritance; and she will give you a thousand dollars to begin your marriage.

Siegm. You are very good, but——

Cleon. Charlotte will certainly make a sensible wife: her failings are few indeed, and her person is far from amiss. But why should I tell you that which you know better than myself? The copy of the will will soon come: are you willing?

Siegm. Certainly—Charlotte is the woman I wish for—I respect you as my father—yet—durst I say so much—I cannot help thinking, Julia is more inclined to *me* than to Mr. Davenport; and Charlotte—Charlotte is *very* kind to the latter. Permit me to add, Julia has desired I would speak to you on the subject.

Cleon. What do I hear! Now I understand why Julia has been so captious. Tell me, I request you, what is to be done? All that depends—I am bewildered! Julia may love you, but Charlotte loves you better.

Seigm. You are right, my dear father.

Cleon. Must Charlotte have two husbands, and Julia none? That would not be well.

Seigm. I am perplexed—I act an unpleasant part. The best would be for you to keep the secret, and defer the affair with Mr. Davenport for a week: in that time, Julia may change.

Cleon. To whom can I speak but to you? Shame will keep me silent.

Siegm. Should Charlotte freely choose Mr. Davenport, I am too *disinterested* to rob her of a husband who would thus establish her fortune.

Cleon. You act nobly. All may yet be well. I am no less willing for you than Mr. Davenport to enjoy the inheritance of Julia. The division will indeed be more equal. Mr. Davenport's possessions will make Charlotte happy, and those of Julia will enrich you. I know not what step first to take.

Siegm. When things are ripe, do you promise Julia shall be mine?

Cleon. Charlotte loves you so much that it is rather her affair than mine; and it would be unjust should you forget her. I cannot conceive how this inconstancy should happen! You must be mistaken.

Siegm. Let us keep the secret a while. I love Charlotte from my soul, and would try every means to have her.

Cleon. We will be on the watch. I certainly think the first arrangement must remain. I will send Charlotte to you; speak tenderly to her, she will gladly hear you. I will once more question Julia, but with great caution. I stay too long, Mr. Simon is alone; but he is too good to take it amiss. [*Exit.*

SCENE XVII.—Siegmund *alone.*

Seigm. All goes well! Julia may be mine!—Handsome, rich, well formed, well bred, noble minded—And yet—if Charlotte should come to a knowledge too soon—would she not hold me in abhorrence?—Oh, no! That's not the danger: she loves me—What ails me? Do the oaths I have sworn to her—Unmeaning oaths, which passion extorts—Oh, Julia, how great are thy charms! To wish to possess thee, can that be wrong?

SCENE XVIII.—*Enter* CHARLOTTE.

Charl. They are both coming. The discovery shall be made. Oh, how will Julia be rejoiced! And you, my friend, do you still love me? Forgive this unnecessary question!

Siegm. Yes, dear Charlotte, I love you eternally; and by the return of my love my fidelity is eternally rewarded! Oh that I could make you perfectly happy! A monarch might envy me this enjoyment! Here they come. Permit me to retire; your father expects me.   [*Exit.*

SCENE XIX.—*Enter* JULIA *and* DAVENPORT.

Charl. (*to* Dav.) Come here, with Julia. I have to offer you—a handsome young and excellent bride, with a large inheritance!

Jul. Is *that* the news?

Dav. And if your bride had ten times her inheritance, my Julia, in a shepherd's hut, would be preferred!

Jul. Indeed! You hear her. Who knows how fortunate you may be! I congratulate you both. Who is it, Charlotte.

Charl. A charming girl, well bred, and with an estate of fifty thousand dollars!

Jul. Excellent! And—— Her name?

Charl. And as beautiful as yourself!

Jul. Why tell me that? If I am beautiful, let the looking-glass tell me so: it is not conversation for sisters. You might have informed Mr. Davenport of this by himself; it is not necessary I should be present. (*going.*)

Dav. Do not go, dear Julia; or, I must follow.

Jul. That must not be! The lady with the fortune, who has fallen in love with you, may take it amiss. It is very fortunate that you have been exercising yourself in making professions of love: it will now give you but little trouble to repeat them.

Charl. This brings me to the point. I will describe the young lady that will please Mr. Davenport. First, her eyes are large and blue, like yours; her person finely formed; her manners elegant; her mien victorious; her hands round, plump and small *.

Jul. (*Looks at her hands.*)

Charl. She delights Mr. Davenport, but she prefers her liberty.

Jul. Really, I cannot understand you! Do tell me her name at once.

Charl. Oh, her name is Julia.

Jul. You are treating me like a child.

Charl. No, Julia; I am the messenger of great good fortune! Your late aunt has left you, by will, her whole estate. Mr. Simon brought us the news, and I requested of him to give me the pleasure of first informing you both. My dear sister, may every happiness that riches can give be yours! And, oh, Mr. Davenport, may Julia be your own!

Jul. Her whole estate! And nothing to you? Is it not divided? Are you sure? Certainly I've misunderstood! Why has she left my sister nothing?

Charl. She loved you the best; the inheritance is yours, and was long intended so to be. Give me my Siegmund, not embittered by poverty, and I have enough. My father, dear Julia, will think every minute an age till he may wish you joy: for I entreated him to take no notice till I had first informed you.

Dav. Amazement! Happy were it for me, perhaps, had there been no such will. Oh, lovely Julia, must I lose you!

Jul. Charlotte, the inheritance shall be divided between you and my father: I do not wish for it; do not deserve it. Vexatious will!—I was

---

* *The text is,* kleine volle runde hände, *which I have followed: these hands are not thought handsome in England.*

uneasy before, and now am more so. (*looks at* Davenport.) What say you, Sir?

Dav. Say, dear Julia——

Charl. Oh, you are getting into the vapours again. My father will be quite impatient.

SCENE XX.—*Enter* CLEON.

Cleon. Why do you stay here, dear children? The coffee waits.

Charl. Do not be angry, dear father; your children are in good company.

Jul. Oh, my father!

Cleon. What is the matter? Shall I not wish thee joy? I have wept with pleasure. Dear child! Pray go, Charlotte, to Mr. Simon, or he will depart to procure a copy of the will. You, Sir, will also be so good as to keep him company.

Dav. Most willingly. (*Going with the sisters, but* Cleon *beckons to* Julia.)

SCENE XXI.

Cleon. Well, my daughter, what says your heart? Is it not rejoiced?

Jul. Yes; for now I can part the inheritance between you and my sister.

Cleon. Sweet girl! For my part, keep what thou hast: but something given to thy sister will be but right. My small house will have enough while I live. But what says Mr. Davenport? Is he not highly pleased?

Jul. I think he is rather the reverse.

Cleon. True, true: he had enough before! But thou must not forget, he loved thee while thou wert poor. Ah, hadst thou heard all the good his guardian has related of him, thou couldst not but return his love. I did not think him well informed, he spoke so modestly, so little like my brother; but I am assured his knowledge is great, and the books he has read almost innumerable. Who could have thought it!

Jul. I have known it long, and know my own deficiency. Perhaps he seeks the same qualities in a wife, rather than an inheritance.

Cleon. How thou talkest! Women do not pursue the studies of men. Thou canst play, sing, dance, and speak French: canst write a good style, and legibly; understandest household duties, art intelligent, of a good family, well bred, cheerful, and now thou art rich. What more can a man desire? He loves thee; let me then have the pleasure to call *him* son, and *thee* a bride.

Jul. A bride? What can I say? Does he really love me? You are too partial to your child! My sister is superior to me.

Cleon. That is not the question. Mr. Siegmund is hers, and she is satisfied. Give her but a small part of thy wealth, then will she be perfectly contented; and she shall this day be affianced. But, perhaps, thou wouldst prefer Mr. Siegmund thyself?

Jul. Mr. Siegmund! How could you have such a thought ? If I must love, why should I not love Mr. Davenport? Is he not much the more meritorious? Nay, even were Mr. Siegmund preferable, which he is not, how could I with honour think of *him ;* since he and my sister love each other so tenderly ?

Cleon. It delights me to hear thee! I am a happy father! (*patting her cheek*) Continue thus to think, my charming girl, for thou thinkest rightly. Ay, ay, thou lovest Mr. Davenport much better than Mr. Siegmund, dost thou not ? The latter appears to me a little changeable—or something worse. I spoke concerning him with Mr. Simon, and——

Jul. Dear Sir, should I determine to love, I give you my word it will be just such a man as Mr. Davenport. But the loss of my liberty ! If I could but find out whether I love him or not.—No ; I do not love him, yet. Though so rich an heiress, I do not find myself more happy. Perhaps, I am a little ill ?

Cleon. Oh, people may easily be ill of love: but love *returned* is a cure for that. When I was ill myself that way, I only said *yes,* and was well again.

Jul. Ah, papa !

Cleon. Ah? I tell thee, *ah* is not the word, but *yes.* He is delighted with thee, and will love thee tenderly !

Jul. But—will he always be delighted ?

Cleon. That depends on thee. Why hesitate ? Art thou afraid he should hereafter change ? Never! His guardian has told me how often thy lover has declared he should not think himself a man, should he ever swerve from virtuous principles. He will be faithful to thee for life: he will not break a *solemn vow.*

Jul. I hear no vows from him. Would not his protestations be addressed to me, if——— ?

Cleon. So, he has not protested ? Excellent ! He is the more to be believed. In love, a public avowal is *more* than an oath. He will this day pledge himself, if thou wilt do the same.

Jul. I am so—irresolute—aukward—I cannot agree with myself: pray give me time.

Cleon. Till supper: but, then, declare at once yes, or no. I am serious, have opened my heart, and given my consent: act for thyself. Thy lover will be in search of thee: give me thy hand: come. It is a pleasure to me once more thus to lead a bride. [*Exeunt.*

END OF THE SECOND ACT.

ACT III.

SCENE I.—Siegmund, Julia.

Jul. WHAT do I hear! It cannot be!

Siegm. Yet it is true.

Jul. Did he say so himself? How unhappy am I!

Siegm. He did not tell me so *exactly in words;* but he greatly prefers Charlotte to you. I could easily pardon him this offence, though it is a deep one, if it were not a crime to you. Dear angel, how I pity you! I know how honourable your intentions are, and will rely on you not so much as to whisper my name in the affair.

Jul. Was this the cause of his affliction? Faithless at last! What advantage could he gain by thus betraying an innocent heart? If through passion he had taken my life, I would have forgiven him; but to deceive me under the mask of love and sincerity is detestable.

Siegm. Be assured, he will deny it.

Jul. Deceitful man! Oh yes! Deny! I shall never hear it from himself— I will not punish him: no, his conscience will be his tormentor.—How! He! To whom I this day resigned my heart!—No, no; I never loved him. Yet how often has he sworn that he loved me!—Is the word of man of no greater worth than this?

Siegm. Dear Julia, do not impute infidelity to our whole sex. Could you but know my heart!—Oh, anger itself only makes you more charming!

Jul. Dear Mr. Siegmund, pray leave me; I will—— And thou, Charlotte, art thou silent!—Oh, love, thou scourge of man, this is thy work!—Leave me: I give you my honour not to betray you, but rather to admire your honest proceeding. Let me see you again presently.

Siegm. As soon as I suppose you are a little cool.   [*Exit.*

SCENE II.—*Enter* Davenport *unperceived.*

Jul. At the very moment when he gave me the strongest promises of love to be faithless!—And yet I cannot hate him: is it witchcraft?

Dav. Do you not see me, Julia? Of whom are you speaking?

Jul. Of a faithless man, whom I might have loved, had I known him less. (*softening*) Is it possible you should deceive me! I! who had begun to prefer you to your whole sex? Why have you acted so cruelly and awakened inclinations in me which, while I feel them, I cannot but despise. Yet, to show you what a heart you have injured, I freely tell you I shall not, cannot perhaps, ever hate you; and, though I cannot but grieve at my weakness, shall wish to hide your failings even from myself.

Dav. Unfortunate man! Is faithless the title I deserve? I will not condescend to excuse myself; but conscious pride bids me declare my heart scorns the slightest infidelity. I will not even ask who can have inspired you with such opinions. Time will discover my rectitude.

Jul. So haughty!

SCENE III.—*Enter* CHARLOTTE.

Dav. (*to* Charlotte) Come, dear Madam, that you may also begin to hate me. Julia tells me I am a deceiver.

Charl. Oh, you have been quarrelling a little! Ay, about the first kiss, I suppose.

Dav. Complain of me to your sister; relate all my guilt.

Jul. Charlotte, perhaps, would afford me little consolation.

Charl. Ah, Julia, had my late aunt known thou wouldst have quarrelled on the day of being affianced to thy bridegroom, she would not have left thee one acre of land. These wars, I hope, will soon be over; naturally, thy heart is fond of peace, but love is rather fretful.

Jul. Your jokes are out of place.

Charl. Do look at her, Sir! Have you vexed her by too small a protestation of love? If so, please her by doubling the quantity. Tell *me* at least, sister, what is Mr. Davenport's fault; or, if you are so very much offended at a kiss, return the offence; give it him back; you will then be quits.—What is the matter with you both?

Jul. The matter! That must not be told when you are present. I scarcely can believe you have given him any such opportunity. Neither, indeed, is it any fault of his that you are more charming than I am. To be faithless is no crime; it is a merit. He would not love you but that he cannot forbear to love the most excellent. I do not blame him.

Charl. Sweet girl, am I your rival? This afflicts me! I will tell you the whole secret: but first say whether this accusation against your lover did not originate with Mr. Siegmund? I see the whole. He has pretended a passion for you, that he might discover your real affections, and artfully made you believe Mr. Davenport was in love with me. Forgive the joke; he has played his part well.

Jul. Nay, he seemed in earnest, and——

Dav. You see what a deceiver I am.

Jul. Yet——

Dav. Do you still doubt? How little do you know me?

Jul. I—Mr. Davenport——

Dav. Is that the reward of my love ?

Jul. How reward? Do you hate me? Should I have been jealous if——
So you have not deceived me? My heart was indeed your warm advocate.

Charl. Ay, ay; caught at last, my dear sister. You are still in pain, I
perceive, that you have not asked your lover to forgive your warmth. I will
do it myself. (*to* Davenport) Be`so good, dear Sir, as to forgive Julia, for
having loved you more tenderly than she supposed.

Jul. No, indeed; when I have faults I will confess them myself.

Dav. And do you love me?

Jul. Yes, beyond—rhyme or reason, and will no longer keep the secret
from your father and guardian, if the telling of it will give you pleasure.

Dav. My Julia! 'Tis too much happiness!

Jul. If I had not already won your heart I would beg for it, so highly do
I esteem it !

Dav. Excellent Julia! I am—— Oh, it is impossible to thank you as I
ought! The greatness of my joy robs me of utterance!

Charl. (*kissing* Julia) Dear sister, may this love be eternal! Set me an
example of tenderness and content. May you, dear brother, be as happy
even as my sister. Remain the friend of Mr. Siegmund, and by your sincerity promote our peace. Let us seek my worthy father : how his happy
heart will beat when he shall hear of Julia's compliance!—I see Mr. Simon
coming; pray be gone, and give me the pleasure of relating to him all that
has happened.   [*Exeunt* Julia *and* Davenport.

SCENE IV.—Charlotte, *Mr.* Simon.

Mr. S. I have the pleasure, at last, to bring you an abstract of the will :
I fetched it myself. Can you read and not be greatly affected? (*gives the
paper.*)

Charl. (*reading to herself*) How! I the heiress? I!

Mr. S. Yes, dear young lady; you, not Julia. Your godfather, the
counsellor, who first gave me the information, must either have been mistaken or have contrived this artifice to increase the joy of his god-daughter.
You are certainly the heiress; and no one can more sincerely congratulate
you than I do. You deserve it all, and more.

Charl. Oh, unfortunate mistake! Will not my dear sister grieve? Will
not Mr. Davenport——

Mr. S. Hey day! You were more rejoiced when I brought you the first
and false account! If you read the will, you will find however that, though
you are the heiress, there is a bequest of ten thousand dollars to your sister,
to be paid on the day of marriage.

Charl. That rejoices me; but she shall have much more rather than she
should take the loss to heart. Oh, happiness! What will my feelings be

when Mr. Siegmund shall thrill to hear this news! How happy am I! Provided only that my dear sister will not be afflicted.

SCENE V.—*Enter* SIEGMUND.

Siegm. Julia, I am told, has at length consented: is it true? How delighted I shall be!

Charl. (*to Mr.* Simon) Yes, at length she has gratified Mr. Davenport; and you, Sir, will be invited to the wedding. But here, Mr. Siegmund, is a copy of the will. Are not you a little vexed that my aunt should have forgotten us both?

Siegm. Not in the least. You are more to me than the wealth of worlds.

Charl. Should Julia offer us something from her inheritance, ought we not to be pleased?

Siegm. Being affianced, she has lost that right.

Mr. S. Oh, Sir, be assured, my ward will give her the full power to be liberal and grateful. He does not seek happiness in the excess of wealth, but in the noble disposal of it; and would have preferred Julia had she not been an heiress; nay, perhaps, would then have thought himself most fortunate. Would that all lovers were as noble-minded as himself!

Charl. You hear, Mr. Siegmund, what a worthy brother we shall have.

Siegm. The honour is no less to his guardian than to ourselves.

Mr. S. I own I am proud of him. Since he was ten years old, he has lived in my house, has all my cares so richly rewarded, and has given me such true enjoyment, that I know not which of us is the other's debtor.

Charl. To any body else I should envy this praise; and, were my dear father to die, would be your ward myself, could I obtain the same. How delightful is the intercourse between the noble-minded! Dare I, Mr. Simon, in your presence, take a liberty which love commands and justifies? Yes, you are worthy to be a witness of the pure emotions of my heart. (*embracing* Siegmund*) At last, my friend, I am happily able to reward your faith and affection as they deserve! You loved me when poor. Providence has to-day bestowed an inheritance upon me, of which I cannot make a better use than by presenting it to you. I know how worthily it will be employed. Here is a copy of the will, in which I am declared the heiress instead of my dear sister, as we had supposed. In short, except a bequest of ten thousand dollars to Julia, it will be all your own. Now what says your heart?

Siegm. Without my Charlotte's love, the present would be indifferent.

Charl. And well do you deserve that love. If nothing be wanting to your happiness but my affection, you cannot be more happy.

---

* *The manners of Germany render these tokens of fondness in the fair sex very admissible, and not unfrequent.*

Siegm. My heart is overpowered! With you, love and fortune are happiness indeed! Why cannot you make the whole world as dignified as yourself! The most unworthy would then, in their own despite, be compelled to resemble you. That you have given me yourself merits my eternal thanks. With your permission, I will hasten to your worthy father, and now——

SCENE VI.—*Enter a Servant.*

Serv. (*to* Charlotte) Here is a letter, Miss: it came by the post.

Charl. A letter by the post!

Siegm. I saw the letter-carrier in the hall, as I came here.

Charl. With your permission, gentlemen—(*breaking the seal*).

Mr. S. I will retire, and congratulate my ward.

[*Exeunt Mr.* SIMON *and Servant.*

SCENE VII.

Charl. (*after reading*) Oh, my friend, some one is determined to embitter my joy! I am envied, and you are calumniated. The blow is wicked! Yet I welcome it, since it will afford me a new opportunity of giving you a proof of my truth and love. I will read the letter; it is only two lines, as you see. (*reads*)

" Do not trust your lover, Mr. Siegmund, he is a deceiver. N. N."

Siegm. How! I a deceiver!

Charl. (*taking his hand*) I know how much you are above being moved by this hateful accusation: it is to you a panegyric. Oh that I might always meet such deceivers!

Siegm. But who, on such a day as this, could make this wicked attempt? If—ay, should it be Mr. Simon himself? Perhaps he loves you! Does he covet your fortune? Why did he go when the letter came? Ought I to forgive such a crime? Had he accused my understanding, I might have thanked him for the mortification; but rectitude of heart and honour, to rob me of them is to administer poison. I! I a deceiver! It will be seen who is deceitful, I or the writer of this letter. Is this the noble-minded guardian!

Charl. I entreat you, in the name of love, be calm: forbear to suspect Mr. Simon: it is not possible that he should be guilty of such malignity. His character is dignified. It may be, you have some enemy who has this day been informed of *your* love, and *my* inheritance.

Siegm. But why excuse this guardian? Did you not remark him when he said, " Would that all lovers were as noble-minded as my ward!" Is not this a shameless attack upon me?

Charl. Indeed you will offend me, should you suspect him but for a moment. From what I have observed, and Mr. Davenport has reported, he is a man whose whole life has been dedicated to honesty and honour.

Siegm. But may he not be betrayed into unjust designs? I remarked what strict attention he paid to every action, every word of yours. Another singular circumstance concurs: in the note he wrote this morning to your father, he said he had received good news from court; of which he has since given an account to your father, but not to me.

Charl. I am certain of his rectitude: pray do not let him be suspected.

Siegm. Why did he not tell *me* that he had been appointed to a respectable office, with a high salary, at court? If he did not mean to undermine me, what was his meaning?

Charl. I forgive your failing, which originates in love, but will listen to you no longer. The attempt shall be turned to our advantage: your enemies will be sufficiently punished by their ignorance of your worth; therefore, pray be satisfied. We cannot better revenge ourselves than by not taking the least trouble to discover the detractor. Dismiss your anger; and let us, in the presence of my father and the company, confirm the ties of affection in despite of our enemy. [*Exit.*

SCENE VIII.—SIEGMUND *alone.*

Siegm. Cursed fortune, what a blow! Yet it does but give me courage. Julia is lost!—Well, but Charlotte and the inheritance are mine!—I have not been false: no! I only wavered.—All circumstances considered, I acted well—nobly.—But where is Charlotte? Should she hear more of my infidelity—— (*in haste*) I will make all secure. [*Exit.*

SCENE IX.—JULIA, DAVENPORT.

Jul. (*repeating after* Siegmund) "Where is Charlotte? Should she hear more of my infidelity—I will make all secure."—Vile man! You heard his confession! We desired to see how he would conduct himself, after receiving the letter. Oh, had this odious conduct never been discovered! Poor Charlotte! To bind thyself to a man who, under the mask of honesty, conceals so bad a heart.

Dav. I told you how unworthy I thought him: he has practised the height of deceit. I entreated him like a brother, in the forenoon, to aid me in gaining your consent; instead of which, he entreated your worthy father to protract every thing for a week; and spoke as if you, my Julia, were in love with him. Is this the friend whom I have more than once invited to partake my fortune, and make my house his own!

Jul. And he pretended, to me, that my *sister* was *your* favourite. I am now convinced he did not act the part that Charlotte had assigned him: yet, poor girl, she will never think to the contrary. Who shall make the discovery to her? Will she believe what she hears? And, if she does, how great will be her misery! How I pity her!

Dav. So do 1; yet you must tell her; or, if you are silent, I must and will speak.

Jul. Think how unhappy my dear sister will be! Pray say nothing. Perhaps—perhaps he is not wicked in nature. Misled by my inheritance, he might——

Dav. His infidelity is still the same; and, in my estimation, the man whom hunger makes a robber is infinitely less guilty. If he could be insensible to the tenderness, the bewitching innocence, and the noble friendship of your faithful and virtuous sister, he would hereafter, urged on by avarice, poison a father, a wife, or a bosom friend.

Jul. Oh, my sister!—Pray forbear!—I tremble——

Dav. Lovely Julia, you are to me the most precious thing on earth; yet, forgive me when I tell you, rather than see your sister united to misery with such a worthless man, I would forego riches, honour, ay, and even yourself! I will speak, how great soever her distress. The letter was written by my guardian, at my particular request. Your worthy father and uncle, who were supposed so simple by him, first remarked his base intentions; and your father therefore informed my guardian of them, who both hates and detects the slightest deviations from rectitude.

Jul. Has the man then no excuse?

Dav. Not the smallest: every thing has been thoroughly examined. (*indignantly*) He is a deceiver, and merits a deceiver's punishment. How! Shall men, by hateful deceit, triumph over the affectionate innocence of woman, which both virtue and honour command them to defend?

Jul. How must my sister proceed with the faithless man?

Dav. Let her punish him by contempt, and make him feel the villainy of attempting to deceive a noble heart.

Jul. Suppose she were to pardon him, would not that be still more noble?

Dav. She need not publish his crime; but, while subduing her revenge, let him be eternally renounced. He is no man.

SCENE X.—*Enter Mr.* SIMON.

Mr. S. I am greatly distressed! The letter has not answered our purpose; she loves him still better than before, and determines to think him innocent. She entreats her father to conclude the match: he, good man, loves his daughter, and, in the greatness of that love, may perhaps forget all precaution and advice. If nobody else will venture to brave the storm, I will.

Dav. And I.

Jul. Oh that my sister would come, I would—— But she loves him with such affection! What will be the feelings of her heart to separate!

Mr. S. Painful indeed! Affection cannot be more sincere; but that is because she holds him worthy of her love. Let her be convinced of her error, and reason, her love of virtue, and her abhorrence of a faithless heart, will gain the victory. She will then despise what now she loves. We must all once more speak with your father, before he gives his consent.

Jul. Noble-minded sister! Oh, that I could share thy misfortunes! How mournfully to me does this day end!

Mr. S. Do not lament the loss of such a man. Charlotte is fortunate in it, and would indeed be unhappy were it otherwise. Pray try, Mr. Davenport, to entice her from her lover, and bring her here.

Dav. I will; it is the only way.

Mr. S. A word, before you go. Have you read the copy of the will which I have brought?

Dav. No, Sir.

Mr. S. Nor you, Julia?

Jul. No.

Mr. S. Then you are not informed that the first account was false? Julia, do not be alarmed—you are not the heiress.

Jul. How! Not! Why have I been deceived? Is every thing to-day unfortunate? Mr. Davenport—You do not speak! Am I no longer your bride? Cannot love endure misfortune? I hoped to have shared with my father and sister; the best apartments in the house that was left me were designed for them. Oh, Sir, what joy did I imagine to myself I should feel, while taking you by the hand, and leading you through all my possessions! Have I now none?

Dav. All that are mine are yours! Forget the inheritance; that can effect no change. I am pleased to think it is not yours. People might have supposed my love was rather to that than to my Julia, and her virtues; this cannot now be suspected. The world will esteem you the more, my dear bride, to find it is yourself I choose and honour. Lead me by the hand to my own house, for that shall be your inheritance. Oh were Charlotte but relieved! Till then I cannot be at peace.

Mr. S. Charlotte is the heiress.

Jul. My sister! I could almost envy her. The thought is odious! No! I rejoice sincerely. Being yours, what can I wish for more?—Oh let all be hers!

Dav. Including me, dear Julia?

Jul. You my sister's husband? Oh, no; I am not yet so disinterested: neither would it be virtue. But pray go to my sister.

Dav. Willingly: love for a moment shall be sacrificed to friendship.

[*Exit.*

SCENE XI.

Jul. Was he serious? Resign him to my sister? How could he hint such a thing! The inheritance is hers. I love her dearly; but if she should ask me to resign Mr. Davenport it would be too much. I could never do it.

Mr. S. Harbour no such thoughts: she will make no such demand. I must further tell you, the will bequeaths ten thousand dollars to you on the day of your marriage.

Jul. That is as it ought to be: yet, could I restore faith and truth to the lover of my sister by resigning this money, how willingly should it be given! Base man! When he shall find Charlotte lost to himself, may he not contrive that Mr. Davenport shall be lost to me? Though he is faithless, I am not to blame.

Mr. S. Have no such fears! Depend on what I say. Charlotte is to be pitied; but better lose her lover than her happiness. Were she but here!

Jul. Who can restore her peace? I love her dearly; but why should I lose my lover? No; I can never be so generous as that: I cannot resign, cannot forget him. She might be happy, but I should not. He said, " Love for a moment should be sacrificed to friendship." What did that mean?

Mr. S. Fear nothing; he is yours: you deserve him; and hereafter we shall feel that love and friendship, when guided by virtue, contain the greatest enjoyment and happiness the world can afford.

SCENE XII.—*Enter* MAGISTER.

Mag. Mr. Simon, I would impart a word. Or I do mistake, or I have this day made the remarkable discovery that the enjoyment and possession of wealth hath great power over the human heart.

Mr. S. I fear, Sir, I know this quite as well as yourself.

Mag. I made it while ruminating in my study.

Jul. Can you remedy the evil, dear Sir?

Mag. Mr. Siegmund must be punished, that he may be amended.

Mr. S. The proper punishment will be contempt.

Mag. Nay, but, the powers of will in him: how shall they be rectified?

Mr. S. Is not contempt the proper means?

Mag. I will not too hastily answer. But are not you, Sir, of opinion that the Stoics rightly maintained there was but one vice: or that, where one vice ruleth, other vices are all rendered subservient. Only observe Mr. Siegmund: doth he not exemplify this paradox?

Mr. S. Yes, Sir; but our business is to separate him and Charlotte, who will not yet believe him faithless.

Mag. Among possibilities, that is one. How happeneth it that men are not astonished at the near relationship which doth subsist between vice and vice? Mr. Siegmund, being told of the will, became avaricious. Vice the first. He attempted to suborn Julia, and possess himself of her inheritance. Proof of inordinate self-love. Deceitful himself to Charlotte, he casteth about to render Julia faithless. Vice upon vice. The first vice cannot be rendered effectual but by deceit and treachery. *Ergo*, he deceiveth his friend, deceiveth his father-in-law, deceiveth you, deceiveth me, deceiveth all having once deceived virtue; and, that all these deceits may proceed, it was necessary he should lie and calumniate. All this he hath done. How unholy is the combination that doth link the vices together! Were not the Stoics right?

Mr. S. Who doubts it, Sir? You see these things in a very learned light. However, you first discovered him to be faithless, and Julia, I, and all are your debtors. Can you now discover the means to separate Charlotte from this Mr. Siegmund?

Mag. I will think thereon. Credulity in Charlotte hath been active; but, from this event, she must be taught how much it doth become all those to hold the human heart in doubt, who have not laboriously studied the generation of covetousness. We, the learned, have this way learnt truly to reason: a knowledge of the *Will* is no less necessary. Is not the will as essential a part of the soul as the understanding? When the understanding doth comprehend, then hath the will an impulse.—The man, who knoweth these things, knoweth his essence; and, also, knoweth the means that tend unto perfection. I call upon you to declare, niece, if I have not, on manifold occasions, informed you that Mr. Siegmund had laid no foundation in philosophy? The bitter fruit of ignorance doth now appear.

Jul. My dear uncle, did you feel this treachery like myself, you would not ask me such questions at present. You read me a fable to-day, and I could wish you would remember the fable of the boy, who fell into the water. Instead of aiding us in our danger, you teach us the origin and hateful nature of vice. Pray do not take my freedom amiss.

Mag. From you, niece, I profess to take nothing amiss. To the word offence appertaineth the appertaining knowledge of the nature of the offence. In this knowledge you are deficient; therefore, your discourse is an offence, and is not.

Mr. S. But how will you proceed?

Mag. It shall be thus. Antecedent to the promise, which my brother might make of Charlotte, I will briefly, and positively, inform him, that my consent shall never be bestowed; and, by this, he will certainly be reduced to protract his own. [*Exit.*

Mr. S. Do so.

SCENE XIII.

Jul. I will follow my uncle; he may be too slow and formal. When she comes, pray discover this afflicting event to Charlotte. I will take care her faithless lover shall not disturb you; and, when I think it the proper moment, will come with Mr. Davenport to your aid.

Mr. S. Honest intentions shall be my guide; and, should I be treated

with the utmost scorn by your sister, and the most degrading revenge by Mr.
Siegmund, I will rather forget myself than the cause I have undertaken.

[*Exit* Julia.

SCENE XIV.—*Enter* CHARLOTTE.

Charl. What are your commands? Is it any thing concerning the ten
thousand dollars I am to pay my sister? Let me hear your proposal; I am
ready.

Mr. S. We will speak of that another time. Are you persuaded that I
wish you well, and that my motives are honourable? These questions may be
thought strange, yet are necessary, considering there is so much danger that
you will not patiently listen to me.

Charl. How, Sir, can I serve you? Speak freely. I owe you no less respect
than I owe my father, and will be exceedingly thankful if you will give me
an opportunity to prove my esteem. I have as high an opinion of your
honour as of the honour of Mr. Siegmund: what can I say more to induce
you to speak?

Mr. S. It is of him I would wish to speak.

Charl. Perhaps your ward desires that part of the estate which lies near
the town? Ay; that leads me to guess why he behaved so coldly toward the
good Siegmund. Why not speak to *me?* He shall have it on those terms
which you yourself think just. Let us join the company. With respect to
the wicked letter, I am determined, in your presence, to resign my heart and
myself to Mr. Siegmund, and convince his enemies that mine is not love for
calumny to shake.

Mr. S. 'Twas I who wrote that *wicked* letter.

Charl. Rather than believe you, I would think it had been written by my
father, dearly as he loves me! You joke.

Mr. S. No, Miss; the affair is much too serious to be joked with. Avoid
and hate me if you please, but I repeat, your lover has not acted honestly
toward you.

Charl. You certainly mean to have the pleasure of trying my constancy,
and endeavouring to frighten me: yet you ought to know I am not to be this
way frightened.

Mr. S. I am not in sport. I will speak still plainer: your lover is deceitful.

Charl. (*offended*) You go too far, Sir. I will answer for his truth, and
would have you know that, by offending him, you offend me. Nay, even
were he faithless, I should hate the person as much who convinced me of
it as him who had betrayed me. But I am too soon angry: no, Sir, you
cannot descend so far. As certainly as I live, you are not in earnest.

Mr. S. *As certainly as I live, I am.* He is unworthy to be loved by you for a moment.

Charl. And I will love him eternally.

Mr. S. You do not know him.

Charl. Better than you do, Sir.

Mr. S. Your native rectitude and unsuspecting heart make you believe - him honest; but you are mistaken.

Charl. Do not give me arms against yourself. I have held both you and him to be honest, and I am deceived. But which must I hate? If my friendship be of any worth, say no more: my very heart revolts! You have been particularly kind to me and my family, but you have acquired no right to act with selfishness toward me. Would it not be more like yourself to cherish me in the paths of virtue than to mislead and render me base? Why do you now speak as you do?

Mr. S. Because, till this afternoon, I was not certain. If you will not believe *me*, give credit at least to your sister, and Mr. Davenport.

Charl. Hateful proceeding! Have you made *them* of your party?

Mr. S. Them, and your honourable father; and, rather than suffer you to be the wife of such a traitor, I will encounter the greatest danger. You are much too noble, much too charming for such a man.

Charl. Would you then offer me your own heart? Must he be faithless because, in your eyes, I am charming? Think you that means like these can win an upright heart? Either I must hate you, or no longer love virtue. I shall not long be able to look at you.

Mr. S. Reproach me as you please, your anger only proves the rectitude of your heart. Your mistake is your justification; and perhaps I might have hated you, could you have heard me patiently.

Charl. Sir, your artifice, if it be one, as it cannot but be, is most odious! How! He, whom I love as myself, would you usurp his place? Is it possible?

Mr. S. Bitter as it is, I will endure even this. I own I esteem you more than I can express; but I have a certain means of depriving you of this suspicion. I give you my solemn promise never more to enter your house; and, could I seek by this discovery to gain your affections, there is no punishment too great for such an attempt. After this promise, it would disgrace me to speak another word. [*Exit.*

SCENE XV.—CHARLOTTE *alone.*

Charl. Oh, what is this?—He faithless! Never! No; this guardian is the deceiver, not he. Thou upright heart! Friend of my bosom! Would they entrap me? Why did not the accuser bring his proofs?

SCENE XVI.—*Enter* DAVENPORT.

Charl. Come to my aid; for, should they all conspire against my happiness, you are yet too worthy to be their abettor. How has my Siegmund offended? Speak honestly.

Dav. He is a faithless man.

Charl. You too an enemy! If he have offended you, act at least with justice, and do not accuse him out of revenge!

Dav. My heart is incapable of revenge.

Charl. But not of ingratitude. Has not Mr. Siegmund this day performed the most friendly office for you?

Dav. I wish he had never been so employed; you would then have been more fortunate, and he an avowed traitor.

Charl. Deceiver! Traitor! Are those names for a man whom I have two years known and loved?

Dav. Had I a less sense of my duty, I might use more circumlocution; but honest sincerity will admit of no other epithets. You, my sister, are well worthy of respect; and the man who, having had such proofs of your tenderness and open honest affection, could see them all and still be faithless, is a monster!

Charl. A monster! I am firm. I ask for proofs. (*passionately*) Neither you, your guardian, my sister, nor even my father, shall deprive him of my love: nor will I accept any other proof than his own confession. I am the more confident in his virtue, being certain that a thought of infidelity could not have arisen in his heart, without being discovered by him to me; and, conscious as I am of this sympathy, your attempt will but strengthen my love, if that be possible.

Dav. May the heart of Julia no longer be mine if what I speak be not the truth! I owe that heart to you; but I were unworthy the enjoyment of it, could I consent to see you wretched.

Charl. You must think me very light and fickle, could you believe I should waver in my love from mere accusation. Have *you* or *I* had the most opportunities to know the heart of Mr. Siegmund? Why do you accuse him when he is absent? Call him here, and tell me then of his infidelity. He is more noble of soul than the best of us, and love him I must.

Dav. Your demand is just; I will seek him. [*Exit.*

SCENE XVII.—*Enter* JULIA.

Charl. Indeed! And will he call him? I begin to tremble! (*mournfully*) And you too, sister! Do *you* not love me? (*kissing her*) Must I again listen to the same hateful story? Oh, no! Yet why silent? Why does not Siegmund come?

Jul. Give up, I conjure thee, the love of a man who——

Charl. Suppose him to blame, must he be unworthy my love? No, sister, he will certainly prove his innocence. Will you not plead for him? Have you forgotten the part he took this very day in your behalf? Why should he now be faithless, I being rich? Why not a deceiver sooner?

Jul. It was while he thought me the heiress. Dear sister, how happy should I be wert thou but undeceived.

Charl. Is it so certain? (*positively*) Once more, no!

Jul. I long struggled with myself; I excused him to my own heart, to Mr. Davenport, his guardian, and our father; and, from my love to thee, wished to think them all deceived: but it is no longer possible. Here, in this place, being alone, he lamented that thou hadst received the letter; and spoke of his own perturbation and *infidelity*. He did not hear me coming. Oh, had he been eternally silent!——My dear sister!

Charl. Speak! Did I rightly hear? Has he accused himself? Is he faithless? If he were, could I still love him? No, no; 'tis certain that our love is mutual: from me he has received every proof of affection. (*scornfully*) Why torment myself with thoughts so horrid? What has he done? Nothing, nothing!

Jul. He has tried, in a most artful manner, to separate Mr. Davenport from me, and supply his place. He insinuated to my father that I loved him; that Mr. Davenport was your favourite; entreated the ceremony might be delayed for a week; and asked my hand for himself.

Charl. What! At the very moment he so earnestly seemed to entreat for mine! You hate us both!

Jul. Yes, entreated when he knew the will was in your favour.

Charl. Then his heart was governed by the will, and not by love? It is unjust to condemn him unheard. The best of hearts are not free from failings, of which they soon repent. (*sorrowfully*) Dear sister, is he quite unworthy of forgiveness? Oh, prove him innocent, and, however wretched, I will renounce him. How willingly would I give him all that is left me, had I but the joy to find him honourable! Oh love, is this the reward of fidelity!

SCENE XVIII.—*Enter* Siegmund.

Siegm. Shall I be happy enough still to have your consent? I have gained your father's. Generous angel, do you still love me?

Charl. Am I beloved by you?

Siegm. Time has given you proof of my affection, and you cannot but know that the first wish of my heart is to possess your love.

Charl. But—My sister—Why do you shrink?

Siegm. To think you should not remember I was prompted to the artifice that offends you by yourself. Was it not appointed, as the part I was to act, that I should make love to her? Speak, Julia, in my justification!

Jul. That is past my power. Recollect what you said to me, to my father, and but just now, leaving this place, to yourself, not seeing me. All I can do is to entreat my dear sister to pardon your faithless conduct.

Siegm. I faithless! (*greatly disordered*) I! and to the best of women! Who! I! Have I spoken to your father? What dreadful mystery is this?— You behold me with anguish! Do you not love me? Do you hear me deny all this unmoved?—Has what I say no weight?—Am I not innocent?— Who are my enemies?—I appeal to my own heart, to love, to all—— Yet pleading for myself will but increase suspicion. Oh, believe me without oaths! May I lose my peace, my love, and you, if I am faithless! Will you not yet believe me?

Jul. Mr. Siegmund, are oaths at your command?

Charl. He must be innocent!

Siegm. And am. I love you, and seek *my* happiness in *your own*. Would you increase that happiness, be yourself again; and renounce suspicions, which I would pardon in no one but yourself. Shall I have the transport to call you mine?

Charl. (*looks at him in grief*) Me!—Call me yours?—Yes.

Jul. Sister!

Charl. Be quiet. Mr. Siegmund, I wish to speak a word with my father; we then may put our enemies to shame.

Siegm. I will go for him: shall I bring the rest of the company? for we must observe all legal ceremonies.

Charl. Yes; but first let me speak with my father; and then I request you will bring them all.   [*Exit* Siegmund.

SCENE XIX.—*Enter* CLEON.

Cleon. Now, children, if all obstacles are removed, I wish you both to be affianced; and then we may sit down to table properly paired. Oh, Charlotte, who in the morning would have thought that, before night, thou wouldst have been an heiress! But 'tis all as we could wish. Julia, being but poor, gained the heart of a wealthy and honourable man; and thou, being rich, bringst a fortune to thy poor lover. What could be better! Thy Siegmund will be grateful for thy fidelity. Well can he describe a tender faithful heart! Eloquent lover! How often has he kissed my hand! How dutifully did he ask my consent!

Charl. That is worthy of him: it revives me. Yet tell me, dear Sir, did he to-day ask my sister's hand? 'Tis what I cannot believe.

Cleon. Why, yes, in a *half and half* kind of manner. He could not but think Mr. Davenport had cast a favourable eye on thee, and that thou wouldst *prefer a wealthy man.* At first, I felt indignant; but he presently *talked* me into good humour. However, the guilty must all be forgiven, when they repent. Here our guests come.

SCENE XX.

Enter SIEGMUND, DAVENPORT, MAGISTER, *and Mr.* SIMON.

Cleon. At length, I have the happiness which I have so long desired. My words shall be few. You are all acquainted why we meet. On you, my eldest child, I first bestow my blessing and consent. (Charlotte *weeps*) Nay, weep not, Charlotte.

Charl. My tears are tears of love. Has my choice your consent? Your child thanks you from her heart.

Mr. S. Recollect, Miss—Will you—— What shall I say?

Dav. Oh, dear sister, let me entreat——

Charl. For what? For Julia at my hands? (*leading her to him*) Here she is: I bring you love that will never end! Mr. Siegmund——

Siegm. I accept your heart with boundless gratitude, and beg your hand with——

Charl. Unworthy man! My wealth I can bestow, but not my heart. Ask of my father and the company, who have all severely felt the wrongs you have done to me, how treachery ought to be rewarded! I have been but too ready at blind forgiveness. (*to Mr.* Simon) Sir, I honour your integrity! If I should ever again think of love, your claims to my affections are the first. (*to Siegmund*) Be so good as to leave us without reply.

Siegm. Willingly.——Accursed love!   [*Exit.*

Dav. Treachery you ought to say. You have your reward.

Charl. (*speaking after* Siegmund) To-morrow I will send you sufficient money to prevent your having the least cause, hereafter, to deceive an affectionate and honourable heart.

Cleon. Oh Charlotte, how happy thou makest me! I have not thy prudence.

Jul. Dear sister, what a noble mind is thine! Indeed I have not been to blame. Could I but see thee as happy as myself!

Mag. I am satisfied to find that vice, by me discovered, should by itself be punished. Thus it is. Whoever doth not subdue and punish errors in their origin will find at length errors will subdue and punish him.

Mr. S. (*to* Charlotte) Dear Madam, I would now remind you of my future claims over your heart, had I not already given you my promise to be silent. My reward indeed is great, that you should no longer think me unworthy, and that you have punished a treacherous lover.

Charl. Oh may he escape the harm he too well deserves! How sincerely did I love him! And how unhappy has that love made me! No; 'tis the folly of my lover that has made me wretched. Pity me.   [*Exeunt Omnes,*

THE END.

REMARKS.

THE plan of THE TENDER SISTERS is too simple for the English Stage, at present, which requires intricacy of plot, a succession of incidents, and is seldom satisfied without attempts at greater variety of character. In this Play, *Cleon, Mr. Simon,* and *Davenport,* have no pretensions to humour: nor is there much originality in the remaining persons. The *Magister* is a formal pedant, in which the touches are frequently pleasant, but rarely strong. The two Sisters are highly amiable; but, except in the strength of her affection and a few occasional sallies, *Charlotte* has little to distinguish her. *Julia,* however, is charmingly drawn, and with but little alteration might be transferred to the Stage with excellent effect. *Siegmund,* at first, appears insignificant; but, when he supposes *Julia* the heiress, it is he that gives the chief interest to the plot, and rises as a character, but, as a man, sinks into the most painful baseness and contempt. The Author has entitled it *a Comedy,* and the Germans affirm it was the first *sentimental Drama* that appeared among them; nor can it be read without leaving a favourable impression of the heart and talents of GELLERT, as an early and successful reformer of the grossness, buffoonery, and absurdity, which then reigned in Germany; or without leaving a fine moral feeling in the mind.

The translation here given of the above piece is rather free than literal: the character of the MAGISTER is occasionally a little heightened, and a few deviations have been made, where idiom, manners, or effect seemed to demand them, but they are inconsiderable; nor can the play by any liberties here taken be supposed to produce as much effect in English as in the German. In a word, the feelings and intentions of the author, rather than his phraseology, have been studied.

DRAMATIC BIOGRAPHY.

SOMÈ ACCOUNT OF GELLERT *.

WHEN Gellert first attained celebrity, the literature of Germany had attracted little notice from the rest of Europe : its authors were then, much more even than at present, exuberant in words, spreading them over paper, and teaching little that had the least claim to originality. They seemed to delight in the prattling of childhood, or garrulity in which old age indulges itself, to the great annoyance of listeners.

Gellert was among those men of a more improved taste, the number of whom, during his life, began greatly to increase ; till, at present, Germany holds a distinguished rank in the republic of letters : nay, among its *own writers of inferior genius*, it *now* repeatedly, vainly, and absurdly, claims an absolute pre-eminence. Its progress has indeed been great ; but much greater tasks must yet be performed, before this proud claim can with justice be recognized.

Born in the year 1715, at Haynichen, a small town in Upper Saxony, the son of a clergyman who had thirteen children, Gellert first went to school in his native place ; where he could have learned little, had he not been assisted by his father. Here however he wrote for lawyers to obtain money, and in his thirteenth year composed his first poem on the birth-day of his beloved father. In 1729, he went to Meissen ; at which place there is one of those seminaries called *Fürsten-schulen*, or Electoral Schools, in Saxony. Here however he could make but little progress, in the acquirement of ideas, or taste ; for, though the classics were *read*, their merits *were not felt:* the dead letter, and not the spirit, of these writers was studied ; and no author thought of cultivating his mother tongue.

---

* Chiefly extracted from a German work, entitled *Handbuch der Poetischen Litteratur der Deutschen*, by *Von Veterlein :* KOETHEN, 1800.

At this school, however, Gellert became acquainted with Gaertner and Rabner ; which acquaintance soon increased into friendship for life.

At fifteen, Gellert went to the university at Leipsic, to study divinity, where he heard the famous Hofman lecture on philosophy; at whose profound researches he greatly wondered, though, as he afterward owned, he little understood them.

In four years time he returned to his father, and began to exercise the clerical office, but without inclination.

After living some time with a noble family in Dresden, as *hofmeister*, or first gentleman, he returned home, and during two years became tutor to his sister's son ; with whom, in 1741, he went back to Leipsic, partly to instruct the youth, partly himself, and again to hear his admired Hofman, but who died at that period.

During this part of his life, he appears to have laid the foundation of his fine knowledge of the human heart, his pure taste, and his excellent and pleasant style.

The author, in whose works he most delighted, most studied, read aloud, and translated for his improvement, was Cicero. Rollin in the French, and in English the Spectator, were likewise his favourites ; while an intercourse with his well-informed friends, particularly *Gaertner* and *Elias Schlegel*, greatly assisted his progress.

About that time Gellert published his fables, in *Die Belustigungen des Verstandes und Witzes* * ; which, *on their first appearance*, were universally applauded.

On his second arrival at Leipsic, he gave private lessons, and, finding his facility and love of study increase, dedicated himself entirely to letters ; for he took but little delight in the clerical profession. In 1745, he by general consent became a public teacher, and lectured *on eloquence and poetry*. In the same year we find him one of the association of young poets, who published a work, at Bremen, under the title of *Beiträge* ; and in the following year a collection of his fables first ap-

---

* A periodical work, which appeared in the year 1742.

peared, by which he rendered immortal honour to, and promoted the good taste of, Germany.

This period of his life, till the year 1751, was especially
marked by activity of mind; those hypochondriac affections,
by which it was afterward so much embittered, not having
yet appeared. Then it was that his *Fables, Dramatic Works,
Life of a Swedish Countess, Essays in Prose, Collection of Letters, Moral Poems, Religious Odes,* and *Lyrical Performances,*
were written.

This noble-minded and active man, though almost oppressed
by external cares, incessant labour, and the decline of a weak
constitution, after continual intercourse with the young students, who by his instruction, and after his example, became
an honour to Germany, yes, the services of this man of genius
were at length recollected by the court; and in 1751 a pro-
fessorship in philosophy was given him, with an annual stipend
of a hundred dollars! about *sixteen pounds sterling.* During
the seven years' war, however, this pittance was no longer
paid; and the envoy *of a foreign nation*— an Englishman, Mr.
Mitchel, who had read his writings, exerted himself that his
pension might be restored. Afterward indeed, toward the
end of his life, a pension more worthy of his merits was allowed.

From private persons, Gellert received many proofs of gratitude and good will * : Prince Henry honoured him, and sent
him a horse, that he had taken at the battle of Freiburg.
Gellert was himself one of the kindest and most friendly of

---

* One wintry day, a Saxon peasant came to Leipsic with a cart load of
wood, stopped at the door of GELLERT, and asked him if he was not the
gentleman who made such fine fables? Hearing it was him, the man leapt
for joy, made many excuses for being so free, and begged he would accept
the wood in return for the pleasure the countryman had received. The King
of Prussia thus describes him in a letter: This blunt GELLERT is really an
amiable man. Like the owl, he cannot easily be drawn from his retreat;
but, having him, he becomes a mild and cheerful philosopher, acute, original,
and no imitator. His heart is melting; candour and truth are on his lips,
and equity and humanity are painted on his forehead: yet, the moment four
persons are present, he becomes embarrassed, and, when the babbling begins,
timid, confused, melancholy, forgetful, and silent.—*Nouveau Dic. Hist.* CAEN,
1789, *Mot* GELLERT.

men. He died December 13th, 1769. Germany lamented his
loss, and wept his death.

His writings were, *Tales and Fables: Dramatic Pieces:
The Life of a Swedish Countess,* a novel : *Letters to various Persons :
Moral Poems: Religious Odes,* and *Lyrical Poems: Essays in
Prose :* and these were all collected and published by himself *.

Five posthumous volumes afterward appeared ; which may
be procured separately by those who, having his own edition
of his works, wish for the remainder. Parts of them have
been translated into English, French, and Italian : though
THE TENDER SISTERS now first appears in an English dress.

ACCOUNT OF NEW PERFORMERS.

YOUNG ROSCIUS.

CONSIDERING the suddenness and shortness of his career,
ample materials have already been industriously collected to
form a theatrical biography of this extraordinary boy ; who
well deserves to be called extraordinary, first for his early
exhibition of talents, but more for what may be modestly
called the whimsical sensation he has excited, the inordinate
curiosity that has intoxicated all ranks of people, and the exaggerated encomiums that are echoed from mouth to mouth.
Not that he does not deserve uncommon praise, heart-felt applause, and an assiduous cultivation of the talents which he
has so decidedly announced ; but it might seriously be wished
that these should be all attended by the sober judgment ; and
that a nation should not be in such a state of moon-struck
madness as to be entirely incapable of rational inquiry. However, as there is little hope but that every attempt to inquire, which does not end in inexplicable rapture, will be
treated as odious prejudice, calumny, malignity, and all the
agreeable words of the same kind which memory can supply,
prudence would prescribe patience, and a silent shrug. Yet
let not the adorers of the charming boy be too much alarmed at

---

* In five volumes; Leipsic, 1769 : from which edition his portrait, given
in this number, is taken.

these remarks, lest they should end in cynical and odious detraction; for it would be my disgrace, not Master Betty's, were I to take any other course than the honourable road of sincerity, candour, and justice. Author, actor, painter, or any other person, who appears before the public, appeals to the understanding, and is highly honoured by fair critical discussion. His theatrical career first demands attention; and the facts recited of him in the following memoir are chiefly collected from accounts, already published, by Mr. Jackson of Edinburgh, Mr. Merritt of Liverpool, and Mr. Harley, an author and actor at Birmingham and Sheffield.

William-Henry-West Betty, or the Young Roscius, was born at or near Shrewsbury, September 13th, 1791 *. His grandfather was a medical doctor at Lisburn, near Belfast, Ireland; and his father, removing from Shropshire, was a farmer, and engaged in business relating to the linen manufactory, near Ballynahinch, in the county of Down. It deserves *particular notice* that his mother and sisters were frequently accustomed to amuse themselves by *reciting plays and poetry* †; and that she and her husband were attached to theatrical entertainments, and in occasional habits of intimacy with some of the most eminent professors of the dramatic art, in Ireland and England. " Hence," Mr. Merritt observes, " it is natural to suppose that " the subject of acting would be frequently introduced in the " family; and [that] Master Betty must necessarily have im- " bibed some notions respecting it, and perhaps some inclina- " tion toward it, at a very tender age. Mrs. Betty being " herself an accomplished speaker, *he was exercised at an* " *early period* in the habit of reciting passages from the best " authors, and was taught to pronounce the language with " propriety." Mr. Merritt however affirms that the child was by no means intended to be educated for the stage. This appears, to say the least, a very doubtful circumstance ‡.

---

* Dramatic Strictures, by J. Jackson, p. 17; third edition, 1804.

† Memoirs, &c. by J. Merritt, pp. 16, 17. Liverpool, 1804.

‡ " The Young Roscius is completely studied in thirty principal characters; " and, what is still more surprising, he was perfect in them when but eight " years old."—*Morning Herald, Dec.* 12, 1804.

Those, who are much accustomed to children, know with
what eager delight they imitate those things which excite the
pleasurable surprise of infantine curiosity.   Master Betty, a
child of acute sensibility and retentive memory, was in the
habit of hearing plays, observing players, and imitating what
he heard and saw, by reading or repeating aloud.   Every person, who is so situated, having a child, must have observed
how the youthful faculties are stimulated, exhilarated, and improved at a very early age, by such practices.   A boy of four
years and a half old amused his father and mother, in my presence and repeatedly, by having heard a play read and pretending to enter the door in the character of an old man to
scold his young ward.   Imitations like these are common to
intelligent children.   Some months before, having seen a puppet-show in the street, he came home and most whimsically,
for several days, continued to imitate what had given him
such unexpected pleasure.

Thus educated, and having these propensities, Master Betty,
in the summer of 1802, being then nearly eleven years old,
was taken to see Mrs. Siddons perform Elvira, at Belfast.   Is
it astonishing that Mrs. Siddons should leave an indelible impression on the mind of a boy, that mind having been thus
repeatedly acted upon, and enthusiastically prepared ?   He
spouted Elvira, spoke of nothing but Elvira, became every
hour more vehement and uncontrollable in his desires, and said
he should certainly die if he must not be a player.

In the pages of his various biographers, epithets are re-
echoed which never were truly bestowed on man : *heaven
presented, intuitive precocity, the brightest luminary that ever
beamed upon a stage,* with every inexplicable extravagance,
are assiduously collected.   These adulators do not comprehend the deep injury that they are liable to bring on this truly
charming boy : a recital and cool observation of facts are safer
guides.

His passionate desire for the stage induced his father to
send for Mr. Atkins, the manager of the Belfast theatre,
before whom Master Betty repeated passages of Elvira.   Not
thinking himself a sufficient judge, or not having the talent of

discovering *intuition*, Mr. Atkins sent his prompter, Mr. *Hough*, for whose judgment he had a considerable deference, that he might have his opinion. Mr. Hough was pleased, gave him a few instructions, advised him rather to study Rolla than Elvira, and so much delighted Master Betty by the knowledge he communicated, that he told Mr. Hough *he was his guardian angel*. Master Betty was not *himself aware* that his genius was intuitive. Nothing further at present occurred: the father and son returned from Belfast to Ballynahinch, and Master Betty, finding plays in the house, took delight to study Rolla, Osman, and other characters.

His father, still intent on the plan he had conceived, sent a pressing invitation to Mr. *Hough*, to pass some time at his house, *and give the boy instructions*. The docility, sagacity, and aptitude of the youth, were highly pleasing to Mr. Hough, who, I should suppose, was very desirous to produce his pupil, and gave lessons with that view. This, though given as a conjecture, must in the nature of things have been almost inevitable.

That the aptitude of the boy was extraordinary has been fully proved; but had his genius been intuitive Mr. Atkins had no such gift, for he still hesitated so much about suffering him to appear at Belfast that he complied only as a last resource, when the assassination of Lord Kilwarden had created so deep a sensation in the country as to render people very indifferent concerning plays. The manager then complied, and announced the tragedy of Zara: *the part of Osman to be undertaken by a young gentleman only eleven years of age.* Curiosity attracted a crowd, the applause was great, and the childhood of the hero, together with his acting, produced a strong sensation.

He next performed young Norval, in Douglas; then Rolla, and afterward Romeo, with equal or increasing success.

Mr. Jones, the Dublin manager, being, as managers are and ought to be, desirous of attracting auditors, engaged him to play nine nights at the Theatre Royal, Crow-street. Finding the boy's talents of such importance, Mr. Betty solicited *Mr. Hough* to become Master Betty's *constant tutor and attendant;*

and Mr. Hough, strongly attached to the boy and impressed
with sanguine hopes of success, acceded and resigned his situation at Belfast.   " From that time to the present, he has di-
" rected *his whole time and attention* to his celebrated pupil ;
" and their strong attachment to each other is a proof that the
" appointment was mutually agreeable.   On the nature of Mr.
" Hough's abilities, as an instructor, the public are enabled to
" decide : he is certainly entitled to great credit, for the care
" and judgment with which he has fulfilled his trust."

In the present infatuation of enthusiasm, this Mr. Hough
(totally unknown to me in person and connections, I cannot
therefore speak from personal kindness) to whom Master
Betty, his father, and the public, are so deeply indebted, is
now wholly forgotten ; and those, who are so eager to as-
cribe the exclusive merit of this excellent young performer
to unintelligible and absurd causes, ought to blush at their
injustice.   The boy's merits are entirely of that kind which
his own enthusiastic ardour, a charming countenance, a body
well constructed, a fine articulation, and *an able instructor*, were calculated to produce.   For his clear articulation,
and for something more, he appears to be indebted to his
mother.

The next fact particularly worthy of attention is the number
of nights, and places, at which he has performed, with the
strong stimulant of increasing success and applause, before he
came to London.   Leaving Belfast, he afterward appeared
nine nights at Dublin ; nine at Cork ; four at Waterford ; six
at Londonderry ; fourteen at Glasgow ; fourteen at Edinburgh ;
fourteen at Birmingham * ; eighteen at Sheffield † ; and fourteen at Liverpool.   A boy travelling thus from place to place,
his fame flying infinitely faster than himself, echoed and re-
echoed as a prodigy, first because his talents were truly uncommon next by being heightened by parents who dearly

---

* Mr. Harley's account says thirteen, but hitherto my documents are
chiefly selected from Mr. Merritt.

† Harley.

love their child, friends who partook of their ecstasy, a tutor
whose own fame he had first supposed to be intimately united
with that of his pupil, managers whose treasuries were filled
by his success, writers and newspapers officious to proclaim the
wonders they had beheld, and the kind and generous feelings
of the public, who saw him only to admire : I say, a boy thus
impelled, thus worked into visionary exultation and superiority, caressed as supernatural, heralded as a miracle, and
proclaimed an emanation of a divine nature, must have been
very different from Master Betty, had he not attained real and
undoubted excellence. Let this excellence be most liberally
praised, assiduously nurtured, and amply rewarded ; but surely
justice still is due to all; and I confess that, in affairs of such a
nature, I have never felt injustice more deep, and pointed, than
when I have heard and read it repeatedly affirmed *that Master
Betty exceeds all other performers.* Master Betty has been well
taught, and perhaps has himself well observed, the points
where actors generally gain applause : but the grand mystery
of the art of acting, that of continued discrimination, which
few actors indeed thoroughly understand, he has yet to learn.
There can be no candid disinterested and discerning mind that
does not revolt at hearing him so indecently granted an exclusive preference. Not to mention many, whose names are deservedly dear to the public, can we so lightly and so soon
forget Cooke, Kemble, and that inimitable pair Mrs. Jordan
and Mrs. Siddons? Must victims like these be sacrificed to
the blind adoration of a novel deity ? May he become a more
than Garrick ! Nay Garrick himself was his inferior ! At least
inconsiderate and pernicious praise has affirmed this ridiculous
absurdity. The poison has been largely administered to the
charming boy ; but may he, his father, and his dearest friends,
find a healing antidote; and may sound judgment, noble emulation, and dignified candour, be to him as guardians and
guides.

The Monthly List of the Plays at the conclusion of this number, will show how often he has performed in London during
December, on the first of which month he made his appear-

ance in Barbarossa at the Theatre Royal, Covent Garden. His success has no doubt equalled his and his parents' most sanguine expectations. Let them remember that curiosity is a turbulent but a shadowy being ; that suddenly appears, feeds voraciously, and vanishes nobody knows where, or why.

Master Betty has a fair complexion, an easy address, and a pleasing countenance ; but it appears to be shaded with melancholy, though by no means depressed. When he is not a stage hero, accounts concur to picture him as juvenile in his desires and sports, and loving play and the company of boys. This is an excellent sign ; for to stimulate young subjects to a certain excess is to destroy the stamina both of mind and body.

In consequence as it was said of a severe cold, Master Betty could not perform at the Theatre Royal, Drury Lane, on December 18th ; and though every precaution of posting and distributing bills was taken, it required great exertion on the part of the manager, Mr. Wroughton, to appease the impatience of some and the disappointment of the remainder. He is to perform, it is said, after the holidays. During his illness bulletins of the state of his health have been published as if he were a royal personage, or at least some high officer of state.

PIECES

FIRST PERFORMED OR REVIVED IN DECEMBER 1804.

THIRTY THOUSAND ; OR, WHO'S THE RICHEST?

A COMIC OPERA BY MR. T. DIBDIN.

THE plan of this Piece, as far as it can be said to have any, is founded on one of Maria Edgeworth's Popular Tales ; but of which Tale little use is made, while such varieties as suited the author's purpose are introduced. On some few former occasions, Mr. Dibdin has discovered comic powers, which only wanted, what he perhaps has never been able to command, thorough leisure and independence, added to a more perfect consideration of what he intended to do, an intercourse with fashionable life, and an approved knowledge of the principles of good taste, to have classed him among eminent dramatic poets. The present opera was certainly never intended to endure the test of criticism ; for it has no one quality of dramatic excellence. It is highly to be regretted that the dramatic authors of the present day should so repeatedly inspire disgust, by having no better means to catch applause than the wretched trick of punning.

The author has laboured to form his plan so that as many as possible of the eminent comic performers and great singers of the theatre should be chained and obliged to drag together ; but they exhaust their powers in vain. Instead of uniting their strength, they are obliged to pull in such different directions, one at one time and another at another, that the fantastic yet heavy machine does not move, till the passengers become impatient ; some enraged, some hopeless, and some asleep.

Much of the music was excellent. Incledon, as a singer of the yet half-formed English school, has uncommon merit. Storace may be said to be *nella mettà* ; half English half Italian : but she always gives great pleasure, and would give much more were her knowledge of the stage combined, occasionally with some few marks of diffidence ; or were she in a less degree obtrusive of herself. Miss Davies gives high promise of becoming a chaste and excellent vocal performer. Braham is an admirable singer ; but the art of singing is in a declining state, and it has been the whole study of his life and education *to increase* that decline ; which he sometimes shows himself most ably and competently fitted *to reform.* For this the public are much more to blame than Mr. Braham ; and the public of England are misled by the best of the present Italian singers, who, instead of resting their fame upon the fine sostenuto, the delicate feelings of discrimination, and the noble pathos which form together the perfection of song, introduce the meretricious ornaments of rapid divisions, shakes which the hearer fears will never end, and cadences that are nearly all alike, though trick and contrivance are continually labouring to give them variety, till the ear is satiated, and the man who recollects what pure taste and the powers of the passions are, despairs lest they should never again be cherished and rewarded by the public. By what magic power Admiral Nelson, the battle of the Nile, and General Abercrombie, themes of so high a nature to the historian, the poet, and the patriot, find their way into a punning farcical opera is not easily to be imagined; but there they are, with many other things almost equally surprising. The song however, to which I allude, describing the death of Abercrombie, affords Mr. Braham an opportunity of demonstrating how exquisitely he can perform, in the very best style of singing.

Having made the above strictures, which I believe to be just, it is likewise just to add that, labouring under great disadvantages, Mr. Dibdin has been a persevering, prolific, and successful writer for the stage; and that, however unequal to his best productions this opera may be, there is not the slightest reason to suppose his powers on the decline. If an unthinking public will continue to delight in puns, vulgar ribaldry, allusions the repetition of which is become nauseous, braggart stage valour, to which English magnanimity listens with indignation, and stale insipid sentiments, which are only adopted because they contain some trite eulogium on generosity, bravery, or any virtue common to the human heart, which gives folly or vice an opportunity of pretending to such qualities by applauding them, it may truly be said that the author, being at the mercy of this public, is sincerely to be pitied, and deserves perhaps to be excused:

For those " who live to please must please to live."

THE ART OF ACTING.
CHAP. I.

Introduction: On the Requisites necessary to Performers of both Sexes: Heroes, Gentlemen, Lovers, Tradesmen, Clowns: Heroines, Fine Ladies, Hoydens, Chambermaids: Characters of middle and old Age, Male and Female.

INTRODUCTION.

AMONG the numerous works which have hitherto appeared, on the Art of Acting, there are few if any that treat on that art with sufficient method, and perspicuity. In general, such works have been but essays; and, though the personating the characters which poets have pourtrayed has been acknowledged to require high powers of mind, an appropriate education, peculiar personal qualifications, and uncommon accomplishments, yet those who have *written* on the subject have chiefly confined themselves to indefinite sketches, while they have acknowledged it required uncommon abilities as well to execute as to describe the dramatic art.

It is easy to point out the deficiencies of works that have appeared, but it is difficult to avoid similar or greater defects. To attempt improvement, in any art or science, is a commendable task; and the knowledge and perseverance by which improvement is accomplished generally obtain, at least some part of, the praise which they deserve.

With an ardent love of the scenic art, a zealous desire to promote it in all its branches, an unconquerable anxiety that it should be well understood both in principle and practice, a strong hope that those who have hitherto treated it with levity or abjured it as pernicious may change their opinion, and with something like a prophetic spirit that announces its future influence on the morals and happiness of man, the present work is begun. These propensities, and a life in great part devoted to a study of the subject, form the chief pretensions of the writer of the present work. It may be added that this study has been comparatively little in books, but indefatigable in the nature of the art itself, as it is at present exhibited on the stage, and as it might be. It is not meant to be insinuated that the work here undertaken will establish high claims to superiority; though great efforts are intended to be made, to promote the object in view, and to deserve approbation.

NECESSARY REQUISITES.

The first *grand requisite*, for a dramatic Artist, is power of mind: but this subject must be reserved for future consideration, and it is then intended to be insisted upon, and inquired into, on that extensive scale which a gift so essential to the formation of a great Actor demands. The next, which is almost equally indispensable, though so infinitely inferior, is a perfectly distinct articulation. Some mistakenly imagine that this is always the result of a sound intonation, and power of voice. Intonation and power of voice, when accompanied by distinct articulation, are invaluable to an Actor; but by no means so absolutely necessary. Articulation, tone, and power of voice, must each of them likewise be treated of hereafter, and apart: as must all the various heads recapitulated at present, for they all demand research, development, and detail.

Classes might be multiplied almost at pleasure, but they will all appertain, more or less, to the following:

Heroes, lovers, gentlemen, tradesmen, clowns: heroines, fine ladies, hoydens, chambermaids: characters of middle and old age, male and female.

A sketch of the qualities necessary to each of these classes is only at present intended.

Heroes. No performer can personate a hero truly unless, did events favour him, he be capable of actually becoming a hero; or, did not his reason and inclination prefer different pursuits. Let him be possessed of this magnetic power of mind, and his defects of voice and person must be excessive, if they are unconquerable. Give him that mighty power, and a distinct articulation, clearness, compass, and strength of voice, an athletic and correct symmetry of person, with pliant yet pleasing features capable of all the varieties and the full force of expressing the various passions, and this *imaginary actor* will be one who has never yet been beheld. Many performers however are on record, male and female, who, were the pictures given of them by their admirers correct, have approached if not attained, nay surpassed this perfection! Roscius was the father of a numerous progeny; for many have assumed or willingly accepted his name. That he was himself the essence of all that is perfect we must now take upon trust. Admiration, in all ages, might more truly be painted blind than justice: like a stone cast into still water, it begins with

raising a small circle, and from circle to circle spreads, till it
necessarily dies away, because it can extend no further.

Lovers. In the lover all the exterior charms, which can
steal upon and enslave the female heart, should be combined :
a smiling, prepossessing, yet anxious face, beauty of form, elegance of manners, sweetness of voice, passionate eyes, and
susceptibility of heart, should all enrapture his mistress. Add
to these the feminine beauties, graces, and accomplishments,
and the description will be suitable to the other sex.

Gentlemen. The requisites to *personate this character completely* are many, and difficult indeed to attain : they are, perfect ease of deportment, even under the most embarrassing circumstances; manners that conciliate, and gain universal
esteem; good breeding so disciplined as never to be thrown
from its guard, or, except on the most extraordinary occasions,
betrayed to the discovery of passion; a smooth and flowing
enunciation; a bland gaiety of heart, that no trifles can disturb; a flattering, yet not officious, attention to every person
present; and all those charms of address and demeanour which
cannot fail to win our affections. There have been almost *as
few gentlemen* on the Stage *as heroes.*

Tradesmen. In a certain sense, all the characters of middle
life are affiliated to this class : but, as it is not here intended
to individualize them, this subdivision will be deferred. The
qualities of a tradesman are such as most performers, who have
abilities for the dramatic art, may easily personate. Habit
induces the mere tradesman to be subservient in his manner,
especially to the wealthy, and on extraordinary occasions servile : he renders contradiction smooth, listens to it patiently,
intends to flatter but does it aukwardly, complies with any
request if his interest be not compromised, is always ready
with the tradesman's bow, not only at meeting and parting but
wherever it can be intruded, and his eye, attitudes, and slightest actions, wherever his interest is concerned, are all anxiously
intent on and subservient to that eager desire of gain which
habit has rendered a predominant passion. · By the nature and
extent of this, his deportment is regulated. His propensities

appear on all occasions; but they appear slightly, earnestly, or extravagantly, in proportion to supposed loss or gain. It is not by this intended to depreciate a class of men, but to describe habits, which are inevitably fostered by barter and sale, unless counteracted by superiority of mind, or extraneous circumstances; and to give a picture such as an actor, who literally personates a tradesman, ought to have in contemplation.

Clowns. Rustic appearance, vacant or gazing eyes, an open mouth, arms dangling yet the shoulders raised, the toes turned inward, a shambling gait with a heavy step, great slowness of conception, and apparent stupidity of mind and manner, characterize the absolute clown. The varieties of this class, like the last, are interesting subjects of study for the stage; but are too frequently misunderstood. Vary the portrait by red ribbands, yellow petticoats, timidity, and maudlin freaks, and his counterpart is seen.

Heroines. Give feminine dignity of person, and all the qualities described under the title *heroes*, with that pervading force of sensibility which shall never vanquish though it shall often endanger heroism, and the heroine will be nearly perfect.

Fine ladies. The fine lady is, or should be, even a more fascinating character on the stage, than that which has been pictured under the head *gentlemen*; for, to the almost unattainable graces of the gentleman, she should add a continued playfulness. a visible coquetry, which, though perfectly at her command, should appear spontaneous, and an ample mixture of delightful caprice, which she evidently indulges only to make herself more captivating. Should the actress suffer the least vulgarity to appear, in either walk, attitude, dress, or enunciation, the fine lady instantly vanishes. Her *dress* is of so much consequence that, the moment she appears, her character should be visible; and this *art of dress* is only to be attained by the study of that which is almost simplicity itself; or would be, were she but to take away a very few ornaments, tastefully selected and admirably placed, by which she intends to be distinguished.

Hoydens. A hoyden exhibits herself by an impatient readi-

ness to romp, eagerness to contradict, fretfulness if contra-
dicted, vehement wishes to enjoy, dress that is ridiculous by
exceeding the fashion, and, while absurd in manner, loud of
voice, and a total stranger to good breeding, by an air of
excessive self-satisfaction.

Chambermaids. Volubility, pertness, a prevailing sense of
self-importance, irksome curiosity, uncommon acuteness in all
that relates to family secrets, extreme ignorance of every
thing beyond her sphere, impatience to prattle, timidity when
overawed, and a pleasure in being rude when she dare, are
most of them what the chambermaid supposes to be her peculiar airs and graces.

Middle and old age. In the various stages of declining life,
though the passions are less strong, many of the evil habits of
youth become rooted, and should appear mingled with the
propensities which prevail in age. Among these propensities
are, anxiety concerning trifles, increasing avarice, obstinacy,
a petulant inclination to contradict, a gradual disregard of good
breeding, ceremony, and dress, uncontrollable peevishness,
and change of voice, walk, and carriage; all which qualities
are to be regulated partly by age, but still more by the mental
strength or debility of the character supposed.

In the personification of the above classes, and of all the
characters which are allied to them, the peculiar study of the
actor should be directed to understand the limits of insipidity
and exaggeration.

Some of these delineations may appear to refer only to the
mind: but a good performer well knows that the body is
entirely regulated by that which passes in the mind; and, so
true an interpreter is action, that words, after they are spoken,
seem only to elucidate what appeared before, though it had
been but imperfectly understood.

SOME ACCOUNT

OF THE RISE AND PROGRESS OF THE GERMAN STAGE.

IT is not here intended to investigate the origin of the dramatic art, in Germany; where, as indeed in almost every country of Europe, its origin was probably in those ignorant ages when few memorials were left of an art which was considered as insignificant, and sometimes as dangerous. A periodical work was begun at Paris, in 1782, and concluded in 1785, entitled *Théatre Allemand,* to which is prefixed a historical abridgment of the German theatre: from this abridgment that which follows is chiefly taken. I may perhaps find occasion to insert facts or observations which are not to be found in that work; but, those excepted, the remainder will be a translation. When other sources are employed, or remarks not there to be found are inserted, the passages containing them will be placed between single inverted commas.

Among all nations, the dramatic art rose by degrees: persons, in grotesque dresses, began by travelling from town to town. Encouraged by ignorant and rude auditors, the children of Thespis afterward continued to rest in one place, and elevate themselves on their tressels; where every mode was employed that could amuse greedy and indelicate spectators: gestures, postures, gross jokes, frequent obscenities, and extravagancies of every kind, were the most certain to succeed. Long did barbarous ignorance continue in stupid admiration of this rude state of the art; till, at length, a happy revolution began to take place. The darkness of ignorance gradually disappeared before increasing good taste: the nation, better understanding itself, inquired into the manners of its more enlightened neigh-bours, among whom the fine arts were further advanced; but, still diffident of its own powers, taking them for guides, and servilely copying them as models. Better understanding her native powers, Germany at length disdains this foreign support, and dares to fly upon her native wings.

' It must not, from what is said above, be inferred that all
' foreign aid is now rejected in Germany; for there seldom
' appears a successful tragedy, comedy, or dramatic piece, in
' England or France, of which some use is not made for the
' German theatre; and which is not, in perhaps a majority of
' instances, rather a barren translation than an improved and
' well-adapted novelty.'

Such has been the progress of the German stage, which has
long been obliged to struggle against a barbarous and false taste,
before it could obtain that decency which at present prevails,
and that estimation in which it is now held. It is not fifty
years * since the Germans began to study the best works of the
French and English, and to make attempts to imitate such models. The difficulties they had to encounter were endless; the
writers in polite literature and in science communicated with
each other in Latin, and neglected their vernacular tongue: the
multitude delighted only in the rude and ridiculous farces to
which they had been accustomed; and sovereign princes, by
whom such farces were justly despised, afforded no favour except to companies of foreign comedians. Hence it will appear,
from the following chronological abridgment, that it is scarcely
thirty years since Germany could flatter itself with possessing
a national theatre, or dramatic pieces of German origin.

The first traces of German dramatic writings, if such pieces
deserve the title, are found in their *Carnaval Sports;* which
have much correspondence with the pieces performed by the
Troubadours of France, so celebrated in the thirteenth century.
Their title indicates their origin, and purpose. The disguises,
assumed at this season of folly, might naturally suggest the idea
of imitating, or mimicking, manners and persons. Their first
attempts were those of gesture: words were afterward added;
and, to increase laughter, the vilest pleasantries and jokes were
soon indulged. The rude and gross vices of the times were represented, and the prospect of success was increased in proportion as the ridicule became exaggerated.

---

* Dating from 1782.

Among the most ancient German authors, of this kind, was HANS ROSENBLÜTH whose first piece, which still exists, appeared in the year 1430. This and the author's other works consisted of gross imitations of the ordinary actions of life, and of disgusting satires on all ranks of men; popes, bishops, electors, and every different class of society, down to the page and the peasant. They usually concluded by an anxious and pathetic exhortation which entreated the spectators not to send the plate empty away, that was to be carried round.

A translation of Terence, which appeared in the same year, likewise subsists.

In the sixth century, the famous poet HANS SACHS, a shoemaker by profession, wrote for the theatre. There are nearly two hundred pieces by him; and, though the plan and conduct are absurd in the extreme, they still contain some characters decidedly drawn, and well supported. In the subjects taken by him from the Old and New Testament, we must pardon the faults he has committed against history; for the ignorance of his age will plead in his excuse. He was the first who distinguished comedy from tragedy*.

In the course of the same century, two translations were made, which still remain: one in 1520, from a Spanish piece, entitle Celestina; another in 1535, from the Aulularia of PLAUTUS.

Some time about the commencement of this sixteenth century, companies of comedians began to collect, and to perform different pieces, translated from the Spanish, the Flemish, and the Italian; among others, the PASTOR Fido of GUARINI. They were represented in 1619.

OPITZ, the father of German poetry, translated the Trojans, in verse, from SENECA. In 1650, a translation of the Cid, by the great CORNEILLE, appeared; which was the first made from the French language.

GRIPHIUS and LOHENSTEIN, at the same period, devoted themselves to the tragic muse; but, though possessed of genius, they

---

* The author speaks I suppose of the Germans.

retarded the progress of the German stage. The emphatic tone, which predominated in their works, dazzled and seduced, before the reign of good taste had begun.

In 1669, the Students of Leipsic performed, at their college, a translation of the *Polieucte* of Corneille. The most remarkable event, in this performance, was that it suggested, to VELT-HEIM, the plan of forming the first regular company which appeared in Germany, and which company existed at the beginning of the eighteenth century. To this manager we are likewise indebted for the first translation of the comedies of *Molière*, which were performed at his theatre.

The pieces that were then played were most of them detached scenes and burlesque extemporary effusions, in which the tragic and the comic were ridiculously mingled. These pieces the comedians pompously entitled *Politic and Heroic Dramas* *: monstruous productions, which, to our disgrace, long held possession of the German stage. Thirty years ago, they were the delight of many cities, nay of some courts, and were prefered to *Rodogune, Brutus, Alexandre,* and *Sertorius*. These French pieces it is true were but imperfectly translated. The enthusasm was such, and comedians were then thought so desirable, that when they travelled from city to city, the magistrates received them at the gates, complimented them, and defrayed their expences. At this period, there was a manager named ELENDSOHN, who was so beloved, by the elector of Cologn, that he raised a mausoleum of black marble to his memory.

(To be continued.)

DRAMATIC ANECDOTES.

MR. Thomas Sheridan, father to the present Mr. Sheridan, used to relate the following anecdote. When the famous Thom-

---

* The author has employed the word *Drama* erroneously; at that time, it was not in use.

son, author of the Seasons, had his tragedy called Tancred and
Sigismunda performed at Drury-lane Theatre, several friends
joined Mr. Sheridan to entreat Thomson to shorten speeches
which they foresaw would weary the audience: but they offended the poet without effecting their purpose. Garrick, who
played the part of Tancred, listened and said nothing; but at
rehearsals, though apparently perfect in his part, continued occasionally to take the prompter's copy and read. The first
night, however, without a whisper of his intention, he curtailed
his own part wherever his judgment directed, and the applause
he received was great; while Mr. Sheridan, and other actors who
had long and tedious parts, laboured on with great difficulty.
The conduct of Garrick saved the piece, and Thomson, though
enraged when he heard the first omissions, in the end returned
Garrick his hearty thanks.

Having in another part of this number delivered opinions
concerning the young Roscius, they may in some degree be
strengthened by what follows, in which the great force of early
impressions appears.

Nicolas Etienne le Franc, surnamed *Ponteuil*, was the son of a
rich notary of Paris. Some have imagined that he received
impressions, even before he was born, which induced him to become a comedian. When his mother was pregnant, the family
lived on the *Quai de la Mégisserie*, where every Sunday certain
puppet-show buffoons erected scaffolds and acted their farces
all the afternoon, which she observed from the windows; and
thus, as people have said, the child in early infancy employed
himself with nothing but puppets. " My testimony may be
believed," says the author of *La Bibliothèque des Théâtres*, " for
" having been his fellow-student, I often assisted at his farces,
" one of which I shall never forget, for it had nearly proved
" fatal. In this piece, of his own invention, Punch, having re-
" ceived a mail with news from Flanders, seats himself on it to
" speak to the courier. As it was intended to play Punch a
" trick, instead of letters, gunpowder and crackers were put into
" the mail, which being lighted set fire to the paper and paste-
" board scenery, burned the apparatus of the young comedian,

" and we were in great danger of being suffocated by the
" smoke."

Le Franc, following his propensity, began first to perform in
private societies, travelled afterward to Poland, married there,
and, returning to Paris, appeared in the part of Œdipus, in
1701. He was received by the company of comedians, in 1703,
notwithstanding the remonstrances made by his family. He
was tall and handsome, a little inclination to squint excepted,
performed kings and peasants equally well, and is said to have
been among the first who introduced natural declamation on the
stage. He died in 1718, aged 44, at *Dreux.*

The following is a much more remarkable instance of similarity :

Most lovers of Theatrical History well know that a French
actor, named *Baron,* was the fine gentleman of the company
superintended by the immortal *Molière,* and the most famous
performer of his day. *Baron* began by being *the infant Roscius*
of that age. When a child, his relations, wishing to get rid of
him, articled him for five years to a woman who had a company
of children performers ; and so great were the abilities of
Baron that he drew vast multitudes to the theatre, and filled
the pockets of his mistress. She however presently emptied
them with a lover, and in her distress applied to Molière, whose
known generosity was great, requesting him to lend her his
theatre only for three days, that she might hire another with
the profits. The first day was fortunate, and on the second the
theatre and stage were so crowded that her profits exceeded a
thousand crowns. Molière, being indisposed, had not seen
Baron ; but, hearing the young actor so highly praised, he
attended at the third representation. The comedians of the
company were all present, and exceedingly surprised ; especially the actress, *Du Parc,* who invited *Baron* that night to
supper. The young actor, hardly knowing how to behave
under so many caresses, gave his promise to go with her ; but
Molière also invited him to supper, and so great was his influence that Baron durst not say he was engaged. Nor was

Du Parc offended at the breach of promise. Molière observed and questioned the boy all supper-time, gave him a bed at his house, and sent for his tailor, who received an order to bring a new suit of clothes for Baron by nine o'clock the next morning. When the hour came, the boy was no less amazed than delighted at the change; and, prompted by the tailor, went to return thanks to Molière, who not only received him kindly, but gave him six louis-d'ors for pocket-money. All this was like a dream to a child of twelve years old, who had long been with persons of a different description, and by whom, had he remained with them, his genius for the stage would have been ruined. This thought affected Molière; and he asked the boy what he most desired? *To stay with you for ever*, replied Baron, *that I may show my gratitude.* " If so," answered Molière, " you shall have your wish: I have already obtained his ma-" jesty's order for that purpose." Molière was as intimate and as much a favourite with the king as a man so situated could possibly be. The former mistress of Baron, enraged at the loss of such a source of wealth, entered the chamber of Molière furiously, with a pistol in each hand, declaring she would shoot him through the head, if he did not give her back the boy. Molière, tranquil and unmoved, said to his servant, *Take that woman away.* His fortitude had such an effect on her that she suddenly dropt the pistols, threw herself at his feet, implored him with tears to restore Baron to her, and drew a picture of the misery to which herself and family must be reduced, should he not comply. Molière showed her the order of the king; and, finding she had no hope, she entreated Molière to let Baron play three days for her profit. " Not only three " but eight," replied Molière, " on condition that he do not go " home with you, and that the person I send with him shall bring " him back to me, each day as soon as the play is ended." By these eight performances she obtained a sufficient sum to settle herself at Paris. The kind and virtuous Molière took no less care of the morals than of the education of the boy, who became a worthy man, and after his benefactor's death long continued the chief support of the stage.

Till very lately there used to be no seats in the pit at Paris. At the fourth representation of *La Rapinière*, a comedy, by *Jaques Robbe*, first performed in 1682, a person in the pit, fearful lest his sword should be stolen, held it above his head; but the crowd was so great that he could not lower his arm, and he was obliged to stand with his arm and sword suspended in the air till the end of the piece.

An actor who formerly wrote for the *Comèdie Italienne* at Paris, in one of which comedies he performed the part of Scaramouch, dedicated his comedy to the *Duc de Saint Aignan*, who liberally rewarded authors. This author-actor went one morning to pay his devoirs to the duke, but *the Swiss*, or porter, suspecting his intention, would not suffer him to enter. Scaramouch, however, moved his compassion, by promising a third of the recompence he might receive. He next encountered the *first lacquey* of the duke; who, being no less selfish than the Swiss, Scaramouch was obliged to promise him another third. Having thus made his way as far as the *Valet de Chambre*, this Valet informed him that *Monseigneur* was not to be spoken with; nor could Scaramouch proceed, till he had promised the remaining third. He then was suffered to address the duke, to whom he presented his piece, with the dedication, humbly requesting he would bestow a hundred strokes with a cane upon his shoulders. This singular request, from so singular a person, surprised the duke, who insisted upon knowing why it had been made. Scaramouch fully explained, the duke sent for his servants, gave them a severe reprimand, and, that the author might keep his word, sent a hundred louis as a personal gift to his wife.

When the Misanthrope of *Molière* was first performed, the immortal *Molière* and the great *Racine* were unfortunately at variance. A parasite, thinking to please the latter, told him, after the first representation, that the piece had failed. " I was " there, and can assure you nothing can be more cold." Racine replied, " You were there, and I was not; yet I do not believe you. It is not possible for Molière to have written a bad piece. See it again, and consider it better."

=====

Pont-Alais was author, actor, and manager of the mysteries in the fifteenth century. His repartees, and manner of delivering them, procured him admission to the first families; nay, he had the honour of frequently approaching Louis XII. and Francis I. of France. He was deformed; and one day saluting a Cardinal, who was the same, he placed himself so as to touch back to back, and said, " You see, *Monseigneur*, that, in despite " of the proverb, mountains may meet." Before it was customary to print play-bills, an actor used to accompany a drummer to squares, thoroughfares and public places, make an eulogium on the piece, and invite the public to see it performed *. One Sunday morning, *Pont-Alais* had the audacity to cause his drum to be beaten, and a new piece announced in sermon-time, in the open place opposite the church *Saint Eustache*. The curate, seeing the people crowd out of the church, left his pulpit, went up to the actor, and asked "who made you daring " enough to beat your drum while I preach?"—' And who ' made you daring enough to preach while my drum is beating?' replied *Pont-Alais*. This insolent repartee rendered the curate silent for the moment; but, on application to the magistrate, *Pont-Alais* was six months imprisoned. The barber of *Pont-Alais* complained that the parts given him to perform were too insignificant; on which *Pont-Alais* gave him the part of one of the kings of the East, seated him on a high throne, and maliciously standing behind his shoulders repeated,

> *Je suis des moindres le mineur,*
> *Et n'ai pas vaillant un teston ;*
> *Mais le roi d'Inde le majeur*
> *M'a souvent rasè le menton.*

> I'm the least of the least,
> Not a sixpence to save me;
> But this king of the East
> Very often has shav'd me.

---

* This has been done within my memory in the small country towns of England.

MISCELLANIES.

To explain the nature of one department of the THEATRICAL RECORDER, which might be otherwise misunderstood, it will be necessary to speak a few words on *Costume*. In the province of the Dramatic Art, the scene occasionally extends itself over all nations, and ages; and as it is peculiarly required of the poet to be attentive to the manners and customs of the people he personifies, so is it equally incumbent on the performer to adopt similar accoutrements, appear in those dresses, and use the same weapons, as those that were in use at the time and among the people where the scene is laid. Such attentions are indispensable to classical correctness and good taste, and have their full reward from an audience; for they delight the multitude, give pleasure to the scholar, and reality to the scene, while they highly contribute to fill the treasury of the theatre. All parties therefore would find themselves benefited by their observance. In numberless cases, when states were greatly subdivided, it would not now be possible to discover those minute distinctions by which each was known to the other: but the times must be very remote, or the nations almost unknown, of which we have not general records.

On mature consideration, the length of time which would be necessary to give pictures of the costume of nations, by a single print in each number, has presented itself as a difficulty: it has therefore been thought more advisable to omit the colouring, of which we have little accurate knowledge, and, instead of a single coloured costume, to give an etching of three dresses on the same plate; by which means, in three or four numbers, the costume of the principal orders of a nation may be exhibited. Colours in all ages have been subject to the fancy of the people, and therefore may be the same to their stage representatives; though in a few instances, as among the Turks, some colours have been prohibited, except to certain orders of men; and these rules and exceptions ought to be known to all theatrical performers. In modern times, the dresses of the middle and upper ranks among European nations have a general resemblance; but the lower orders keep themselves remarkably distinct from each other, as perhaps in the course of this work there will be various occasions to shew.

The costume of Eastern nations is chosen to begin with, because, the people being remote, it is imperfectly understood, and has been too much transgressed against upon the stage. It will be necessary to state on what authority every example of costume is given. The *Ooria Brahmun*, in the present number, is taken from a large folio volume, of which it is affirmed there are only three copies in England, and which was etched and printed at Calcutta, on Indian paper, from designs made after the people themselves, purposely to describe their dress and manners, by a person named *Solvyns*. Whether Mr. Solvyns was a native of India or of Europe does not appear; but it is evident that he was thoroughly acquainted with his subject. His designs extend further than to costume alone, for they include architecture, shipping, and other objects, that explain the manners of the Hindoos. To the plate annexed he adds the following explanation:

" An Ooria, or Orissa, Brahmun, offering his devotions to
" the Sun. The back-ground represents the style of the archi-
" tecture of the *Munders*. It is universally known that the
" Brahmuns are the priests of the Hindoos; and that, by the
" tenets of their religion, to them are assigned the duty of
" teaching and reading their sacred books, of sacrificing, of
" assisting others to sacrifice, of giving alms if rich, and if
" indigent of receiving gifts. They are forbidden trade, ser-
" vice, and a performance of all menial offices."

The author has given five plates of the Brahmuns belonging to different countries or sects. He further informs us that, though these are the principal, there are subdivisions of the cast; and that, while held in respect and veneration by the Hindoos of every part, the inhabitants of one country will not eat and drink from the hands of a Brahmun of a different tribe.

When the nature of the piece subjects costume to the fancy of the performers, it will then only be necessary that the performers should be consistent with each other; and this kind of subjection happens whenever the author has not marked, with some precision, the period at which the events he describes take place. The Afterpiece, entitled Matrimony, which is a free translation from the French, and which was brought out with success at the Theatre Royal, Drury Lane, in November 1804, is of the above indefinite description. The dress chosen by Mrs. Jordan, and here represented, which she wore in her first scene, is well imagined, picturesque, and proper.

By long custom, the Theatrical Christmas is obliged to be pantomimical, or holiday joviality and children from school would be deprived of their highest enjoyment. The lovers of Harlequinades, however, were disappointed at Drury Lane, where, on December 26th, they were presented with nothing more than a pantomime ballet called Old Harlequin's Fire-side, and which, by being pleasing, was thought much too short. The very juvenile performers, Master Byrne and Miss Bristow, convinced the unprejudiced and the observing that children are capable, by the means of instruction, of imitating any thing except those passions of which they cannot have had any experience.

On the same evening, Harlequin Quicksilver was the novelty at Covent-Garden, and was intermingled with dialogue which, whatever criticism may affirm, cannot be ill employed whenever it effectually contributes to give pleasure. In this instance, it was only explanatory. The fertile Mr. T. Dibdin is said to be the author, and certainly deserves great praise for his fertility; though it were to be wished he would concentrate and give full force to his powers. The music was by Mr. Davy, who has long been acknowledged to possess talents that deserve a more determined and persevering cultivation. It is hoped the reader will not wish any further account of these mushrooms of poetical ground.

The intelligence that is occasionally received concerning provincial theatres seldom contain any thing very remarkable; and it is hoped that the pages of this work will not be incumbered with articles of too trifling a nature, though whatever claims *public attention* will be noticed. Investigations of the individual merits of the London performers will be incidental, as occasion may require; and particularly when their talents are called into action by any species of novelty.

MONTHLY LIST, FOR DECEMBER, 1804.

DRURY-LANE.

DEC.

1. Busy Body - - - - - - - - - Matrimony.
3. Hamlet - - - - - - - - - - -
4. Belles' Stratagem - - - - - - Matrimony.
5. School for Scandal (by Com.) - Cinderella.
6. Provoked Husband - - - - - Matrimony.
7. Bold Stroke for a Wife- - - - Matrimony.
8. She Stoops to Conquer- - - - Matrimony.
10. Douglas - - - - - - - - - - The Citizen.
11. The Heiress - - - - - - - - The Caravan.
12. The Rivals - - - - - - - - - Richard Cœur de Lion.
13. Douglas - - - - - - - - - - Of Age To-morrow.
14. The Heiress - - - - - - - - Matrimony.
15. Barbarossa- - - - - - - - - The Spoiled Child.
17. Pizarro - - - - - - - - - - The Citizen.
18. Barbarossa * - - - - - - - - Matrimony.
19. The Stranger - - - - - - -- The Devil to Pay.
20. The Beaux Stratagem - - - - Richard Cœur de Lion.
21. Rule a Wife and have a Wife - Doctor and Apothecary.
22. The Way to Keep Him- - - - The Prize.
26. The Busy Body - - - - - - Old Harlequin's Fire Side, and Richard Cœur de Lion.
27. Richard III. - - - - - - - - Ditto, and Caravan.
28. Bold Stroke for a Wife - - - Ditto, and Sultan.
29. The Land we Live in (first time) Cinderella.

COVENT-GARDEN.

DEC.

1. Barbarossa - - - - - - - - - - The Horse and the Widow.
3. Ditto - - - - - - - - - - - -
4. Douglas - - - - - - - - - - Birth Day.
5. Lovers' Vows - - - - - - - -
6. Ditto - - - - - - - - - - - - Follies of a Day.
7. The Blind Bargain - - - - - - The Escapes.
8. Douglas - - - - - - - - - - The Sultan.
10. Thirty Thousand - - - - - - The Will for the Deed.
11. Ditto - - - - - - - - - - - - The Midnight Hour.
12. Ditto - - - - - - - - - - - - The Child of Nature.
13. Ditto - - - - - - - - - - - - The Miser.
14. Ditto - - - - - - - - - - - - Raising the Wind.
15. Ditto - - - - - - - - - - - - Animal Magnetism.
17. Ditto - - - - - - - - - - - - The Prisoner at Large.
18. Ditto - - - - - - - - - - - - Two Strings to your Bow.
19. Ditto (by Command) - - - - The Guardian.
20. The Blind Bargain - - - - - - The Tale of Mystery.
21. The Cabinet - - - - - - - - - The Irishman in London.
22. Thirty Thousand - - - - - - Raising the Wind.
26. George Barnwell - - - - - - Harlequin Quicksilver.
27. Beaux Stratagem - - - - - - Ditto.
28. Dramatist - - - - - - - - - Ditto.
29. The Blind Bargain - - - - - Ditto.
31. Richard III. - - - - - - - - - Ditto.

Changed to The Wonder, *on account of Master Betty's illness.*

THE

THEATRICAL RECORDER:

BY

THOMAS HOLCROFT.

CONTENTS OF NUMBER II.

London:

Printed by C. Mercier and Co. No. 6, Northumberland-court,
Where the Work may be procured;
And at all the BOOKSELLERS;
And published for the Author, by H. D. Symonds, Paternoster-row.

PHILIP THE SECOND:

A TRAGEDY,

IN FIVE ACTS,

TRANSLATED FROM

THE ITALIAN OF ALFIERI,

BY FANNY HOLCROFT.

DRAMATIS PERSONÆ.

PHILIP II.

CARLOS, his Son.

PEREZ, the Friend of CARLOS.

GOMEZ, the King's Favourite.

LEONARDO, an Inquisitor.

ISABELLA, the Wife of PHILIP.

Counsellors.　　　Guards.

SCENE—The Regal Palace.

PHILIP THE SECOND:

A TRAGEDY.

〰〰

ACT I.

SCENE I.—Isabella.

Isabella.

ANXIOUS fears, restless wishes, impious hopes,
Avaunt!—What I, the wife of Philip, break my vow!
What I love Philip's son!—Oh God!—Yet who
Could see the prince, and not admire? Sublime
Of mind, humane of heart, in genius rich!
A heavenly form enshrines a spotless soul!
Ah, why did nature stamp thee so divine?
But what are thoughts like these? Is't thus I seek
To chase his gentle image from my breast?
Oh, were the fatal secret to escape!—
'Tis true that sadness blights my faded cheek,
And, when we meet, he sees the swelling tear
With pain restrain'd. But sees he not I fly?
And knows he not that smiles and festive joy
Are crimes denounc'd in Spain's fanatic realm?
Who can unveil my heart? Oh that I could
Myself enjoy the ignorance of others!
That memory were lost! Thought buried in
Eternal night! Oh wretched Isabel!
Thy tears alone can sooth the horror of
Thy fate; which tears, alas, are blackest stains
Of guilt.—I'll seek some lone recess, and there
Indulge a while my grief—Just Heav'n!—The prince?
Alas!—I'll fly—In ev'ry word and look,
My heart might speak.

SCENE II.—*Enter* Carlos.

Carl. (*aside*)   Oh Isabel!—What, lady,
Do *you* avoid my sight? Do *you* frown on
My woe?

Isab.　　　　Prince—

Carl.　　　　　　　　In my father's court, I know
That enmity and hate have mark'd me base :
O'erlook'd and poor in royal Philip's love,
I marvel not to read contempt half hid,
And rancour ill conceal'd, in ev'ry eye.
But you were of a softer mould ; a clime
Far milder gave you birth ; for bigot rage
Had not possess'd your soul, nor vile deceit.
Who could suppose that, in a form so fair,
So full of winning grace, there beat a heart
Estrang'd to sympathy !

Isab.　　　　　　　You know the life
I lead in these abodes : the new and strict
Decorums, of this gloomy court, have not
Yet stifl'd, in my soul, the dear innate
Affection, which we bear our native soil.
That you're unhappy, prince, and that your wrongs
Are great, no less I grieve : what can I more ?

Carl.　　　　　　　　　　　For me ?
Oh joy ! Now ev'ry care is flown ! Nor have your woes
Less strong been felt ; how oft have I suppress'd
The torments of my soul to mourn your fate,
And wished——

Isab.　　　Time yet may sooth its rigour, prince ;
My sorrows bear no poise to *yours* : restrain
Your pity.

Carl.　　Does compassion then in *me* offend,
While *yours* revives my sinking heart ?

Isab.　　　　　　　　You set
Too high a price——

Carl.　　　　　Oh no ! What virtue can exceed
That trembling sense of human woe which thrills
In ev'ry noble breast ! which fortune's frowns,
Or smiles, can ne'er destroy ? Oh, matchless gem,
Which leaves not him a wretch, whose griefs are sooth'd
By tears of sympathy !

Isab.　　　　　　Carlos, this bosom too
Can thrill ! These eyes o'erflow !—Alas !—Think not
Cold apathy benumbs my soul ! These lips
Should plead your innocence, if my weak voice
Could reach a Sire too angry to be just.

Carl.　　Who dares to plead for *me* ? And if you would,
The task should not be yours. Oh, cruel fate !
From you alone my woes arise ; from you,
My only friend, yet you can not console !

Isab.　　From *me* your woes arise ? From *me* ?

Carl.　　　　　　　　　　You know
It well. The fatal day on which, betroth'd,
They tore you from my arms brought endless woe.

Isab. Out hopes, like transient sunbeams on a wintry **noon,**
Were soon eclips'd by clouds, portending tempest.

Carl. From infancy I lov'd; you were my all;
'Twas Philip bade me love; yet dar'd to break
The ties which, in the face of Heav'n, he made!

Isab. And you?

Carl. A subject and a son, I wept,
In silence, woes I could not heal. My soul
Repin'd: I hush'd its just complaints: I still
Rever'd the hand that gave the mortal wound. The **king**
Became your lord! what tongue can tell the pangs
Suppress'd, the stifl'd rage, that rent my heart?
Of conscious virtue proud, for more it was
Than human fortitude. I bore my wrongs,
And rein'd my sorrows, so that never once
I stray'd from honor's path. Yes, God, who reads
The naked heart, can vouch that mine was pure.
The languid day, the restless night, were spent
In sighs and tears. Oh, fruitless grief! As my
Affliction grew, my father's *hate* increas'd.

Isab. Prince, hatred blackens not your father's heart.
Vile sycophants, with malice fraught, who feel,
And feeling dread, your worth, with all the rage
Of envy raise distrust in Philip's breast.

Carl. You little know, and may you *never* know,
The king: nor are the crimes of this vile court
Within your sphere. The spotless heart can ill
Conceive, or yield belief to, vice so wanton!
More cruel than the servile herd he rules,
Philip rejects his son: *he* wills each blow,
Which abject envy aims. The father he
Abjures; yet still I feel he is my father.
Ah, should I e'er forget that sacred name,
Cast off respect, and give my wrongs full vent,
I'd not complain of sullied honor, fame
Destroy'd, or of a father's most unnatural most
Unheard-of hate, but, misery to think,
But of a stab still more implacable!
Of you—of you he robb'd me!

Isab. Prince, a son——

Carl. Forgive the ravings of a tortur'd mind.
How long my griefs have canker'd in my breast!
To you, alone——

Isab. You must not tell, nor must
I hear——

Carl. Oh, lady, you *have* heard in part:
Why then refuse the rest? Th' impassion'd heart
Will find a tongue, or break.

Isab. No more! Be gone!

Carl.   Alas!
I must obey: but, ah, how much I yet
Could tell! One last poor hope remains——
    Isab.   What hope in you
Is not a crime?
    Carl.   You do not hate?—
    Isab.   My lord,
If you *presume* to love, I'm *bound* to hate.
    Carl. Chastise me then; warn Philip of my love.
    Isab. The king?—I dare not e'en pronounce your name.
    Carl. So great you deem th' offence?
    Isab.   Do you *alone*
Offend?
    Carl. Oh, Heav'ns! Your heart then shares—
    Isab.   What can I say?
Too much I've said; too much you have presum'd.
Think I'm your father's wife; respect yourself;
For, while you dare to speak, and I dare hear,
We sanctify revenge.
    Carl.   If passion rack'd
Your heart like mine, if in anothers arms
My image still pursu'd, how light would seem
Th' offence of seeking to approach and gaze,
Till sense grew wild, on that enchanting face,
To sometimes give a momentary pause
To grief, in pure and chaste effusions of the soul!
    Isab. Alas!—Away!—Fly from this fatal realm;
At least, till I'm no more: and soon I feel
Death's welcome hand will strike.
    Carl.   Do you reflect?
Think you 'tis easy to elude the king's
Distrust? Were I betray'd, my flight would be
A new offence; and, ah, my father seeks too much
To find me criminal. The sole offence
Of which he *might* complain he does not know.
    Isab. (*with great passion*) Oh that I knew it not!
    Carl.   You soon will be aveng'd.
Oh, leave me to my fate! If sorrow find
Me not an early grave, my father will;
For in his savage breast my death is seal'd.
Oh let me dwell still in these dark abodes,
Which borrow light from you! Ah let me breathe
The air you breathe!
    Isab.   My soul recoils! Alas,
I tremble for your life! To stay is death!
An inward voice forebodes your hapless fate.
You say you love: oh, grant my first, my last,
Request; fly Philip's vengeful ire!
    Carl.   It cannot be.

Isab. Then carefully avoid my sight: preserve
My fame and yours unblemish'd: let your deeds
Bely the sland'rous tongue of envious rage:
Clear yourself to Philip. Live, I charge you,
But sully not the only gem I wear,
A spotless mind! Oh, leave one raft to save
A sinking wretch! My heart, my soul, my thoughts,
Will all be yours. With fate I cannot war;
But seek me not. This meeting be our last.
Only to Heav'n the fatal myst'ry's known:
Oh let us hide it, prince, from ev'ry eye;
Nay from ourselves; and, if you can, e'en blot
The recollection from your heart!
    Carl.   What, must we meet
No more? Oh misery! And thus you leave
Me?—Cruel fate! At once thou mak'st me blest
And curst!

SCENE III.—*Enter* PEREZ *in haste.*

    Per. You're watch'd, my lord!—But, say? What moves
You thus? You are unlike yourself!—Oh, speak!
This heart will share your sorrows.—How, you're silent!
From infancy, our pains and pleasures have been one:
Did you not call me friend?
    Carl.   And dar'st thou speak
Of friendship in this court? A word of guile,
In courts corrupt and base, and but usurp'd.
Thy faith avails me not; 'tis ruin to thyself:
Steer not against the tide: kneel with the servile crowd:
Adore the sovereign idol, and exalt
Thy voice in strains of welcome praise;
'Twill serve thee best.
    Per.   Oh, sink me not so low!
Confound me not with sycophants so base!
I swear—But vows are here a current coin,
Which ev'ry man alloys: each tongue will pledge,
And ev'ry tongue is perjur'd: better proof
This heart, this arm, will give: what peril shall
I brave?—Point out the foe, who most offends?
    Carl. 'Tis Philip—Ay, 'tis he! His insolent
Dependants merit not the name. To him
I owe respect; to them contempt.
    Per.   Prince, Philip is
Deceiv'd; you are traduc'd: the traitors stab
With craft; 'tis they excite the king's unjust
Displeasure. I'll unmask them, and proclaim
The truth——

Carl. What say'st thou, Perez ? Philip knows
The truth far better than thou think'st : he hates
It more ; nor will he hear a voice in my
Behalf——
      Per.   The voice of Nature——
      Carl.   Moves him not :
His heart is pitiless. To innocence and Heav'n,
Who smiles benignant on th' oppress'd, I trust
My cause. Were I with truth accus'd, thou shouldst
Alone for Carlos plead. What greater mark
Of friendship can I give ?
      Per.   Oh, let me share
Your fate, whate'er it be : 'tis all I ask ;
What honor else can this vile court bestow ?
      Carl. But know'st thou Carlos ne'er again shall smile ?
That peace and fortune are for ever flown ?
      Per. I seek not fortune, but to serve my prince.
Ah, if a sep'rate grief prey on your heart,
Our tears, at least, shall flow in sympathy.
      Carl. A grief lies here which saps the root of life,
Which yet I cherish : oh, that I could pour it in
Thy soul !—A friend more noble never man
Possess'd, yet I can not requite thy truth
With confidence. Now go : why dost thou still
Persist in love so pure, yet so ungently borne ?
My claims are bankrupt ; prithee go : dost thou
Forget it is a mortal crime to pledge
Thy faith to him the monarch hates ?
      Per.   And know
You not, the man who keeps that faith, and braves
The monarch's wrath, attains immortal glory ?
Your secrecy afflicts, but can not shake, my soul.
A sorrow mines your days, which you can not
Impart ?—I'll ask no more : but surely you
Can not refuse to let me share your woes,
And die with you ?
      Carl.   . Is such thy wish ?—Then take
My hand, the luckless pledge of luckless friendship.
For thee I grieve ; but war no more with fate
And Heav'n, who grant me such a friend. Oh, Philip,
Thou art more wretched than the wretch thou mak'st !
Though, rob'd in stately pomp, thou proudly sway'st
Hispania's rich domains, while slaves in myriads kneel,
I view thee not with envy, but compassion ;
For sacred friendship never touch'd thy soul.   [*Exeunt.*

END OF THE FIRST ACT.

ACT II.

SCENE I.—Philip, Gomez.

Philip.

WHAT hast thou most at heart?
   Gom.   Your favour, Sire.
   Phil.   How think'st thou to retain it?
   Gom.   By a prompt
Obedience, and an anxious zeal.   'Twas thus
I long have won my sovereign's grace.
   Phil.   I need
Them both to-day.
   Gom.   The task is light.
   Phil.   I know
That, hitherto, thy ardent faith has been
Unmatch'd; but *now* high thoughts revolve within
My soul: I shall perhaps entrust to thee
A charge so consequent, and new, that it
Behoves me to recal *thy duty* briefly
To mind.
   Gom.   Th' event will justify the trust
Great Philip places, in his faithful slave.
   Phil.   The task will not be difficult to thee.
Alone my consort comes; thou'lt hear us long
Converse: mark well; note ev'ry look, and change,
And fix on her that searching eye that oft
Has read thy sov'reign's inmost thoughts, and met
His yet unutter'd wish.

SCENE II.—*Enter* Isabella.

   Isab.   My lord, I wait
Your pleasure.
   Phil.   Think, lady, 'tis no light cause
For which I call you here.
   Isab.   My liege? What is't?
   Phil.   You soon shall know—May I depend on you?——
But wherefore doubt? Where could I seek advice
More just, or more sincere?
   Isab.   Advice! From me?
   Phil.   From you. You know your judgment stands the first
In our esteem; and, if you have not shar'd
The cares of state, think not your consort poor
In love, or that your king wants confidence.
I'd spare you toils so irksome to your sex.

But now the day is come in which th' affairs
Of state most nearly touch our royal blood,
And your advice becomes most exigent.
But first, say, which you hold most awful, most rever'd,
A sov'reign's will or father's sacred right?

Isab. They're equally rever'd. Who doubts?

Phil. One who
Perhaps should most have known their force. But tell
Me, queen, ere I unfold my soul—be frank—
Has Carlos—Philip's son—your hatred, or—
Affection?

Isab. Sire!

Phil. I understand! Were you
To listen to your heart, and not high virtue's voice,
The name of *mother* would be wormwood to
Your soul.

Isab. Oh no! you wrong me, Sire. The prince—

Phil. Is dear to you? You, Philip's consort, have
The *virtue* to regard his son with all
A *mother's* love?

Isab. You guide my thoughts; you love,
Or think you love, the prince: no less do I.

Phil. Since your pure heart feels not th' unjust dislike
Step-mothers bear, nor yet a *mother's* blind
And doting tenderness, be you his judge.

Isab. His judge! I!

Phil. Hear me? Long I center'd each
Fond wish in Carlos; till, forsaking noble
Honors' path, he kill'd my dearest hopes! Oh,
How oft paternal love excus'd the wrongs
Of this self-will'd audacious son! But, now,
His rash and daring arrogance spurns all
Control; and stronger measures must, alas,
Be us'd. A new offence is added to
The rest, which all exceeds; to which all words
Are poor; which break all ties of blood! But how?
You tremble, yet unknowing? Listen, and you'll
Shudder. 'Tis five years now, or more, since that
Vile race, who plough the marshy lands that lie
The lowest on the coast, first dar'd to brave
My pow'r. Rebellious to their God and king,
Crime follow'd crime. You know the blood and treasure
This war has vainly cost; and, tho' myself
And empire were to perish in the strife,
The perfidy of those vile slaves shall be chastis'd!
I've sworn to sacrifice the impious race
To violated Heav'n! Who cannot stoop
T' obey must learn to die. Who would believe!
My son, my only son, leagues with my direst foes!

Isab. The prince!

Phil. E'en he! The many papers found,
His secret conf'rences, th' audacious language
He in public holds, all confirm his guilt.
Oh, think how agony must rack the father, and
The monarch, thus betray'd. Say, what does such
A son deserve?

Isab. (*aside*) Oh, wretched Isabel!—
And must I then decide?

Phil. You must: on you
His fate depends. Speak freely, queen; fear not
To wound the father's heart, or irritate the king! Pronounce.

Isab. I only fear to be unjust. In courts
We often see the innocent confounded with
The base. Your son——

Phil. How, lady! Can you doubt
My regal word? Who more can wish to find
Him guiltless? Prove, oh prove, the accusation false!

Isab. Has he acknowledg'd then——?

Phil. What pow'r could force
Him? Obstinate and proud, he not alone
Disdains reply, to certain evidence,
But will not urge the shadow of excuse.
I would not, in th' intemp'rate heat of passion, charge
Him with this last offence; but, tho' the burst
Of indignation was suppress'd, the cooler voice
Of Justice must be heard.—Oh God!—Still! Still
I feel I have a father's heart!

Isab. Oh, give
Those feelings vent, the noblest man can boast!
I'll pledge my life, he yet is innocent. Oh, Sire,
You'll find you are deceiv'd! He cannot thus
Have strangely err'd! He is belied! But you
Will hear the prince; for Nature has a syren voice;
To her the eloquence of angels would
Be tame. If haughtily he met reproof,
And spurn'd at censors, oft malignant, you
He will respect. To you his heart will yearn,
And yours will cherish confidence, and love.
The prince is rarely suffer'd to approach
You, Sire; and you more rarely deign to greet
Him with a gentle word: with awe he comes,
With sorrow he retires; this silence, fatal as
Ill-judg'd, creates restraint, and fear, while sweet
Affection wanes. If now he rest unfam'd,
Wanting renown, it is for you to rouse
His slumb'ring virtue. He's your son,
And ev'ry noble spark cannot be dead,
Since Philip's blood flows in his veins! Trust not

To ruder hands a charge so dear! Preserve
Your majesty to strangers, but cast off
The king's stern aspect, when your son appears.
What may not gen'rous treatment win, from gen'rous minds?
You think he greatly err'd: And who errs not?
Be yours, alone, the task to reprimand.
A father's wrath is mild, and yet the son
With trembling meets his frown: a word from you,
One kind reproach, will sink more deep into
His noble heart, and kindle more remorse,
Than all th' opprobrium malice can inflict.
Let but your courtiers know the prince is dear
Still to their king, that you esteem his hot
And youthful ardour, worthy high applause
No less than blame, then will you hear each voice
Rais'd to extol. Dismiss suspicions not
Your own: leave kings to brood o'er dreaded treason who
Deserve their fate!
  Phil.   'Tis worthy of you, queen!
It well behoves you thus to raise the flame
Of Nature in the father! None but you,
Kind lady, pleads her force! Alas, the monarch is
A scepter'd slave! He not alone must curb
His strongest thoughts, but must not dare to breathe
A sentiment unfetter'd by restraint:
Nay often is oblig'd to tamely feign.
Yet, mark, the moment comes when breaking from
Rude bonds, too long endur'd, he firmly acts.
You have unveil'd the truth more fully than
You think. Ah, since your heart absolves my son,
All doubt is nearly clear'd. Go, call the prince.
         [*Exit* Gomez.

SCENE III.—Philip, Isabella.

 Phil. You soon shall see I am a father still.
Should much offended majesty be forc'd
To act, more than my son's this heart will grieve.
  Isab. He comes, permit me to retire.
  Phil.   Not so:
Remain.
  Isab. With freedom I have spoken as
You bade: Why should I stay? Step-mothers are
Unwelcome mediators, and my presence here
Is now not wanted.
  Phil.   You're much deceiv'd; 'tis
Most necessary, queen. Step-mother is
With you *a name,* and e'en the name you may
Ere long forget. Your sight will glad the prince.

He comes; nor shall the champion of his fame,
And *purity of heart,* evade his thanks.

SCENE IV.—*Enter* Carlos *and* Gomez.

Phil. Approach, Don Carlos—say, when shall I call
You by the tender name of son? My brow
Is stern: alas, the fault is yours: cold rigid forms
Replace a father's love; but should you hate
Your Sire, why fear you not your Lord?
 Carl.   My Liege,
Tho' accusation oft has reach'd my ear,
I know not yet th' offence with which I'm charg'd.
In silence I have borne my griefs; for, if
You think me guilty, doubtless, I have err'd.
'Tis true, my heart feels not remorse, or guilt,
But deepest anguish, that you should suppose
Me base! Oh, that I knew in what my woes,
Or say my faults, originate!
 Phil.   You love
Your country little, and your Sire still less;
And lend too quick an ear to artful flatt'rers:
From thence arise your faults.
 Carl.   I joy to think
You do not charge me with a wayward spirit.
The past may be retriev'd: I yet may learn
What tribute of regard my country claims.
To chase those sycophants who dare deceive
You, and traduce their prince, because their arts
O'erpow'r the voice of truth.
 Phil.   Rash youth—your thoughts,
Your actions, nay your very looks, proclaim that you
Assume far far beyond your right. This I
Should hold a venial fault; but, as your years
Increase, your sense grows younger still and you
More rash. I'll call th' offence I now deplore
A juvenile transgression; though it bears,
Perhaps, the face of studied mischief.
 Carl.   Sire!
Transgression!—What transgression?——
 Phil.   Can you ask?
Know you not, prince, that I have trac'd each step,
Search'd ev'ry thought, and prob'd the most conceal'd?
Acknowledge, queen, his gravest fault is, not
In having err'd, but, in self-will'd denial
Of guilt.
 Carl. Of guilt! What have I done?
 Phil.   Are your
Offences then so many that you know not which

I mean?—Say, have you not a secret league
Where treason fiercely flames? Where lies are forg'd
With impious zeal?—Did you not grant within
These very walls, by stealth, ere break of day,
An audience, long and criminal, to vile
Batavia's envoy? That base wretch, who, if
You yield him faith, comes here our friend, but who
Broods hatred and deceit, in his false heart!

    Carl. Oh, father, is each action then of mine
Ascrib'd to guilt? 'Tis true I long convers'd
With the Batavian envoy; and 'tis true
I mourn'd with him his people's fate: nay mourn
It still; nor would you less, perhaps, did you
Know all they have endur'd; for years oppress'd
By rulers, haughty, timid, inexpert,
And absolute, beneath whose iron yoke
They groan.   I'll not deny I sorrow for
Their woes; but would you have the son of Philip boast
A vulgar soul, or wear a heart of rock?
Perhaps the hope of rousing your compassion,
By freely giving utt'rance to the truth,
Makes me presume too far: but how can I
Offend my father, in supposing him
Alive to pity's voice? If you are Heav'n's
Vicegerent here on earth, what brings you nearer to
The Deity than sweet compassion? Yet,
If you still think I've err'd, my fate is in
Your hands; but charge me not with treason, I
Conjure you, Sire.

    Phil.   A noble pride exhales
In ev'ry word—but you cannot embrace,
Nor is't for you to penetrate your king's
Sublime designs.   Henceforth, restrain your rash
Impetuous spirit: check that restless wish to force
Advice, unask'd, on us, with daring arrogance;
And learn to not make traffic of your thoughts,
However just.   If, on some future day,
The world is to behold you on the throne
Which bears the palm o'er Europe's ample realms,
Learn wariness; then you will be rever'd.
The rashness, prais'd in youth, then would create
Severest blame. 'Tis time methinks to change.
You call on me for pity: pity you
Shall have, but for yourself; all merit not
So much: leave *me* to judge of what is right
And wrong.   The queen has long been pleading, nor
In vain, in your behalf: she deems you worthy still
No less of my affection than her love.
You owe your pardon more to her than me—

To her!—I hope you'll learn to estimate
My favour, and deserve it more. You see,
Oh lady, that I yield ; and, taught by you,
Not only learn to *pardon* but to love my son.
   Isab.   My liege——
   Phil.   The merit's yours and yours alone :
I have repress'd my anger for your sake,
And warn'd him with paternal tenderness.
Oh, may I ne'er repent!—Now, Carlos, mark!
Fulfil her hopes, and prove your gratitude.
You, queen, must see the prince more frequently;
That he from *good* to *better* may advance :
Converse together ; give him sage advice. You will,
My son, attend ; nor shun her sight—'tis my
Command.
   Carl.   *Pardon!* 'Tis an ungentle sound.
But since I hear it from my Sire, and since
The queen implor'd, I must submit; but, oh,
I hope that Fate (for Fate it is and not
My guilt) will ne'er degrade me thus again !
   Phil.   You should not blush at having been forgiv'n,
But to have err'd.—Enough—retire ; think well
On what I've said. Return, oh queen, to your
Apartment, I'll be with you soon : I'm call'd
A while to more important cares. [*Exeunt* Queen *and* Prince.
   Phil.   (*to* Gomez.)   Heard'st thou ?
   Gom.   I heard !
   Phil.   Saw'st thou ?
   Gom.   I saw !
   Phil.   Oh rage ! My doubts—
   Gom.   Are doubts no more.
   Phil.   And Philip still lives unreveng'd !
   Gom.   I think——
   Phil.   I've thought. Away ! *   [*Exeunt.*

END OF THE SECOND ACT.

———

ACT III.

SCENE I.—Carlos, Isabella.

Carlos.

OH, queen, excuse this new and daring step.
If at an hour so late, so strange, I sent

---

* The two copies of this tragedy in our possession have different modes of
ending the act. Nothing can well be conceived finer than the above: the
other is far inferior.

Faithful Elvira to request a moment's
Audience, 'twas for reasons most important.

    Isab.   What would you, prince?—Why am I summon'd;
Is not my peace sufficiently destroy'd?
Why are you here?—And why am I?

    Carl.   Oh, be
Not angry, lady: briefly I will speak, and then
Return, hard fate, to solitude and tears.
This morn, you dar'd to plead in my behalf
To Philip: great was your imprudence! And
Of this I came to warn you. Heaven grant
It's ill effects may fall on me, alone!
Pompous compassion was insidious deceit:
The pardon he bestow'd was pledge of hate
More bitter. Your pure heart suspected not
How galling Pity's breath is to the tyrant's soul.
Now mark it well: forbearance, in the king,
Is the forerunner of each cruel act.
From that dread hour, strange fears have prey'd upon
My soul!—Oh God!—What can it mean? He spoke
Unlike himself: and show'd unusual love!
Oh, never, I conjure you, speak again
To him of me!

    Isab.   'Twas he first spoke, and forc'd
Me to reply: but then his wrath seem'd wholly to
Subside: and ere you came, he wept and prais'd
You with a father's warmth. He gave you life;
And can I, prince, believe a father does
Not love his only son? 'Tis passion blinds
You: it imagines hatred which can not
Exist!—You see your father with dislike;
And I, oh misery, create this strife!

    Carl.   Oh, Isabella, ill you judge us both.
I fear, 'tis true, but do not hate the king:
I envy him the gem he snatch'd from me;
Too rare for such a hand, which throws it by,
Unconscious of its worth. Were you content,
Alas, my sorrows would be less.

    Isab.   Again
You break into complaints: I'll leave you, prince.
Be calm: I'll study ev'ry word and look,
Should Philip ere renew his last discourse.
I fear him too; but *you* still more I fear.   [*Exit.*

SCENE II.

    Carl.   Oh, noble heart! Ill vers'd in mean distrust,
Where hast thou fallen?—But who comes here?
What now?

SCENE III.—*Enter* GOMEZ.

Gom. I wait the king : anon he will
Be here.—Permit me, prince, to share the joy
You feel, at being fully now restor'd
To royal Philip's grace : my influence
And pow'r have ever been exerted in
Your favour. Deign t' accept——
　　　[*Exit* Carlos, *who passes* Gomez *with an indignant and*
　　　contemptuous air.

SCENE IV.

Gom. 　　　　　Haughty enough !
But, still, more rash.

SCENE V.—PHILIP, LEONARDO, PEREZ, GOMEZ :
Counsellors *and* Guards *at a distance.*
[*They all sit.*]

Phil. 　　　　Ho ! Guards ! Let none intrude
Upon our privacy. Ye few but faithful friends,
You're call'd upon, in this strange hour and place,
To hear a cause most urgent, and most high.
Attend ! (*pause.*) Black horror creeps upon my soul,
Congeals my blood ! Turns ev'ry tear to stone !
My feeble voice dies on my trembling lips,
And wavers still, amid contending passions.
And must I speak ? Oh, yes ! My country wills,
Not I, the cruel task !—Who would believe
I sit in accusation here, a judge ?
'Tis past conjecture ! Who but I wou'd dare
Accuse so high a criminal ?—You shrink !
Aghast you look !—What will you say, when I
Shall name *the prince ?*——
　Leon. 　　　　Your only son ?
　Per. (*with all the warmth of honest indignation*) When did
He e'er transgress ?
　Phil. 　　　More happy than your king,
Domestic peace is yours ; of that I'm robb'd,
By my ungrateful son ! How vainly have I tried,
With gentle words and mild reproof, to move
This disobedient boy ! To pray'r and kind
Advice he shuts his ear ; and menace still
More daringly defies. Offence crept on,
Offence, and bold presumption grew ; till, at last,
He now has broke all bounds. This very day,

On which I gave no dubious proof of lenity,
Too great, he chose to crown his base exploits
With impious guilt.   The glorious sun, bright herald of
My deeds, scarce hence had mov'd t' illume my vast
Domains, and night the traitor's friend had spread
Her sable robe, when horrid thoughts rose in
My son's black mind.   Thirsting revenge, because
He had receiv'd the pardon of his guilt,
Silently he mov'd toward my chamber,
The murd'rous weapon naked in his hand.
Close at my heels he slunk; his arm was rais'd
To strike, and soon he would have plung'd the steel
In his defenceless father's side—Aloud
A voice exclaim'd Beware! Philip! Beware!
'Twas Roderic who came; and then I heard
The jarring clang of falling steel.   I turn'd
To look, and lo a dagger glisten'd at
My feet! Then, by the glimm'ring light, I saw
My son steal cautiously along the gallery!
My tale is told.   If any of you can
Accuse the prince of other crimes, or can
You prove him innocent of this, oh speak!
I conjure you, freely speak! So may Heav'n
Inspire your tongues! A fearful task it is!
Oh, weigh it well, ere you decide! From you
My safety—and my son's, at once I claim.
     Gom.   What do you ask, oh Sire? Can we betray
Our sov'reign, and ourselves?—Yet, can we pierce
A father's heart? Oh force us not to such
A dread extreme.
     Leon.   The day may come, oh king,
When you may grieve, and we repent, your having heard
The truth.
     Per.   Her voice can never harm: the truth
Is ask'd; let truth be heard!
     Phil.   The father hears
You not; the king attends.
     Gom.   Then I will first
Begin, first brave the father's wrath; for you
Are still a father, and we read your brow
More agitated than severe: if you arraign
The prince, the son is still absolv'd.   You will
Not, haply can not, number all his crimes.
To treat with vile Batavian rebels was
Too petty an offence, to satisfy
Your son.   Behold this paper, taken from
The prince, in which he signs our ruin and'
His shame.   With France he dares negotiate!
With hated France! Navarre, rich Catalon,

And other provinces no less renown'd,
The conquest of our valiant ancestors,
And which with valiant blood we have maintain'd,
Oh shame, he pledg'd : the most detested price
Of most detested aid, lent to a son
Against his Sire ! So great a part of these
Domains will fall a prey to the proud Frank ;
The rest, unable to resist, will groan beneath
The yoke of this implacant son, that would
Dethrone a king, whose arm and genius not
Alone a part but e'en the whole of this
Vast globe could sway ! Such the fate that threats us !
Most necessary, dear, and sacred, are
Your days to us, oh king : but no less sacred is
The glory of Hispania's noble realm.
T' attempt a father's life is horrible
Excess : but to have sold his honor and
His country, suffer me to say, perhaps,
Is e'en as horrible. Philip might that
Forgive : it touches him alone : and this ?—
May have the pow'r to overlook—Yet, when
Black crimes like these are prov'd, what sentence dare
These lips pronounce, but that of death ?
   Per.   Death ! What
Words are these ? Death !
   Phil.   Oh God !
   Leon.   Who would believe
That, to the names of *traitor, parricide,*
And *rebel,* I could add one more detested still ?
A name that no man dare pronounce !
   Phil.   What is't ?
   Leon. Of Heav'n the sacrilegious foe, he scorns
Our holy faith !—Oh God, omnipotent,
Inspire thy vile but faithful servant, and
Unseal his lips, to oracle high truths !
The moment now is come, when, with a nod
Tremendous and almighty, thou'lt destroy
Impiety and pride ! On me thou call'st,
Thy violated sanctity to now defend !
Thou warm'st my icy breast with fire divine,
And worthy of thy cause !—Oh king, respect
In me the awful voice of the most High,
And tremble while you hear ! The prince (I dare
Not call a wretch so harden'd Philip's son),
The prince, with tongue of fiend, each day blasphemes
The ministers of Heav'n, nay Heav'n itself !
His hell-born heresy dares interrupt
Our holy rites : he scorns our ancient faith,
Applauds the new, and, should he e'er be king,

He'll overthrow our sacred altars, and
With impious foot will trample on whate'er
We honor, now, with incense and our vows.
We shall behold—What is't I say? Though God
Suspend a while th' exterminating sword,
'Twill fall, at last, and sweep him from the earth.
I never shall behold the sacred veil withdrawn,
Which guards from vulgar eye immortal truth,
Beyond the powers of thought, which men no less
Revere: nor that tribunal laid in ruins
Where Heaven's justice is administer'd
To man with tenderness which but corrects
To save, where we untainted keep our faith,
Though Hell and Carlos vow its fall! Oh, Heav'n, avert
The horrid vow! Hell, may'st thou hope in vain!
—Oh, Philip, raise your mind to Heav'n's eternal King,
Life, honor, empire, all he gave and all
He can withdraw! Is he, who braves his pow'r,
A son?—The dire decree is pass'd: for you
It is to sign; delay not, Sire—The hand,
That dares retard th' avenging sword of Heav'n,
Turns on itself the mortal blow.

    Per.   Bold truths
But rarely spring on slav'ry's soil: nor do
The free of soul as freely always speak:
Yet base submission oft puts on the mask
Of independence. Listen, Sire, and know
What freedom is: from *me* a different language you
Will hear.—This paper, Sire, is forg'd; the crimes,
Alleg'd against the prince, but ill agree.
If he, oh monstrous guilt, prepar'd to aim
His hand against a father's sacred life,
Why treat with rebels? Why demand the aid
Of France? Why barter the paternal realm?
Why rob himself?—For if, by these base means,
He hop'd to lighten his sad destiny,
Why thus attempt this horrid parricide?
Why but attempt? Would he so far have gone
And then shrink back?. What obstacle oppos'd?
—If so he did, it was the act of phrenzy, not
Of guilt. He knows that ev'ry eye and ear
Watch for a monarch's safety, e'en when not
Belov'd, because from him all honors, wealth,
And power, flow. You saw him fly?—Oh 'twas
A lying vision, conjur'd up, my lord,
By traitors to your peace! Oh, let him come!
Let him be heard! He'll justify himself.
That he not thirsts your blood I swear: my head,
Nay more, my honor, which is far beyond

The grasp of kings, or priests, I'll stake upon
His innocence.   How shall I speak of that
Ferocious pride, which, in the garb of meek
Insulted sanctity, begs, for compassion,
To drink a martyr's blood !—I say—but what
Avails that I repeat, such wicked men
Veil base designs beneath religion's cloak,
Entangle private pique with sacred things,
And make themselves the sanguinary tools
Of vice ? Who knows it not ? The prince has ever shown
A gallant mind, and sympathetic heart.
His gentle manners grace a noble form :
From earliest age, his father's joy and pride,
In excellence he grew. You sung, my lords, his praise,
And thought him noble : so I think him still.
A mind once dignified can ne'er descend
To crimes so black.   Contempt, nay outrage, oft
He bears in silent sorrow, and respect.
'Tis true that grief is often made a crime,
And is but fuel to an angry mind.
Oh, Philip, he's your son ! Appease your wrath !
Take pity on his woes ! He is not guilty ;
But, ah, he's most unhappy ! Were he more
Tenfold more vile than these fair-speaking lords
Would prove, a father cannot, dare not, take
The life he gave.
  Phil.   At length, one pitying heart
I find : oh bless'd compassion ! I'll yield to
Thy pious dictates ! I a father ! and
Will be a father still ! Myself, my kingdom,
All I resign, to Heav'n's impervious will.
My son, perhaps, is but the instrument
Of dread Jehovah's wrath, which I've incurr'd.
Perish Hispania, perish Philip, so
Carlos be but sav'd ! He's now absolv'd.
 Gom. Would you be greater than the law ? Why call
Us here ? You can without our sanction break
The laws. Acquit, acquit the prince ! But, if
You should, some fatal day, repent this pity.
 Per. Pity, indeed, wou'd not avail ; for here
It wears, methinks, a lying mask. Decide
Among yourselves, I dare no longer sit
In a such a court. I still hold honor dear ;
For life I care not : that I never bath'd
My hands in guiltless blood the world can vouch.
Remain who will. To Heav'n I raise my vows ;
To Heav'n, that knows the truth. But why make this
Appeal ? Is Heav'n *alone* not ignorant ?
Can I not read, on every face, that ev'ry man's

Convinc'd; tho' every man is dumb? Has it
Not long been deem'd a capital offence
To hear or speak the truth?
    Phil.   Know'st thou to whom
Thou speak'st?
    Per.   The father of Don Carlos:
    Phil.   And thy lord!
                                    [*Exit* Perez.

    Leon. 'Tis true, my liege, you are the prince's sire;
And who reads not a father's anguish and
Despair in every look? But you are too
The father of your people, and they venerate
That sacred name, tho' it is slighted by
The prince. He is but one, and numberless
Are they; he is in safety, while the rest
Stand on the brink of danger; he is guilty, *they*
Are innocent. Can you debate to save
One, or *the whole?*
    Phil.   Oh cease to stab me to
The heart! Alas, my strength forsakes me. I
Must call another council, where I shall
Not sit, and where the holy ministers
Of Heav'n shall give their voice. They are not sway'd
By mundane passions! Truth will issue from
Their lips; and truth alone they'll hear. Away,
And judge the prince. Were I to come, I should
Disturb the course of justice, or expose
My courage to a trial most severe.   [*Exeunt* Counsellors.

SCENE VI.

    Phil. How many traitors are ye? Perez, dar'st
Thou brave me? Haply, he has read my heart!
No, no.—In what a dauntless tone he spoke!
Can souls like these exist? Where I am king,
Can such a man continue long to breathe?   [*Exit.*

ACT IV.

SCENE I.—Carlos *alone.*

Carlos.

OH, night, more genial to this horrid court
Than day, I hail thy welcome shades! Not that
Thou bring'st a momentary pause to grief;
But thou dost veil from sight the hideous forms

Of cruelty and vice, that crowd in these
Abodes. Elvira says I may expect
Her here : she comes on Isabella's part.
What would she say ? How awful is this calm !
Oh, gentle sleep, canst thou descend 'mid restless cares,
Remorse, suspicion, and black crime, to smooth
The traitor's and the tyrant's couch ; while thou
Still fli'st an innocent oppress'd ?—But I
Regret thee not : fond mem'ry visions every charm
And mental grace my soul adores ! What spell
Confines me to this spot ? 'Twas here she stood ;
'Twas here her lips at once spoke misery
And bliss ! Since that ill-fated moment, I
Have been less wretched—but, alas, less pure !
Whence rise these coward fears ? Are they the just
Reward of guilt ?—Of guilt !—When did I e'er
Transgress ? My tongue avow'd the passion of
My heart ; but who could love like me and not
Avow ? Who comes ? Elvira ? No ! What noise
Is that ? Whose steps are those ? What blaze of light ?
In arms ? To me ? Traitors, avaunt !   [*Draws his sword.*

SCENE II.

CARLOS, PHILIP, (*followed by Soldiers with arms and torches.*)

Carl.   Oh Heav'ns,
My father ! Thus attended !
    Phil.   Now ! What seek
You here, alone and arm'd, at such an hour ?
What would you ? Whither go you ? Your intentions !
    Carl. May soon be told. The sword I drew in self
Defence, against this arm'd escort, falls from
My palsied hand before my father ! I
Resist not, Sire. But say, need you a poor pretext ?
And what ? Oh, father, subterfuge becomes
Not kings ; but mean excuse still less becomes
Your son.
    Phil. You add defiance to your guilt !
'Tis well ! Such daring is the last resource
Of harden'd villainy. Formerly, you
Veil'd your rebel thoughts ; mask'd the blackness of
Your heart in feign'd respect. But throw it off ;
'Tis better you should break all barriers to
Your rage, shed all your mortal venom, dauntless
Avow each fell design, and glory in
Your magnanimity !
    Carl.   What must I, Sire, avow ?
Oh, father, spare me useless outrage ! I'll

Submit to all your vengeance can ordain,
And call it just, if grateful to your soul!
   Phil.   Alas, in age so tender, how have you
Arriv'd at perfidy so great? Where have
You learn'd iniquity thus black, that now,
Detected by the king in such abhorred
Deeds, you dare to meet his eye unchang'd?
   Carl.   Where
Learn'd iniquity? Sire, this palace gave
Me birth——
   Phil.   I know it, wretch, to my disgrace
And woe!
   Carl.   Then why delay to end your grief?
Why shed you not your son's pure blood? 'Twill make
You happy!
   Phil.   My son! You!
   Carl.   Speak! What is my
Offence?
   Phil.   You ask of me! Of me! Is not
Your heart torn by remorse? Ah, no! Long has
It been a stranger to your breast: if aught
You feel, 'tis rage that I've escap'd your murd'rous arm.
   Carl.   What is't I hear? I seek my father's life?
I charg'd with parricide?—But you do not
Believe—Oh no! What proof have you?
Whence rise these horrid doubts?
   Phil.   Doubts! Certainty
Lies in the hate you bear me.
   Carl.   Father, force
Me not, oh, force me not to pass beyond
The awful bar, which Heav'n and man have plac'd,
Between the subject and the king, the son
And father! Make me not a wretch!
   Phil.   You have
With sacrilegious foot, long overstep'd
Those bounds. What is't, I say? You never knew
They did exist! Quit Virtue's lofty strain,
It fits you ill; speak as you feel! Unveil
Your treasons plann'd, and those you have achiev'd!
Be brief. Fear you that I'm less noble than
You are base? If you speak truly, without
Disguise, you still may hope: but if you're silent, or
Attempt concealment, then beware!
   Carl.   I'll speak:
I'm driven to excess!—I know myself
Too well to fear your threats, and *you* too well
To hope. Take back the life you gave! Oh fatal gift!
'Tis yours; my honor is my own. You gave
It not, nor can rob me of it. Were I

From cowardice to own myself a parricide,
I were a wretch indeed !—You here shall see
Me breathe my last; prepare a death opprobrious, long,
And cruel: Carlos still shall be himself.
You, my father, alone unmov'd will see
Me die.
    Phil. Is't thus, rash boy, you speak your lord ?
Is't thus you justify your crimes ?
    Carl.   My crimes !
You hate me: that's my only crime. Blood is
Your beverage: thus, Sire, I justify
Myself: your pow'r is absolute ; hence you
Have right.
    Phil.   Holla ! Arrest him, guards !
    Carl.   This is
The answer of a despot. Sire, load me
With chains ! Behold, my bosom's bar'd : come, plunge
Your sword ! Why do you hesitate ? Is this
Inhuman act your first ? Has not each day
Of your black reign been mark'd with blood ?
    Phil.   Be gone,
I say ! conduct him to the tow'r, and cast
Him in the blackest dungeon : on your lives,
Obey.
    Carl. Fear not ; your ministers are cruel as
Yourself.
    Phil. Force him away !   [*Exeunt* Soldiers, Carlos.

SCENE III.—Philip, Isabella.

    Isab.   Oh, Heav'ns ! What is't
I see !
    Phil. (*sternly*) Why come you hither, queen ?
    Isab. (*timidly*)   I hear
Sounds of distress and mournful lamentations.
    Phil. 'Tis true; you hear.
    Isab.   The prince forc'd from your sight ?
    Phil. 'Tis even so ! 'Twas he—
    Isab.   Your son ?
    Phil.   Do you
Grow pale and tremble at the sight ?
    Isab.   I !
    Phil.   Well
You may. Your terror is *no little* proof,
To me, how well you *love*. You tremble for
Your consort : but, be calm ; the danger's o'er !
    Isab. The danger ? What ?
    Phil.   It was extreme : but now
My life——

Isab.   Your life!
Phil.   So *dear* and *necessary* to
You, queen, is safe.
    Isab.   The traitor?
    Phil.   Will receive
His just award. Fear not my heart again
Should yield to feminine compassion. No,
The season's pass'd : the voice of justice, loud
And terrible, shall now alone be heard!
    Isab. But what's the prince's crime?
    Phil.   Oh, Heav'ns! Perhaps,
'Twas not alone my life he sought! The wretch,
Who thirsted for his father's blood, would not
Have spar'd his father's wife—if her he view'd
Alike with envious hate!
    Isab.   Have spar'd? What say
You, Sire? Oh, wretched me! The prince—
    Phil.   Ungrateful to
Us both, forgets the many *favours* he
Receiv'd—But calm yourself; be happy: I
Will take upon myself th' important office to
Secure *your everlasting peace and mine.*   [*Exit* Philip.
    Isab. What language! What a frown!—I scarcely can
    recall
My troubled senses! What said he? Can he
Suspect my love?—Oh no! 'Tis too conceal'd.
And yet his threat'ning eye, so fix'd
On me.—Oh, wretched Isabel! What meant
He by his everlasting peace and mine?
My peace?—Oh, Heav'ns! And what escap'd my lips?
Did I not name the prince? What horrid fears
Congeal my blood! Where is he gone? Ah, where?
Why speeds he thus away? What shall I do?
I fain would follow—but my feet refuse
To guide my trembling frame.

SCENE V.—Isabella, Gomez.

    Gom. Forgive th' intrusion, queen :
I thought my liege was here.
    Isab.   He was e'en now.
    Gom. I then with haste must seek him ; for he waits
To learn the great event.   [*Going.*
    Isab.   Event?—Oh, stay!
What is't?
    Gom. If you have spoken with the king,
He must have told you how impatiently
He waits the final judgment.

Isab.   No; he spoke
Ambiguously of treason, but he——
   Gom.   Did
Not tell the traitor's name ?
   Isab.   The prince——
   Gom.   You know
Then all. I now come from the council——
   Isab.   Come ?——
What council? What bring you ? Alas !——
   Gom.   They long
Discuss'd th' important cause, and all at last
Agreed——
   Isab. To what ? Explain.
   Gom.   Here is the sentence ;
The king has but to sign——
   Isab.   It dooms ?
   Gom.   The prince
To death.
   Isab. To death ? Wretches !—To death !—What is
His crime ?
   Gom. Did not the king explain?
   Isab.   Oh, no!
   Gom. He has attempted Philip's life !
   Isab.   Oh, Heav'ns !
The prince ? Carlos !
   Gom.   It is the king himself
Who makes the charge ; and lays before us proof——
   Isab. His father ? And what proof? fictitious proof!
Alas, there surely is some other cause,
Which you conceal ? Oh tell his *real* offence !
   Gom. His *real* offence ?—And dare I speak, if you
Are uninform'd ? It might betray my life.
   Isab. Oh, what say you ? How can you fear I should
Betray ?
   Gom. If I but speak a word, I shall
Betray the king! my sov'reign lord !—But why
Seek *you so ardently* to learn the truth ?
   Isab. I seek ?—'Tis but a woman's wish.
   Gom.   What can
I tell you, queen ?—The prince is in great danger;
Nay, likely he may fall. But what are *you*
To him ? He's not *your* son—his death cannot
Harm you ; nay, it may place your future sons
On Spain's illustrious throne. Believe me, queen,
His *criminality* lies in the *love*——
   Isab. What say you ?——
   Gom.   Philip bears you: gladly he
Would have a son of yours succeed him, which
Can never be, while Carlos lives.

Isab. (*aside*)   I breathe !——
Dare you suppose I have a mind so base ?

Gom.   'Tis Philip's thought, not mine, I thus explain.
But——

Isab.   Then that which I could never believe
Is true ; a father can abhor his *own*,
His *only* son !

Gom.   Oh, lady, much I pity you,
If you before so little knew the king !

Isab.   What say you! Whom do I trust?

Gom.   Nay, since I
Read true compassion on your brow, I'll speak
The horrid secrets that oppress my heart.
'Tis true, alas, too true, the prince, ill-fated youth,
Is only infamous in having such
A sire !

Isab.   You make me shudder !——

Gom.   I too shrink !
Know you whence rises this unnat'ral hate ?
From dastard envy ! The pure virtues of
The prince inflam'd the king's imagin'd greatness.
He finds his son too diff'rent from himself,
And rather, oh impiety, would have
Him die, than live more great !

Isab.   Oh, sire unmatch'd,
In ruthless cruelty ! but still more vile !
Why does the council doom the innocent
To die ?

Gom.   What council dare oppose a king
So absolute? He brings the charge himself.
Each knows 'tis false ; but each, in terror for
Himself, by silence gives assent. On *us*
The shame of this vile sentence falls : *we* are
The guilty instruments of *his* revenge.
We shudder while we strike ; but 'tis in vain :
Who dar'd refuse would soon fall victims to
His rage.

Isab.   Is this a dream ?—Amazement ties
My tongue ! Is there no hope ?—Must he unjustly fall ?

Gom.   In artifice, the king's supreme indeed !
At first, he'll seem to doubt, make specious show
Of sorrow, and compassion, nay perhaps
He will delay, ere he pronounce his death :
But fools are they who think his grief sincere ;
Or hope, because a while he still forbears
To strike, his deep and inward wrath is cool'd.

Isab.   Ah, if your heart is not of rock, like his,
Take pity on the prince !

Gom.   What can I do ?

Isab. Perhaps——

Gom.   With fruitless tears, in secret mourn
The noble victim's fate: no more is in
My pow'r.

Isab.   Oh, God! What age has heard, what eye
Beheld, atrocity so black!

Gom.   Could I
But save the prince, no danger would I fear!
And, Heav'n's my judge, remorse, the legacy
A tyrant's fatal friendship leaves, corrodes, nay wrings
My heart; but——

Isab.   If you really feel remorse
It may afford the prince no little aid.
Nor need you sacrifice yourself. Philip
Suspects you not: you may clandestinely
Abet the prince's flight: who could betray?
Who knows? The day may come in which the king
Again may be himself; and nobly would
He recompense the man, whose courage sav'd
His glory, and his son.

Gom.   And, grant I dar'd,
Would the prince consent? Know you the contempt,
Th' indignant rage with which he'll spurn at flight,
And brave his doom? No fear of death can shake
His lofty mind. He'll obstinately perish,
And all advice or aid, from *me*, would be
Suspicious, and receiv'd with scorn: he thinks
Me Philip's slave——

Isab.   Is this the only bar?
Suffer me to see him; lead to the tow'r,
Where you have free access: my pray'rs, I hope,
Will move him to comply. Oh, grant my urgent suit.
The night is far advanc'd: prepare for his
Escape, and keep this fatal paper from
The king, who may not yet expect 'tis giv'n.
Oh, let us try—I pray you let us haste,
And angels be our guard!—Delay not, I
Conjure you.

Gom.   Who would not fulfil a work
So pious! At my peril I will make
Th' attempt! Come, lady! Heav'n will not desert
Th' afflicted mortal who deserts not Heav'n!   [*Exeunt.*

END OF THE FOURTH ACT.

ACT V.

SCENE I.—*A Dungeon.*

Carlos.

OH, death! from thee alone I now must hope.
Oh, could it be an honorable death!
But infamy, alone, I must expect
From cruel Philip.—One dread thought preys on
My soul more agonizing still! Perhaps
He knows my love! Unusual rage, in his
Despite, blaz'd from his dark ferocious eye.
His speaking with the queen, then calling me,
And watching—Heav'nly Powers, how shall I act?
The queen! Alas! barbarian! he, perhaps,
Ere now, has wreak'd on her the vengeance of
Imaginary guilt: for tyrants strike
If their suspicious minds but dream offence.
But how should Philip learn a secret known
To none, perhaps, and scarcely to ourselves?
My sighs may have betray'd my heart; but are
The gentle sighs of love a language tyrants know?
Need *such* a father *such* a cause to act
A part unnatural and black?—His hate
Is mortal, and I see the day is come
In which my blood must satiate his rage.
Oh, fickle throng of fortune-smiling friends,
Where are you now? A sword is all I ask;
But none of you will bring the friendly steel,
To snatch me from disgrace! What noise is that?
The hinges creak—the massy bars give way—
What have I to expect!—I'll listen—Heav'ns!

SCENE II.—*Enter* ISABELLA.

The queen! *You* Isabella here! who was
Your guide? What brings you hither? Love, your duty,
Or compassion? How gain'd y' access?
   Isab.   Alas,
You know not all the horror of your fate!
You're branded with the name of parricide.
Your father makes the charge: a wicked council dooms
You, prince, to die; the king has but to sign.
   Carl. If so, my time is short.
   Isab.   And you are still
Unmov'd?

Carl.   I long have center'd ev'ry hope
In death: to breathe my last near you, you know,
Was all I wish'd.   The horrid crime with which
I'm stigmatiz'd, may grieve but not surprise.
Yes, die I must; and can I shrink when you
Are come t' announce my death?
    Isab.   Oh, if you love,
Speak not of death; yield, I conjure you,
To these fearful times.
    Carl.   Yield! Too well I see
The cruel task to vilify is yours.
My unrelenting father sends you to——
    Isab.   How! Think you I'm the minister of Philip?
    Carl.   He might compel, or by his arts prevail
On you to try me thus: but, if not so,
What could induce the king to let you come?
    Isab.   The king? Oh, Heav'ns! Were he to know——
    Carl.   Alas,
To Philip, lady, all is known.   What say
You! Who presum'd to break his lord's command?
    Isab.   His fav'rite Gomez.
    Carl.   Gomez!—Heav'nly pow'rs!
Oh, lady, what an odious name you have
Pronounc'd! A name most fatal and terrific!
    Isab.   He's not your foe, as you suppos'd.
    Carl.   Oh, God!
If e'er I thought he was my *friend*, shame more
Than rage would dye my burning cheek.
    Isab.   Yet he,
Alone, takes pity on your fate: 'twas he
Reveal'd the king's atrocious plot.
    Carl.   Oh, too
Incautious, too believing Isabel!
What have you done? Why did you trust in such
Compassion? If he told you true, the viler tool
Of a vile king, it was but to insnare.
    Isab.   To what effect? If you will grant my suit,
He soon will give no little proof that he's
Sincere: he led me hither, secretly,
And now prepares to favour your escape.
I urg'd him to't: lose not a moment! Fly
From Philip, death, and me!
    Carl.   Oh, fly yourself,
While yet you can, far from this place! The feign'd
Compassion Gomez show'd was treach'rous as
Himself.   In what insidious nets you have
Been caught! 'Tis now *indeed* I tremble? Oh,
What horrid doubts arise! The myst'ry of
Our love is known to Philip—and——

Isab.   Ah no!
The moment you were forc'd away, anon,
We met: his wrath was fearful, and my soul
Recoil'd. The dread *you* feel then seiz'd on *me*;
But afterward, more calm, I thought on what
He said, and am convinc'd my terror was
Unfounded: for he charg'd you, not alone
With having wish'd to take his life, but with
Designs on mine.
     Carl.   Could I unravel this
Most intricate and demon's web, my soul
Must be as vile, or viler, than his own.
But I'm too sure your coming here conceals
Some horrid fraud: that which might be surmise
Is now confirm'd, be what it may. Retire,
And quickly, from this fatal place. In vain
You think, or hope, that Gomez will assist
My flight; and still more vainly, even if
He would, that I should e'er consent.
     Isab.   And am
I doom'd to pass my melancholy days
In such a court?
     Carl.   Alas, you are! But linger not.
Away, if life is dear.
     Isab.   Life dear to *me?*
     Carl. My *honor*, then, and your unblemish'd fame.
     Isab. Can I abandon you, in such an hour?
     Carl. Why brave you danger thus? To what effect?
You seek destruction, for you cannot save.
Breathe on the clearest crystal, and 'tis sullied:
So is the purity of woman by
A breath. Let not the tyrant triumph, e'en
In thought, o'er fancied guilt. Go, hide your tears;
Stifle your sighs; and hear the tidings of
My death with stoic calm. To virtue consecrate
The mournful days you may survive; and, if
You seek for solace to your grief in this
Vile court, *one* honest man remains! 'Tis Perez.
You know him well: in secret you may weep,
And speak of me—But prithee now depart.
Retire—force not unmanly tears—give not
Ten thousand deaths in one! Receive my last
Farewel!—and leave me!—Go! I now have need
Of all my courage, for the fatal hour
Of death draws nigh.

SCENE III.—PHILIP, ISABELLA, CARLOS.

     Phil.   'Tis come, vile wretch, 'tis come!
I bring it thee!

Isab.   Oh sight! oh treachery!
Carl.   I am prepar'd: now kill me!
  Phil.   Miscreant,
Thou di'st! but first, perfidious pair, you shall
Be call'd to terrible account.   I know
You well! I long have known the impious flame
Which burns within your veins; and, tho' repress'd,
The fury that consumes you.   How oft
Have I subdu'd the rage I felt, and borne
A long and painful silence!—But at length,
You're fall'n within my pow'r: why should I grieve?
Are vain complaints the arms I ought to use?
Vengeance I wish, and vengeance I will have.
Quickly shall it fall, and heavily!—
But, first, I'll triumph in your shame! Think not,
Vile lady, that I e'er have lov'd thee: or
That jealous rage distracts my heart.   A thing
So abject as thyself ne'er fix'd the high
Affections of a Philip! Nor could she,
Who merited his love, betray.   In me
Thou hast not wrong'd thy lover, but thy lord.
Thou hast disgrac'd the sacred title of
My consort.   I ne'er wish'd thy love; but still,
The fear thou ow'st thy king shou'd so have aw'd,
Thou shouldst not e'en have dar'd to think of love.
Thou, base seducer, art beneath reproof.
Nought can surprise from thee: a crime so black
Was worthy of thy heart.   The guilty sighs
Ye both in secret heav'd, the silence, and the grief,
I well observ'd, and even now can see
You cherish in your impious hearts, were but
Too certain proofs of your offence.   Why do
I waste the moments in mere words: you've sinn'd
Alike; alike shall be your fate.
  Carl.   What is't
I hear? She's innocent! Not e'en the shadow of
Offence is hers! Her spotless heart, I swear,
Fed not a flame impure: she scarcely knew
I lov'd: she had——
  Phil.   I know how far ye each
Have gone; I know you have not yet presum'd
In thought to violate my royal couch.
Had you done this, would you be here? But words
Of ardent love flow'd from thy serpent mouth;
She listen'd; that's enough.
  Carl.   You're wrong'd by me
Alone.   I'll not deny a transient ray
Of hope gleam'd in my heart; but soon the queen's

Pure virtue broke the charm. She heard me, it
Is true; but only to reprove, and chase
The fatal impious passion from my breast.
Fatal indeed! Alas, too fatal now!
But once it was legitimate. She was
My bride! You know it well; you gave her to
My arms; and you had more the right to give
Than rob me of the gift. I'm guilty ev'ry way!
Yes, I adore her!—You have seiz'd my all!
What can you more?—Feast on revenge, and drink
My blood to quench your jealous rage:
But spare the queen; she's innocent.
  Phil.   She fail'd
In courage, but her guilt match'd yours. You speak
Not, lady, in your turn? But silence best
Convicts you: impious love (denial is
In vain) burns in your bosom. When I spoke,
Not long ago, with studied art, to you
Of Carlos, you did wantonly betray
Yourself. You bad me recollect he was
My son. Perfidious as you are, you durst
Not say your lover! Had you less in thought
Betray'd your duty, honor, and the laws——
  Isab. My silence does not rise from fear. I'm lost
In wonder, at the unexampl'd rage
And artifice of your impervious heart. At length,
Bewilder'd sense returns! I am your wife,
And for that heavy sin must now atone.
I have not wrong'd you. In the face of Heav'n
And Don Carlos, I spurn imputed guilt!
But, in my heart——
  Carl.   Oh, hear her not! Weak pity prompts
Her words!
  Isab. In vain you seek to save: each word
You say pours poison on the cank'ring wound.
Excuse avails no more; I wish but to
Escape the matchless torture his dire sight
Inflicts.—Could tyrants feel so pure so dignified
A sentiment, I'd tell you, king, 'twas you
First taught us love: 'twas you, from earliest age,
That influenc'd my thoughts: in him you bad
Me centre each fond hope: with him I thought
To spend a life of bliss! 'Twas then my duty, and
Your law, to love the prince. Who made it now
A crime? You, by dissolving ties so holy.
Men must submit to arbitrary pow'r,
But will the heart so quickly change? The love
I had imbib'd was strong; but, when your wife,
I buried it within my breast. I hop'd

That time, my virtue, and, perhaps, that you
Would chase——
   Phil.   I then will do what neither time
Nor your *pure* virtue could effect; yes, I
Will quench the impious passion in your blood.
   Isab. You rule with terror, and delight in blood.
Are these allurements, think you, to induce
Me to bestow on you the heart I might
Recover from the prince? On *you*, unlike
Your son, as virtue is to vice! You e'er
Till now have seen me trembling, and confus'd;
But now I fear you not. I hitherto
Conceal'd the impious flame; for such I thought
It was; I now proclaim it! since I find
You are more impious still.
   Phil.   Oh, pair immaculate,
Ye well are match'd! It now is to be prov'd
If ye can die as *bravely* as ye speak.

   SCENE IV.—*Enter* GOMEZ *with a bloody sword in one hand,*
           and a bowl of poison in the other.

   Phil. Mark'd you, Gomez, what I said? Are my
Commands obey'd?
   Gom.   This moment Perez fell, pierc'd to
The heart: this sword is recking in his blood.
   Carl. Oh, sight of horror!
   Isab.   Cruelty unmatch'd!
   Phil. The clan of traitors is not yet destroy'd:
But you may see the recompence reserv'd
For your accomplices.
   Carl.   Alas, how many deaths
Am I condemn'd to bear, before I die!
Thou too, oh Perez! Rage! Despair! Soon I
Shall follow thee! Where is the fatal sword?
Oh bring it quick! and may my blood alone
Assuage this tiger's quenchless thirst!
   Isab.   Oh, sword!—
Let mine appease his ill-born rage!
   Phil.   Cease this
Ignoble strife, the poison'd bowl or sword
Are at your choice. Thou, mocking boaster, first
Decide.
   Carl. Oh, sword, still warm with guiltless blood,
Thou'lt bring me liberty and peace. For thee,
Unhappy queen, death only now remains!
Too freely thou hast spoken: but I pray
Thou'lt take the bowl; death will be thus more easy.
This is the last request of inauspicious love.

Rouse all thy fortitude—Behold! *(stabs himself)* I die.
Now follow me—The bowl!—The bowl!—Delay
Not—
                                            [*Dies.*
   Isab.   Oh!—Yes, I will follow thee! Death, how
Welcome art thou!
       [*Going to take the bowl, which* Philip *suddenly seizes and
        dashes to the ground.*
   Phil.   Live! Live! in thy despite——
   Isab.   Away!—Oh, cruel destiny!—He dies,
And I must live?——
   Phil.   Yes, thou shalt spend long years
Of ling'ring woe, torn from thy minion.
Thy sighs and tears will yield a banquet to
My soul. When time shall have allay'd thy grief,
And life again is dear, then thou shalt die.
   Isab.   *I* live with thee? *I* bear thy odious presence?—
No! Never!—I will die!—The deadly draught
Is spilt, but, yet—(*rapidly seizing* Philip's *sword, and stabbing
     herself*) the sword remains.
   Phil.   Forbear!
   Isab.   I die!
   Phil.   Oh, Heav'ns! What is't I see!
   Isab.   Thou see'st
Thy wife—and son—expire—both innocent—
Both slain—by thee!—Belov'd—Carlos—I come.   [*Dies.*
   Phil.   A stream of blood, and, oh, what blood o'erflows!
I have revenge, most amply horrid! But,
Am I at peace?—Gomez, let the foul deed
Be hid from ev'ry eye. Thy silence may
Save Philip's honor and perhaps—*thy* life.   [*Exeunt Omnes.*

THE END.

REMARKS.

AMONG the black actions which stain the memory of Philip the
Second, there is none that has given so much employment, to invention, as the death of his son Don Carlos, and his queen the
unhappy Isabella. To this the Abbé Saint Réal, in his historical novels (a species of writing which when it intermingles truth
and falsehood deserves to be severely reprehended) has chiefly
given birth: but the character of Philip was, in its general
tendency, so black, cruel, and atrocious, that even the imagination of a poet can with difficulty equal the truth. ALFIERI, not
alone with honest indignation, but, feeling a dignified moral

horror against such a man, has painted him with some of the vices that distinguished his character; particularly with the blackest fraud, and the most cold-blooded cruelty. His master vices, ambition and bigotry, could not unfortunately become a part of the present subject: nor could the poet sufficiently affix on his name that detestation with which it has been impressed by his actions, because it is not known how Don Carlos and Isabella perished: but, that Isabella had been affianced to Carlos, that Don Carlos died violently, and that Isabella did not long survive, appear to be indubitable facts. As Don Carlos is here depicted, the rashness of which his father and his enemies accused him is scarcely apparent. That which meaner minds might call rashness, the poet has made a noble fortitude, and contempt of death, by combining it with a full conviction, on the mind of Carlos, that his father was fully determined to take away his life ; and only endeavoured, by the most vicious yet profound dissimulation, to draw from the lips of Carlos some confession, which might aid to colour or extenuate the crime, Isabella recollects, but not quite sufficiently as a profound cause of her affection for Carlos, the contrast of situation of having actually married the father and that of having espoused the son : to whom she was first affianced, by Philip himself. In such a woman, this distracting thought must have been continually torturing the mind. Gomez and Leonardo are fine and true examples, of the dangerous depravity which such a master as Philip must create. Perez has not a sufficient part in the fable to display his magnanimity; nor does it by any means equal that which the German tragic poet, Schiller, has given to the *Marquis della Posa*, in his tragedy of Don Carlos, which character is most admirably drawn. That Alfieri possessed the highest qualities of the human mind, the enthusiasm of the poet, and the inestimable moral dignity of man, those who read this tragedy will scarcely deny. I feel a delightful, and I hope a just pride, when I inform the public that this translation is the work of one of my daughters, and that the corrections made by me have been very few and purposely sparing. To impose the joint labours of two persons as the performance of one or the world would be moral turpitude.

DRAMATIC BIOGRAPHY.

SOME ACCOUNT OF ALFIERI.

I AM sorry that the documents I possess, concerning this man of genius, are so few. I have indeed none, which are printed, except what are contained in his own works, and what are already before the public in a HISTORICAL MEMOIR ON ITALIAN TRAGEDY *, a work which is or deserves to be well known, for the mass of information it contains on a subject that is highly interesting to literature, yet one with which English readers in general are but little acquainted.

Of the time when, or the province where, our poet was born I have seen no account. The title page to his works runs thus, " *Tragedie di* VITTORO ALFIERI DA ASTI :" and, in a letter prefixed to them, written by *Ranieri de' Calsabigi,* and signed Naples, August 20, 1783, he is addressed by the title of Count. To this letter he writes an answer dated September in the same year. These letters relate to the opposition and the success with which his four first tragedies were received, by the critics and the public; and the manner of acting tragedy, and pronouncing heroic verse, in Italy. To his *Bruto Primo* he prefixed a dedication " *Al chiarissimo e libro uomo, il Generale Washington:*" literally, *To the Renowned Free man, General Washington:* which dedication is dated Paris, December 31, 1788. ALFIERI is now dead : at least I fear so ; for, within some months, his death was announced in one or more of our daily newspapers. The following is the account given of him, in the above-mentioned historical memoir †.

" Impatient of the tœdium of an inactive life, and nobly ambitious of fame, "Count Vittorio Alfieri of Asti ‡, while yet a youth, struck into the dramatic walk. ' *Ciò che mi mosse a scrivere da prima,*' says he, ' *fu la noja, e il tedio d'ogni casa,*

---

* Quarto, London : 1799.   † Page 294.

‡ Asti may have been either the place of his birth, his residence, or from which he took his title.   EDITOR.

misto a bollor di gioventù, desiderio di gloria, e necessità di occu-parmi in qualche maniera, che più fosse confacente alla mia incli-nazione *.' " Such was the ardor with which he engaged in
" this new pursuit, that he produced, in less than six months,
" a tragedy, entitled Cleopatra, which was he candidly con-
" fesses what might be expected from his ignorance, and pre-
" sumption,"—' *un mostro*' [A monster.] " Yet this play, he
" informs us, was twice represented on the public stage in
" Turin, where," ' *sia detto a vergogna degli uditori, non meno*
' *che dell' autore* †,' " it was not only heard and tolerated, but
" even applauded. Thus suddenly transformed, to use his
" own words, from a dissipated youth into a tragic author, he
" determined to endeavour at qualifying himself to support his
" new character. In order to this, much was to be done. He
" had little Latin, but no Greek—was totally ignorant of the
" English, and had paid so little attention to the cultivation of
" the Italian language, that his knowledge of the ' *pura lingua*
' *toscano*' was '*presso che al abbicci* ‡." " He therefore thought
" it necessary to abstain from his favorite indulgence—the
" perusal of French authors—and devote himself to the study
" of the best Italian writers with a view to acquire the means
" of clothing his ideas in a suitable garb. He did not, how-
" ever, neglect the book of Nature: indeed he must be allowed
" to have studied it with uncommon success. He seems to
" have explored, with the inquisitive eye of genius, all the
" recesses of the human mind, and to have noted, with anxious
" care, the workings of the passions in all their various modi-
" fications. Hence the power which he acquired over them.
" But, however ardently he might have labored to attain the
" mastery of his vernacular tongue, he undoubtedly failed in
" the attempt; for even in his most elaborate works, his diction

---

* I was first excited to write by the irksome weariness of an idle life, added to youthful enthusiasm, the love of glory, and the necessity of employing my time congenial to my inclination.

† Be it spoken equally to the disgrace of the audience and the author.

‡ Was almost in its infancy.

" is harsh, inelegant, and sometimes ungrammatical." ' *Peccato,*'
" says an Italian critic, speaking of the beauties of our author's
" tragedies, ' *che tante gemme siano state legate in piombo, che col suo*
' *tristo coloro abbate ed infievolisce il loro stupendo splendore* *.'
" His language, nevertheless, is nervous and appropriate: in fact
" in his ' hoarse rough verse' we often hear a mighty voice,
" at whose pealing sound vice stands appalled.

   " In the construction of his dramas, our author departs from the
" ancient model. He rejects the chorus, and is heedless of the
" unities. Sparing of confidants, he abounds in monologues; and,
" from mismanagement of his situations, he often fails in illusion.
" Still however his genius predominates: his dramas, with all
" their faults, seldom fail to produce the intended effect."

Four or five years ago, at Paris, I frequently heard of the
fame of Count Alfieri. A Milanese nobleman spoke of him in
such high terms, and so decisively pronounced him to be incomparably the best tragic poet Italy had ever produced, that
we were determined to procure his works; and in them his
poetic character appeared so grand that my daughter was induced to translate the Tragedy of Philip II. According to the
authority of the above-mentioned Italian, the style of ALFIERI
was so concise, and the construction so difficult, that he could
not be understood by many of his countrymen: he had in
reality created a new poetic language. The Italians ca him
their Shakespear.

We were further informed that, in the beginning of the
French Revolution, he was ardent and indefatigable to promote
what appeared at first to be almost so miraculously to the benefit of mankind: but that, after being a witness of the atrocities
committed by the French in Italy, he became so disgusted, and
so deeply grieved, that he retired to his country seat to lament
the catastrophe in silence. We had friends who, when at
Siena, were personally acquainted with him; and, if memory
do not fail, they informed us he was then between sixty and
seventy, and a pleasant amiable old gentleman.

---

   * It is a pity that jewels so numerous should be set in lead; the gloomy
tint of which dims their dazzling splendor.

The following sonnet was given me by a friend, in London; and perhaps it will not be easy to find so severe a satire, in so short a space: it likewise pourtrays the turn of his thoughts, relative to the influence of bad governments on men.

Vuota insalubre Region, che stato
Ti vai nomando; arridi campi incolti
Squallidi, muti, estenuati volti
Di Popol reo, codardo, insanguinato;

Impotente non libero Senato,
Di astuti vili in fulgid' ostro avvolti;
Ricchi Patrizi e, piu che ricchi, stolti;
Prence che fa sciocchezza altrui, beato!

Città, non Cittadini; augusti Tempi,
Religion non gia; leggi che, ingiuste
Ogni lustro cangiar vede, ma in peggio;
Chiavi che, compre un dì, schiudeano agli Empi
Del Ciel le porte, or per età vetuste;
Non sei tu, Roma, d'ogni vizio il seggio?

I give the following not as a poetical translation, but as nearly a literal one as the construction of language appears to allow.

Desolate sickly waste, that dost continue
To call thyself a State, uncultivated,
Arid region; exhausted, squalid, mute,
Cowardly, blood-thirsty race; impotent,
Enslaved Senate, in cunning base, altho'
In purple cloth'd; wealthy patricians, yet
In folly far more rich; Beatic prince,
That mak'st holiness a farce *; City, with
Not a single patriot; Temples august,
But no religion; Laws, of such injustice
They ev'ry lustre change, to laws still worse;
Keys, procur'd to open t' impiety
The gates of Heaven, useless now from age;
Rome, art not thou the seat of ev'ry vice?

---

* Or   *Beatic prince,*
So Folly has pronounc'd thee;

ACCOUNT OF NEW PERFORMERS.

An author can scarcely impose upon himself a task more delicate, than that of estimating the merits and demerits of new performers. Among the stimulants to excellence, public applause is perhaps the greatest; and public applause depends on public opinion, which, if it be swayed to the prejudice of the actor, excludes hope and palsies the rising faculties. All observers of the theatre have remarked the feeble and defective manner in which actors have originally begun, and the slow advances they at first made, though they have finally become ornaments to their profession, and the support of the stage. The actors, that appear on the London theatres, have generally obtained some celebrity in provincial towns; but in these it was easily obtained; and, when they appear in London, they are not themselves at first acquainted with the species of character which they are best enabled to represent. It is sometimes the discovery of accident, but more generally of frequent experience.

From these premises, it must be evident that censure, if severely inflicted, must kill progressive merit; and that praise, if lavishly bestowed, may dangerously mislead and lull young performers to sleep. Scarcely any human being is so forgetful, of the mischief he may commit, as the man who calls himself a critic, when he takes up his pen, perhaps to encourage, perhaps to bestow as he imagines a severe flagellation. Praise and blame are necessary to the actor; but a chaste and conscientious rectitude are no less necessary to the critic.

The principal new performers, that have appeared during the present season, are Miss Duncan, Mr. Elliston, and Mr. Mathews; all at the Theatre Royal, Drury-lane. They have been seen sufficiently often to have obtained a certain degree of public favor; and, as remarks of the present kind are of little use except to the meridian of London, many of these remarks are not required.

The figure of Miss Duncan is highly to her advantage:

she is above the middle size, is finely formed, and well proportioned. Her face is such as a stage heroine might wish;
for the features are marked, prominent, and capable of great
variety. Her qualities for the stage have been carefully cultivated; for she sings, dances, and treads the stage, sufficiently
well to display the accomplished young lady. Her voice is
clear, and her articulation good; but they may both receive
considerable improvement. She is deservedly in favor with
the public; but she will no doubt remember that this favor can
only be insured and increased, by an assiduous cultivation and
increase of talent. Neither applause nor talents can remain
stationary: they must increase, or decline. She will not, it
may be hoped, be so unfortunate as to suppose herself already
a perfect actress; for then public favor would gradually lessen
till she might become one of those half and half performers
who appear, and disappear, merely to fill up the routine. If
she would peruse any one part, and, at every single period, or
phrase, would put the precise questions—" how many different
emotions does this period contain? and what variations of
voice, manner, and look, are required?" she would sometimes
find a vast difference between the answer and those emotions
and varieties which she at present adopts, and perhaps under-
stands. That she will acquire the habit of putting such important questions to herself there is every apparent reason to
hope; and the gratifying reception, she has hitherto met,
cannot but act as a high inducement to the delightful task.

Mr. Elliston, by having played so long and such a distinguished line of characters at Bath, has happily acquired a
knowledge of the stage, which admits of little improvement.
He is always at his ease, scarcely liable to be thrown off his
guard, has a good articulation, a sonorous yet clear-toned voice,
an agreeable middle-sized person, and a spirited manner;
which manner may be called so voluble that it does not give a
common spectator time to inquire for defects. The volubility,
here meant, is not so much of utterance, as of utterance combined with gesture, agility, and change of demeanor. These
qualities, by ensuring a certain share of success, have seduced

him into the error of never profoundly studying his author. To tragedy, this profound study is indispensable; but his spirit and ease, in comedy, frequently give the severest critic much satisfaction. In the present state of the stage, Mr. Elliston may be truly considered as a great acquisition: but, by a determined and persevering course of study, his talents may still be very highly improved.

Mr. Mathews is a young performer, and has not yet acquired that full possession of himself, and that firm confidence, which are absolutely necessary to the fine display of comic power. He should endeavour to acquire force, no less than variety; as well as the mode by which comic points come with their full impression upon an audience; yet not to depart from that chaste and simple style, which he at present very luckily appears to make his study. These qualities are by no means incompatible, as some performers have erroneously supposed them to be. Many living instances might be cited, to prove this assertion; and the late Mr. Weston possessed these opposite powers in so high a degree that Garrick, who had been many years famous in Abel Drugger, and Scrub, was so well convinced of Weston's superiority as to renounce such characters ever afterward, in Weston's favor. This at least is what I have very often heard repeated, while they were both living; and by those performers who, from their situation at Drury-lane Theatre, could scarcely have been mistaken. Mr. Mathews is sufficiently in favor with the public to encourage him to every exertion; and that he has a just ambition to distinguish himself he has given sufficient proof. His voice is scarcely loud enough, nor are his features sufficiently large, for the cast of characters in which he best succeeds: but the voice may be greatly improved, and even the features rendered much more pliable, and marking, by an assiduous course of well-planned study.

Actors unfortunately shew, by their practice, how continually they suppose that study (abstractedly, and almost wholly, the words which they are to repeat excepted) is a thing but little required of them: though by facts we are daily taught that perfection is not to be attained, in any art, not even in that of the lowest mechanic, without unremitting perseverance of thought and practice combined. The actor should be intently studious of the peculiarities, caprices, and oddities, and of the manner in which they display themselves, wherever they can discover such qualities to exist, in any human being: and, perhaps, there is no human being in whom they do not exist. How vast the volume, then, which an actor has to study! These peculiarities are frequently observed, to a certain degree, and imitated, by actors, for the private diversion of themselves and friends. How strange it is that they do not oftener think in what manner the whims of an individual might be incorporated with, and form a prominent feature of, such a character, or such another, which they have publicly to personate. May the performers to whom the foregoing remarks relate make the study of their profession their highest enjoyment, their daily and luxurious banquet, till they are able to give a no less delightful feast to the public! May they remember it is really the banquet of pleasure; and the only banquet in which they can indulge without restraint, and free of all expence!

PIECES

FIRST PERFORMED IN DECEMBER 1804, AND JANUARY 1805.

THE LAND WE LIVE IN:

A COMEDY, IN FIVE ACTS, BY FRANCIS-LUDLOW HOLT, ESQ.

THE Comedy of "THE LAND WE LIVE IN" appeared, at Drury-lane, on the twenty-ninth of last December, and was only once performed. Few pieces have received a more severe condemnation, than this unfortunate comedy. It was unfortunate, because the opposition to it began before it could have been justly decided how far it might deserve the fate that befel it; and unfortunate, because it was too inveterately con-

demned, with scarcely a possible chance, had the latter part
been the finest writing that poet had ever imagined, of being
fairly heard.   Perhaps, we must seek the origin of these misfortunes in the managers, proprietors, and authors themselves.
The flagrant practice, at present, is such that, unless an audience, who may highly disapprove, proceed to an almost excess
of acrimony in their condemnation, the piece they have condemned is again obtruded upon the town; and the daring
assertion, " that it had been received with loud and universal
applause," is read the next morning, and continued to be read,
at the bottom of the play-bills, as long as means can be found
to bolster up the ill-formed embrio.   Let the gentlemen, who
make those public assertions, settle the account how they can
with their own rectitude and delicacy.   To a tumultuous mode
of condemnation, therefore, an audience is reduced; or, to the
alternative of thus having their judgment revoked, and insulted.   The gentleman who, being asked concerning the success of a new piece, replies it has completely failed, blushes to
read it triumphantly announced the next morning, and to see
the lie publicly posted to an opinion which was given, the
night before, by every body present at the representation.

Mr. Holt has published his comedy, and by this means has
enabled the public to judge of it, as a composition.   It is to be
hoped that he does not himself consider it as deserving to have
appeared repeatedly before the public; for, should he continue
in this mistake, it would probably lead him into similar errors
in future.   These would merit regret the more by his having
proved, in the present instance, that he has a vigorous and
manly style, is a man of acute remark, and is an attentive
observer of those vices, and follies, to correct which is the
duty of the comic muse.

The chief defect of " THE LAND WE LIVE IN" is a vacuity
of plot and incident, such as should connect the various parts,
so as to form unity and fulness of design.   The attention of an
audience cannot be kept alive, either by brilliant wit or broad
satire, when it cannot be discovered to what they tend; and
when no story is in the recollection, the end of which we are

desirous to hear. The feeble attempt at interest, which the author endeavoured to create, by introducing a husband divorced from his wife, he immediately destroyed, by informing the audience that this husband was become anxious to be again united to his wife; and the death-blow to all interest was still more securely given by the wife, when she expressed the same prompt alacrity. Perhaps he did not intend this to be the main plot of his piece, but that the interest should be excited by the marriage, which was to take place, between the daughter and son of two old friends. If so, it is certain no person could be interested for beings who were so wholly indifferent to each other; and who were so little worthy of entering the marriage state.

Having noticed this essential mistake, it would be unnecessary to proceed; except earnestly to hope that the author will hereafter be more attentive to his fable, and the public less inclined to give eager, hasty, and severe decisions.

THE SCHOOL OF REFORM; OR, HOW TO RULE A HUSBAND:

A COMEDY, IN FIVE ACTS, BY THOMAS MORTON, ESQ.

IT is peculiarly gratifying to an author, who has frequently received great and decisive testimonies of public favor, to meet with a similar reception at every new effort he makes; and this high gratification was received by Mr. Morton, on Tuesday, the 15th of January, when the above play was first represented. The piece Mr. Morton has last produced, like most of those which he formerly wrote, is a strong mixture of the serious and the pleasant: or might, perhaps, more emphatically be called a tragi-comedy. Voltaire, in his preface to ' The Prodigal Son,' *L'Enfant Prodigue,* has given an opinion more liberal than is customary with French critics, and which perhaps he would not have given had it not been applicable to his piece, which opinion ought to be generally adopted. Speaking of dramatic pieces, he says, " Were I required to pronounce which species is the best, I should answer that which is the best executed." Were this rule made the test of merit, by critics, we should hear less of the unities, and more concerning the excellence or the failure of effect, and its causes.

There is indeed a unity which, when it is observed, never fails of receiving its due reward; and this may be either called the unity of action, or, more properly perhaps, the unity of story, or fable. When every scene and incident, throughout a dramatic piece, contribute to produce one effect, it must be very strange if that effect should be feeble. Should an audience be made to laugh and cry, at various passages of the same piece, this, instead of being a defect, cannot but justly be considered as effecting the best purposes of dramatic poetry, whose double province is the imagination and the passions of man.

These effects however should be produced by natural, and probable, and not by forced, incongruous, and impossible, events. When writing "THE SCHOOL OF REFORM," these simple means were not sufficiently present to the mind of the author: at least, he has failed in imagining and giving them a due arrangement. He has most judiciously been intent on producing the planned and double reform of his two heroes; but he has not scrupled to employ very romantic suppositions, for that purpose. A boy, brought up by the Philanthropic Society, saves the life of a lord; this lord is the father of the boy so brought up. The thing is not impossible, but it is an event which appertains to romance or novel writing. The lord, in gratitude, makes him his secretary: the lord's servants pretend to know him to be the son of a thief; and this too is rather strange. The youth openly avows himself to be such, which is still more strange, perhaps; but it is truly dignified and moral; and, while it decides his character, insures his favor with the public. The young hero delivers another gentleman from danger, by securing a highwayman, which highwayman proves to be his supposed father; and not only the supposed father of the youth, but the former and long lost dependent of Lord Avondale, formerly a farmer, and a tenant to this Lord Avondale, but who, at that time, was only Mr. Radnor. The persons the youth had delivered were General Taragon, and his daughter, who had been affianced by the general to Lord Avondale. This daughter, however, and Frederick (the youth, her deliverer) fall inordinately in love with each other, at first sight. The highwayman, Robert Tyke, when brought to be examined, being instantly known to and knowing Lord Avondale, is abruptly acquitted of those felonious intentions which Frederick, the general, his daughter, and the servants, had all witnessed, and has an apartment assigned him, in the house of Lord Avondale, in which he appears to be entirely at his ease, and does not scruple to make use of his lordship's wardrobe, nor to tell an entire stranger that he has Lord Avondale under his thumb. The reason that Tyke, the highwayman, has this power over Lord Avondale is the grand secret, on which the plot hinges. This Lord, while he was plain Mr. Radnor, had privately married a beautiful young woman, who had accompanied him when he was appointed secretary to an ambassador abroad; to which embassy Mr. Radnor was afterward raised as the principal agent; and then, ambition seizing him, he caused his wife to be falsely accused, and shut up in a convent, after she had brought him an infant son. This infant son, Frederick, Mr. Radnor, afterward Lord Avondale, committed to the care of Robert Tyke, with a large sum of money, at the time that Robert Tyke was a remarkably industrious and honest farmer. Why the child was thus exposed is left to be imagined by the audience. Tyke became a dissipated, gaming, racing, profligate, and a criminal; and, being tried for his life, escaped with transportation. When aboard the ship, and about to sail, he relates the manner in which he saw his father die. Frederick had been put under the old man's care, who we afterward find came to life again; yet Frederick was exposed to poverty and want, though we do not clearly understand how that happened. However, the improvident Tyke, before he parted with the child, Frederick, marked his neck by gunpowder with an F.

Emily, the mother of Frederick, after having been confined

such a number of years, gets released from the convent, returns to England, brings all her certificates and papers, and
arrives, by accident, in the very neighbourhood of his lordship, and obtains admission, either as a lodger or a friend, we
do not well know how or why, at the house of Mr. Ferment.
Lord Avondale gives his picture, not as he now is, but as he
was when a youth, and only Mr. Radnor, to Frederick ; and
prevails on him, after some struggles on the part of the youth,
to present it on Lord Avondale's part to Miss Taragon, who
shows it to the injured Emily, and she at the first glance discovers in it the portrait of her husband ; but, as it appears,
is too ill to speak of her discovery. Miss Taragon presents
a purse to Frederick, to bestow as he thinks proper : her reason for making this gift we do not comprehend, but it was
necessary afterward for Frederick to have such a purse.

The father of Tyke is introduced, overcome with age, grief,
and poverty; and the bailiffs are sent to his cottage, to seize
his effects. Frederick gives the purse, and the debt is paid.
Tyke enters, and discovers, after talking to him for some time,
that his father is alive.

By the means of General Taragon and Mr. Ferment, Lord
Avondale is informed that an inquiry is to be instituted, against
the wretch who had deserted Emily. Conscious that it was
himself, though they are ignorant of it, and dreadfully alarmed
for his fame and fortune, he becomes anxious to devise any
desperate means, by which he may obtain the certificates and
papers of his wife, which are deposited at the house of Ferment. For this purpose, he provides a cloak and pistols, and
has no doubt but that he can bribe Tyke to make a forcible
entrance, and steal them. He is mistaken : Tyke, after finding his father, repents, and resolves never more to commit
such crimes. His lordship then endeavours to seduce Frederick, but his attempts are equally vain ; and, at last, seizing the cloak and pistols, Frederick being present, he despe-
rately rushes out to perpetrate the act himself. Frederick,
watching for him with the highest perturbation, at length
hears a noise ; a pistol is fired, and Lord Avondale returns,

after having seized the papers, expressing a hope that he had *killed* the man by whom he was pursued ! His pistol had failed, the pursuers arrive, the doors are endeavoured to be forced, and he purposes to kill himself; but Frederick prevents him, seizes the pistols, puts on the cloak, persuades Avondale to retire, and personates the thief, in order to shelter his patron and friend.

Frederick is sent to prison, where he hears the bells ringing to celebrate the marriage between Lord Avondale and Miss Taragon, and therefore refuses to make his escape, though Tyke is come purposely to aid him. However, in their passionate debates, Frederick, being unbuttoned and his shirt open, Tyke discovers the F on his neck. Frederick is reconciled to life, finding Avondale to be his father. The jailor enters, who will not be bribed, but is so benevolent that he will let his prisoner escape. The meeting and explanation between father, wife, son, and lovers, take place, and all ends to our hearts' content.

This recapitulation I believe to be accurate; but, if my memory should have committed any mistake, it shall be publicly avowed, and I shall be heartily sorry for the blunder.

Should the reader imagine I have been thus minute purposely to prejudice him against the play, he will be greatly deceived. That these crowded and multifarious events, thus combined, are nearly impossible is true; and yet the play, on the whole, produced continual and strong effects on the passions, and was justly received with enthusiastic applause. There are two species of probability ; the probability of events, and the probability of the passions and emotions of the human mind. In the first of these probabilities, Mr. Morton has been very defective ; but to the last he has been delightfully true, and therefore deservedly triumphant. There are few plays in which the feelings, comic and tragic, have been more frequently or powerfully excited. He who should write a more regular piece, but with a heavy abatement of the pleasure which Mr. Morton has the art to give, might boast perhaps that he had greater skill, but certainly could never pretend to equal genius.

In giving an account like this, the strictest attention ought to be paid to the justice which is due to the world, and the justice which is due to the author. By such conduct, the progress of good taste will be accelerated, and the principles of honor never injured.

It can scarcely be possible to remember the performance of this play, and not bestow the most heartfelt applause on the acting of Mr. Emery. This acting was so natural, so devoid in the serious parts of all stage sing-song and whine, so distant from the appearance of studied trick, so justly conceived, and so powerfully felt, that praise can scarcely be excessive. Of his comic excellence the town had received sufficient proof; but the wonder and delight that were expressed, at seeing him so capital a tragedian, gave a *haut gout*, an inestimable value, to the contrasted parts of the performance. Robert Tyke was the real hero of the piece, as well in the writing of it as in the representation.

The character of Lord Avondale does not give sufficient display to the great abilities of Mr. Cook, whose talents can scarcely be too much admired.

Mr. Lewis was as usual exceedingly pleasant, and did perhaps all that was possible with his part. I know not why the author, by his title, induced the audience to suppose that *how to rule a husband* was the subject of his play, while in reality it is only a slight, inefficient, and superfluous episode.

Mr. Charles Kemble gave great satisfaction in the part of Frederick, and is an attentive, studious, and improving young actor.

Mr. Munden can scarcely personate a character without making it pleasant: the picture he several times gave, of an old good-natured officer, who was willing at a moment's warning to cut any man's throat, was happily sketched; but the character itself is only an outline, which the author appears not to have had time to fill up.

Mr. Murray gave an agreeable portrait of a feeble good old man. The remainder of the men's characters were of little importance in respect to acting.

Of the principal woman's character, Mrs. Ferment, performed by Mrs. Litchfield, it has been whimsically observed, that her dumb method of ruling her husband was nothing more than the old recipe of sullenness: but Mr. and Mrs. Ferment do not appear to have produced so full an effect as had been preconceived.

Mrs. Gibbs made the little she had to say and do, in Emily, interesting. She is an actress of great feeling, and knowledge of stage effect; except that she has not sufficiently cultivated her voice, so as to render it clear, powerful, and penetrating.

Miss Brunton, and the other female characters, had still a less share in the business of the play : but the little there was to do seemed to be done with propriety.

Mr. Morton has declared himself the enemy of the German plays; yet he is eminently, and almost devotedly, a student in the German School. That there is a mixture of virtue and vice, in all men, is true; but virtue and vice ought not to be confounded : when servants, bailiffs, jailors, and all classes of people, are described as sentimental and generous, those precious qualities become too common; and the danger of being false to nature is imminent. When such people are really so, they should be given as exceptious, and drawn with force and at full length.

Mrs. Davenport, who made the housekeeper a very respectable old woman, had escaped my memory; as had likewise the strange discovery of Emily, at the altar, when Lord Avondale is leading up his bride to be married. How there came to be folding doors before an altar, and by what means the lady procured admittance to place herself in an attitude behind them, are among the inexplicable events before enumerated, which I must conclude with repeating that, though they injure, they do not destroy the sterling merit of the play.

The Epilogue was admirably spoken by Mrs. Lichfield, who appears to have no mean comic powers.

THE ART OF ACTING.

CHAP. II.

Action, *Tragic*, *Comic*, *and unimpassioned*.

ACTION is held to be so high a qualification that some have affirmed it to be the first, and almost the exclusive, art of an orator. This opinion is extravagant; but that appropriate action, on various occasions, produces unexpected and forcible effects is daily proved, as well by orators as by stage performers.

Severe investigation will perhaps demonstrate that the deportment of the orator, and his organs of speech, are equally under the guidance of the mind; that passion, whatever its nature may be, as well as comic humour, are never forcibly and adequately expressed but when the mind, at the moment of delivery, has a strong, powerful, and clear conception of the thoughts, and passions, which are personated; and that it can never accurately pourtray them, but when it is itself under this kind of enthusiastic impression. The rules therefore for action and intonation must be intrinsically the same.

All this appears to be true: but it likewise appears that the mind may partially conceive; and that, when it is either ignorant or inattentive, the organs of personification whether of action or of intonation are in a like proportion deficient. Every art must be studied in detail; and only as far as it is thoroughly understood, in its minute parts, can unity and perfection be the result. Different performers are found to be deficient in different ways, and degrees. The person, who would instruct, must not be too much afraid to speak of seeming trifles; or of being thought tedious: nor must the person, who is in need of instruction, complain of the labor and delay of reading, before he arrives at those rules of which he thinks himself most in want. Knowledge, like mountains, is composed of small and seemingly insignificant particles. The great misfortune is, in the students of this and all other arts, that, having overcome their first impediments, they imagine themselves to be in no

farther need of excellence, and treat advice as intrusive impertinence.

Action is either tragic, comic, or unimpassioned. The parts
of which it is composed are, standing, walking, running, attitude, and gesture : for the proper conduct of all which it is
necessary to understand the use and management of the eye,
the arm, the hand, the knees, legs, and feet, and the proper
deportment of the whole body.

To express the imperious and uncontrollable passions is the
province of tragic action. It is never the intention of persons,
who are under the dominion of passion, to make themselves
the subject of laughter. There are many instances in which
they produce this effect, unintentionally; but they belong
to the ignoble passions, and are within the province of comic
action, and comic personages : for the same passions, when
felt by persons of a different character, become dignified, terrible, and destructive; and therefore cannot excite laughter.
Avarice, which in some instances is highly comic, in others
becomes the scourge and desolation of kingdoms. Many poets
have well delineated the ridicule to which the jealous sometimes subject themselves; though few passions of a private
kind have more frequently produced scenes of tragic horror.

The nature of tragic action, therefore, is energetic, daring,
and impetuous, to excess. That which would be extravagant
and ridiculous, in persons of equal and calm minds, is frequently an appropriate, necessary, and true expression of passion. The impassioned person may be remarkably reasonable,
and sagacious, in some parts of his behaviour, the moment
preceding an act of phrenzy.

Of this remarkable instances are afforded. In Paris, wretches,
frantic and in the last paroxysm of despair, when about to dash
themselves on the pavement, from garrets six or eight stories
high, have on several occasions warned the passengers below
to take care of themselves. A dreadful but a fine lesson this
to actors; who, by the working of the features, their gesticulations, and their whole deportment, although they appear by
the words they speak to be in the full possession of their un-

derstanding, may exhibit to the audiehce an inward convul-
sion of nature, that threatens and forebodes destruction.

In stage personification, nothing can more offend than the
tame rant, and composed recollection, with which the crimes
of passion are perpetrated. Instead of feeling and picturing
the violent frantic and sudden emotions of passion, actors, with
very few exceptions, are continually impressed with the
wretched and ignorant persuasion that a long stride, a uniform
swing of the arm, and a monotonous clamorous bellow, are
the grand requisites of a tragedian. This persuasion is so
strong in them, and they are so self-satisfied, that they appear for ages to have aped each other.

This they fully conclude is all that appertains to or can be
achieved by tragic acting ; and the spectator, or the critic,
who should affirm there is a deficiency of knowledge and execution, in any one of them, would immediately be accused of
an endeavour to deprive a meritorious individual, who lies at
the mercy of the public, of the means of subsistence. It is
true indeed that any spectator, or critic, who shall decry performers in general terms, and not point out their defects in
any clear and distinct way, by which they may be understood
and corrected, ought rather to be deemed cynical than serviceable. Against this kind of critic all public men have a
just right to exclaim. Were such general criticism which
does not discriminate reprobated, and held in contempt, the
task of a critic would then become as respectable, and as beneficial, as it is too often at present nugatory, defamatory,
and destructive of good taste.

It should be the first business of an actor deeply to investigate each character which he pretends to perform, and embue
his whole soul with recollections never to be erased, of the
number and the nature of the wild starts of passion, to which
the character to be represented is subject : he should note them
in his books, explain them to himself, and memorandum them
immediately, and at that happy instant when he conceives them
in their fullest force; should study all the various ways in
which they show themselves, and in fact make himself a most

profound and masterly commentator on the passions, their consequences, and their marks, prognostics, and appearance.
What a labour would it be thus to study no more than Macbeth, Hamlet, Lear, and Othello. Yet these characters, we
daily find, every beardless stripling is eager to represent ; and
imagines he may fret and strut his hour upon the stage quite
as well as another: neither is he, in general, very far from
the truth.

Comic acting has likewise its fits and starts ; but of totally a
different nature : yet there is this grand similarity, that he
alone can be successful who makes man his study. Excellent
comic actors, however, are far more numerous than excellent tragedians ; and the reason appears to be plain : men take a pleasure in observing the follies of others, which follies are almost
continually before their eyes ; while the exhibition of the tragic
passions gives so much pain that it is shunned, if possible, and,
to give peace to the mind, endeavoured to be buried in forgetfulness. Laughter can likewise be excited by oddity of action ;
such as may accompany almost any habit, or caprice of mind,
without destroying but rather tending to give a zest to that
habit, or caprice; therefore, though the follies of men are
daily present to the eye, superficial observers have no knowledge of the particular gestures, attitudes, or demeanor, that
are most usually found to appertain to each different class of
humorists.

There are indeed some general rules, that cannot be mistaken : such as that age is feeble, has bent knees, a faltering
voice, a curbed body, and a discontented countenance; but,
the countenance excepted, these properties may as well belong
to a man of the soundest understanding, and most rational demeanor, as to a man of the most eccentric habits.

Truly to class, and effectually to personify, the different
gesticulations, attitudes, and modes of deportment, of the different species of humour, which generally prevail, the volume
of nature must be industriously studied ; and the labours of the
comic performer will be no less than those of the tragedian, for
they will both be endless.

Were this great task executed in any tolerable degree, comic actors would not be, what they almost all are, such mannerists that one of them cannot long be mistaken for another: they would so transform themselves, so embody each character, have such various modes of gesticulation, such change of demeanor, and be so entirely different each time from any thing that they had ever been before, that, speaking of spectators in general, the comedian would defy them to any certainty of guess as to the name and person of the performer, unless indeed some one actor should be so superior to all his companions, in this art of transformation, that he would always betray himself by his excellence.

What then should the duty of a comedian be? To note down, with a keen eye, the various gesticulations, and modes of deportment, of every individual in society; and to memorandum every turn of the face, every motion of the eye, and every posture of the body, with the turn of mind and occupation of the person to whom they belong.

Were they to carry their inquiries no further than to all the persons of whom they have some personal knowledge, and, having a character to perform, would adopt the deportment, gesticulation, grimace, look, and tone of voice, of a different individual for every different character, suiting each with each as their judgment should direct, how infinitely greater and more delightful would the variety be, than that uniformity which at present prevails.

Of unimpassioned action little need be said, more than will be found, hereafter, among the remarks on general deportment.

In the following chapters of this work, the detail of action will be considered, under its various heads. The intention, in what has been said, is to strongly impress the importance of this branch of study upon the mind of the actor; and to convince him, if possible, that should he neglect it, or treat it in a light and superficial manner, he never can arrive at perfection in his profession.

AN

ESSAY ON DRAMATIC COMPOSITION.

INTRODUCTION.

IT may be asked, why is this subject, on which so much already has been written, again intruded on the public? Have not *Aristotle*, *Quintilian*, *Horace*, and other ancient authors—have not *Boileau*, *Racine*, *Dacier*, and a multitude of French writers—have not a crowd of English critics, not forgetting the prefaces of the immortal *Dryden*, all treated this subject? Can laws and rules create a poet? or what is there now to be said that can be esteemed as new information?

It may be difficult to answer these questions satisfactorily : but it may truly be alleged, that rules are much more easily given than remembered ; that, being the offspring of man, rules themselves are liable to be defective; that it is scarcely possible to say when inquiries into any subject ought to cease; that it is not novelty for which we ought to seek, but truth, so clearly stated and arranged, if possible, as not to be mistaken ; and that therefore every new effort, to accomplish this desirable end, may rather deserve praise than blame.

There is still a farther reason for treating the subject anew ; which is that there appear to be well-founded doubts, among men of liberal inquiry, whether the rules that have been so dogmatically given, and so long received as the standard by which perfection may be attained, be not in many respects so faulty as to be almost incapable of being observed, in the noblest efforts of the dramatic art. Attempts, therefore, to decide this point, will scarcely be considered as superfluous; and if any true criterion could be made public, by which good may clearly be distinguished from bad, a most desirable end would certainly be attained.

Of the Purposes for which Tragedies and Comedies are or ought to be composed.

In all the works of man, his present pleasure and his future happiness are consulted; and, in our best dramatic works, these purposes are combined: but too many of our inferior compositions seldom have any thing but present pleasure in view, and are so far defective in their construction. The pleasure, given by a dramatic work, scarcely can be exquisite, unless the future happiness of man be kept in view: that is to say, unless some essential moral truth, or truths, are inculcated. To the unprejudiced, it needs no effort of the understanding to demonstrate that this high purpose, in most if not all of our best dramatic writings, has been nobly effected. To the dreadful consequences of *envy, deceit, concupiscence, revenge, jealousy, ambition,* and all the frantic passions of the mind, no man can be insensible, or remain unwarned, who shall read *Venice Preserved, The Orphan, The Fair Penitent, Zanga, Measure for Measure, Macbeth, Lear, Othello,* and a multitude of those masterly works that exist, as well among the neighbouring nations as in the happy and highly cultivated English language. The first rule, therefore, that a dramatic poet has to observe is, that it is his duty to effect this double purpose, of giving present pleasure and promoting future happiness.

Of the different Species of Dramatic Writing.

Though tragedy and comedy appear to have formed the two grand classes of the dramatic art, it is nevertheless true that, among all modern nations at least, there have continually been other branches, which, though of the same tree, are distinct, in their nature and often in extent. To *mysteries, moralities, masques, intermedes,* and *interludes,* have succeeded *comic operas, farces, speaking pantomimes,* and particularly *plays,* or serious *dramas:* beside an innumerable progeny of *ballets, dumb pantomimes,* and *spectacles,* in many of which the eye and the ear are chiefly consulted. Into the nature and end of these different classes it will be good to inquire, and, by inquiry, to endeavour to afford some light that may guide the adventurer, in paths which confusion and indecision have often darkened.

Of the Moral Nature of Tragedy.

Of all the works of man, it may be doubted whether there is any species of an equally impressive and dignified moral nature as tragedy. The epic poem might equal, if not surpass it, in the closet ; but, as epic poems cannot be represented before multitudes, by whom from their nature they have little chance of being read, their moral influence must be greatly and inevitably less. Every thing that is noble, in the heart and actions of man, is the proper subject of tragic composition. All the dreadful errors into which his passions can lead him are there necessarily contrasted, with the purest emanations of his soul ; the consequences of each are developed, and, while terror and compassion, at the portraits which it gives of vice, seize the heart, that heart is relieved, delighted, and embued, by the purity and dignity of virtue, as well as by its comparative and everlasting tendency to happiness. It is scarcely possible to compose tragedy, so as to be received and applauded by the public, without more or less producing this beneficial result.

Unless this can be denied, it follows that the duties of the tragic poet are among the most sacred which the human mind has conceived, and his rank and office of the highest nature *. It should however be added, the more unassuming he shows himself, in society, the better proof he gives of his poetic

---

* It is related of Piron, a French tragic and comic poet, that being one day conversing with a minister at his levee, a nobleman came in, and that the minister then invited them to his cabinet. Unacquainted with Piron, the nobleman bowed, and insisted on his going first. Piron returned the compliment, and the minister, turning round, said to the nobleman, " Pray take the lead, my Lord, Monsieur Piron is only a poet." On which Piron instantly stepped forward and exclaimed, " Since my rank is known, I will take my place."

dignity.   True genius will neither affect hypocritical modesty, nor be debased by any symptoms of inflated pride.

Of the Moral Nature of Comedy.

There may perhaps be rational doubts entertained, whether the moral effects of comedy might not be greater even than those of tragedy ; in which case, comedy would deserve the preference.   Tragedy appears to be better calculated to exhibit the grandest efforts of virtue, as well as the most fatal effects of vice : but, in the present state of morals at least, these grand efforts and fatal effects are less familiar, not so often required or seen, nor so productive of general benefit, as the subordinate but diurnal morality, which it should be the province of comedy to teach.   It is indeed true that, when the mind can be made to feel the higher virtues so impressively as that they can never be forgotten, it scarcely could be greatly erroneous in subordinate principles, and practice.   Comedy, however, has a so much wider range, can insinuate precepts by such familiar and multifarious means, and enforce them so powerfully by satire and ridicule, that it might become a most incomparable engine, for the destruction of vice, if properly employed in dramatic poetry.

There is another point of comparison, which must not be overlooked.   Of the different powers required for the tragic and the comic poet, it seems difficult to pronounce which are required to be the most numerous and the highest, supposing that, in each of them, perfect specimens were to be demanded : but, if we except SHAKSPEARE, the powers of the tragic poet, with respect to invention, variety, and knowledge of the human heart, seem generally to have been inferior to those of the comic.   To both, this knowledge of the human heart is the source of power.   It is true, there are a few tragedies, besides those of SHAKSPEARE, among which *Venice Preserved* is perhaps the first, which contain so fine a volume of this knowledge that the candid might be inclined to doubt which way they ought to decide : but, on a summary view, perhaps, including the whole works of SHAKSPEARE, and especially taking

MOLIERE into the account, we should say the comic muse has far outstripped her sister.

(To be continued.)

SOME ACCOUNT

OF THE RISE AND PROGRESS OF THE GERMAN STAGE.

(Continued from No. I. p. 71.)

TOWARD the year 1708, the harlequin of the Italians began to be introduced on the German stage; and was so thoroughly naturalized, by one STRANITZKY, that, till the year 1730, neither tragedies nor comedies were performed, to the perfect satisfaction of the spectators, in which harlequin was not allowed to mingle his ridiculous and often indecent buffooneries.

We shall not mention a multitude of small companies of comedians, which were formed about that period, and who, till the year 1726, wandered from town to town in their poverty and barbarous state throughout Germany; but we shall be satisfied with relating an anecdote which was rather singular. One of these ambulatory troops had strayed into Sweden, and there performed the story of *Adam and Eve*. This drama made so great an impression, on the minds of the spectators, that, when they beheld Justice and Mercy personified, they fell on their knees before them.

The year 1727 became famous, by the first appearance of an actress, whom Germany may regard as the person who founded its theatre. This was MADAME NEUBER, the daughter of a doctor of laws of *Zittau*. She engaged herself to perform in the company of SPIEGELBERG, in which she soon became distinguished. Tragedy was preferred by her; and it may be said, in her praise, that she was the first who taught the actresses of Germany the true tone of declamation. She afterward obtained a privilege from the Elector of Saxony, and undertook to reform the theatre. With this intent, she drew together the best actors ; among whom there soon appeared several, who deserved to be distinguished in the history of the German theatre. One of the first was the famous KOCH, who, after having been five and twenty years the manager of one of the best companies in Germany, died at Berlin, January 3, 1775, bearing to the grave the reputation of a celebrated actor, and the still more glorious title of a truly honest man.

In 1727, GOTTSCHED likewise appeared, who was a professor of philosophy, at the university of LEIPSIC : a man of much erudition, pedantic, and vain, but without genius. He perceived the lamentable state in which the German language then was ; despised by the great, who only understood French, and neglected by the learned, who preferred the Latin. He determined to do honor to his mother tongue, and to become the reformer of German literature. To effect this purpose he devoted himself. Though his talents and merit in general did not surpass mediocrity, he cannot be justly refused the glory of having planned a route for the guidance of those men of genius whose works have consigned his name to oblivion.

The arrival of MADAME NEUBER, at Leipsic, he considered as highly favorable to his design ; while the title of Creator of the German Theatre flattered his vanity, and induced him to obtain it by the merit of industry. He assumed a high tone, and drew the attention of the Germans, not to the beauties of foreign works, but, to the mechanism and rules according to which they were composed. Himself and his wife gave a number of very defective translations, and prevailed on MADAME NEUBER to have them performed. In this manner, he effectually gave a new form to the German theatre; but he retarded its progress.

The first piece performed by MADAME NEUBER, who followed the advice of GOTTSCHED, was a translation of the *Regulus* of PRADON. Though the style was wretched, the piece was well received ; which success was due to the pomp with which it was performed. From this period, 1727, to 1739, there was a succession of *The Cid, Brutus, Alexandre, Cinna, Iphigenie, Be-*

Venice, Les Horaces, Brittanicus, Le Comte d'Essex, Polieucte, Alzire, and a number of foreign chefs-d'œuvres, the transla- tions of which were scarcely supportable. In the year 1731, the first original production of GOTTSCHED appeared, called Cato Dying; a pitiful tragedy, ill versified, and consisting of a strange assemblage of English and French scenes. It was applauded however with transport, because the reputation of the author at that time was high; but it was applause that soon died away : taste became more refined ; men of genius resorted to ancient and foreign sources, and obtained distinc- tion by real excellence. The tragedy of GOTTSCHED was then reduced to its just value; that is, it was placed much below mediocrity.

The year 1737 was made remarkable by the banishment of Harlequin, whose reign till then had been triumphant. GOTTSCHED, who from ignorance confounded his copy with the true Italian Harlequin, chose rather to banish them both, with- out mercy, than to give more delicacy to this character, and thus prepare the nation for good comedy. Harlequin was afterward avenged for this affront : Counsellor MOESER under- took his defence, in a treatise entitled, *Harlekin; oder die Vertheidigung des groteske komischen**: a work which alone announced more taste, and knowledge of the theatre, than all the writings of GOTTSCHED.

The defeat of Harlequin was the last triumph of this dic- tator of literature. The deceitful charm, by which he had fascinated the mind, suddenly disappeared ; and his disputes with MADAME NEUBER gave the first wound to his fame. He would force her to perform a bad translation of ALZIRE, made by his wife, in preference to another, that was much superior, and that had already appeared with success. Equally consi- dering themselves as the creators of the German theatre, equally inflated with their individual merit, and persuaded that their fame was now at stake, they made open war on each other. GOTTSCHED wrote bitter criticisms on all the pieces that

---

* Harlequin ; or an Apology for Grotesque Comedy.

MADAME NEUBER presented to the public; but he had unfortunately given his enemies too much advantage, for the laugh not to be on their side.

At this time, in order to support his staggering fame, GOTTSCHED determined to lay his dramatic works before the public; and they were printed in six volumes, which fortunately are now forgotten. Among them was a number of translations, from the French; such as *Iphigenie*, *Cornélie*, *Le Tambour Nocturne**, *Zaire*, *Alzire*, *Le Dissipateur*, *Les Horaces*, *Le Misanthrope*, *Le Cid*; all wretchedly versified, by GOTTSCHED and his spouse. This collection only contains two or three original pieces, that still deserve to be read; and they were not by GOTTSCHED.

In 1739, the first tragic author that Germany possessed appeared; who doubtless would have contributed to the perfection of the theatre, if death had not too suddenly cut short his career. His name was John Elias *Schlegel*. He had not finished his studies when, in imitation of Euripides, he wrote his tragedy of IPHIGENIA IN TAURICA; which was represented at Leipsic in 1739, and which, amid many feeble parts of a first attempt, announced the true genius of a tragic poet.

This year was likewise remarkable by the misfortune of MADAME NEUBER, who did not long enjoy the pleasure of having triumphed over GOTTSCHED: it was occasioned by an invitation she received to go to Russia, and which she very imprudently accepted. Two years after her arrival there, the Duke of Biron, her protector, was disgraced, and she was obliged to return to Germany; where, when she arrived, she found a new company formed, during her absence, under the management of *Schoenemann*. This company became famous by the performers that composed it, many of whom are still alive.

The actor among them, who merits first to be named, was the famous Eckhof, the Roscius of Germany. This sublime

---

* Which is itself a translation of Addison's Drummer, or The Haunted House.

and inimitable actor was born at Hamburg, in 1720, and appeared first at Luneburg, in 1740: superior talents, added to severe study, soon made him the first actor of Germany; and his excellence was equal in tragedy and comedy. He died the 16th of June, 1778. Melpomene still deplores her three favorite sons; GARRICK, LE KAIN, and ECKHOF; who all died in the same year *.

DRAMATIC ANECDOTES.

AMONG foreign nations, particularly the French, a mode of criticising new pieces is adopted, which, when it is restrained within the bounds of decency, is highly advantageous to good taste and the progress of the dramatic art. When a new piece meets with success, at one theatre, a parody upon that piece has frequently appeared, at another; or critical speeches have been put into the mouths of the performers of such old pieces as would admit of the interlopation. A tragedy, called *Gustave Vasa*, written by the famous Piron, was performed in 1733; and the comedians of the Italian theatre soon produced a criticism, in verse, to the following effect; which, as it cannot but singularly remind us of the style of composition adopted by our own poets of the present day, will probably amuse the reader.

" When a hero shall arise from the bosom of the North, his
" refulgent light will efface all others: the great Gustavus
" will astonish by his beauties, and even by his defects; all in
" him will delight, even to his dress. Ye Gods! What a rich
" abundance of improbabilities, of common-place sentiments,
" happily linked, of incidents such as have never been beheld!
" A dream, a rencounter, monologues more than enough, a long
" funeral oration to celebrate a living prince, disguises, con-
" spiracies, imprisonments, and proscriptions. A sedition, by

---

* That is, in 1782.

" which all is suddenly changed; an elopement, a flight, a
" combat on the ice, where, like a diver and by a happy pro-
" digy, the daughter of Stenon sinks and disappears, full dress-
" ed, then returns to light and day, her clothes all very dry,
" to inform us how it happened; and, by a last event wor-
" thy of being vaunted, after so many perils, fracas, and furious
" affairs, by which the agitated public are held in suspense,
" the piece finishes very peaceably ; and, one poor dying confi-
" dent excepted, the actors all retire safe and in good health."

Piron, discontented with the performance of Sarrasin in the
above tragedy, and knowing that actor had been an Abbé in
his youth, called aloud from the amphitheatre—" That man,
" who was not worthy of being consecrated at twenty-four, is
" equally unworthy of being excommunicated at sixty." All
actors in France used to be excommunicated. Sarrasin how,
ever is said to have been an excellent comedian.

At the performance of this Gustavus, the Abbé Desfontaines
met Piron much too richly dressed, as he supposed; and, coming up to him, said—' Poor Piron! Really, that dress is ill
' adapted to you!' " That may be," answered Piron ; " but,
" really, in return, Mr. Abbé, you must allow you are as ill
" adapted to your own." The Abbé wore the clerical habit.

When the art of poetry by *Dacier* first appeared, an author,
named *De Brie*, read nothing else : his contempt for *Corneille*
became excessive, *Racine* was but little more in favor, and he
despised the French exceedingly, for having admired both
these poets. " We have not a single good tragedy," exclaimed
he; and determined out of pure compassion to write one. The
subject he chose was the *Heraclides*, in which all was measured
by line and rule, in full deference to the remarks of *Dacier*.
This regular and scientific piece was only played once.

The same author wrote a comedy, of one act, entitled *Le
Lourdaut*, which was little more successful. These two pieces
gave occasion to the following epigram, by *Jean Baptist Rous-
seau:*

Pour disculper ses Oeuvres insipides,
De Brie accuse et le froid et le chaud;
Le froid, dit il, fit chéoir mes Héraclides;
Et la chaleur fit tomber mon Lourdaut:
Mais le Public, qui n'est point en défaut,
Et dont le sens s'accorde avec le nôtre,
Dit à cela—Taisez vous, grand Nigaud;
C'est le froid seul qui fit chéoir l'une et l'autre.

Weeping his children, poor De Brie has told
How both have perish'd, or by heat, or cold:
Frozen my poor Heraclides lies dead!
Lourdaut expir'd by fever in the head!
The public, hating ignorance and sloth,
Cries silence, fool! the cold has kill'd them both.

———

After the appearance of the *Abderites,* a comedy of one act, performed in 1732, written by the academician *Moncrif,* a critic, addressing himself to the author, says—" The comedies " of *Molière* made us laugh; and we cry at those of *La* " *Chaussée:* but we neither laugh nor cry at your Abderites. " Like *Theognes,* called by the Athenians the poet of snow, " you keep us in perfect apathy, without exciting the least " emotion either of grief of joy.

———

At the performance of *Abdilly,* in 1729, a tragi-comedy by *Madame Riccoboni,* the pit called aloud to an Abbé, who was in front—" Down, Mr. Abbé, down!" The Abbé took no notice at first; but, as the cries increased, he turned and addressed the rioters, saying — ' Gentlemen, having already been ' robbed of my gold watch in your company, I would rather ' quit the theatre than risk my snuff-box.' The cries were immediately changed to applause, and the Abbé kept his place.

———

The famous *Favart,* during his dramatic labors, wrote a comic opera, in one act, entitled *Acajou,* the subject of which he took from a tale by *Duclos.* It was first played, at the fair of *St. Germain,* in 1744; but a prohibition afterward appeared, by which the actors of the comic opera were not suffered to speak, and at the following fair this opera was re-written all in *Vaudevilles.* In the month of October in the same year, it was performed with great satisfaction on the theatre of *L'Académie*

Royale de Musique. It then became so popular that, on the evening when the theatre was to close, the barrier which separated the, orchestra and the pit was broken. Endeavours were made to repair it, but in vain : while one part of the spectators were made to give way another rushed forward, and in the confusion it was not possible to give their money back to those who had been obliged to leave the theatre. Several demanded it with threats, and six of the most mutinous were arrested. M. *Monet* conducted himself, on that occasion, with much prudence : he caused those who had been sent to the guardhouse to be released, and paid the discontented by a harangue, partly pleasant partly pathetic, which appeased every body. It is said there never was so lucrative a performance. Every person paid six livres [five shillings] and the stage itself was so full that there was only room for one actor at a time. There was neither symphony nor dance, nor could any thing be heard, not even the actor who came to return thanks : yet all was applauded, and every body satisfied ; most especially the manager.

A person, named *Cadoret,* known by the anagram *Terodac,* was so perfect a mimic that the authors imagined they really saw and heard the actors, whom he parodied. In his part of *Métromane,* he so finely caricatured the actors of that time that this was an additional reason for forbidding the actors of the comic opera to speak, and confining them to song. It was imagined that, by this means, the scene of *Métromane,* which so highly offended the actors who were imitated, would have been suppressed. But the author here found little difficulty ; for, as the comedians then, as they do at present, rather sang than spoke, the author set their declamation to music ; and the notes so nearly agreed, with the inflexions and rant of the tragic actors, that the difference was scarcely perceptible. Thus, instead of injuring the comic opera, its success was increased.

MISCELLANIES.

THE dress of Miss Duncan, in Charlotte Rusport, exemplifies the principles of true taste : it is not encumbered by false ornament, but is flowing and elegant, yet simple, as displayed in the coloured print at the beginning of this number.

Purchasers and students of Costume, it is presumed, will be satisfied with the change adopted, of giving three plain specimens, instead of one coloured : the subject is so voluminous that little progress could be made, by a single figure monthly. The subject of Indian Costume cannot but interest the stage, where the scene is so frequently laid in India. The work, from which the examples are given, has been noticed in No. 1. The author of that work says of it, in his preface—" It will serve to " illustrate the character, customs, manners, persons, and dresses " of the inhabitants of Indostan—their implements of husbandry, " manufacture, and war—their modes of conveyance, by land " and water—their religious sectaries, and the appearance of " their country." All this cannot be effected on the small and cheap scale of the present work, but while exemplifying costume the back-ground (as in this number and the last) of the scenery, as given in the grand folio from which they are taken, may afford instruction. Of the three figures here engraved that work contains the following description.

" *A Srotery* Brahmun of Bengalee, with the *Garrah,* and the *Cossa*, or *Agrah;* utensils used by them in their offerings. The Srotery possesses seven goons, or sciences ; the Koolen nine."

" The *Kanoge* Brahmun. The shrub represented is the *Tulsee,* held in great veneration by the Brahmuns."

" A *Drawer* Brahmun ; the back-ground shews the manner of prostrating themselves in their *Munders*, or *Pagodas*."

Indian Costume will be continued so as to afford full information on the dress of the people, Gentoos and Mahomedans.

MONTHLY LIST, FOR JANUARY, 1805.

DRURY-LANE.

DEC.
31. She Stoops to Conquer - - - - - Old Harlequin's Fire Side, and Richard
JAN. 1805. Cœur de Lion.
1. The Mountaineers - - - - - - - Ditto, and The Citizen.
2. The Wonder - - - - - - - - - - Ditto, and Doctor and Apothecary.
3. The Stranger - - - - - - - - - Ditto, and The Irishman in London.
4. The West Indian - - - - - - - Matrimony, and Old Harlequin's Fire Side.
5. The Soldier's Daughter - - - - - Old Harlequin's Fire Side, and Prize.
7. Pizarro - - - - - - - - - - - - Ditto, and Fortune's Frolic.
8. The Suspicious Husband - - - - Ditto, and No Song No Supper.

9. The West Indian - - - - - - - Ditto, and A House to be Sold.
10. Hamlet - - - - - - - (2d time) A new Allegorical Dance The United Britons, and Spoil'd Child.
11. The Belles' Stratagem - - - - - Old Harlequin's Fire Side, and Of Age To-morrow.
12. The Suspicious Husband - - - - The United Britons, and Deserter.
14. The West Indian - - - - - - - - The Mock Doctor, and Old Harlequin's Fire Side.
15. The Beggar's Opera - - - - - - The United Britons, and The Citizen.
16. The Marriage Promise - - - - - Who's the Dupe? and Old Harlequin's Fire Side.
17. The Provoked Husband - - - - The United Britons, and The Irishman in London.
18. The Rivals - - - - - - - - - - Two Strings to your Bow, and Old Harlequin's Fire Side.
19. She Stoops to Conquer - - - - - The United Britons, and The Liar.
21. The West Indian - - - - - - - - The Apprentice, and Old Harlequin's Fire Side.
22. The Mountaineers - - - - - - The United Britons, and Anatomist.
23. As You Like It - - - - - - - - - The Humourist, and Old Harlequin's Fire Side.
24. The Clandestine Marriage - - - The United Britons, and The Citizen.
25. The School for Scandal - - - - - Of Age To-morrow, and Old Harlequin's Fire Side.
26. The Jew - - - - - - - - - - - Old Harlequin's Fire Side, and Richard Cœur de Lion.

COVENT-GARDEN.

DEC.
31. Richard III. - - - - - - - - - - Harlequin Quicksilver.
JAN. 1805.
1. John Bull - - - - - - - - - - - Ditto.
2. The Man of the World - - - - - Ditto.
3. The Heir at Law - - - - - - - Ditto.
4. The Blind Bargain - - - - - - Ditto.
5. The Cabinet - - - - - - - - - Ditto.
7. Romeo and Juliet - - - - - - - Ditto.
8. The English Fleet - - - - - - Ditto.
9. The Cabinet - - - - - - - - - Ditto.
10. Thirty Thousand - - - - - - - Ditto.
11. The Man of the World - - - - Ditto.
12. The English Fleet - - - - - - Ditto.
14. The Poor Gentleman (by Com.) Ditto.
15. The School of Reform - - - - - Ditto.
16. Ditto - - - - - - - - - - - - Ditto.
17. Ditto - - - - - - - - - - - - Ditto.
18. Ditto - - - - - - - - - - - - Ditto.
19. Ditto - - - - - - - - - - - - Ditto.
21. Ditto - - - - - - - - - - - - Ditto.
22. Ditto - - - - - - - - - - - - Ditto.
23. Ditto (by Command) - - - - - The Paragraph.
24. Ditto - - - - - - - - - - - - Harlequin Quicksilver.
25. Ditto - - - - - - - - - - - - Ditto.
26. Ditto - - - - - - - - - - - - Ditto.

A fine Head of ALFIERI, *after a print by* Morghen, *beautifully embellished by* H. THOMPSON, R. A. *and engraved by* Messrs. Cooke, *will be given with No.* III.

THE

THEATRICAL RECORDER:

BY

THOMAS HOLCROFT.

London:
Printed by C. Mercier and Co. No. 6, Northumberland-court,
Where the Work may be procured:
And at all the BOOKSELLERS;
And published for the Author, by H. D. Symonds, Paternoster-row.

1805.

AVARICE AND OSTENTATION:

A COMEDY,

IN FIVE ACTS,

TRANSLATED FROM

THE ITALIAN OF CARLO GOLDONI.

DRAMATIS PERSONÆ.

COUNT CASTELDORO.

MARQUIS DEL BOSCO.

CHEVALIER DEL BOSCO.

GIACINTO.

FRONTINO.

FIORILLO.

TAYLOR.

JEWELLER.

ARAMINTA.

ELEONORA.

DORIMENE.

VISITORS and a NOTARY who do not speak.

SCENE—Paris.

AVARICE AND OSTENTATION*:

A COMEDY.

~~~~~

ACT I.

SCENE I.—COUNT, *solus.*

Count.

AT last I am determined to marry. How! I marry! I, who have always avoided expence! I, who have detested every intercourse with the ladies! Well, in this case, I am hurried away in my own despite. Ambition has induced me to obtain a title; therefore, should I die without children, my money is lost! and children themselves will but bring trouble! (*calls*) Frontino!

SCENE II.—*Enter* FRONTINO.

Front. Here, Sir!
Count. Hark ye!
Front. I have found a taylor, Sir, as you ordered me; and a taylor of the first notoriety.
Count. Will he come directly?
Front. Very soon. He was obliged first to wait on a duke. I was lucky enough to find him at home when he was about to step into his coach.
Count. His coach!
Front. Yes, Sir.
Count. His own coach? His own horses?
Front. Beyond all doubt. A superb carriage, and excellent nags.
Count. O Lord! He's too rich. Is he in repute?
Front. In the greatest! He works for the first families in Paris.
Count. But his honesty?
Front. On that subject I have nothing to say. But why, Signor Count, did you not employ your own taylor?

---

* The title in the Italian is *L'Avaro Fastoso*; THE POMPOUS MISER.

Count. Fie! My own taylor on such an occasion! I have need of several suits; and, as they must be grand, magnificent, and made in full perfection, shall I, if any one should ask who is my taylor, shall I answer *Signor Taccone;* whose name nobody knows?

Front. Then, Sir, from what I hear, you are soon to be married?

Count. So soon, that this very day, and in this very house, I am to sign the contract: I have therefore called you to give the necessary orders. On this occasion, I shall have a great company to dine with me; and must have such a dinner—in short, brilliant! grand! splendid! Not that I would satiate the indiscreet, or gorge my guests: but I would surprise, by an air of grandeur—you know what I mean.

Front. Yes, Sir, tolerably well: but to do all this will not be quite so easy. I must inquire whether the cook——

Count. No, no, Frontino, I would not have thee be dependent on the caprice of a cook. Take the direction of every thing upon thyself. I know thy talents, the readiness of thy wit, and thy zeal for thy master's interest. There is not in the whole world a man like Frontino! Thou canst work miracles: and on such an occasion wilt surpass thyself.

Front. (*aside*) Ha! His usual mode! Coaxing me when he wants me; but afterward——

Count. Here is a list of the guests, whom I have invited. My sister lives in this hotel, and my future spouse and her mother have the adjoining apartments. Here is a note of the other guests. We shall be thirty at table. Hasten to them all, and get a positive answer from each, that, in case of refusals, other persons may be invited.

Front. Thirty guests! Do you know, Sir, how much a dinner for thirty will——

Count. Perfectly; and will employ thy discretion to combine economy and magnificence.

Front. For example, you gave a supper a few nights ago to three gentlemen, and——

Count. Ay, that was a trifle: at present I would be talked of.

Front. But this trifling supper you thought so dear that——

Count. Lose no time in useless words.

Front. You threw the account in my face, and have not yet——

Count. Here is my sister. Be gone!

Front. (*aside*) Oh Lord! Oh Lord! What will become of me! This time, friend Frontino, by way of recompence, prepare thyself to be kicked out of doors. [*Exit.*

SCENE III.—*Enter* DORIMENE.

Count. Good morning, dear sister ; how do you do?

Dor. Perfectly well. How are you ?

Count. Never better. Fortunate and happy man ! I am to possess a bride of high birth and merit.

Dor. Then you are determined in favour of Eleonora.

Count. Ay, sweet sister! She is your relation ; you proposed her to me, and I therefore have reason to give her the preference.

Dor. (*ironically*) Her and one hundred thousand crowns to her portion, with as much more perhaps at the death of her mother.

Count. You will allow, sister, that such conditions are not to be despised.

Dor. True, but you, who are so——

Count. I understand you. A man like me, having sacrificed a considerable sum to obtain a title, should have endeavoured to marry into an illustrious family. I have thought much, and long combated this reigning inclination ; but I know the prejudices of the old nobility : I must have dearly paid for the pompous honour of such an alliance.

Dor. That is not what I wish to say.

Count. I am determined to marry the charming Eleonora.

Dor. But if the charming Eleonora should feel no love for you ?

Count. My dear sister, I do not think myself a person to be despised.

Dor. But the inclinations are whimsical.

Count. Has Eleonora told you she cannot love me ?

Dor. Not precisely told me, but I have great reason to doubt.

Count. (*to himself, vexed*) This is a little strange

Dor. Why are you angry if you take in ill part——?

Count. No, no, you mistake me. Speak freely and sincerely.

Dor. You know the confidence you have placed in me. Having discoursed together concerning this family, I wrote to Madam Araminta, with an invitation for herself and daughter to pass a few days at Paris.

Count. And they have been a fortnight with you. This I know must give trouble, and bring expence ; and, as you have done it for my sake—I—my duty—my obligations are eternal.

Dor. By no means, brother. The expence is trifling, and the inconvenience little. I love this family, and, beside being related to my husband, am greatly interested in its behalf. Eleonora is the best girl on earth, and her mother is no less respectable. A good heart, economical, and to the most exact economy she unites no less prudence and regularity of conduct.

Count. Excellent : and so has been the education of her
daughter. But now tell me——

Dor. Sincerely, brother, in my opinion, Eleonora neither
loves you much nor little.

Count. On what do you found this strange suspicion ?

Dor. I will tell you. When your name is mentioned, she
looks down and gives no answer.

Count. Bashfulness.

Dor. When she hears or sees you coming, she changes colour, is in a tremor, and wishes to hide herself.

Count. At her age that is not extraordinary.

Dor. When this marriage is mentioned the tears are in her
eyes.

Count. The tears of a child ? Can any thing be more equivocal ?

Dor. And though so equivocal and so full of doubt, will you
dare to marry her ?

Count. Certainly, without the least difficulty.

Dor. It seems you love her to distraction?

Count. I love——I do not know how much.

Dor. You have scarcely seen her twice.

Count. Is not that enough to a feeling heart like mine ?

Dor. Ah, brother, I know you.

Count. Your penetration is a little too quick.

Dor. I do not wish hereafter you should have to reproach
me.

Count. Yonder is Frontino.

Dor. If you have business——

Count. (*affected kindness*) Will you go ?

Dor. We shall meet again. I only wish you to think a
little on what I have said, and before you marry——

Count. Fear nothing, dear sister. Do me the pleasure to
dine with me to-day. I will send to invite Madam Araminta
and her daughter. We shall have many guests. The notary
will be here after dinner, and the contract will be signed.

Dor. To-day ?

Count. No doubt : Madam Araminta has pledged her word.

Dor. (*ironically*) I give you joy. (*aside*) I will never
suffer Eleonora to sacrifice herself for my sake. If I could but
truly understand her heart—— I will try.   [*Exit.*

SCENE IV.—*The* COUNT, *and then* FRONTINO.

Count. Poor girl ! A little too diffident of me. Does not
think me capable of subduing a tender and inexperienced heart !
Beside, she carries her delicacy rather too far : in marriages
of convenience, not the heart but family interest is consulted.
Well, Frontino, what have you to say ?

Front. The taylor is come, Sir.

Count. Where is he?

Front. At the door, sending away his coach, and giving orders to his servants.

Count. His servants!

Front. Yes, Sir.

Count. Apropos: that reminds me that thou must write immediately to my country steward, that he may send me six handsome youths, tall, well made, the best he can find on the estate, that the taylor may take measure of them for liveries.

Front. Six clowns in liveries!

Count. Yes, to honour my nuptials. Tell the steward that all the time they stay here their country wages shall be continued, beside having their board. Thou knowest this sort of people: take care not to overload their plates.

Front. Never fear, Sir, they will not die of indigestion.

Count. Hold. Take the key of the closet where the plate is kept; let it be displayed, and all brought on table.

Front. But, Sir, your plate is so antique, and so black— it will be necessary at least to have it new polished.

Count. Oh, silver is always silver—here comes the taylor, I suppose.

Front. Yes, Sir. Enter, Signor, enter.

SCENE V.—*To them the* TAYLOR.

Tayl. I am the most humble servant of your most illustrious lordship.

Count. Come near, Sir. I was impatient to see you. I want four suits for myself, and twelve liveries for my servants.

Tayl. It will do me honour to serve you, and have no doubt but it will be to your heart's content.

Front. My master pays well.

Tayl. I have the honour to know him. Who is it that does not know the illustrious Count Casteldoro?

Count. The occasion requires all possible display of magnificent splendor.

Tayl. I will show you stuffs of gold and silver.

Count. No, no; I do not wish to look as if caparisoned in gilded leather. The dresses must be noble and rich, but nothing with a shining ground.

Tayl. You prefer embroidery?

Count. I do: four embroidered suits, but in the best possible taste, the patterns rich and delicate.

Front. (*aside*) Hey day; I do not know my master.

Tayl. Rich, but light embroidery?

Count. No, Sir: point of Spain, ample, massive, and of the best workmanship; well designed, splendid, but nothing that shines.

Tayl. Every thing that you can desire. Shall I take your measure ?

Count. Yes—on one condition.

Tayl. What is it ?

Front. (*aside*) Ay, let us hear the condition.

Count. You must slightly tack on the embroidery, that it may not be spoiled. I would have no buttons of false diamonds. I shall wear my four suits each of them twice during the first eight days of my nuptials, so that your embroidery will still be new, and may again be sold as such. You must now tell me what you will charge for the cloth, the making, and the use of your ornaments.

Front. (*aside*) Yes, yes, he is still himself.

Count. But first concerning the liveries.

Tayl. With your permission, I wish to have the honor of speaking to you in private.

Front. (*angrily to the* Taylor) If I must not stay, I can go.

Count. By no means. Frontino is part of the family : you may speak before him.

Front. (*to the* Taylor) You see, Sir ! Hem !

Tayl. No, friend ; I did not mean you, but—look to see if we have no listeners. (*slily gives* Frontino *a crown.*)

Front. (*aside*) A crown ! It is long since I had so much.

Tayl. Sir, I comprehend the nature of your project. You are not naturally inclined to pomp ; but, sagacious and prudent as you are, you willingly sacrifice to appearance and convenience. I esteem myself most fortunate in having the honor to serve you. I venerate gentlemen who think like you, and laugh at those who ruin themselves, while I give them every aid in my power, that they may be ruined in style. In me you have discovered the only man fit for your purpose : set your heart at rest ; I have the means to satisfy you.

Count. (*aside*) If I do not mistake, this is a most smooth-tongued, artful——(*aloud*) Well then, you will make my four suits ?

Tayl. Pardon me, Sir, your idea is not practicable. I could not avoid paying extremely dear for the embroidery ; and my delicate conscience would never permit me to sell it again as new.

Count. (*aside*) His delicate conscience ! Why did he come to me ?

Tayl. I will confide a secret to you which I have treasured up with jealousy ; for, were it known, I cannot tell you how much it would prejudice my character and credit. I, who am the court taylor, taylor to the principal nobility of Paris, I secretly, and under a borrowed name, carry on a flourishing trade in old clothes.

Count. An old clothesman keep his coach !

Tayl. Which is maintained by that very means.

Front. (*to the* Count) You see, Sir, I have found you a man of sincerity; a man whose heart is as open as his face; a man who merits all your confidence.

Count. (*aside*) I perceive— (*aloud*) Should I find this to be my interest?

Tayl. I will show you two dozen of most magnificent suits, all new, that never were worn but once or twice at the most.

Count. Will they be known again?

Tayl. No danger of that; every thing that enters my magazine assumes a new face. I export the most splendid samples that France produces; and I import the spoils and riches of the principal cities in Europe. You shall see suits the most superb, and stuffs of the greatest rarity. It is a pity you will have neither gold nor silver.

Count. Nay, should it be any thing of uncommon beauty and taste, gold and silver would not offend me.

Front. To be sure, if the streets were to be paved with gold, we must walk.

Count. But the price.

Tayl. See, admire, and select; act just as you please. (*aside*) I have found the very man I wished for. I will soon be back, dear Sir. (*aside*) Paris is the place; every thing a man wants is there to be found.

Front. Have you by chance any thing that will sit genteel, and make me look like a gentleman's gentleman.

Tayl. (*aside*) I will clothe you from head to foot, only be my friend.

Front. Your friend! On such conditions who could refuse.

ACT II.

SCENE I.—DORIMENE *and* ELEANORA.

Dorimene.

COME here, my dear Eleonora, I wish to speak to you alone. My brother, I believe, is gone out: (*looks off*) he is not in his cabinet.

Eleon. (*aside*) What can she have to say? She has a friendship for me, but I believe her interest is more for her brother. I can expect no consolation for myself.

Dor. We are alone, and may speak freely. Permit me first to observe that within these few days you have had a serious melancholy air, which seems but little to suit your expectations.

Eleon. It is natural to me, Madam; a little more, a little less, I am always so.

Dor. Excuse me; but on your arrival at Paris you had no such gloomy appearance in your face. You are entirely changed, and certainly not without cause.

Eleon. Dear no; there is no such change.

Dor. My good young friend, you conceal the truth, and want confidence in me. Be a little more just, and rest assured that, though I proposed a marriage between you and my brother, no foolish ambition makes me wish it should succeed at the expence of your heart. Tell me openly what are your wishes; speak freely, and you will see whether I am your friend.

Eleon. (*aside*) If I durst but—— No, no.

Dor. Have you any dislike to my brother?

Eleon. I have not long had the honour of his acquaintance, Madam.

Dor. His age, for example, may seem a little too great when compared with your own.

Eleon. The age of a man does not appear to me a thing of great consequence.

Dor. You observed that my brother has rather too much economy.

Eleon. You know, Madam, I have been educated in economy.

Dor. If so, my dear Eleonora, to my great satisfaction, I have been entirely mistaken, and you will be perfectly happy with my brother.

Eleon. I!—Do you think so?

Dor. No doubt, it cannot be otherwise. I have questioned you with the best intentions, and you have answered—sincerely—as I must believe.

Eleon. Oh!—Certainly.

Dor. Then be at peace; your heart tells me you will be happy.

Eleon. (*affected*) My heart, Madam!

Dor. Your heart.

Eleon. Ah! I do not understand my own heart.

Dor. Why are you so much moved?

Eleon. (*looking off*) Am I not called?

Dor. Called? Where? By whom?

Eleon. (*going*) Perhaps my mother;—perhaps somebody——

Dor. No, no; pray stay: your mother knows you are with me, and therefore cannot be in fear. I have something more to say to you.

Eleon. (*aside*) How difficult to disguise my feelings!

Dor. Remember, your heart has told me——

Eleon. (*timorously*) What, Madam?

Dor. You are in love with another.

Eleon. (*confused*) I, Madam!

Dor. You: your blushes confirm it.

Eleon. (*aside*) Heavens! Have I betrayed myself? (*aloud*) You will not tell this to my mother? I shall be lost!

Dor. No, no; fear nothing: though you have discovered that you cannot confide in me, I love you tenderly, and am incapable of giving you needless pain. Here your mother comes: let us consider between ourselves.

Eleon. Ah, Madam! (*embracing.*)

SCENE II.—*Enter* ARAMINTA.

Aram. Well, child! I fear you are troublesome?

Eleon. Pardon me, but——

Dor. We are friends, and I entreated her to keep me company.

Aram. You are kinder to her than she deserves. I cannot understand her! She is become so melancholy and dull!

Dor. The air of Paris may not agree with her.

Aram. Do you think so? Since she left the place of her education, she is no longer the same! Nothing pleases, nothing diverts her! Music, reading, and drawing, are all forsaken! I have spared no expence, and have taken no little delight in perceiving her progress; while, at present, I am equally surprised to see her thus negligent. I willingly incur expence for any good purpose; but no one can be more angry than I am at squandering money.

Eleon. (*aside*) It is very true! I no longer know myself.

Dor. Nay, Madam.

Aram. If she wishes to return to her retirement, why not say so?

Dor. Oh, no, Madam; she has no such wish.

Aram. But why then, child, are you so gloomy; so indolent! You are soon to be married, and to govern a family: this requires activity, attention, and order, as you may see by my example. I am busy, from morning to evening, here and there, going, coming, helping, commanding, and sometimes obliged to find fault: but, by these means, all goes well.

Eleon. (*aside*) I hoped to do the same; but all my hopes are flown!

Dor. Oh, Madam, when your daughter's heart shall be at ease——

Aram. At ease! What does she want? Is not the marriage-contract to be signed to-day?

Dor. Here comes my brother! He can best inform you——

Eleon. (*aside*) How miserable am I!

SCENE III.—*Enter the* COUNT *and a* JEWELLER.

Count. I am happy, ladies, to find you together; I came purposely to ask your advice.

Aram. On what subject? Ladies are sometimes excellent advisers?

Count. (*to the* Jeweller) Show your case of jewels.

Aram. (*aside*) Jewels! He may well ask advice in such articles; it is easy to deceive.

Jew. (*presenting the case to* Dorimene) Please to examine if diamonds can be more pure and perfect.

Count. Pray give me your opinion.

Dor. I think them admirable! What say you, Eleonora?

Eleon. (*with indifference*) I do not understand such things.

Aram. I do—show them to me. Though I never wore any diamonds, commerce has made me well acquainted with them. (*taking the case*) These are fine, indeed! Perfectly assorted, and of a beautiful water. What is their price?

Count. Oh! that is a secret between ourselves: (*to the* Jeweller) is it not?

Jew. My Lord——I have nothing to say.

Aram. (*aside*) So much the worse; the Count will be the more easily imposed upon. He comes to ask advice, and then refuses to hear it!

Count. (*apart, to the* Jeweller) My good friend, will you trust your diamonds with me three or four days?

Jew. (*to the* Count) If the ladies think them good, and well chosen, I should prefer——

Count. Nay, friend, jewels of this value must not be purchased without reflection. Knowing me, you cannot be afraid.

Jew. By no means! They are at your service.

Count. Be pleased to return at the end of the week: I know the price, and you shall then have the money or the diamonds.

Jew. I am much obliged to you, Signor.   [*Exit.*

SCENE IV.

Count. (*aside*) Excellent! just as I wished! (*to* Eleonora) Will you do me the favour, Madam, to wear the jewels I have the honor to present you, at least for to-day.

Dor. To-day?

Count. It is the day on which we are to sign the contract, and we shall have thirty persons at table.

Aram. Thirty!

Count. At least, Madam.

Aram. (*aside*) He will ruin himself! But I will hear more.

Count. (*presenting the case to* Dorimene) Dear sister, let me request you to trouble yourself with this case, and to kindly attend at the toilet of this lady, to assist in arranging the diamonds. Will you do me the pleasure, charming Eleonora, to accept my sister's aid?

Eleon. (*coldly*) My mamma never wears diamonds.

Aram. Do not be silly, child. I did not wear diamonds, because my husband was too prudent to indulge in such expences: but, if the Count think differently, complaisance requires your acquiescence.

Eleon. But, you know, mamma——

Aram. Oh! I know—I know, child, you do not know good breeding. Accept them gratefully.

Eleon. (*aside*) Unhappy me! (*to the* Count) Signor—I am greatly obliged.

Dor. (*apart, to the* Count) Are you satisfied with such a cold manner?

Count. Perfectly.

Dor. Have you no dissatisfaction; no fears?

Count. Not the least.

Dor. (*aside*) What a singular man is my brother?

SCENE V.—*Enter* FRONTINO.

Front. Here is a letter, Sir.

Count. With your permission, ladies.

Aram. By all means! (*to* Dorimene) Let us examine the jewels a little.

Count. (*to himself, having read the letter*) The Marquis comes at an ill time! After a dinner of thirty guests, I must give him a supper! He asks it with so little ceremony too! How can it be managed?

Dor. What is the matter, brother?

Count. (*affecting cheerfulness*) Nothing, nothing. I have just received news, which gives me pleasure. The Marquis Del Bosco is arrived, and coming to sup with me this evening.

Eleon. (*agitated*) What do I hear?

Aram. I know the Marquis; his country seat is not three miles distant from mine.

Count. You will see him this evening; with the Marchioness his daughter, and the Chevalier his son.

Eleon. (*still more agitated*) The Chevalier! Oh, Heaven!

Count. I hope they will be in time to be present, when we sign the contract.

Eleon. (*still aside*) Fatal trial! How shall I support it?

Aram. What is the matter, daughter?

Eleon. Nothing—not much—a swimming in the head.

Count. (*to* Araminta) For Heaven's sake, take care of——! (*to* Frontino) Don't go.

Aram. The open air will revive her.

Dor.   Let us walk into the garden.

Aram.   By all means.

Dor.   Is the door open, brother?

Count.   No ; but here is the key.

Dor.   (*aside*)   He will trust it to nobody, but has it always in his pocket.   Come, Eleonora.   (*aside*)   This may be a proper opportunity.   (*retiring, with* Eleonora.)

Count.   (*to* Araminta)   I hope, Madam, this attack is trifling ; but the young lady should not be exposed to the least danger.   If you think proper, we will defer the dinner of to-day, and have a supper instead.

Aram.   Just as you please—but your dinners and suppers— I have much to say to you on such subjects.   My daughter may want me ; I will return presently.

SCENE VI.

Count.   (*earnestly*)   Hark ye, Frontino !   Send messengers, immediately, to inform the guests I have invited that, instead of dinner, I entreat them to honor me with their company at supper.

Front.   So, so !—But it will be difficult to find them all, so late in the day.

Count.   No matter.   Those who may come to dinner must be told of the change.   They will return to supper, or not, as they please.

Front.   Yes, Signor.   (*aside*)   Admirable !   Quite in character !   [*Exit.*

Count.   This visit comes at a lucky time !   Nothing could be more fortunate !

SCENE VII.—*Enter* Araminta.

Count.   Well, dear Madam !   Eleonora ?

Aram.   All I hope will be well.

Count.   Then I shall be happy ; for health should be our first care.   I have sent round to the guests, with an invitation to supper this evening.

Aram.   Thirty persons at supper !

Count.   I hope so, Madam.

Aram.   Permit me to speak openly, and tell you all I think.

Count.   You cannot give me greater pleasure.

Aram.   Is it not extreme folly to assemble thirty persons, twenty of whom, at least, will make a jest of you?

Count.   A *jest* of *me ?*

Aram.   Beyond all doubt.   Do not think I am avaricious : thank Heaven, that is not my defect ; but I cannot endure to see money squandered.

Count.   But, on such a day, and under such circumstances,

Aram.   Are they your relations, whom you have invited?

Count. By no means. A select company: The nobility! The literati! The magistracy! All persons of distinction.

Aram. Worse and worse! Vanity, ostentation, folly! My good friend, you do not know the value of money.

Count. (*smiles*) I not know the value of money!

Aram. Alas, you do not! Your sister made me believe you were economical: had I known the truth, I should never have married my daughter to a spendthrift.

Count. So you think me a spendthrift!

Aram. I first perceived it by the considerable sum you threw away in the purchase of a title; which sacrifice to vanity has no beneficial end.

Count. How! Are you not aware, the rank I have acquired will impress a character of respect on myself, your daughter, and our descendants?

Aram. Quite the reverse. I rather would have given my daughter to you, as Signor Anselmo Colombani, a well-known merchant, than to the Count of Casteldoro, a newly-made nobleman.

Count. But, Madam——

Aram. Your ancestors have saved what you will scatter.

Count. Scatter! I! You are mistaken, Madam. You do not know me.

Aram. Oh, yes, yes. I saw the manner in which, without any knowledge of diamonds, or asking the least advice, you were led away by the jeweller.

Count. Oh, with respect to the diamonds——

Aram. Ah, ay! I know your answer. They are to decorate the Countess of Casteldoro. And who is the Countess of Casteldoro? My daughter, Signor, has been well educated, but with no such expectations. Every thing has been done, in abundance, that could contribute to convenience, decency, and information; but nothing to pomp and vanity. The ornaments of my daughter ever will be modesty, obedience, and that self-respect, which she could not but acquire from such an education.

Count. (*a little moved*) But, Madam——

Aram. (*very warmly*) But, Signor—(*softening*) I ask your pardon—Perhaps, you may think me too warm; but I see you hurried into a gulph of expence that makes me tremble. My daughter's happiness is concerned: I give her a hundred thousand crowns in marriage.

Count. (*somewhat haughtily*) Am I not able to settle an equal sum upon her?

Aram. Yes, at present. But wealth will diminish; and especially when we have the vanity to be profuse, grand, and magnificent.

Count. I once more assure you, Madam, you do not know me.

Aram. Signor, had you been a different person, I had con-

ceived an excellent plan. My annual income is five and twenty
thousand livres: I might have lived with you and my daughter, and the two families might have become one; but, at present, Heaven preserve me from taking such a step!

Count. (*aside*) She will drive me mad! (*to* Araminta)
Pray hear me. (*whispering and cunningly*) You mistake my
character. Few people indeed understand economy so well as
I do, as you will soon be convinced. I willingly close with
your proposal, and——

Aram. By no means! You try in vain to persuade me
against conviction. Respecting my daughter—I have promised—we shall see—but for myself it is different. Not all
the gold on earth should induce me to make such an arrangement, with a man who does not know the use of money, but
lets it slip through his fingers faster than chaff through a sieve.
                                                        [*Exit.*

Count. This is admirable! I never imagined I should pass
for a prodigal.   [*Exit.*

ACT III.

SCENE I.—*The* Count *and* Frontino.

Count.

Frontino.

Front. Signor.

Count. Go and inquire how Eleonora does.

Front. One of your guests is without, and desires to speak
with you.

Count. Who is he?

Front. The young gentleman who lately read you a comedy,
written by himself.

Count. Oh! Signor Giacinto. Bid him enter.

Front. Please to come in, Signor.   [*Exit.*

SCENE II.—*Enter* Giacinto.

Count. Good morning, Signor Giacinto. I am very sorry that
the messenger, sent by me, did not find you at home: he came
to inform you that an accident has occasioned me to put off the
dinner, but that I hoped to see you at supper.

Giac. It is just the same to me, Signor. Meanwhile, permit me the honor to——

Count. I hope to see you, without fail, this evening.

Giac. I am infinitely obliged to you; but, having now the
good fortune to find you alone, and at leisure, I wish to lay

before you certain alterations made in the epistle dedicatory : as I have nothing so much at heart as your satisfaction.

Count. Well, Signor Giacinto, since you are absolutely resolved to dedicate your comedy to me, I have thought—it would be best to inform you—of certain particulars respecting myself. Not from vanity ! Oh, no ! Heaven preserve me from that ! But solely to give an opportunity to your eloquence, and lustre to your work.

Giac. You see, Signor, I have made a good use of the materials which you have so kindly furnished : but I have done something more.

Count. Have you mentioned my pictures ?

Giac. Oh yes.

Count. And my library ?

Giac. Certainly.

Count. Including the books which I told you I should purchase ?

Giac. But—Signor—a catalogue of books in a dedication—

Count. Where is the difficulty ? You may say, in a note at the bottom of the page, the Count of Casteldoro possesses—a superb library, of not less than ten thousand volumes. A man of wit, like you, knows how to take advantage of every thing. The supper of this evening, for example, may furnish some new ideas : something animated, witty, poetical.

Giac. That may be possible ; but I have been employed on a subject more essential : I have written your genealogy.

Count. (*coldly*) My genealogy ? No, no, friend. I have not a taste for that science. You might, I grant, say things that should happen to do me honor ; but I am an enemy to vanity, and would prefer forbearance ; especially on the question of genealogy.

Giac. As you please ; but I have made discoveries, that have cost me much time and study ; of which I thought you might wish to be informed.

Count. (*with curiosity*) Discoveries that relate to me ?

Giac. That relate to you, Signor.

Count. My dear Signor Giacinto, let me hear.

Giac. Your true family name is not Colombani.

Count. I grant it may have been changed.

Giac. Do me the favor to listen. The great Columbus, who discovered America, and who was ennobled by the king of Spain, had two brothers, and various relations. Now, in looking through authors to discover annotations for my Life of Petrarch, I found that one of the relations of Christopher Columbus went from Genoa, his native place, to the city of Avignon, in France. By corruption of the termination, I find the name of Colombo, or Columbus, has been changed to Colombani ; and I demonstrate, beyond all doubt, that you are a descendant of that ancient illustrious family.

Count. (*much pleased*) You have demonstrated it !

Giac. Here are my proofs. (*presenting papers.*)

Count. (*receiving them*) From the little I can now recollect, I believe you are right. Ay, ay ; it might be. I do not love ostentation, as you perceive, but I shall be highly pleased if your discovery can do yourself honor; I therefore have not the courage to forbid the publication. Have you presented your comedy to the comedians ?

Giac. Yes, Signor.

Count. And they certainly received it with approbation ?

Giac. On the contrary, Signor, it has been peremptorily refused.

Count. Refused !

Giac. You have heard it read : does it deserve such a reward?

Count. If the comedy be good, why is it refused ? Their interest should oblige them to accept it, with thanks.

Giac. What can be expected from such ignorant judges? But I will have my revenge ! It shall be printed ! The public shall decide !

Count. Bravo ! You are right ; have it printed. It might not be greatly successful on the stage, but in the closet it will delight. Your sale will be prodigious.

Giac. Since you approve and encourage me, Signor, would you but have the goodness to pass your word for the expence of printing, and——

Count. (*with a determined tone*) There is no need of that: apply to a good bookseller ; let him have his profits, and he will answer for the whole.

Giac. To speak the truth, Signor, I have in vain applied to more than one. At last, a bookseller has agreed that, if the Count of Casteldoro will make himself responsible, he will undertake to publish it on my account.

Count. How ! Have you mentioned my name ?

Giac. I could not avoid it.

Count. You have done very ill. Should it be known that I take an interest in the comedy, it would be said I did so because of the dedication ; and I should then appear ridiculous. Drop all thoughts of the press at present; a more favorable opportunity may occur.

Giac. But, Signor——

SCENE III.—*Enter* FRONTINO.

Count. Well, Frontino, what answer ?

Front. The young lady is rather better, Signor.

Count. Rather better ! But is she well enough to—— I will go and inquire myself. (*to* Giacinto) You see, Signor, a young lady is ill in my house, and the supper must be deferred. Another time—— (*going.*)

Giac. Then, if the manuscript be useless, Signor——

Count. True ; it shall be returned. (*going.*)

Giac. I beg you to recollect the time and trouble it has cost me.

Count. (*returning the manuscript*) Very right! You are fond of your own works: I am glad they give you satisfaction, and cannot but thank you for any labor taken on my account. Whenever I can serve you, pray command me.

Giac. Infinitely obliged to the generosity of Signor Count Casteldoro. (*aside*) What ingratitude! Sordid fellow! He shall pay for this, or I am mistaken.   [*Exit.*

Count. One guest the less. But I must inquire after Eleonora. (*going.*)

Fior. (*without*) Why house! Is nobody to be found?

Front. This is Fiorillo, the servant of the Marquis.

SCENE IV.—*Enter* Fiorillo, *in a travelling Dress.*

Fior. (*bows*) Signor Count, my master, the Marquis del Bosco, is coming. I rode before, as you perceive, to inform you that his carriage will soon arrive.

Count. (*coldly*) Arrive! What here? And in his coach? Does he come to make any stay?

Fior. No, Signor. To-morrow morning he must be gone to Versailles; for he has affairs at court.

Count. (*aside*) I am glad of it! (*aloud pompously*) I hope the Marquis will do me the honor to remain with me to-night, in company with his son, the Chevalier. With respect to the Marchioness—I'll speak to my sister, and hope she may also be accommodated, as becomes her rank.

Fior. The Marchioness *Del Bosco* does not come with her father; she is with the Countess *d'Orimon,* her aunt, and is to remain at her hotel.

Count. (*aside*) So much the better. (*aloud*) That is unfortunate. I hope, however, I shall have the pleasure to see her.   [*Exit.*

SCENE V.—Frontino *and* Fiorillo.

Fior. Your master, like your kitchen, smells well!

Front. We are to have a magnificent supper to-night; no less than thirty guests.

Fior. Indeed! Your master is superb. A rare service! Much to eat, and little to do! Then, as to wages—you will make your fortune, Frontino!

Front. Fortune! I can't say——Perhaps!

Fior. You have been long with this master.

Front. Very true: I have an attachment to him.

Fior. And so have I to mine; but without the hope of

saving a farthing in his service. If 'it were not for the profits of the card-tables, I should certainly leave him.

Front. Then you have much play?

Fior. A great deal.

Front. And no less profit?

Fior. Hum—Tolerable; but not equal to you.

Front. I! Shall I speak plain to a fellow-servant? I have little wages, and no vails.

Fior. Then you are foolish, Frontino. In Paris, so clever a fellow as yourself may find a hundred services, in which they may profit a hundred different ways.

Front. Do you know any *one* ?

Fior. Certainly: but you are attached to your master?

Front. To part with him would not break my heart.

Fior. If he pays so ill, he does not like you.

Front. That's a mistake: I am his prime minister, and favorite.

Fior. What do you mean? Were he miserly, so be it; but a generous——

Front. Generous! You little know my master.

Fior. How so? A supper for thirty guests——

Front. Ah, did you know what it will cost me!

Fior. You! Cost you!

Front. Me. Grumbled at, cross-questioned, put to the torture, almost afraid of my life, when I give in my bill. I tremble but to think of it!

Fior. So, so! Very different with us: our master is easily satisfied, and always gay and good humoured. He has an odd manner of speaking, indeed, and never tells you more than half what he means. He has favorite words, which, right or wrong, he always uses. Every body laughs at *him*, and he laughs at himself.

Front. I wish I had such a master!

Fior. The worst of it is, he is poor, and seldom has any money.

Front. Yet you say he plays?

Fior. Very true: he always finds money for that. I hear a coach.

Front. Which way does he——

Fior. (*at the window*) Be quiet! Yes, they are here.

Front. I want to hear more.

Fior. Run and tell your master.

Front. (*aside*) I shall hear it all; he can't hold his tongue.

[*Exit.*

Fior. Frontino is a good fellow, but he talks too much; that's his fault.

SCENE VI.—*Enter the* MARQUIS.

Marq. Where is he? Where is the Count?

Fior. His servant is gone to tell him you are here.

Marq. Go, go; see—— Good, good, excellent!—His servant——?

Fior. Will soon be back.

Marq. Meanwhile—— My horses—Nothing to eat—Poor
devils—Time to—— Good, good, excellent!—Provender—
My son——?

Fior. Is coming. *(aside, and going)* It is not every servant could understand him.   [*Exit.*

SCENE VII.—*Enter the* CHEVALIER.

Chev. My dear father! How can I thank you, for all your
kindness?

Marq. Say no more—Father to be sure—Few words—
can't express all one feels.

Chev. Most true! Had you not discovered my passion, I
scarcely should have dared to own it.

Marq. Keen eyes—Why not, dear boy? Why not?—
Know Eleonora—Know her mother——

Chev. I am a little known to the latter, but not enough to
speak on such a subject.

Marq. A lady that—— Are you sure of the daughter?

Chev. Perfectly. I have met her at her cousin's, and—we
have corresponded.

Marq. Good, good, excellent! We shall want—— The
Count is my friend.

Chev. And I am acquainted with his sister, Madam Dorimene. I will beg her to entreat for me. Here comes the
Count.

SCENE VIII.—*Enter the* COUNT.

Count. Pardon me, Marquis, but——

Marq. Ah! Count! Good day—Good day—Your health—
Mine—You see! Hope! Hope!

Count. Still the same! Always cheerful!

Marq. Soul—Life—Good, good, excellent!

Count. And you, Chevalier.

Chev. Always at your commands.

Count. Is the Marchioness with you?

Marq. My daughter?—With her aunt—Good company—

Count. True: I have the pleasure to know her, and will call
and pay the ladies my respects.—Hope to have the honor of
their company to supper.

Marq. Always obliging—Good, good, excellent!—Ought to apologize—Come suddenly—No ceremony, I beg.

Count. None on earth. I shall only give you my ordinary supper.

Marq. Good, good, excellent! Family meals—Friendly—

Count. The apartments here, on the right—Oh! I forget—To-morrow you go to Versailles?

Marq. I do.

Count. I am sorry to lose you so soon : but, as I was saying, these apartments shall be yours.

Chev. Permit me, Signor Count, to pay my respects to your sister.

Count. You will do me an honor, and give her pleasure.

Chev. *(to his father)* Have I your leave, Sir?

Marq. Certainly. *(aside)* Poor fellow! He is—— Ay, ay—I was just the same—Youth, nature.

Count. We may all go together, if you please.

Marq. Ha! *(aside)* No; must not spoil sport. *(aloud)* Go by himself.

Chev. *(going)* I know my road.

Count. You will meet a young lady there, with whom perhaps you are acquainted.

Chev. *(eager to go)* Indeed! So much the better!

Count. I have something to tell you concerning her, which perhaps you do not know.

Chev. *(aside)* Too well! I am on the rack!

Count. But which you will be glad to hear.

Chev. *(aside)* Heavens! Perhaps, Eleonora may have discovered our passion to her mother.   [*Exit.*

SCENE IX.—Count *and the* Marquis.

Marq. Now we are alone——*(looking round)* Have you time?

Count. I am at your disposal.

Marq. You are my friend.

Count. The title does me honor.

Marq. Good, good, excellent!

Count. *(aside)* He is sometimes very ridiculous.

Marq. I have a favor to—— Friendship—Liberality—Frankness.

Count. *(aside)* So, so! He wants to borrow money.

Marq. You know my family——

Count. Perfectly.

Marq. A son—must be thought of—A daughter too—Good, good, excellent!—The Chevalier—I pity him—You understand me?

Count. I believe I do. You are seriously thinking of establishing your family, which is highly commendable. And, talking of establishments, I think it but right in me to inform you of my approaching marriage.

Marq. Oh, oh!—that way inclined—You too—Good, good, excellent !

Count. I am this day to sign the contract, and think myself fortunate that you, Signor Marquis, will be present, and——

Marq. Very happy—but, wheanwhile—Could you do me the pleasure to——

Count. You well know, Signor Marquis, the various expences of these occasions: they are endless. To own the truth, I find my pocket empty.

Marq. Good, good, excellent !

Count. Good ! I find it exceedingly ill.

Marq. Hear, hear—You are the friend of Madam Araminta.

Count. True; and she, for example, is remarkably rich : she might be of service to your house.

Marq. Precisely so—My very thought—— Would you but speak to her, but without—— What is her daughter's name ?

Count. Eleonora.

Marq. True—Bad memory—Eleonora.

Count. (*aside*) If I had not much penetration, I could never guess what he means. (*aloud*) I will speak privately to Madam Araminta.

Marq. Ay, but—— In a particular manner, so that—— You understand me ?

Count. I will speak with all possible caution, and hope she will comply—provided she has good security.

Marq. Security !—I—She—As to—my estates.

Count. What sum do you wish ?

Marq. I heard that—— Ay—A hundred thousand crowns —Quite satisfied !—Would not wish for more !

Count. (*aside*) A hundred thousand crowns ! I would not wish for more ! She will scarcely consent to that.

Marq. When will you speak ?—I have a project—— No sooner said than done—It is in my nature.

Count. I will inform her to-day.

Marq. And you hope she—— Good, good, excellent !

Count. I think Madam Araminta will comply, if possible; first out of regard to yourself, and next to me, who am soon to become her son.

Marq. Ha !—What ?—You ?—

Count. I am to marry her daughter.

Marq. Marry !—When ?—That true ?—That possible ?

Count. Why so excessively surprised, Signor Marquis ? Do you see any reason to the contrary ?

Marq. I—— No—(*aside*) My son !—Fine affair !—Stupid folly !

Count. Madam Araminta intends indeed to give a hundred

thousand crowns with her daughter, but do you think she will
have a sum beside so great to lend you?

Marq.   Lend me!—Zounds!—Lend me!

SCENE X.

The CHEVALIER, *making Signs of Disappointment and Silence to
the* MARQUIS, *enters and goes off without being seen by the* COUNT.

Count.   But, if you please, I will speak to her.

Marq.   (*to the* Chevalier) Yes, yes; I understand.

Count.   (*supposing the answer was to himself*) And will tell
her——

Marq.   By no means—Don't think—— No, no.

Count.   Yes and no! I do not understand you, Signor.

Marq.   Lend me!—I may—— I am—— Quite another
meaning—Good, good, excellent! Did not come to——

Count.   If you will excuse me, I have business. Those are
your apartments. (*aside*) I never met so unintelligible a person!   [*Exit.*

Marq.   Lunacy—Cross purposes—Good, good, excellent!
                                                   [*Exeunt.*

ACT IV.

SCENE I.—*The* CHEVALIER *and* FIORILLO.

Chevalier.

WHILE my father reposes, I will visit my sister; tell him
this, when he wakes.

Fior.   Yes, Signor.

Chev.   Do you know whether the Count is at home?

Fior.   Yes; I saw him just now going to speak with Madam
Dorimene.

Chev.   (*aside*) Surely he is not a rival to be feared. At
least, I am secure of the heart of Eleonora, and will not yet
despair of gaining her mother.   [*Exit.*

Fior.   So, young gentleman! I see how it is with you. I
pretty well guess your intentions, and how they are thwarted.
Ay, ay, I shall have enough to satisfy the curiosity of Frontino.
.(*sits in the back-ground at his ease.*)

SCENE II.—*Enter* COUNT.

Count.   (*not seeing* Fiorillo) I am wearied, teased! Nothing
but indifference; and, instead of perfect satisfaction, some-

thing like contempt. A man like me, who had but to choose!
So advantageous a marriage! (*seeing* Fiorillo) Is the Marquis
at home?

Fior. Yes, Signor: being rather fatigued with travelling,
he is taking a nap.

Count. (*aside*) How amiable is his daughter! How charming! I felt affected and confused at the courtesy and kindness
with which she and her aunt received me. The visit made me
cheerful, happy, and reconciled to myself. What a difference
between the politeness of these ladies and the common and trivial manner of Araminta and her daughter; who neither understand civility nor good breeding. Ah! were the young
Marchioness but as rich as she is handsome and engaging—
who knows? I have a thought——Should her father but be
reasonable and easy to manage—Here he comes.

SCENE III.—*Enter the* MARQUIS.

Marq. (*rubbing his eyes and calling*) Fiorillo!
Fior. Signor.
Marq. My son?
Fior. He is gone out.
Marq. Why did not he—— Where is he gone:
Fior. To visit the Marchioness, his sister.
Marq. I too wish—— My coach!
Fior. The horses, Signor——
Marq. (*angry*) Good, good, excellent! My coach!
Fior. I will go and see. [*Exit.*

SCENE IV.—*The* COUNT *and the* MARQUIS.

Count. Do you wish to go out, Signor Marquis.
Marq. See my daughter—Much to say—Tell her—Good,
good, excellent!

Count. I have just had that honor. It was long since I
had seen her. She fully answers the charming promise of her
childhood: her sweetness has increased with her years, and
the progress of her talents is wonderful. Permit me to congratulate you on possessing such a treasure.

Marq. Oh, Count—— Ay, ay; good girl. If she chose
—but—rank, manners—— Good, good, excellent!

Count. With such talents, so much merit, and blooming
eighteen, you should think of a husband for her.

Marq. No doubt—For my part, I—— Apropos; what has
just past—you remember—— I borrow!—Lend me!

Count. It appears to me that you suddenly changed your
opinion.

Marq. I tell you, no—I mean to—speak, fully, plainly,
clearly—Always my way.

Count. In any case, Signor Marquis, I shall be happy to serve you. I have not spoken to Madam Araminta; for, to own the truth, I am not quite pleased with her daughter. I begin to feel a certain dislike.

Marq. Oh, oh!—A different thing—Well?—hay?—Why not?

Count. I have done every thing to gain their esteem and friendship. A house so richly furnished, carriages and horses the most rare, diamonds worth a hundred thousand livres——

Marq. Is it possible!

Count. 'Tis true: they were shewn. Madam Araminta was amazed.

Marq. Grand!—Superb!—Good, good, excellent!

Count. Injustice and ingratitude have been my reward.

Marq. Good, good, excellent!

Count. (*aside*) Curse the phrase!

Marq. (*aside*) In that case——if Eleonora——if my son—— (*aloud*) If so, Signor Count——candor——frankly and freely tell them—— You understand me? Cut matters short.

Count. Had I paid these attentions to a lady of rank, and merit, I should have acted much more wisely.

Marq. Ay, ay—If—— Certainly!

Count. Do you think a man of rank and fashion, a man like yourself for example, would refuse me the hand of his daughter?

Marq. Rather—— A person of worth—a person that—Who can say more?—Certainly not.

Count. Signor Marquis, thus encouraged.

Marq. Oh I—— If so—I'll go this moment!

Count. Where, Signor?

Marq. To my daughter. (*calls*) Fiorillo!

Count. And may I hope?

Marq. (*calls louder*) Fiorillo!

SCENE V.—*Enter* FIORILLO.

Marq. My coach.

Fior. The coachman is not here, Signor.

Marq. How so? (*to the* Count) Can you lend me——? Soon return.

Count. It is not a hundred yards: you can easily walk.

Marq. Walk!—Hundred yards!—Enough—Adieu—Soon be back— (*going*) Diamonds! A hundred thousand livres!

[*Exit with* Fiorillo.

SCENE VI.—*The* COUNT, *then* FRONTINO.

Count. Courage! The Marquis is enraptured; the daughter's won! All goes well. But I must not lose sight of——

(*calls*) Frontino! No, no; she must not get possession of the jewels. Frontino, I say!

Front. (*entering*) I was busy in planning the dessert.

Count. Go, immediately, and tell my sister I beg her to come here: I have something interesting to communicate. And add, but in a whisper, that I request she will bring me the jewels, which I committed to her care.

Front. But the supper, Signor! I must be every where, and look to all!

Count. True: is every thing prepared?

Front. To your wishes; two essentials excepted.

Count. Which are——?

Front. Coffee and *liqueurs.*

Count. *Liqueurs* inflame the blood.

Front. But coffee?

Count. Blockhead! Coffee at night? It prevents sleep.

Front. Surely, Signor! Not give coffee! Forfeit your character as a liberal host, for such a trifling expence?

Count. Go, Mr. Liberality; do what I bid you.

Front. (*aside*) No coffee! I would rather pay for it out of my own pocket. Yet, no; he would even swear I had filched the money from other articles. [*Exit.*

SCENE VII. Count, *alone*.

Count. Dreadful! Luxury is come to such a height! Thank Heaven, I have not spent one farthing from whim or caprice. I always pay money with prudence and circumspection. I do not yet know the character of the Marchioness, but, being once the Countess of Casteldoro, I will teach her my method; which is to esteem myself, and to despise and laugh at other people.

SCENE VIII.—*Enter* Dorimene.

Dor. I am told you want me, brother?

Count. Pardon this liberty—Where are the diamonds?

Dor. Here: do you want them back?

Count. (*taking them*) Yes, yes! You shall know why.

Dor. You need not take the trouble to tell me, for it is not possible to persuade Eleonora to accept them.

Count. So much the worse for her: she will repent. I have a secret to tell you.

Dor. You know how greatly I am interested in your happiness.

Count. I have seen the Marchioness del Bosco, and have great reason to believe that, whenever I please, I may obtain her hand.

Dor. Indeed! What will the Marquis say?

Count. Oh! He will say, Good, good, excellent! I am sure of him.

Dor. You know the disorder of his affairs! Will you marry her without a portion?

Count. Oh, no! Thank Heaven, I have not lost my wits.

Dor. What will you do then?

Count. Listen and learn. First, let me tell you, I am neither blind nor foolish. I perceive the affections of Eleonora are given to another, and I do not think I am greatly mistaken when I suppose the Chevalier her favorite. Omitting to notice the impertinence of father and son, in visiting me under the mask of friendship, I must tell you it may contribute to aid my project, which is this. Let you and I persuade Madam Araminta to give her daughter, with a hundred thousand crowns, to the Chevalier, on condition that his father receives the money, and that he redeem all his mortgages. I will request the Marchioness his daughter from him, with these said lands; and, by this means, the son and daughter will both be gratified, and the Marquis will not disburse a guinea. What say you, sister; is not the plan a good one?

Dor. Well imagined, but difficult to execute.

Count. Do not fear that; all will be right. The Marquis is gone purposely in search of his daughter: I will join them, and, I have no doubt, all will be concluded this very day. These jewels—may be of— Sister, you shall see wonders. [*Exit.*

Dor. What does he mean? But, if every one be made happy, I shall be the same.

SCENE IX.—*Enter* ELEONORA.

Eleon. (*at the door, timidly*) Are you alone, Signora?

Dor. I am, my dear: come in.

Eleon. My mother is busy, writing——

Dor. Have you any thing to tell me?

Eleon. Forgive my curiosity; have you taken away the jewels?

Dor. Yes; the Count asked for them. Are you vexed?

Eleon. On the contrary, delighted.

Dor. Then you are averse to diamonds?

Eleon. Not at all; but—— You know my secret.

Dor. There are things in expectation, my dear——

Eleon. What, what? Ease my heart, if possible.

Dor. My brother feels you do not love him.

Eleon. That I can easily believe.

Dor. And suspects the Chevalier.

Eleon. Heavens! He will tell my mother!

Dor. Your mother, my dear, must and ought to know it; and you ought to conquer your inclinations.

Eleon. Conquer! Oh! It is not possible.

Dor. I love you, as you know, but cannot——

Eleon. (*suddenly, and looking off*) Ha! I must go.

Dor. What is the matter?

Eleon. (*going*) Don't you see the Chevalier?

Dor. Yes, yes! You are right. Be gone!

Eleon. (*aside and slowly going*) I die to stay.

SCENE X. *Enter the* CHEVALIER.

Chev. Signora—(*discovering* Eleonora) Heavens! Does Eleonora see me and yet go? (*his eyes fixed on* Eleonora.)

Dor. Your pleasure, Signor? (*turns and sees* Eleonora *not gone*) Young lady, your mother expects you.

Eleon. (*timidly*) Pardon me, I would speak one word.

Dor. Well, speak! Make haste!

Eleon. (*gradually approaching*) The jewels will not be returned?

Dor. I do not fear the return *of the jewels.*

Chev. Ladies, if I incommode you, I'll be gone.

Dor. (*a little angry*) As you please, Signor.

Chev. (*going slowly aside*) This treatment is rather severe.

Dor. (*ironically*) Well, Mademoiselle, have you any thing more to say?

Eleon. No, Signora: but—— What offence has the Chevalier committed?

Dor. Really, my dear, you make me smile.

Eleon. I—I cannot smile.

Chev. (*returning after looking into his father's apartment*) My father is not there.

Dor. You will find him at the house of your aunt.

Chev. I just came from there; my aunt and sister are gone out.

Dor. (*more angry*) Young lady.

Eleo. (*mortified, and curtsying; her eyes fixed on the* Chevalier) Pardon me.

Dor. (*ironically*) Excellent, upon my word!

SCENE XI.—*Enter* ARAMINTA.

Aram. (*surprised, aside*) Ah, ha! (*aloud*) The milliner is waiting, daughter: go and look at what she has brought.

                [*Exit* Eleonora, *mortified.*

Aram. Pray stay, Chevalier: I would speak with you.

Dor. Ay, pray do; it is right I should justify myself before you. I see, Madam, you understand what I am not blind to; but I assure you I am no party concerned, and that this meeting, though accidental, I think is highly improper.

Aram. (*kindly taking her hand*) I know you, Madam.

Chev. I am sorry, ladies, I am so unfortunate.

Aram. (*softly to* Dorimene) Do me the pleasure to follow

my daughter. Poor child! I vex her sometimes, but I love her dearly! Try to console her.

Dor. Most willingly, Madam.   [*Exit.*

SCENE XII.   ARAMINTA *and the* CHEVALIER.

Chev. I did not think, Signora, that my conduct——

Aram. Let us speak plainly, Signor. What are your pretensions to my daughter?

Chev. Oh, could I but hope to merit her hand——

Aram. Of yourself, nothing more could be desired: your birth, character, and conduct, are all in your favor; and I should think it an honor to call you my son. Permit me only to say that the affairs of your family——

Chev. I own it. My father is the best of men, but has been greatly mislead.

Aram. Then, being sensible of this truth, you, better than any person, should be aware of the confusion and distress which might be brought on a young woman, of a good family, and with no contemptible fortune. Would you willingly expose this fortune to the evident danger of being ill managed, and soon dissipated?

Cher. Hear me but a moment: I will speak frankly. I have spent some years in the army, which I have been obliged to quit, because I could not properly support my birth, and military rank. Returning home, I have lived privately, without complaint, and concealing my situation. A family friend, interesting himself in my behalf, suggested that a proper marriage might enable me to appear again at my post; and thus excited me to mix with the world, and declare my purpose. I heard of you, Madam, of your daughter's merit, and of the fortune which she was to have. I saw her, and was so enraptured by her charms, and mental qualities, that every interested motive instantly ceased, and love alone took possession of my heart. I then, indeed, wished I were rich, and deeply felt the distress of my family. My friends saw my distress, pitied me, would not forsake me, spoke of your goodness, and encouraged me respectfully to declare myself, and my hopes. I listened to their advice, or rather to love; and hoped that gratitude and respect would, some time, acquire for me a daughter's love, and a kind mother's consent.

Aram. I approve your candor; yet, do not hope I can give you my daughter, though I am greatly affected by your situation, and disposed to favor you, as far as prudence will permit.

Chev. Your goodness consoles me! but, oh Heavens! Do you refuse me that precious gift, your daughter?

Aram. You must not hope to have her, Signor. It may be ten years before you are in a state to marry. Live in freedom, and leave my daughter to her destiny. If you approve it, thus much I can offer. I will lend you the sum necessary to purchase military rank, and even a regiment; depending for repayment upon circumstances, and your word of honor.

Chev. I may die, Madam.

Aram. And I may lose my money; but not the recollection of having done justice to merit, and a worthy gentleman.

Chev. Noble generosity! Yet——Your daughter——

Aram. I speak absolutely—You must not think of her.

Chev. Surely it is possible that love and constancy——

Aram. Let us examine, what sum will you want? You have friends?

Chev. A few.

Aram. I may increase the number. Let us retire where we can speak more freely.

Chev. Wherever you please. (*calls*) Fiorillo!

Aram. Poor youth! The victim of his father's imbecility!

[*Exit.*

SCENE XIII.—*Enter* Fiorillo.

Chev. Hark you, Fiorillo! Tell my father—— Here he comes. I have not time to speak to him. Say I am with the ladies. [*Exit.*

Fior. With the ladies! He is unusually gay. Perhaps his affairs have taken a lucky turn.

SCENE XIV.—*Enter the* Marquis.

Marq. Well, the coachman—— A rascal!—Returned yet?

Fior. The coachman is not to blame, Signor.

Marq. How so? I am—— Good, good, excellent!—All gone out.

Fior. Who, Signor?

Marq. My daughter, and—— What did the dog say? So soon—Zounds!

Fior. You should not be angry, Signor. I met him loaded like a porter: his horses hungry, and not fed, he went to buy corn.

Marq. How?—Very fine—The Count——The stables——

Fior. Oh yes: none can be finer; but without a single oat, nor dare the coachman buy any, without an express order from his master. Oh the miser!

Marq. Who? Who? Good, good, excellent! A miser!

Fior. There is not such another on earth.

Marq. Who, I say? Blockhead! Fool! The Count—a man! —Go, go, numscull!

Fior. Every body I have spoken with in the house, and out of the house, servants, tradesmen, or neighbours, all say the *same.* Nay, Frontino, his chief favourite, can stay with him no longer.

Marq. How! Know—— He refused me his coach.

Fior. From avarice. He walks, for fear of laming his horses.

Marq. A hundred thousand livres in diamonds!

Fior. Yes; the jewels he has showed to his bride——

Marq. Well?

Fior. And which he will never pay for. Frontino told me they were not bought, but borrowed.

Marq. Borrowed! Damn! Good, good, excellent!—A concealed miser—Hypocrite! Damn, damn! A fellow—odious—despicable—My daughter? Oaf! Sup with him?—Great feast—No oats for the horses—Go and see the poor beasts.

Fior. Not that way, Signor. The stables are in the other court.

Marq. Double court—No corn—Great palace—No oats for his horses?   [*Exeunt.*

ACT V.

SCENE I.—*The* COUNT *and* FRONTINO.

Count.

MAKE haste! Place and light those candles, that there may be a splendid illumination!

Front. But I want help, Signor.

Count. Pshaw! Thy activity and talents, Frontino, are quite sufficient.

Front. (*aside*) So much for compliments.

Count. I am vexed at again not finding the Marchioness and her aunt at home. Surely they will come to supper? See how the candles waste; shut the doors and windows.

Front. The evening is so warm!

Count. No matter; do as I bid you.

Front. (*aside*) He has odd modes of saving.

Count. I feel myself quite animated. The supper grand! The illumination grand! The—— Some of my guests, and those not mean ones, will acknowledge and do justice to my dessert. I grant the expence is great, but expence, once properly incurred, will long serve. (*to* Frontino) Should any one ask for me, I am here with the Marquis. (*to himself*) Let me but finish affairs with him, and the difficulty with his daughter will be but little.

SCENE II.—FRONTINO, *and then* FIORILLO.

Front. (*calls*) Fiorillo!

Fior. (*entering*) Here am I. What do you want?

Front. (*giving him a light*) Help me to light the candles.

Fior. Willingly. (*both lighting and speaking fast.*)

Front. Gently! Gently! Mind how you turn that chandelier; the candles are only short bits fastened on coloured sticks.

Fior. Do not fear. I hope we shall sup together?

Front. Should any thing be left. The dishes are large; the contents small.

Fior. We shall have a bottle at least?

Front. Zounds! If we have, I must pay for it.

Fior. Among so many, how can one be missed?

Front. I will tell you. The Count has a bag with a certain number of pellets; one of which he puts in a different bag as the bottles are emptied.

Fior. Oh, the devil!

Front. (*seeing the* Count *return*) Hush!

SCENE III.—*Enter the* COUNT.

Count. (*angry and aside*) Might this be expected? A man of my rank and riches? Rudeness so great! Contempt so visible! Tell me his daughter is not for me! Will not come to supper, and then to sneer and laugh at me! He too! So weak and foolish! Talk of nothing but oats; a reiteration of oats, oats! (*to* Fiorillo *haughtily*) Your master wants you. Go!

Fior. I have had the honor to help my comrade, Signor.

Count. Have the complaisance now to help yourself, and be gone. [*Exit* Fiorillo.

SCENE IV.—*The* COUNT *and* FRONTINO.

Front. (*aside*) We shall have bad weather; there is something new in the wind.

Count. (*to himself*) What a blockhead was I! Absurd design! Is not money worth more than ruined antiquity? Oh yes! I will marry the captious beauty; marry her in despite of her and of myself. No more attentions; no more respectfulness; no more complaisance for any one. (*to* Frontino) Put out the lights.

Front. Put them out, Signor?

Count. Do as you are bid! Make haste!

Front. Very pretty! (*begins to extinguish.*)

Count. (*aside*) Deceive me! Laugh at me! Once more for Madam Araminta. (*to* Frontino) Will you never have done? (*puts out some candles with his hat.*)

Front. But the supper ? Every thing is ready.

Count. How many dishes ?

Front. I have brought out all the silver, as you ordered ; and, large and small, though most of the last, there will be forty.

Count. (*putting out a candle*) They will serve forty days.

Front. But, Signor——

Count. Silence babbler ! (*puts out the last, and they are in the dark.*)

Front. So, here we are, and here we may stay.

Count. Why did you put out the last candle ?

Front. I do not think it was I, Signor.

Count. Go for a light

Front. Nay, but how to find the door.

Count. Stop ! Stop ! I hear somebody.

SCENE V.—*The Stage dark : Enter* FIORILLO.

Fior. What can this mean ? All in total darkness ! Perhaps there will be no supper ?

Front. (*aside to the* Count) I think it is Fiorillo.

Count. (*softly, and holding* Frontino *by the arm*) Stay where you are, and speak as if I were gone. (*aside*) I may make some discovery.

Fior. (*stumbling on* Frontino) Who is there ?

Front. 'Tis I.

Fior. Frontino ! Why have you put out the lights ?

Front. Because—because it was too early.

Fior. 'Sblood ! Your master is a miser indeed.

Front. How ? Jackanapes ! My master a miser !

Fior. Why you told me so yourself.

Count. Ah, rascal ! (*shaking* Frontino.)

Front. Oh the liar ! I capable of——

Fior. Hold your tongue, and patiently hear. I have thought of a way by which you may crib a bottle of wine, in spite of the pellets.

Front. Vile cheat ! What are you talking about ?

Fior. Really, my dear Frontino, you are no longer the same. Change thus in a minute ! You speak as if your master were here.

Front. I speak as I have always spoken. I love my master, obey my master, respect my master, and—and—he's a generous gentleman.

Count. (*shaking him with great anger*) Scoundrel !

Fior. And all you have said of his avarice is false ?

Count. Villain ! (*shaking* Frontino *till he falls.*)

Fior. What now ? Where are you ? What has fallen ?
[*Exit the* Count, *feeling till he finds the door.*

SCENE VI.—FRONTINO *and* FIORILLO, *then the* COUNT.

Front. (*aside*) The devil take you! (*feeling about*) Where are you, Signor?

Fior. Who are you talking to?

Front. Signor, where are you?

Fior. Hey day! You have taken a cup already, my friend.

Front. Ah! Ah! Here he comes. God help my poor back.

Count. (*entering with a candle, speaks softly*) Traitor! Dog! (*aloud*) Hark you, Frontino!

Front. (*afraid*) Ye—ye—yes!

Count. (*aside*) If we were alone! (*aloud*) Go and tell Madam Araminta I wish to speak to her, either in her cabinet or my own.

Front. Yes, Signor. (*aside*) I will not trust his looks. (*to the* Count) Do not think——

Count. (*disdainfully*) Deliver your message.

Front. (*aside*) I see how it is. You must pack off, my friend Frontino. [*Exit.*

SCENE VII.—*The* COUNT *and* FIORILLO.

Fior. You have a faithful servant there, Signor.

Count. You do not know him, friend. An ungrateful fellow, to whom I have been kind and generous in vain. A professed liar! I discovered him, gave him warning; and, to revenge himself, the rascal speaks ill of me. (*going with the light he brought.*)

Fior. Excuse me; this room is dark: permit me to light another candle.

Count. Certainly. I can't tell why they were all put out.

Fior. Frontino is a good servant, and knows how to manage.

Count. (*aside*) The hound! I would send him to the devil if I could find a servant for as little wages. [*Exit.*

SCENE VIII.—FIORILLO, *then the* MARQUIS.

Fior. If I had not got this light, here I might have stayed.

Marq. (*entering*) I should like to know——? (*to* Fiorillo) Did you not say——? Tell him to come here.

Fior. Who, Signor?

Marq. My son.

Fior. Yes. (*aside*) He is not always to be understood. (*aloud*) First suffer me to light a candle.

Marq. Another—I love—— Good, good, excellent! See clear. (*lights a third himself.*)

Fior. Some one may come to put them out.

Marq. Out! Who?

Fior. (*laughing*) The illustrious Count!   [*Exit.*

Marq. True!—The oats.

SCENE IX.—*Enter* ARAMINTA.

Aram. (*speaking as she enters*) He is in his cabinet. Marquis, your obedient——

Marq. Humble servant—All well? All well?

Aram. As you see.

Marq. Good, good, excellent! I wished to—— My son will tell you.

Ardm. Your son, my daughter, and Dorimene, have so stunned and tormented me that I can hear no more.

Marq. If so, Madam—But—you know me—I have not—Very true; but—my property—my estates—Forest, lordship, brooks, waters—High lands, low—Pasture, arable—A barony. Good, good, excellent! Two millions of livres!

Aram. What matter your millions? My husband made a fortune from nothing : you, with millions, are ruined! He took care of his own affairs; I managed the house. But permit me to say, Signor Marquis, in your family all has been disorder.

Marq. The Marchioness, Heaven bless her!—Piquet, basset—Poor woman! Always lost. For my part—the chace—good hounds—fine horses—Then—my son—Good, good, excellent! Oh, a brave boy!—Some day or other—our estates—Ay, ay.

Aram. Had I the management of them, they would soon free themselves.

Marq. Good, good, excellent! Take—act—give 'em up— Oh, with all my heart!

Aram. Surely you do not imagine, Signor Marquis, it becomes me to be an agent?

Marq. Did not say so. You are yet—Your cheeks fresh—I —Not old—Understand me.

Aram. You are jesting.

Marq. Jest when I——? Good, good, excellent!

Aram. I have no intention to marry ; and, if I had, it would not be vain titles, but happiness, that I should seek.

Marq. Right—if you—no one interfere—Mistress of every thing—carte blanche. Good, good, excellent!

Aram. Carte blanche?

Marq. Without restriction.

SCENE X.—*Enter the* CHEVALIER.

Chev. My father sent for me.

Marq. You see, Madam! Only son—Good youth,

Aram. I know it. and know his merit,

Chev. Ah, Madam! (*to the* Marquis) Did you, Sir, know the kindness, the liberality, with which this lady overwhelmed me, how would you be surprised!

Marq. All is concluded. Eleonora—thine. (*overjoyed.*)

Aram. Not too fast, Signor Marquis: I have told you how tenderly I love her, and that I will not risk either her happiness or her fortune.

Marq. But—Speak boy—Our affairs—— Good, good, excellent! Speak the truth; this lady may—— As for me—here I am—My heart, my hand, carte blanche.

Chev. To which, dear father, I willingly subscribe. I leave every thing to your discretion. (*flying to the side scene*) Approach, dear Eleonora; conquer your fears; join your prayers to ours, and move the heart of a mother, who doubts only through delicacy.

[*Enter* Eleonora, *and* Dorimene, *who remains in the back-ground.*

Eleon. (*falling at her mother's feet*) Oh, my mother! You know my heart, and how religiously I have always obeyed your commands. You would unite me to a man whom I can never love: virtuous affection has taken possession of my soul. I ought to have told you, but fear and respect forbade me; yet my feelings, however ardent, I was determined should be sacrificed to obedience to that affection which I have ever felt for you, and that tender attachment in which I have been educated. Ah, do not force me to a marriage I detest, and which will render me the most disconsolate and wretched woman on earth.

Aram. (*aside*) Poor child! Did she know my heart!

Marq. (*wiping his eyes*) Now—if—— Good, good, excellent!

Aram. Be it so on one condition. The carte blanche—

Marq. (*presenting his hand*) Sign it—Pray accept——

Aram. Your hand?

Eleon. My dear mother, your superintending prudence and goodness will secure our felicity.

Chev. Oh yes. Your orders shall be respected; your example the rule for our conduct; your advice our guide.

Aram. (*aside*) My child! My child!

Marq. (*still tenderly presenting his hand*) Madam!

Aram. (*cheerfully*) Signor Marquis—I am yours.

Marq. And I—— Good, good, excellent!

Dor. (*coming forward*) Permit me, ladies and gentlemen, to say I have thus far been silent, being desirous to promote this young lady's happiness: but I think you will remember my brother ought to be, in some degree, consulted in this affair.

Eleon. Heavens! What say you, Madam?

Aram. My daughter should have been his, had he been less pompous.

Marq. And my daughter—But—a miser.

Eleon. (*sees the* Count *coming*) Oh, my mother!

Marq. Fear nothing—I'll speak——Know how—hear me fully—Good, good, excellent!

SCENE XI.—*Enter the* Count, *and afterward* Frontino.

Count. (*aside*) She is here; now is the time to oblige her to determine. (*to* Araminta.) I sent a request, Madam——

Aram. I was coming, but was stopt by the Marquis.

Marq. Yes, Signor Count, I have to inform you——

Count. Pardon me, Signor: I have business with this lady. (*to* Araminta.) The notary will soon be here, and we must sign the contract.

Aram. And do you still persist to claim my daughter? Have you not renounced her?

Count. No, Signora. My design, of which my sister may have informed you, was to propose conditions honorable to all parties; but these the Marquis disapproves.

Marq. Hear me speak. You required——if you had—— Why not? But oblige me so far—Good, good, excellent! No anger—A hundred thousand livres, diamonds, and—Oats— Oats!

Count. Why do you thus reiterate oats? I cannot comprehend you; can you, ladies?

Dor. (*to the* Count) Your coachman, brother, may have refused—

Count. (*to the* Marquis) How! Have your horses not been fed? If so, am I responsible for my coachman's error? Must I be thought a miser—I—(*aside*) My servants have babbled, and I shall lose my reputation,

Front. (*entering to the* Count) Persons without are asking for you, Signor.

Count. (*aside*) My supper guests perhaps: the moment is favorable to the support of my honor. (*aloud*) Is the notary among them?

Front. Yes, Signor.

Count. Bid him come in. Show the other persons into the billiard-room. Let the house be illuminated and the supper served.   [*Exit* Frontino,

Marq. Good, good, excellent!

SCENE—*The Last.*

Enter the Notary, *the* Jeweller, Giacinto, *and Others.*

Count. (*to the* Notary) Signor, please to read the contract, that it may be signed. So, Signor Giacinto, you have discovered that my bride is better, and that the supper will take place.

Giac. No, Signor, I have made no such discovery. But I have discovered some literary gentlemen, who, since I am not enabled to print my comedy and your genealogy, will publish the genealogy at their own expence, with all necessary and some remarkable annotations.

Count. (*enraged*) I comprehend him. (*dissembling*) Have you the genealogy in your pocket?

Giac. Here it is, Signor.

Count. (*receiving and concealing the MS.*) Signor—I have a proper esteem for talents——they have ever been encouraged and recompensed by me. (*aside*) A mercenary scoundrel! (*whispers* Giacinto) Accept these five and twenty *Louis*, and let me hear no more. (*tears the paper.*) [*Exit* Giacinto.

Aram. (*aside*) What a man! He would quickly have scattered my daughter's fortune.

Count. (*to the Notary*) Once more, the contract.

Jew. (*advancing with a bow*) Signor Count.

Count. How now! What do *you* want.

Jew. Permission to speak.

Count. (*softly to the* Jeweller) I desired you to come in a week.

Jew. 'Tis true. But hearing you are this evening to be affianced, permit me to observe that, after my jewels have been seen——

Count. Ay, ay. (*vexed and aside*) The rascal knows what he is about. (*privately returns the jewels and angrily whispers*) Here, take your diamonds, and trouble me no more.

[*Exit* Jeweller.

Front. (*entering*) The supper is ready: must it be served?

Count. Wait till I call you. Once more, the contract: with your leave, Madam, we will read it that it may be signed.

Aram. Signor, while I was a widow the power was my own, but now I am once more married.

Count. Married! Who is your husband, Madam?

Marq. Good, good, excellent!—Yes, Signor, 'tis I.

Count. (*aside*) Here's a blow! Oh, all hopes are gone! (*aloud*) Then Eleonora——

Aram. I love my daughter too much to willingly part with her: once to-day you have refused her hand, which I shall now give to——

Marq. Good, good, excellent!—To my son.

Count. (*to* Dorimene *indignantly*) I am derided, sister, disdained.

Dor. I warned you, brother, yet you would persist. Be prudent: you are in the presence of many people; do not risk your reputation.

Count. (*aside*) Very true. Suffer what I will, I must dissemble. (*aloud*) You're happily come, ladies and gentlemen, to witness to the signing of a contract between—the——the Chevalier del Bosco and this young lady. (*aside*) My tongue is parched : I have not the power to proceed. (*aloud*) The honor of contributing to this—ceremony—is mine. (*aside*) Oh, that the house were on fire! (*aloud*) Let us walk into the library till the supper is ready.

Aram.   Ay, ay, Ostentation to the last.

Marq.   Avarice! Avarice!   [*Exeunt omnes.*

THE END.

REMARKS.

THE foregoing piece contains a fund of comic humour, which gives great pleasure to the accurate observer of the human heart ; but the humour it displays is seldom of that bold nature to which our theatres give the loudest applause. The characters are well imagined, but not strongly drawn ; and they are so contrasted as to relieve each other. The vices of avarice and ostentation, existing in the same person, are frequently seen in society ; but they rather assume a littleness of manner, by tempering each other, than acquire those decided and broad features, which at one moment excite great laughter, and at another not less surprise. To represent a man whose usual manners are those of a gentleman, but at times those of extravagant ostentation, combined with equally extravagant avarice, is no easy task either for an author or a performer. Araminta is opposed to the Count so as to produce, in a certain degree, the ridiculous parts of both characters : but her rigid adherence to economy is so nearly allied to sound understanding, that it is difficult to give it an air of caricature, and not to injure common sense and morality. The Marquis del Bosco, whose mind is in a continual state of clear confusion, that is of perfectly understanding itself without the faculty or ability to make itself understood, being too much in a hurry ever to finish a sentence, is a faithful transcript of what is often seen. It also conveys a fine moral truth, to which GOLDONI does not sufficiently advert : that is, that confusion is the sure parent of misfortune. The affairs of the Marquis are in the most disorderly and ruinous state : the poet seemed, rather intuitively than positively, to know that so the affairs of a man, whose understanding was of this kind, must be. The generosity of Araminta to the Chevalier by no means subtracts from the humor (which might easily be made more prominent) that rises out of her habits of thinking and acting. It may not be improper to observe that all the plays which have appeared, or are likely to appear, in this work, may afford, not only excellent hints, but, materials more than half formed for dramatic writers. As the numbers increase, they will contain an increasing fund of intellectual wealth, lying at the free disposal of literary talent.

DRAMATIC BIOGRAPHY.

ABSTRACT OF THE LIFE OF GOLDONI.

THIS author has himself written his life, in three small octavo volumes, which are prefixed to his works: at least to the edition printed at Venice, in 1788. That city gave him birth, in the year 1707: his father (a physician) and mother both inherited small fortunes; but the fortune of the father had been greatly impaired, and that of his mother and aunt lay chiefly at Venice. His parents were great lovers of theatrical exhibitions, and particularly his grandfather, who had comedies and operas performed in his house, and actors, singers, and musicians, as his frequent guests. Children always imitate that which most amuses them, and that which they most frequently see. Goldoni, speaking of himself, says—" Among the comic " authors, whose works I continually read, I preferred those " of Cicognini." This Florentine, little known in the Republic of Letters, wrote many comedies, of much intrigue, intermingled with weeping pathos, and trivial humor *: but they were very interesting; he having the art to excite suspense, and give pleasure by the denouement. To him, therefore, I

---

* *Miste di patetico lagrimoso, e di comico-triviale.*

" was greatly attached, and studied him so much that, when
" eight years old, I had the temerity to draw the sketch of a co-
" medy. My governess thought it very fine, my aunt jeered
" me, my mother reproved but at the same time kissed me,
" and my preceptor affirmed that it contained wit and common
" sense too great to have been hoped from such a child. As
" for my godfather, who had more gold than understanding,
" he would never believe the work to be mine, but affirmed it
" had been revised and corrected by my preceptor.

" The dispute on this subject became too warm, but was
" luckily interrupted by a third person, who was the Abbate
" Valle of Bergamo, a friend of the family, who had seen me
" working at my comedy, and had witnessed my flights and
" fancies. I had prayed him not to mention it. He silenced
" the disputants, and did me justice."

Goldoni says that, in the edition of his works printed by
Pasquali, he had cited the name of the Abbate Valle, who
was still living in the year 1770, in proof of this fact; thinking he might have more friends and relations, by whom it would
not be believed. He further tells us this comedy, or rather
this puerile attempt, was read by all the society who visited
his mother.

After receiving a good education, Goldoni was induced by
his parents to study the law : but, previous to this, Goldoni gives
some anecdotes of himself that deserve to be known.

In the Pope's dominions, women are not suffered to appear
on the stage ; and he had a principal woman's part given him
to perform with the prologue to speak. " This prologue was
" of so singular a kind," says Goldoni, " that I have never for-
" gotten it : literature had become so corrupt that poetry and
" prose were alike subject to bombast : metaphor, hyperbole,
" and antithesis, held the place of common sense. This bad
" taste existed as late as the year 1720 : the following is the
" manner in which I had to address my auditors—' Oh, most
' benignant Heaven, from the rays of your resplendent sun,
' you behold us, butterflies, who, on the feeble wings of our
' conception, take flight toward so beautiful a luminary.' He

adds, " this fine prologue produced a shower of comfits, with
" which the theatre was inundated, and I almost blinded; such
" being the common manner of giving applause in the states
" of the Pope."

Being at *Rimini*, where he was under the care of the professor *Candini*, Goldoni relates the manner in which he became
acquainted with a company of comedians. Their season at
Rimini was nearly over, and the Director, or Manager, informed
him they were soon to remove to *Chiozza*, where they were to
play a few days; and that they should afterward go to Venice.
" To Chiozza!" exclaimed Goldoni.: " my mother, whom I
" long to see, is at Chiozza." Hearing this, the comedians all
loudly called come! come with us, on board of our bark!
You shall be well received and pay nothing; excepting by
helping us to joke, laugh, and sing. " Such an invitation,"
adds Goldoni, " could not be refused. The day came, the co-
" medians were ready, and, when they saw me, they began to
" cry Goldoni! Goldoni! Thus laughing, feasting, and caressing
" me, the sails were set, and farewel to Rimini."

Of the pleasures of this little voyage he gives an animated
picture. On the fourth day, they arrived at Chiozza; and, being fearful he had acted rashly, he entreated the Manager to
accompany him to his mother. Being at her house, they entered, and Goldoni remained in an an anti-chamber, while the
manager went and spoke to his mother. Signora, said he, I
come from Rimini, and bring news of your son—Indeed? How
does he do?—In perfect health—Is he happy?—So so, Signora—
What is the matter?—He longs to see his dear mother—Poor
boy! I wish he were here! (I, says Goldoni, stood listening with
a beating heart)—I offered to bring him here—And why did
not he come, Signor?—Should you be glad to see him?—No
doubt!—But his studies?—He may return to them: beside,
masters are every where to be procured—Then the sight of
him would make you happy?—Beyond expression!—Behold
him, Signora!

" Saying this, he opened the door; I ran into my mother's arms,
" and while she kissed me tears would not suffer her to speak,

"This was a theatrical scene, to which the stage director was "accustomed."

During the progress of his studies, Goldoni relates various adventures, interesting scenes, and critical situaations, from which he sometimes escaped with difficulty. He was several times in danger from artful women, had once determined to become a Capuchin friar, was stimulated, by his parents and friends to study the law, and enjoyed places of some diplomatic importance. The theatre excepted, the law appears to have been his most serious study; and, through the chief part of life, he bore the appellation of the Advocate Goldoni. His first and reigning inclination finally prevailed, and he devoted himself so entirely to the stage that the number of his dramatic works, in the edition of Venice already cited, is almost incredible. Tragedies and comedies in verse, comedies in prose, musical operas, farces, after-pieces, and interludes, amounting to little less than two hundred *, beside those which it seems have never yet been printed, prove the fecundity of his mind, and the prodigious facility with which he wrote.

His chief labors were for the theatres at Venice: he excelled in the Venetian dialect, but, being ambitious to write pure Tuscan, he made many efforts to attain purity; and wrote many comedies to prove it attained, by the reading of which a foreigner, at least, is satisfied they were not written in vain. But, on purity of diction, it very rarely happens that a foreigner can give a just opinion.

In the early part of life, he visited most of the chief cities of Italy, and, while he attentively studied men and manners, could not fail to highly profit by these excursions. After the numerous pieces he had given to the Italian Theatres, and particularly to those of Venice, he was pressingly invited, in the year 1760, to make a journey to Paris; for which city he

---

* It may be more: they are in forty-four volumes; and each volume, when the pieces are of a regular kind, usually contains four: but in some the number is increased. Those which Goldoni calls tragedies are some, if not all of them, a species of heroic drama.

departed, in April 1761, being greatly excited by curiosity, yet deeply regretting to quit the place at which he had gained so much fame. There was a company of Italian players, at Paris, who were desirous of better success, and who imagined it would be secured by the name and talents of Goldoni. It afterward, however, appeared that these hopes were not fully answered; but it also appears that the fault was not with the poet: it rather lay with the public, who could not be expected to understand or enjoy comedies written in a foreign language, equal to those which were nightly before them, in their native tongue.

The genius of Goldoni, though repulsed, was not subdued; for, while in Paris, he wrote a charming little comedy in French, called *Le Bourreau Bienfaisant*, which not only gave infinite pleasure on its first appearance, but which still keeps and will long continue to keep its due rank upon the stage. To write a highly successful comedy in a foreign language affords an undeniable proof of superior powers of mind.

A man like Goldoni could not fail to find protectors among the great, at Paris, where people of rank had long made it one source of gratification to notice and promote the interests of men, whose literary abilities were in high esteem: he was recommended to the royal family, and many years remained preceptor in the Italian language to some of the princesses. I believe he never again revisited his native country; but of this I do not speak with certainty; nor have I any document before me of the year in which he died. In the last chapter of his Memoirs, however, he says, " Behold me arrived at the year " 1787, and the eightieth of my age." In the same chapter he tells us that, having been lately ill, Count Alfieri* paid him a visit; and adds that Sophocles and Euripides were the models of this great poet. Of his own comedies he says—" the appli- " cation which I gave to the writing of them was that which " nature inspired." In the preceding sentence he had indeed said—" I am much more indebted to nature than to study †."

---

* Of whose life an abstract was given in the preceding number.

† If any correspondent will kindly indicate where documents of the death of Goldoni may be found, it will be esteemed a great favor.

BIOGRAPHICAL ABSTRACT

OF THE LIFE OF JOHN TOBIN, ESQ. AUTHOR OF THE NEW
PLAY CALLED " THE HONEY MOON."

JOHN TOBIN was born, January 28th, 1770, at Salisbury.
The maiden name of his mother was Elizabeth Webbe, a
West Indian, and by her he was the third son of James
Tobin, born in London, but an inhabitant of the island
of Nevis. Quitting England for the West Indies, his parents sent him and his two elder brothers to the free-school
of Southampton, where he remained seven years, and was
afterward pupil to the reverend Mr. Lee of Bristol, in
which city his father, returning from the Indies, embarked
in a commercial partnership. Not having been bred to commerce, his father in early life had been devoted to the pursuit
of the liberal arts, and the taste of the son was improved by
residing in his father's house. His inclination, however, for
the law, to which profession he was destined, was by no means
increased. He was for a short period with a Mr. Gautier, who
taught French at Bristol. In 1785, he was articled to an
eminent solicitor of Lincoln's Inn.

After the death of that gentleman, he became a partner with
three other clerks in the office; but, disagreements happening
which ended in a chancery suit, he entered into a new firm with
his friend Mr. Ange.

Finding his health decline, by the advice of his physicians he
went, in 1803, and resided with a relation in Cornwall; but his
disorder assuming the form of consumption, he was induced, in
November 1804, at the earnest solicitation of his friends, to embark at Bristol for the West Indies, hoping benefit from a
warmer climate. In the same ship was the wife of a valued
friend, suffering under the same disease and buoyed up by the
same hopes. Detained at Cork some days, the vessel sailed
from that port on the 7th of December, and on that day
he died. Contrary winds obliged the ship to return to the
Cove of Cork, and he was attended to his grave by the friend
who had accompanied him on this short voyage. Previous to

this disease, his health generally appeared good; but he was always of a spare habit, and, when a boy, indisposed to violent and muscular exercises. When at school he was quick in acquiring lessons, tranquil of disposition, and prone neither to give nor take offence. Delighting to indulge in reverie, his pursuits were of a peaceable and literary kind. On the banks of the Avon, near Salisbury, where he spent his holidays with his grandfather, he acquired a love of angling, to which he was ever afterward devoted; and his ardor for it was increased by the few opportunities in which it could be indulged. Averse to walking, unless when he had a strong motive, his hours were lost in thought, or in the creations of an active mind. Abstracted and constitutionally indolent, he was alike apt to forget forms and neglect pecuniary concerns; yet, having a high sense of moral duty, he never broke even trifling engagements. Of inflexible integrity himself, he detested selfishness, and carefully avoided men of hollow principles, however bland their manners, or brilliant their accomplishments. By taking a part in school performances, and visiting the theatre at Southampton, he acquired a taste for the drama, and his first piece was written before the year 1789. Constantly engaged after this period in dramatic compositions, they were offered to the theatres, but were all rejected except a comedy called The Pharo Table, which was accepted at Drury-lane, though never performed. On quiting London, he left the Honey Moon, the last piece he had finished, with his brother: they had resided ten years together, united by kindred feelings and similarity of sentiment and pursuit. To this brother, who had so often been his unsuccessful negociator at the theatres, he committed the care of bringing the piece on the stage, having received a promise from the manager that it should be performed.

For a mind like his, the court of Chancery had few charms; nor did he follow his profession with that zeal which can this way acquire wealth and fame; but he loved independence, had a just sense of duty, and was punctual, while in health, in attending at the office. His mind indeed might be absent, and when he left the place he ceased to think of such business.

The Pharo Table was chiefly written in bed, during illness, in the year 1795; and his other pieces, between the hours of nine and twelve, after his return from Lincoln's Inn. He frequently composed while walking the streets, and especially songs, which he usually committed to writing when he came home. Animated by society and enjoying rational conversation, yet, as solitude never displeased him, he did not anxiously seek company; though always happy to see a few valued friends, their absence was never perceptible. Unruffled by the accidents of life, possessed of fortitude not easily shaken, and with a mind never unemployed, he was subject to no fits of weariness. " He was altogether the happiest man I ever knew *." Though the progress of the disease alarmed him, he contemplated death without fear or superstition. Hope and fancy pictured to him his future success on the stage, while his bodily powers were wasting and his energies daily on the decline. " He died without a groan." While at Falmouth, he revised some of his works, and wrote notes on Shakspeare, intending to contribute to a new edition of our immortal bard. Two of his unfinished plays it was his intention to complete in the West Indies. A constant reader of Beaumont and Fletcher, and the writers of that age, he was no less an admirer of Farquar and some of his contemporaries. He also read some Spanish comedies, but found little to admire except the ingenuity of their plots. Genuine comedy he supposed might yet find support from the public, and a better taste be revived, notwithstanding the mercenary motives by which it continues to be depraved. Deeply sensible of the moral influence of the drama, he scorned to flatter the base prejudices or the sickly imaginations of the great vulgar or the small.

---

* These are his brother's words.

PIECES

THE HONEY MOON:

A COMEDY, IN FIVE ACTS, BY THE LATE JOHN TOBIN, ESQ.

THIS Comedy appeared at the Theatre Royal, Drury Lane, on the 31st of January, where it was highly and deservedly applauded. It may be said to form an epocha in the annals of the drama, by being a modern attempt to revive the manner of writing which prevailed in the sixteenth century. In his plan the author has totally, and, were but common sense our guide, justly disregarded the vaunted unities of time and place; but, for the greater perfection of his piece, he neglected, that which ought to be sacredly observed in dramatic composition, the unity of action, as it has been named by critics, but which would be more intelligible to young students were it rigidly inculcated as the unity of fable. By this it is understood that there should be but one story, and that every character introduced in a piece should concur in promoting one grand design.

Against this rule also the author has egregiously erred. Instead of one, there are three stories, and as many designs: a design to make a lively coquet play on the feelings of her lover; a design to ridicule and subdue a woman-hater; and a design to correct the haughty and angry temper of a termagant.

This last is the principal design; and in the manner of executing it, the appropriate nature and pleasantry of the sentiments, and the flowing and frequently poetical diction of the author, the sterling merit of the play consists. The plan of the fable is so far from new that it appears to be an absolute imitation of Shakspeare, not only in the characters of the Duke and Juliana, who are literally Catherine and Petruchio drawn in a different point of view, but of Zamora, who is as truly a transcript of Viola in Twelfth Night. In the management of the principal plan, when the scene changes from the palace to the cottage, we are no less forcibly reminded of Rule a Wife and have a Wife, by Beaumont and Fletcher. The imitations, through the whole play, of the authors of that age are too numerous to be cited; but they are frequently so happily made, and often executed with such an air of originality, that, instead of being blemishes, they seem to stamp a sterling merit, and to purify the dramatic gold that had so long and so basely been alloyed.

The Honey Moon possesses another antique novelty: it is chiefly written in blank verse, but interspersed with scraps of prose, which an attentive reader is apt to suspect the author at first intended to versify. He has managed this peculiarity with so great a knowledge, of the blank verse which is proper for the stage, that it possesses so much ease and fluency as not to be perceptible as verse, except to delicate and critical auditors.

Of the execution of the three designs it may be said, that the manner of taming the shrew, which is the chief, gratifies while it delights; that the ridicule thrown on the woman-hater, which the author appears to have intended to make no less effective, is sometimes insipid, and in a place or two offensive; and that the sportiveness of the coquet, in the third plan, is a relief to the moroseness of the shrew.

An incident is introduced in the beginning of the fourth act, of a hostess and an apothecary, who conspire to cheat Balthazar, the father of the three heroines, of his money, by giving him improper medicines after a fall from his horse, to detain him as a guest and patient; and of making him, after having listened to their scheme, oblige the apothecary to swallow his own drugs. This scene, all together, gave displeasure. Dramatic authors should remember that, to introduce an extravagant and almost farcical incident, unless it forcibly and naturally arises out of the subject, is always a very dangerous experiment.

As the poetry of the piece forms one of its striking beauties, to cite a few of the poetical passages may please the reader, or afford him an opportunity of judging should he differ in opi-

ʜion.   In Act I. Rolando, the woman-hater, is seeking for a
simile to a woman's tongue, and his companion asks him,

> *Count.*   Have you found it ?
> *Rol.*   Humph ! Not exactly.   Something like a smoke-jack ;
> For it goes ever without winding up :
> But that wears out in time—there fails the simile.
> Next I bethought me of a water-mill ;
> But that stands still on Sundays : woman's tongue
> Needs no reviving Sabbath.   And beside,
> A mill, to give it motion, waits for grist :
> Now, whether she has aught to say or no,
> A woman's tongue will go for exercise.
> In short, I came to this conclusion :
> Most earthly things have their similitudes,
> But woman's tongue is yet incomparable.

In Act II. Scene III. Balthazar goes in search of his daughter, and the Count says,

> I'll bear you company :
> And as the traveller, perplex'd a while
> In the benighted mazes of a forest,
> Breaks on a champaign country, smooth and level,
> And sees the sunshine glorious, so shall you, Sir,
> Behold a bright close and a golden end
> To this now dark adventure.

The following is a fine drawn picture of the follies in which
the wealthy indulge : it is near the end of the second Act.

> Who then, that has a taste for happiness,
> Would live in a large mansion, only fit
> To be a habitation for the winds ;
> Keep gilded ornaments for dust and spiders ;
> See ev'ry body, care for nobody;   [*feeble*]
> Lose the free use of limbs, by being mewed up
> In a close carriage, next to being bed-rid,
> As if, like mummies, we should fall to pieces
> By taking air ; and, above all, be pester'd
> With those voracious vermin call'd attendants.

At the close of the third Act, the Duke gives the following beautiful picture :

> Thus modestly attir'd,
> A half-blown rose stuck in thy braided hair,
> With no more diamonds than those eyes are made of,
> No deeper rubies than compose thy lips,
> Nor pearls more precious than inhabit them,
> With the pure red and white which that same hand
> That blends the rainbow mingles in thy cheeks,
> This well-proportion'd form (think not I flatter)
> In graceful motion to harmonious sounds,
> And thy free tresses dancing in the wind,—
> Thou'lt fix as much observance, as chaste dames
> Can meet, without a blush.

Many more citations might be made, but the above are sufficient to show the poetical talent of the author.

It is unfortunate that the most pernicious moral is inculcated by this comedy, that of deceiving the mind into virtue, or of doing harm that good may be the result. The Duke, having married a shrew, descends to a continued course of deception, and, without any scruple, repeatedly tells direct falsehoods, that by these means he may reform his wife. The most clear and understanding moralists have maintained, that good ends are not to be produced by such means, and to induce men to make use of them is to administer poison to morality. It has too long been supposed, by dramatic writers, that the grossest falsehood on the stage was merely sport; it ought rather to be plainly made evident that, when falsehood is practised, the consequences are evil.

The three young ladies are all daughters of Balthazar, a painter, of whose great excellence in his art or renown not a word is said; how he came to have Captains, Counts, and Dukes for sons-in-law, and how the three ladies are each so exceedingly different in character from the two others, may be questionable, but likewise may easily be overlooked. Truth requires it to be said of this comedy, that its merits and defects are each of them great, but that the merits are so uncommon that the defects are cheerfully pardoned.

The performers in general were happy in their parts; but Mr. Elliston and Miss Duncan have never perhaps been seen to greater advantage. Miss Mellon scarcely deserves less praise; and, though Miss De Camp did not gain so much applause, it was not from want of talent, but because the part of a love-sick virgin is but ill adapted to her sprightly and playful mind.

An account of the author, the late Mr. John Tobin, has already been given.

THE LADY OF THE ROCK:

A MELO-DRAME, IN TWO ACTS,

PERFORMED FEBRUARY 12, 1805, AT THE THEATRE ROYAL, DRURY LANE.

As the author of this Melo-Drame and the present work is avowedly the same, the account which can best be given in this place is perhaps contained in the advertisement prefixed to the piece itself, which is as follows:

" In a work of great literary utility, called the Annual Re-
" view, edited by Mr. Arthur Aikin, I happened accidentally
" to see an account there given of the Honorable Mrs. Mur
" ray's Guide to the Western Islands of Scotland; in which
" the subject and part of the story of the following Drama
" may be seen. She relates that one of the Macleans, of
" Duart, was married to a handsome and amiable, but, unhap-
" pily, a barren sister of Argyle; that, in those days, barren-
" ness was a high crime in a husband's eyes; that Maclean,
" being determined on her destruction, ordered ruffians to con-
" vey her secretly to a place now called the Lady's Rock,
" which stood nearly opposite to his castle, on a promontory
" in Mull; that she was seen by mariners, who saved and
" conveyed her to her brother, at Inverary; that her husband
" made a grand mock funeral, wrote disconsolate letters to her

" relations, and went in deep mourning to Inverary, to his
" brother-in-law, lamenting, with every show of grief, the
" irreparable loss he had sustained; that Argyle said little,
" but sent for his sister, whose sudden appearance electrified
" the husband; that, being a mild and amiable man, Argyle
" took no revenge, except by commanding Maclean to depart
" instantly, humanely advising him to avoid his brother,
" Donald; and that Sir Donald Campbell afterward stabbed
" Maclean, in a street at Edinburgh, when he was eighty
" years of age.

" The Review observes—' This tale might be dramatized
" with very powerful effect, by a skilful writer.'

" At first, I thought otherwise: an audience would not at
" present listen to a husband, who should complain of the
" crime of being barren; and the incidents, though highly
" dramatic, were insulated, unconnected, and one of them,
" that of exhibiting the distress of the Lady on the Rock,
" appeared too difficult for stage scenery. This opinion I
" afterward changed, and produced the piece which is now
" before the public.

" In the play-bills, it is announced as a piece of three acts;
" the reason of which is, the change of scene from the storm to
" the mountains of Scotland requires time; and it was thought
" much more advisable to make a pause, after the storm scene,
" than to introduce dialogue that might prove either insipid
" or irrelavent: as the utmost caution has been taken, in writ-
" ing the piece, not to say a single word that should not aid in
" giving effect to the story.

" I had originally drawn Dugald that which I thought and
" still think the most natural, an unrelenting villain, who
" made a last attempt to stab his brother, and expired uttering
" curses; but perhaps it is a pleasure to find that hardened
" villainy is so offensive, to public feeling, it could scarcely be
" endured. On the first night, the death of Dugald put the
" piece in some little danger. There was no difficulty in
" making the change, as it is now printed.

" I intended to convey a public moral, and teach parents

" the vice of encouraging their children to be spies, when I
" conceived and gave a sketch of a lovely little girl, innocently
" betraying her mother, for whom she had the tenderest affec-
" tion : but this likewise gave a slight degree of offence, and
" I curtailed the part of the child : for dramatic authors must
" not reason, but comply with the public feeling.

" Enough can scarcely be said in praise of Mr. Johnston,
" the machinist of Drury Lane Theatre, by whose invention
" such apparent reality and distress are given to the Rock
" Scene. Expedients to suggest a storm have long been in
" the possession of the Theatre, but no example was ever
" before afforded of such agitation and terror excited by the
" elements, and of water rising to overwhelm a rock that
" appeared to defy their fury.

" To the ladies and gentlemen, who perform in the piece,
" I sincerely return my cordial thanks : their exertions were
" as friendly and as zealous as they have been successful. The
" powers of different performers are and have always been
" greater and less ; but in their endeavours on this occasion
" they were most amicably united."

TOO MANY COOKS:

A COMIC OPERA, IN TWO ACTS, BY MR. KENNY.

THIS Opera appeared at Covent Garden, on the same evening that the Lady of the Rock was brought forward at Drury
Lane, but was not received with sufficient approbation to
render it attractive, and was therefore withdrawn after the
third night. The author alleges, with great justice, that, if a
piece be written purposely for certain performers, and that, by
any accident whatever, those performers do not accept the
characters designed for them, his intentions are not executed.
Mr. Kenny wished to have withdrawn the piece till circumstances should have been more favorable, but was persuaded
to the contrary, though, when he yielded, he foresaw the
consequences.

TO MARRY, OR NOT TO MARRY:

A COMEDY, OF FIVE ACTS, BY MRS. INCHBALD.

ON Saturday evening, February 16, this Piece appeared at
the Theatre Royal, Covent Garden, and was received throughout with great applause, and with scarcely an audible mark of
disapprobation. The title precisely expresses the tendency of
the piece: the struggle of a man, with himself, concerning
marriage. Sir Oswyn Mortland is a baronet and bachelor, some
years turned of thirty, an orator in parliament, a man enamoured of literature and in habits of retirement, accustomed
to reason on marriage, and consider it as a thing, good perhaps
in itself, but, absurd for him, whose delight is in his library,
and who feels an aversion to be interrupted by female activity,
curiosity, or even affection; amiable of heart, but morose if
intruded upon, as he shows when his uncle enters, and still
more to his sister; and finally apt to be irritated at whatever
disturbs him in his favorite reveries: such is the hero in whom
the interest of the piece almost exclusively centers.

The thing intended to be proved, in the development of
this character, is that recluse men have little regard for, because
they have little intercourse with, women; and that they can
love, even violently, when that kind of woman appears whose
mien and manners do not offend their peculiarities.

To draw this character is by no means a new attempt upon
the stage. The Epicene of Ben Jonson is of that class of comedy; but, still more directly, LOVE MAKES A MAN, or THE
FOP's FORTUNE, by Cibber; and *Le Philosophe marié*, by Nericault
Destouches. Cibber had but imitated Beaumont and Fletcher:
while Mrs. Inchbald has adapted the comedy of Destouches to
the English stage, and, in the year 1789, gave it to be performed at the Theatre Royal, in the Haymarket, under the title
of THE MARRIED MAN. These things are mentioned, not as
derogatory, but, by way of opportunity to remark that it is
absurd to criticize the want of novelty in a subject; the manner of treating it is what ought alone to be considered: for an

old subject is frequently so managed as to give it entirely a different face; better, or worse, as it may happen. Voltaire openly and expressly treated the subjects that had been forestalled by his great rival, Crebillon; and that were then actually before the public. For this some persons accused him of encouraging a spirit of jealousy: it was at least a spirit of emulation; and, as it proved, a conscious superiority.

To display the power of love, or, in more philosophical language, the predominant propensity that man and woman have to each other, Sir Oswyn is exhibited as of somewhat an imperious, resentful, and persecuting spirit, and, by persecution, as having made a mortal enemy of a Mr. Lavensforth, whom he had driven from England, reduced to many distresses, and implanted in his bosom a still higher degree of rancour.

Hester, the only child of this Mr. Lavensforth, is the heroine who ensnares Sir Oswyn's affections, subdues his habits and passions, and makes them all resolve into and even strengthen the passion of love. The simplicity of her appearance first attracts his notice; her orphan state, her want of protectors to rescue her from a marriage she hates, and the artless yet understanding manner in which she answers, first fix his attention, and give him feelings such as he had never before known. These are increased by various incidents, by which love is gradually augmented, till it becomes too powerful for any resistance.

His uncle, Lord Danberry, had extorted a promise from him that, since it was necessary he should have an heir to his estate, he would marry any woman of his recommending; and the uncle, foreseeing that he would yield, which foresight, be it remarked, Sir Oswyn's character considered, offends probability, had brought down Lady Susan Courtly for that very purpose. Lady Susan, on her part, is so determined to marry Sir Oswyn, that she is something like a dun who will take no denial.

Lavensforth returns to England, retires to a hermitage in the neighbourhood of Sir Oswyn, makes an implacable, and surely an offensive, vow to plant a dagger in his enemy's heart; and

that in the presence and hearing of a negro servant, who proposes to commit the murder himself, and save his master, and
thus raises a kind of horrid suspense by rancour so black and
villainous. He likewise dispatches a letter to his daughter,
which she receives in the presence of Sir Oswyn, whose jealousy is excited, understanding that it comes from a man the
name of whom she will not declare, although she must give him
the meeting. Luckily, for an excuse to his inclinations, the
night is dark, and he insists upon accompanying her till she shall
be out of danger. He is shot on the road, and deeply wounded,
as he supposes, by a highwayman, but, in reality, by the negro,
who afterward tells his master he had discovered it was Sir Oswyn. Improbability likewise attaches itself to all the incidents of
the negro. By this expedient, however, the denouement is artfully and finely effected. With revenge so implacable, it was
difficult to foresee how the author could produce a reconciliation between Sir Oswyn and Lavensforth; but the latter, not
recognizing the person of the baronet in a dark wood, there
meets him wounded, administers every office of humanity with
every expression of sympathy, binds up his wound, leads him
into his hermitage, and consigns him to repose. It is then that
he learns from his negro Sir Oswyn is in his power; and in
the first moment his exultation is great, but at the next the
thought of murdering a wounded man under his own roof
shocks every sentiment of honor, and he resolves first to set
him free.

Sir Oswyn comes from the hermitage, almost recovered,
without time or medical aid, and Lavensforth declares himself
and his purpose. Refusing to profit by his momentary cle-
mency, the baronet draws the pistols he had taken with him
to guard Hester, presents the choice of them to Lavensforth,
and, by the dignity of his sentiments, the fortunate arrival of
Hester, and the discovery that Sir Oswyn had been her protector, and was her lover, so entirely softens the odious hatred
that had existed as to induce a frank and perfect reconciliation.

There is an elegant simplicity in the general plan and conduct of this comedy, which, could it have been entirely pre-

served, would have given it a very high value, but some of the frivolous circumstances attending Willowwear, Lady Susan, and other parts, are to the spectator, and must be to the reader, so many insipidities that divert the mind from the story, without the power of affording any adequate amusement; but, as they are not often intruded, Mrs. Inchbald no doubt had a latent consciousness of their true nature. There are many vapid follies which have not sufficient force to excite attention when noticed either in life or exhibited on the stage, and on these dramatic writers too frequently rest the success of their productions. Mrs. Inchbald has rather chosen to depend on the everlasting sources of passion, mingled with the no less everlasting sources of prejudice, from the due mixture of which all humor, wit, satire, and passion result. Sound judgment, a refined taste, and delicacy of feeling, have generally been her guides; for whose sake the deviations into which she has occasionally strayed, though they should not be overlooked, should freely be pardoned. Among dramatic authors, to make females court men, and declare, with very little reserve, the great inclination they have to be married, is a common practice. Is it not a common fault? In a pure state of morals it might be none; but while legal marriages shall continue necessary, for the preservation of society, as they most undoubedly are, while prejudices lead the imagination astray, and while decency and propriety of conduct are no less requisite to make women happy, than gentleness, faith, and affection, it is dangerously to mislead, and in any given case certain to injure them, should they be thus instructed to throw off at present all that reserve which their mothers once held as their indispensable and certain guardian. Mrs. Inchbald has not gone so far in this respect as others, but surely too far for prudence to be perfectly satisfied. To notice mistakes where there is so much merit, is a painful but a well intentioned task.

As an actor, it may be doubted whether Mr. Kemble was ever seen to greater advantage, if so great, as in the two first acts of this comedy; though he had much excellence in many other parts, in these he was beyond praise: he must be seen for his merits to be understood. None of the works of man are perfect, and even in this highly finished picture of the character already described he had little faults: his greatest beauties were seen when he said nothing; yet some two or three times his pauses became rather too long; they by no means reached, but they somewhat approached, monotony. It might not be his fault, but the throwing away the newspaper after the book was also of that kind. A repetition of any little incident, however charming in its nature, must be varied; it then may become highly delightful. To well consider whether the character of Sir Oswyn cannot be made throughout equally, or perhaps increasingly, impressive, is a task worthy of Mr. Kemble.

Mrs. Inchbald ventured to take a bold step, and to introduce an entirely new performer as the heroine of her piece. The event has proved that she was highly justifiable in running this risk: never was there greater want within these thirty years, and perhaps longer, than there has been lately of that class of female performers, which Miss Shuttleworth is likely to become. Mrs. Jordan is a luminary of the first magnitude, but she could neither shine every where nor at all times, nor was she entirely of the class of which Miss Shuttleworth promises to be. The loss of Mrs. Pope [once Miss Young] Mrs. Abington, and Miss Farren, has been severely felt. In figure, Miss Shuttleworth has some resemblance to the last; and of articulation, theatrical talent, and intellect, she has given such charming proofs that public expectation is raised very high. Let circumstances be but favorable and it will probably be surpassed.

Mr. Munden, an actor of sterling merit, rendered Lord Danberry respectable, and no actor could do more.

Mrs. Davenport could only hope not to displease, and she was successful.

The characters performed by Mr. Farley and Mrs. Glover seem, at first, to have been intended as parts of high comedy;

but they are sunk in the general interest of the piece to persons of little significance.

Mr. Cooke gave a faithful and a strong picture of a man labouring under violent passions, contrasted with humane affections. Both he and Mr. Kemble gave dignity to parts which, however well conceived by the author, might have sunk in feebler hands. The dialect of his negro was not good, not characteristic, as delivered by Mr. Brunton; his faithfulness and contrition were better expressed.

ESSAY ON DRAMATIC COMPOSITION.

(*Continued from No. II. p.* 143.)

Of the Moral Nature of Plays.

BY plays is here understood all those theatrical productions, in which there is a prevailing tendency to be serious and declamatory, or tragical. Serious scenes may very properly find their place in comedy; but, when they overpower laughter, humorous incident, and comic character, the piece is properly classed among plays.

Moral utility may be greatly promoted by every species of dramatic writing; but the authors of plays have often improperly claimed a superiority as moral teachers. It has been strangely maintained, by all adversaries of the drama, and even by some of its friends, that, because comedy is employed to exhibit *folly*, and pourtray *vice*, it is the *friend* of folly and vice. Even had authors any such intention, this would only be possible in a relative and inferior degree. A relative and inferior degree of vice and folly, is taught in the temples built and consecrated to the essence of virtue! for, unless the understandings of men were so correct, as accurately to discriminate *where virtue ends*, and where vice and folly begin, to this evil, whoever may be the teacher, those who are instructed must submit. Whatever the place, and wherever seen, vice, when known, is detested, and folly laughed at; and where with so hearty a good will, such branded shame, and such effectual contempt, as on the stage?

There is much laughter in life; and yet there are but few modes of exciting laughter. Some have maintained that the consciousness of superiority is its only source. Generally speaking, a thing laughed at is a thing despised; and who will intentionally imitate that which he despises? Where is there so incessant a fund of laughter to be found as the stage supplies? Or what writings contain, like a comedy, in so small a compass, so vast a volume of morality? Could the manual of Epictetus be sufficiently familiarized to the unlettered, admirable as it is, it might exhibit a less mixture of error, but would even then be of inferior force; for, by the thoughtless multitude, it must still be read as a task: while they will always resort to the playhouse as to a place of supreme pleasure. Even the sermon on the Mount, justly revered as it is by the most ignorant and the wise, perfectly comprehensible for the simplicity and truth of its precepts, and adored as an emanation from divinity, is yet seldom read, little remembered, and, when read, resorted to rather as an act of piety than a source of pleasure.

These considerations seem to decide in favor of the moral utility of comedy, over every other species of public exhibition: plays can only enjoy the third rank; for though they may partake of tragedy and comedy, as they cannot so often produce the moral effects of laughter, nor can to the full attain the dignified and elevated sentiments of tragedy, they must, as they generally are, be deemed inferior.

Of the Moral Nature of the Comic-Opera.

Whatever contributes to the happiness of man is of a moral nature: pleasure, therefore, of every kind, which has no decided tendency to produce future pain, is a good that deserves cultivation, in proportion to its magnitude.

Of the mental pleasures which society at large can enjoy,

literature and the fine arts claim an undoubted precedency. Few indeed are the people who do not derive pleasure from music ; and, by the lower orders, music is seldom heard to such advantage as at the theatre.   Their weariness is relieved, their passions are soothed, and their hearts are delighted, while they listen.   It seems indeed astonishing to recollect that the legislature continues to narrow, and in part to interdict, such sources of innocent delight, and such means of moral instruction.

As in an opera much of the time of performance is devoted to music, and as likewise, in such productions, a strong portion of insipidity has always prevailed, their highest moral utility is still further lessened : when they are well written, however, this utility is not small ; for, as music itself produces the effects already described, a just personification of the manners and follies of men may give such aid, to the part which is good, as to render the whole excellent.

Of the Moral Nature of Farce and Pantomine.

To people unaccustomed, perhaps, calmly and seriously to consider the tendency of the drama, to speak of the moral tendency of farce and pantomime, or even of comic opera, will at first excite derision.   Unless, however, it can be denied that that which contributes to human happiness is good morality, it will be difficult to prove that the morality of such entertainments, and indeed of all moral affections whatever, is not either good or bad.

Any theatrical exhibition which deceives or misinforms is so far bad ; if it amuses, without these bad effects, it is good in proportion as the amusement is great.   Farces have few means of deceiving, except they induce a belief in any degree that vice is virtue.   Such a belief may be induced in a variety of ways : youth, by hearing a character swear on the stage, may be taught to imitate what he hears, or by seeing any other vicious habit treated with humorous levity.   It has already been remarked, that none of the actions of men are wholly pure ; they have some mixture of good and evil, and the balance is in favor of that which predominates.   In some of our farces there has been much ribaldry ; but it may be doubted if there be a single one in which, if it be dispassionately examined, the good does not greatly prevail. Hilarity is itself a good of a high kind, and to attract all orders of men to spend their evening in mental instead of sensual pleasures, is to morality an invaluable art. It would needlessly give disgust to recapitulate the vices into which the thoughtless multitude, great and small, are, when they are unemployed, too frequently seduced. The mind turns painfully from the scenes which the thought suggests.

In pantomimes there is too great an indulgence of objects of deception, and particularly of terror : because pantomimes are chiefly intended for children and youth, and because deception and terror never should be presented before children and youth, unless in the company of those sagacious instructors who can turn them to lessons of real information. Their utility may then be great ; for to the young they are exceedingly amusing, and so far exceedingly good.

Every other species of entertainment may be arranged among the foregoing classes.

(*To be continued.*)

SOME ACCOUNT

OF THE RISE AND PROGRESS OF THE GERMAN STAGE.

(*Continued from No.* II. *p.* 147).

BRUCK appeared in comic parts while Eckhof was on the stage, and deserves to be ranked with the famous French actor Préville : he was long the delight of Germany.

But the art of these actors brought no theatrical reformation : instead of becoming the school and the censor of national manners, it remained in its infancy. Gellert was the first who felt this, and endeavoured to effect a change ; Gellert, whose simplicity, gentleness, and worth, all Europe reveres, and whose memory is ever dear to those to whom he has taught wisdom and virtue. His comedies are not masterpieces, nor do they announce a high dramatic genius; yet he far surpassed his contemporaries in purity of style, in naturally delineating the manners of Germany, and in never putting modesty to the blush, qualities at that time rarely found even in original pieces. *Die Betschwester*, or The Devotee, was his first comedy, and appeared in 1745, which piece drew on him many vexations : calumny was outrageous against this respectable man, though the purity of his intentions, and the candor of his character, were generally acknowledged. He gave his Tender Sisters * the same year, which was the first German piece of the drama species, and which possesses the defects and merits of his other works.

The year 1747 was memorable, for in that year the first comedy of Lessing appeared at Leipsic. Germany honors this great man as the first of her dramatic poets. His works, better than any words, will testify his merit, for they will ever remain the pride of the German theatre. The name of this piece was *Der Junge Gelehrte* [The young Student] and was represented by the company of Madame Neuber. Though it abounds in beauties, it is seldom played, perhaps because the character is too local, and pedantry is not a very interesting subject. About this time Schlegel, before mentioned, gave a collection of his dramatic works, which did not injure the favorable idea that had been conceived of his talents. In a word, this era may be regarded as the birth of good taste in Germany. After this, famous writers were often imitated, and the slow progress which the dramatic art has since made must be attributed to particular causes, particularly to the little encouragement talents meet, being dispersed through so vast a country divided among numerous princes, and not possessing a capital city, like London, or Paris, where merit may find its reward.

In 1749 Gellert published a collection of his comedies, among which *Das Loos in der Lotterie* [The Prize in the Lottery]

---

* See No. I. of this Work.

a comedy which well deserves to be named, the characters being original, and generally well supported.

Schlegel continued his theatrical labors, and, among others, gave Germany two pieces, which merit to preserve their place on the stage; Woman Triumphant, and the Dumb Beauty *.

Toward the end of her course, Madame Neuber found that fortune is no constant attendant on merit; the suffrages of all Germany and the honor of having contributed to reform bad taste could not preserve her from poverty. After suffering many misfortunes, she was obliged, in 1750, to renounce the stage. Continuing to languish, in extreme indigence, ten years longer, she died unknown, in 1762, at a small village near Dresden. Her name might have died with her, if that theatrical enthusiasm for the drama, which has since spread through Germany, had not induced some lovers of the art to raise a monument to her name on the borders of the Elbe, near the place where she expired.

About this time Koch established his theatre, which became famous by a succession of good actors, whose regular conduct procured them that esteem which is now generally felt in Germany for stage professors. Brückner and Madame Steinbrecher, both justly admired, were among the first that appeared: he as a principal tragedian and lover, and she in sentimental characters.

DRAMATIC ANECDOTES.

HAMLET excepted, it is doubtful whether any tragic character is more difficult, for an actor truly to personate, than Macbeth. The following is an abstract of the account, which Mr. Davies gives, in his Miscellanies of different actors in that part—Betterton is celebrated, in the Tattler, as being excellent

---

* The Editor not possessing this author's works, cannot indicate the German titles.

in Macbeth; but Cibber makes no particular mention of him in that character, which he acted to the very verge of life. Mills afterward obtained it of Wilkes; but he was heavy and dull. Quin was monotonous. Mossop wanted variety and ease. Barry had too much amenity for the terrible agonies of Macbeth. Garrick alone could comprehend and execute the complicated passions of this character: from the meeting of the witches to the last scene, he was animated and consistent: the impressions made upon his mind by those supernatural hags were at all times visible. Wilkes had improperly given the part to Mills, while Booth and Powel were doomed to the characters of Banquo and Lennox. One evening, a country Squire, being heartily tired with Mills, seeing his bottle com. panion, Powel, appear in the fourth act, loudly called—" For " God's sake, George, give me a speech and let me go home."

When Garrick was in Italy, he was requested, by the Duke of Parma, to give a proof of his skill in acting: on which, he instantly threw himself into the attitude of Macbeth seeing the dagger of air. The duke was perfectly convinced, by this single specimen, that Garrick was an absolute master of his art.

Of Garrick and Mrs. Pritchard, in Macbeth, Davies gives an animated picture. The commission of the murder was conducted in terrifying whispers: what they spoke was heard; but more was learned from the agitation of mind in their action, and deportment. The dark colouring given, to the short abrupt speeches, made the scene awfully tremendous. The wonderful expression of heart-felt horror, when he showed his bloody hands, only can be conceived by those who beheld him.

Mr. Davies justly remarks that, Shakspeare having produced his witches, Jonson, hoping to excel him, wrote his Mask of Queens. As far as his conduct was open and liberal, it was glorious in him to emulate, and endeavour to excel; but, to us, the task appears beyond human power. Jonson displayed much reading, and some poetry; but his scenes were labored, and bombastic. His witches were all differently attired; some

with rats on their heads, some on their shoulders; with oint-
ment pots at their girdles, spindles, timbrels, rattles, and other
instruments of witchery, making strange gesticulations, and a
confused noise.   The incantations of Shakspeare are awfully
tremendous; those of other poets generally are ridiculous.

=====

A boy taller by the head than himself insulted Cibber, on
which he was rash enough to strike him; but, was soon at the
mercy of the big boy.   Another lad beloved for his supposed
good nature by Cibber being present, called out " Beat him,
" beat him, soundly," which so affected Cibber, he burst into
tears.   When the affray was over he took the lad aside, and
asked him how he came to act so?   To which he gloutingly replied, " Because you are always jeering, and making a jest of
" me to the whole school,"

=====

Mrs. Dancer, afterward Barry, afterward Crawfurd, was
the daughter of an apothecary at Bath.   At seventeen she was
promised marriage by a young nobleman, but disappointed;
after which she became the wife of Mr. Dancer, an actor, who
first brought her on the stage at Plymouth; and going afterward
to Dublin under the tuition of Barry, she was rising into great
favor.   Domestic discontents succeeded: she went out of town on
pleasure with a female friend, was there joined by a famous
male dancer belonging to the theatre, and anecdotes, epigrams,
and witticisms on Dancer her husband, and a dancer her supposed lover, were numerous.   In 1769 she married the famous
actor, Barry: he died in 1777. Garrick wrote a monody on his
death, and this monody for several nights she continued to
repeat, acting her widowed grief.   A year or two afterward
she married Mr. Crawfurd, then known as a young Irish bar-
rister; but much better since, to the theatrical world, as the
manager of the Dublin theatre.   She died on the 29th of November, 1801, and lies interred beside her second husband in
the Cloisters of Westminster Abbey.

=====

A one act comedy, named *l'Accommodement Imprevu*, being
performed in 1737, a spectator clapped with all his force, and at

the same time exclaimed " *Ah! Oh! Vile! Wretched!*" The
people round him asked him what he meant? He replied:
" Gentlemen, I received an order to applaud, and having given
" my promise it shall be kept; but I am an honest man, and
" cannot belie my conscience. Notwithstanding the applause I
" give, I shall now and for ever repeat that the piece is detestable." The spectators round him caught his spirit, and at
once applauded and hissed with equal violence,

Douville, the author of a five act comedy, entitled *L'Absent
de chez soi,* and brother to the Abbé de *Bois-Robert,* hearing
his piece applauded, asked his brother what he thought of it.
Bois-Robert frankly answered, he thought it bad ; as it really
was; and the piqued author replied, ' The pit shall be my judge.'
—" Right," replied the Abbé ; " but you may change your
" opinion, in time ;" and so it happened. *Douville* produced
another comedy, which was hissed, and *Bois-Robert* then asked
him if the pit should be his judge ? ' Pshaw !' replied the
vexed brother, ' the pit has not common sense.' " Ay, ay, you
" have found it out," exclaimed the Abbé ; " I discovered it
" when your first piece was performed."

In a French comic opera of one act, entitled *L'Abondance,*
one character in the piece was *Virtue,* personified. The first
appearance of it being deferred, and the manager required to
say how that happened, he replied—" *Mademoisselle Rosette,*
" who is to play the part of *Virtue,* has just been brought
" to-bed, and we are obliged to wait for her recovery."
The answer becoming public, the part was necessarily suppressed.

MISCELLANIES.

COSTUME.   The dress of Miss Brunton, in the School of Reform, is a specimen of that simplicity in which the admirable
taste of the present times appears to delight. Of the Indian
Costume the first is a Brijbasi Brahmun repeating munters, or

incantations, under the drapery thrown round him, which ceremony, like other Hindoos, he must keep inviolably secret.
This, and the four Brahmuns before given, constitute five of
the heads of their leading sects, and are specimens of the manner in which the Hindoo priests, when brought on the stage,
ought to be clothed. In eminence, next to the Brahmun, is the
K'huttry, who now dresses as the plate represents. Under the
Mogul government this cast was preferred to all others, the
Brahmuns excepted; and, according to their religion, from
among its members princes, rajahs, landholders, and soldiers,
should be selected. They are less numerous in Bengal than in
the northern parts of Indostan. A Byce is the third cast, and
is ordered by their sacred books to be employed in merchandize,
and husbandry. The Costume of the K'huttry and Byce,
therefore, should be accurately noticed for stage representation.

After the temporary recess occasioned by his illness, Master
Betty again returned to the stage, and appeared, January 28th,
at Covent Garden, in Douglas. There is much difference of
opinion, concerning him: even, in the play-bills, he is announced
as Master Betty, at Covent Garden, and as the Young Roscius,
at Drury Lane; as noted in the monthly list here printed. It
may not be amiss to remark that the Roman Roscius was a *Comedian:* a short account of him may at this moment amuse.

Quintus Roscius, a Gaul by birth, and contemporary of the
great Æsopus, was the most famous actor in *comedy* of his age.
It was said of him, by *Cicero,* that *he pleased so much, upon the
theatre, he ought never to have left it; though, he had so much
virtue and probity, he ought never to have gone on it**. *Cicero*
successfully defended him against *Fannius;* and *Piso* and *Sylla*
were likewise his friends. The republic allowed him a large
pension; but, according to *Pliny,* not half so much as to *Æsopus,*
who was a tragedian. Some say *Roscius* was the first who
wore a mask; others deny the assertion: but all allow he was
ugly, and had a cast with his eyes. Some estimate may be
formed of the luxury in which actors then lived, from Pliny, who

---

* This characteristically marks the illiberality of opinion that prevailed,
among the Romans, concerning actors.

relates that, at a repast, given by *Æsopus*, a vessel of pottery was placed on the table, which cost upward of four hundred pounds, and which was filled with birds that had all been taught to sing and speak, and that cost, on an average, twenty-five pounds a piece. The son of this Æsopus is said to have dissolved pearls, for his guests to drink.

A correspondent writes that Master Betty is going to Wolverhampton in June; where, or in which neighbourhood, *Young Roscius the Second* has appeared. No wonder: managers are overwhelmed with letters: hundreds are said to have been received from parents, who every one have a Young Roscius, only wanting to be known in order to be adored.

TO CORRESPONDENTS.

A Correspondent, J. C. T. has kindly warned the Editor that, in his opinion, unless the translated Play be omitted, and more be said of the Actors and other temporary subjects, the THEATRICAL RECORDER *cannot succeed; or that he at least will cease to be a purchaser. After sincerely thanking him for his good wishes, the Editor requests him to consider that the very Plays, which he desires to see omitted, will, if well executed, form a highly valuable Collection, as well for the lover of the Dramatic Art as for those who wish themselves to become Dramatic Authors. Not only the plans of new Pieces do already, and will continually, present themselves, but many characters are there finely sketched, and, some, almost completely ready for the writer, who shall please to select and bring them on the Stage: while, on the contrary, were 72 closely printed pages, monthly, devoted to what can rationally and animatedly be said of new Pieces, new Performers, and temporary occurrences, such subjects could not fill a single Number; unless the Author were to become a babler, spin his materials to a cobweb texture, and indulge in sleepy insipidity Other friends, however, have been of the same opinion with J. C. T. The Editor can only reply—he thinks they have not sufficiently considered the subject: they have neither properly estimated the treasures they wish to reject, nor foreseen how scanty are the materials they would recommend.*

MONTHLY LIST, FOR FEBRUARY, 1805.

DRURY-LANE.

JAN.
28. Hamlet - - - - - - - - - - - The Anatomist, and Old Harlequin's Fire Side.
29. The West Indian - - - - - - - - A House to be Sold, and Ditto.
31. The Honey Moon - - - - - - - Fortune's Frolic.

FEB.

1. The Honey Moon ------- The Irishman in London.
2. Ditto ------------ Richard Cœur de Lion, *changed to the Humorist.*
4. Ditto ------------ The Mock Doctor, and Old Harlequin's Fire Side.
5. Ditto ------------ Richard Cœur de Lion.
6. Ditto ------------ United Britons, and High Life Below Stairs.
7. Ditto ------------ Of Age To-morrow, and Old Harlequin's Fire Side.
8. Ditto ------------ The United Britons, and The Anatomist.
9. Ditto ------------ Ditto, and The Prize.
11. Ditto ------------ A House to be Sold.
12. Ditto ------------ The Lady of the Rock.
13. Douglas (Young Roscius) - - - - The Deserter.
14. The Honey Moon ------- The Lady of the Rock.
15. Barbarossa (Young Roscius) - - High Life Below Stairs.
16. The Honey Moon ------- The Lady of the Rock.
18. Ditto ------------ Ditto.
19. Lovers' Vows (Young Roscius) - The Citizen.
21. Douglas (Young Roscius) - - - Bon Ton.
22. The Honey Moon ------- The Lady of the Rock.
23. Tancred and Sigismunda (Roscius) The Apprentice.
25. The Honey Moon ------- The Lady of the Rock.
26. Tancred and Sigismunda - - - - Bon Ton.

COVENT-GARDEN.

JAN.

28. Douglas (Master Betty's Seventh Appearance at this Theatre.) - Il Bondocani.
29. The School of Reform (by Com.) Hartford Bridge.
31. Lovers' Vows (Master Betty) - The Padlock.

FEB.

1. The School of Reform - - - - - Harlequin Quicksilver.
2. The Mountaineers (Mast. Betty) Animal Magnetism.
4. The School of Reform - - - - - Harlequin Quicksilver.
5. The Mountaineers (Mast. Betty) A Tale of Mystery.
6. The School of Reform - - - - - Harlequin Quicksilver.
7. Romeo and Juliet (Master Betty) The Midnight Hour.
8. The School of Reform - - - - - Harlequin Quicksilver.
9. Romeo and Juliet (Master Betty) The Jew and the Doctor.
11. Tancred and Sigism. (Mast. Betty) The Padlock.
12. The School of Reform - - - - - Too many Cooks.
13. Ditto ------------ Ditto.
14. Ditto ------------ Ditto.
15. The English Fleet ------- Raising the Wind.
16. To Marry, or Not to Marry - - Paul and Virginia.
18. Ditto ------------ Harlequin Quicksilver.
19. Ditto ------------ Marian.
21. Ditto ------------ Il Bondocani.
22. The English Fleet (by Command) The Review.
23. To Marry, or Not to Marry - - The Escapes.
25. Ditto ------------ Harlequin Quicksilver.
26. Ditto ------------ The Turnpike Gate.

THE

THEATRICAL RECORDER:

BY

THOMAS HOLCROFT.

Contents of Number IV.

London:

Printed by C. Mercier and Co. No. 6, Northumberland-court,
Where the Work may be procured;
And at all the Booksellers;
And published for the Author, by H. D. Symonds, Paternoster-row.

1805.

FROM BAD TO WORSE:

A COMEDY,

IN THREE ACTS,

TRANSLATED FROM

THE SPANISH OF CALDERON DE LA BARCA,

By FANNY HOLCROFT.

DRAMATIS PERSONÆ.

DON CESAR URSINO, Florida's Lover.

DON JUAN, betrothed to Lisarda.

THE GOVERNOR OF GAETA.

CAMACHO, }
FABIO, } Valets to Don Cesar.

FELIX, a Servant.

An Alcaide. Servants to the Governor.

Alguazils.

DONNA FLORIDA, betrothed to Cesar.

DONNA LISARDA, betrothed to Juan.

CELIA, }
NISA, } Waiting Women to Lisarda.

FROM BAD TO WORSE:

A COMEDY.

~~~~

ACT I.

SCENE I.

The GOVERNOR, *reading a Letter;* FELIX *in a travelling Dress.*

Governor (*reads*).

" MY dear lord,
" I will relate the particulars of my misfortune without
" reserve, being well assured of your sympathy and zeal to
" serve me. A gentleman, whose name and person are known
" to my domestic, who brings you this, has fled from Naples,
" in consequence of an affair of honor. My daughter, who
" was the accomplice of his rashness, is the companion of his
" flight. I understand that he intends to embark for Spain:
" he may perhaps have taken refuge in your port; if so,
" arrest the fugitives, but treat them as my children. Though
" my honor has been impaired, it is not irrevocably lost."
A confused report of this unfortunate affair had before
reached me; and I am greatly obliged to my friend, Don
Alonzo, for remembering me on such an occasion. I would
give half my estate that the fugitives may have taken shelter
in this port; and I call Heaven to witness that the honor of my
friends shall be my dearest care. A trust so great should be
religiously fulfilled. I am beside indebted to him, for his courtesy to me, in Flanders; and am impatient to return the obligation. But I must know the name of the Cavalier, who has
so cruelly wounded his honor, and embittered his peace.

Fel. It is Don Cesar Ursino, Signor; who has killed a Cavalier, and eloped with Donna Florida, whose charms had
occasioned the affray, and who the same night was missing.
I know Don Cesar by sight; and, if your lordship will grant
me a warrant to search the inns, I have little doubt of finding
him, for I believe he is concealed in this place.

Gov. I will in person aid your research: but, first tell me,
what reason have you to suppose he is in this town?

Fel. I saw one of his domestics, this morning, pass before the inn at which myself and comrade put up : I therefore naturally conclude that Don Cesar cannot be far off.

Gov. Did you follow the man?

Fel. No, my lord, I am known to him ; but I desired my comrade not to leave him till he had seen him safe in a house.

Gov. Well, go and learn all you can ; then return, and I will take the necessary steps to secure Don Cesar. We must act with prudence ; for, if we proceed too rashly, he may evade our search.

Fel. Your caution is excellent, my lord. When I have seen and questioned my comrade, I will attend your lordship*.

[*Exit.*

SCENE II.—GOVERNOR, *alone.*

Gov. Oh, honor, how brittle art thou in the hands of a yielding woman?

SCENE III.—*Enter* DONNA LISARDA, *and* CELIA *her Attendant.*

Lis. My lord !

Gov. Daughter, where are you going?

Lis. I come to wish you good morning. Is my love irksome to you, honored Sir, that you would leave the house without seeing me? You look disturbed.

Gov. Do not wonder at this unusual gloom ; I have a father's heart, and a father's fears. Trembles not the benighted traveller, to pass the spot where foul robbery has been committed? Enters not the mariner, with awe, the gulph where formerly some vessel struck, on treacherous shoals? Shrinks not the bold hunter, when he discerns, by the glimmering light of dawn, the corpse of some poor wretch, mangled by the fierce tiger? Here, like the benighted traveller, I discover certain danger. Here, like the mariner, I see the foundered vessel. Here, like the hunter, I discern the fierce tiger, which lies in wait to destroy me : for, to him who knows how to prize it, honor is all that I have described ; and is hourly exposed to treachery, danger, and death. [*Exit.*

SCENE IV.

Lis. I scarcely know where I am. Perhaps I am discovered, Celia ; and my father, by this ambiguous discourse, means to warn me that his honor is endangered.

Cel. May be so, Madam. His manner and words were se-

---

* In the original, the valets and waiting-maids use *thou*, and *thee*, as familiarly as their superiors.

rious: he has no doubt heard of your imprudent inclination: and, if I may be allowed to speak, he has great reason to be displeased. You are a heretic in love, at the risk of your honor: you wish to fill Don Cupid's quiver with new arrows; but, were you as jealous, passionate, vain-glorious, and wretched as your fathers and forefathers have been, you would not involve yourself in the difficulties and dangers to which your imprudent frolic with a stranger has exposed you.

Lis. If you knew all, Celia, you might with more reason blame my foolish love; and, since you judge me so severely before you have heard my story, you shall be made acquainted with the whole. His majesty, to recompense my father's valour and services, presented him with this government. He came hither; I accompanied him, and met with universal admiration and respect. But I soon felt myself fettered, by the attention that was paid me. Wherever I went, it was whispered—" There goes the Governor's daughter !" Even, at church, my appearance occasioned a general murmur, and all eyes were upon me. I could never be left to myself a moment: whether cheerful or sad, the town were sure to know it. At length, I grew heartily sick of this homage; for vanity itself may die of an indigestion; and I resolved to forget my rank, and sometimes to walk in the public gardens, where, concealed by my mantle and veil, I could speak and enjoy the freedom which that disguise allows. One day, as I was walking near the sea-shore, thus disguised, I perceived my father among the company. Oh, Heavens! that he should be there on that very day! Struck with alarm, I ran into a garden, where I found a Cavalier, who, seeing me frightened, and perhaps thinking me in danger, drew his sword in my defence. I thanked him for his gallantry, and told him it was unnecessary. In a short conversation, I found that he was not only brave and courteous, but elegant and well informed. I say nothing of his rank; for, when I tell you he has these qualifications, you may infer that he is a gentleman. He requested me to confide my name to him: this I declined, but promised to meet him at the same place in a few days, on condition he would neither attempt to follow me, see my face, nor learn my name. To this he politely assented, and, shall I confesss it, I kept the appointment. Whether he lives incognito, or whether he is detained a prisoner, I cannot say: I only know his name is Don Fabio*. For my part, all I seek is to amuse myself, without prejudice to my honor. He is nearly a stranger to me; yet, setting aside prudery, I—think I love him. No, no; the new sensations I feel are not love: they are incomprehensible to myself. But I see no reason that what my father said should induce me, whether I am or am not in love, to visit the young Cavalier no more.

---

* Don Cesar Ursino; the false name is supposed to be for safety's sake.

Cel. I dread the consequences of these follies. Recollect, Signora, that you are betrothed ; and that your bridegroom is daily expected. Your father has ordered the suit of apartments next yours to be prepared for his reception.

Lis. Alas, Celia, I may now with better reason complain of my cruel destiny.

SCENE V.—*Enter* Nisa.

Nisa. A handsome lady, who appears to be a stranger, requests to speak with you, Signora.

Lis. What is her name ?

Nisa. She did not tell me.

Lis. Show her in.   [*Exit.*

SCENE VI.—*Enter* Donna Florida, *veiled.*

Flor. Thus lowly bending, the ground I touch will be to me as the long wished-for port to the weather-beaten mariner, if I am suffered to kiss that beauteous hand. (*unveiling and kneeling.*)

Lis. Rise, fair lady : the earth is unworthy to receive the brightest constellation of heaven *.

Flor. Were I indeed a constellation, you are the heaven above me, and command my respect. Nay, were I your equal in beauty, my hapless fortune would liken me to the modest moon, while you reigned queen of the stars.

Cel. (*aside*) This lady is at no loss for words.

Lis. I rejoice not to suppose myself a sun, which emits its golden ays to illuminate your beauty ; but kind nature rather has made you a planet, and me your satellite. Tell me in what can I serve you ?

Flor. I implore your pity and protection.

Lis. Perhaps you wish to be more private ?

Flor. No : that which hereafter must be known should now be told.

Lis. Speak, Madam.

Flor. I will be brief. You, charming Lisarda, who are as discreet as you are beautiful, ought to know that your favors are worthily dispensed : for, when fortune frowns, the world is apt to judge the poor suppliant with asperity. I am a woman, and as such implore that compassion which the noble never refuse. Oh that he were here who knows the truth of the melancholy tale, which dies on my faltering tongue ! But in his absence let these eyes, which, like two fountains, overflow and inundate my cheeks with tears, be the pledge of my veracity ! I am the daughter of a nobleman, whose name

---

* The Spanish is every where rather more than less florid than the translation.

respect bids me conceal: for I would not spread the dishonor, which is brought upon it, by my imprudence. Among the numerous gentlemen, who sought my favor, was a Cavalier, who, in birth and fortune, was my equal. From the hour when Phebus bedecked his golden tresses with rosy wreaths, till, reclined on the snow-white surge, he esteemed the wide ocean a bed too narrow for his glorious rays, this gentleman enlivened the street in which I lived with serenades, and every gallant show. He was the sun-flower, that graced my windows: a sun-flower by day, but at night an Argus, to whose tenderness and honor, in the face of Heaven, I intrusted my person, and pledged my faith. You will make allowance for my weakness, for I am a woman; and you doubtless know how grateful adoration is to our sex. Thus, for a while, fortune smiled on our love; and those happy moments which mutual confidence secure to faithful hearts were ours! Alas, mystery and danger enhance the lover's joys. A garden was the temple in which we plighted our vows; and the myrtle and jessamine were mute witnesses to my tender fears and doubts. Who would have thought that love so gentle so soon should prove my torment? Or that a fearful tempest lowered beneath so sweet a calm? A noble Cavalier, when my faith and love were no longer mine to bestow, thought proper to pay his court to me. I treated him with disdain whenever he passed my windows. By watching, he at length discovered that my severity toward him did not proceed so much from decorum, as from a preoccupied heart, and he resolved to take a cruel revenge for slighted love. One gloomy night, when the moon was half concealed by clouds, he came a little before my lover to the garden gate, gave the usual signal, and I let him in. Cruel fate, for this unlucky moment brought my betrothed, who, seeing a man enter, guided by the lamp of night, which proved to be the torch of death, in words scarcely articulate demanded—who he was, and what he wanted? The stranger, without vouchsafing a reply, covered his face and laid his hand on his sword. More dead than alive, I was going to answer for him, but their swords were already drawn: never did angry comets, crossing each other in the disturbed heavens, dart quicker fire than that which flamed on the sharp-edged steel. By the will of Providence (or say it was my destiny) the stranger at the first thrust was mortally wounded. "I am a dead man," he cried, and fell lifeless on a bed of withered violets, which, living, had decked the throne of love, and now adorned the couch of death. My lover, seeing him fall, cried to me in a faltering voice—" Now caress your favorite, faithless woman, who sought you at such an hour, and who there lies weltering in his blood! Nor am I sure that one life ought to satisfy revenge!"

Trembling and confused, I attempted to justify myself; but the jealous are deaf to reason. He hurried out of the gar-

den, mounted a horse (shall I say with wings, he flew so fast)
and was out of hearing in an instant. I remained in a stupor of
grief, from which I was roused by the neighbours and servants, who had been alarmed by the noise and the voice of my
father, who called on my name. Not having the courage to
meet his anger, I gave no answer; but, resolved to fly, rushed
out of the garden, and, with a distracted heart, took refuge at
the house of a female friend, with whom I remained concealed
for some days. I heard, mean time, my lover had fled to a
sea-port, intending to embark for Spain. This made me quit
my native city, in the hope of finding and convincing him of
my innocence: but hitherto I have not been able to discover
any traces of my beloved Cavalier; and, being aware of the
dangers to which a woman unprotected is exposed in so wild a
chace, I determined to renounce the mad attempt. The fame
of your amenity reached my ears, and I hoped to live in honorable obscurity under your protection. Your domestics are
numerous; one more added to the number can make little difference, and you are too noble to suffer one of your own sex
and rank to be exposed to insult, and injury. Confirm my
hopes, dear lady, lighten my woes, and relieve my fears! You
are a woman: as such, grant me your favor and protection,
and may you never love, or be your love propitious——

Lis. Rise, fair lady; dry your tears, or Aurora will complain that you usurp her office. Your beauty guarantees the
reality of your misfortunes. What is your name?

Flor. Laura.

Lis. Remain then, Laura, with me; not to serve, but to be
served. Now retire to my apartments, for my father must not
see you, till I have obtained his permission to receive you as
my guest.

Flor. Good angels guard you! Cruel fortune, be satisfied
with the woes thou hast already inflicted!   [*Exit.*

Cel. Though compassion is laudable, I doubt the prudence,
Signora, of admitting this stranger lady into your house.

Lis. What are your doubts?

Cel. Why, I doubt if the world can produce a woman,
virgin or widow, servant or mistress, who will be sincere, when
she thinks it her interest to be the reverse.   [*Exeunt.*

SCENE VII.

*Scene changes to a Garden behind a House, with a Back Door in
View.*

Don Cesar, Don Juan *in a travelling Dress.*

Don J. I am fortunate indeed in coming to this *Quinta**,
since I find you so unexpectedly here, Don Cesar.

---

* *Quinta* signifies a house of entertainment, with gardens, a little way out of
the city.

Don C. My good fortune brought you hither! Once again let me embrace my friend!

Don J. Death alone can dissolve our friendship! But what do you here?

Don C. My story is long and melancholy. You come from Flanders, or you would not be unacquainted with it.

Don J. I had heard you were in difficulties, and am surprised to find you here apparently so satisfied.

Don C. I am far from being at ease, Don Juan: fear and suspicion are my tormentors; and if your heart had not been known to me, I would not have seen you. I am concealed here, till I can embark for Spain. The master of this house formerly served me, and I can depend on his honesty; but, should any stranger come, a boat is kept in readiness, and I can put immediately to sea.

Don J. My arrival is fortunate, since I may serve you. I am a person of some consequence in Gaeta; for I am come to be the fortunate lover and husband of the illustrious Lisarda, who is noble, beauteous, and amiable: in short, she is the only daughter of Don Juan of Arragon. Dismiss your fears; my intended father-in-law is governor of this place, and captain of the king's forces. Beside, the judicial rank of my own father will enable me to befriend you.

Don C. Thanks, my noble friend! I have not now to learn how much I owe you: may you be fortunate in your love, and may you enjoy many happy years! But now, tell me, what brought you to this house, my friend?

Don J. I wished to pass the day here, and divert myself. I have come to Gaeta like a soldier, ill provided with jewels and such-like gallantries; and, though I am very well for a soldier, I have not the appearance of a bridegroom. I therefore propose to remain two days incognito, and not to see my mistress till I am properly equipped.

Don C. How fortunate I am! You can spend these two days with me.

Don J. I would with pleasure, but the alcaide of the fortress is my friend: I have sent him word of my arrival, and expect him here every moment to fetch me. As you must not be seen, I will go and meet him.

Don C. Your caution is prudent.

Don J. Adieu, Don Cesar. I will not fail to visit you in secret, and you may rely on my zeal to serve you.   [*Exit.*

SCENE VIII.—*Enter* CAMACHO.

Cam. Master of mine, your heart I see is in deep soliloquy, your senses and your conscience are in rebellion, and thought has played the devil with memory and common sense. Who is now the sovereign of your thoughts, Signor? The absent

Donna Florida, or the Incognita, who is cousin-german to the Prince of Darkness.

Don C. Your jokes were always ill-timed, and they are now more impertinent than ever.

Cam. What offends you, Signor?

Don C. That you should ask who is the sovereign of my thoughts. Who can it be, if not the lovely Florida?

Cam. If you love her so entirely, why do you engage in a new intrigue?

Don C. Because I am banished from happiness and her charms.

Cam. And, she being absent, you are willing to find a substitute? Such are the ways of man! Ah! and of woman too.

Don C. In one fatal night, I lost my country and my mistress.

Cam. You have done a thing for which every body blames you, Signor.

Don C. For killing my rival?

Cam. No.

Don C. What then?

Cam. For having secured your own safety, and left your mistress to meet the consequences of your rashness.

Don C. It was wrong, Camacho. Yet let those who accuse me love passionately, and find their mistress with another man, then, if they conquer their feelings and act rationally, at so trying a moment, I will plead guilty. Could such an extreme case happen again, I should know how to act; for a man cannot twice commit the same fault. But what is become of Florida?

Cam. Do you forget, Sir, that a traveller informed you, on your first arrival, she had retired to a convent in Naples? But here comes the lady knight errant, who, like the wolf in the fable, does not stand on ceremony.

SCENE IX.

Enter LISARDA *and* CELIA, *both veiled and in Disguise.*

Don C. As Phœbus, veiled in burnished clouds, gives life and harmony to enamelled plains, so you, bright sun, with rays invisible, revive those languid flowers, which hail you queen of love *.

Lis. Your courtesy I, courtier-like, will answer. These flowers, if they greet me with so flattering a homage, have been taught by you, who are the mirror of gallantry.

---

* These mixed metaphors and florid phrases are retained in the translation as characteristic of the author, and of Spanish poetry.

Don C. Since the time you first honored me with your amiable presence, I learned from them how to love, and how to sigh. It is a mistake to suppose they need instructions: every flower has a favorite blossom: it is the breath of love which fans the budding rose. Since all acknowledge the gentle sway of love, do not think me a flatterer.

Lis. Nay, you are a flatterer.

Don C. In what?

Lis. In pretending to love me, though you have never seen my face.

Don C. Is it then impossible to love, without seeing a lady's face?

Lis. Yes.

Don C. I feel the contrary.

Lis. How?

Don C. Very forcibly. Can a blind man love?

Lis. He can.

Don C. As such, then, I love.

Lis. The man who never saw can have no desire to see; and he loves from reflection; but no man having eyes will fall in love in the dark. Not seeing my face, you cannot love.

Don C. By Heaven, you are mistaken! Love so conceived is the more durable.

Lis. It will require some ingenuity to prove your assertion.

Don C. The object most dazzling to a rational mind is the light of the understanding; and this luminary I adore in you. If I had beheld the radiant beauties of your face, my love would have been divided between the charms of your person and the attraction of your wit, and consequently would be less solid. Judge then if I would change rational affection for one less dignified.

Lis. Nay, were your eyes no less fascinated than you say your heart is, your love would but increase.

Don C. I cannot see how!

Lis. If oil be poured on the blue blaze, does it therefore cease to burn? Love is a fire; and, like the mingling brands, our eyes add fuel to the flame.

Cam. (*to* Celia, *concealing his face*) Fair nymph!

Cel. Well?

Cam. Do you, sweet chamber-maid, think fit to imitate your betters? Am I not to see your face?

Cel. No.

Cam. Then we'll be quits: as I am a man of honor, you shall not see mine.

Cel. The thought is excellent!

Cam. Now, by St. Jago, we are face to face in masquerade; and I resign you to Lucifer. If ever you wish to uncover, may his sooty highness, of gigantic stature, spread your mantle in vast circumference wherever you go! May this mantle stick to you like wax! May its rare amplitude enamour Gara-manto! And, for your eternal punishment, may Radamanthus condemn you never to quit it in the regions below.

Don C. You have conquered, lady. Since it is your creed that Cupid's darts take the surest aim from the eyes, you will not think me rude if I offer to lift up your veil.

Lis. Forbear!

Don C. Excuse me, Signora, but I must see your face.

Lis. You may, with this proviso: that you will never see the owner more.

Don C. I am amazed! Methinks the adventure of Cupid and Psyche is in us renewed; or rather reversed. Love, it is said, concealed himself from the idolizing nymph; whereas the Psyche I adore conceals herself from idolizing Love! Throw aside that black veil which is the eclipse of beauty; and, if it is a merit to be fair assert your claims. This envious veil may be a cloud of glory to you, but to me it is the mantle of Pluto.

Lis. Your arguments are very subtile; but again I tell you, if you persist in this boldness, your hopes will end in nothing*, for I will return no more.

Don C. Be the consequence what it will, I must see your face.

Lis. (*unveiling*) Then, look. You see.

Don C. (*in admiration*) Yes! And I cannot imagine why you should selfishly debar poor mortals from the light of the sun. But what noise is that?   [*A noise heard within.*

Lis. It is several persons speaking at once.

SCENE X.—*Enter* FABIO.

Don C. What is the matter, Fabio?

Fab. Fly, Signor! The boat is ready: the Governor is come, in person, to seize you.

Don C. Most likely he has heard of my being here.

Lis. (*aside*) Merciful Heavens! My father! What will become of me? It was not without a meaning he spoke this morning.

Don C. What shall I do?

Cam. Put to sea, and row with might and main.

Don C. Adieu, fair lady! My misfortunes force me to fly.

Lis. Your flight will accelerate mine.

Don C. What is it you wish?

Lis. If you are, as you seem to be, a gentleman, do not desert a woman, whose imprudence in coming to see you exposes her honor and her life. I am not what you perhaps

---

* In the original there is a play upon the word *humo*; which, in one place, signifies *silk*, or *crape*; and in the other *smoke*.

think me; if you leave me defenceless, my death and disgrace are certain. I am pursued, and there is no way to escape.

Don C. (*aside*) Fortune goes from bad to worse! A man may be hurried into error, and be forgiven; but to commit it deliberately admits of no excuse: it shall not again be said that I desert a lady in distress. (*aloud*) Signora, I will protect you with my life. Conceal yourself in the house: I will remain here to guard you; but it is me they seek, not you.

Lis. Quick, Celia, into the house!

[*Lisarda and Celia hurry into the house : Celia. drops her clogs.*

Don C. (*to Camacho*) Take up these clogs.

Cam. A pretty legacy, truly. (*He takes up the clogs and hides himself behind the door of the house.*)

SCENE XI.

Enter GOVERNOR, *followed by* Alguazils *and* Servants.

Gov. Are you Don Cesar Ursino?

Don C. A gentleman never denies his name.

Gov. You are my prisoner.

Don C. I submit; but pray remember my rank.

Gov. I do: you need not deliver your sword. There is a lady with you, whom I must likewise, paying due respect to her sex and rank, detain a prisoner.

Don C. A lady?

Gov. Yes.

Don C. A lady here?

Gov. It is in vain to deny it. I have certain intelligence that she is concealed in that house.

Don C. (*aside*) Heavens! Who can this woman be, who has thrown me into these difficulties?

SCENE XII.

The Alguazils *enter the House and drag out* CAMACHO.

Alg. Here is a man hid behind the door.

[*Exit with his Followers into the house.*

Gov. Who are you?

Cam. The faithful squire of this unfortunate knight.

Gov. Why did you hide yourself?

Cam. Not with any evil design, my lord. I have a foolish trick of hiding myself.

Gov. What have you there?

Cam. Only a pair of clogs, your lordship.

Gov. So, so! These are indications that what I seek is not far off. Where is the owner?

Cam. Here, and please your lordship.

Gov. What, do you wear clogs?

Cam. Shields of cork, I believe, are forbidden, by the just laws of this kingdom, but not clogs. Unfortunate is the sick man, saith a divine proverb, who is without clogs of cork.

SCENE XIII.—*Re-enter* Alguazils, *leading in* LISARDA, *veiled.*

1st Alg. We found this lady in a chamber. (*to* Lisarda) Please to be unveiled, Signora.

Gov. Silence! Lady, do not unveil. I know the respect which is due to your quality, and am sorry that I am obliged to detain you a prisoner.

Don C. My lord, my life is yours, but I cannot suffer that lady to be dishonoured.

Gov. Your tone is too lofty, Don Cesar: it is easier to talk than act. I will excuse your rashness, because of the interest I take in the welfare of that lady. Her father is my friend, and I feel a father's concern for her honor.

Lis. (*aside*) To what will this lead? I fear ruin is certain.

Don C. I had no intention, my lord, to turn your courtesy against yourself: neither would I make a boast of holding life cheap, since it is easy to die.

Gov. Come, Signor, be guided by my prudence and friendly counsel: I do not come as a judge, but as a mediator, who is acquainted with your story.

Don C. I know I have offended against the laws, and am your prisoner; but what has the lady done?

Gov. Do not think you can impose on me: I act from unquestionable information. You, Don Cesar, must follow me to the fortress, where you must remain a prisoner. The lady shall be conducted to my house, and treated in every respect as my own daughter.

Lis. (*aside*) Alas, what is it I hear? Yet it will be less difficult to soften his anger when he is alone. (*aside to* Don Cesar) Signor, I agree to that proposal.

Don C. (*to* Lisarda) If so, I am satisfied. My lord, I accept your offer. The lady, you say, will be received in your house?

Gov. I have pledged my word. (*calls*) Alguazil.

Alg. My lord!

Gov. Conduct the lady in my coach, to my daughter, Lisarda; and tell your lady I beg she will receive her kindly, and keep her company. I must convey Don Cesar to the fortress. [*The* Alguazils *lead off* Lisarda.

Don C. I attend you, my lord, and think myself much honored by your courtesy.

[*Exeunt* Governor, Don Cesar, *and* Servants.

SCENE XIV.—*Manet* CAMACHO, *and enter* CELIA.

Cel. Is she gone ?

Cam. Yes.

Cel. Then I will run home.

Cam. Whoever your mistress may be, by St. Jago you may well rejoice !   [*Exeunt.*

ACT II.

SCENE I.—*A Saloon in the* GOVERNOR'S *Palace.* NISA, CELIA.

Nisa.

HOW, Celia! Returned alone ? Where is our lady? You are silent ! What ails you ?

Cel. I am half dead with fright !

Nisa. What has happened ?

Cel. Why, we were—but I hear footsteps ! I will tell you presently.

SCENE II.

Enter Alguazils *and* Servants, *leading* LISARDA, *who is still veiled.*

1st Alg. Make way !

Nisa. (*aside*) Santa Maria! Is it not my lady?

1st Alg. I must speak with the lady Lisarda. I bring a message from my lord the Governor.

Cel. (*aside*) Now, wit assist me !—My lady is indisposed ; you cannot see her. Deliver your message.

1st Alg. My lord entreats her ladyship to receive this Signora kindly, and to keep her company.

Cel. I will not omit one syllable of what you say.

2d Alg. Hark ye, young woman ! (*aside to* Celia) This lady we bring is a prisoner : inform your mistress that my lord begs she will take great care of her.

[*Exeunt* Alguazils and Servants.

SCENE III.

Nisa. (*to* Celia) Is it my lady ?

Cel. Yes.

Lis. Take my veil, Celia. Do you, Nisa, give me that mantle.

Nisa. What strange masquerade is this? You, my lady, a prisoner in your own house, and committed to your own custody? Pray, dear lady, explain this enigma! I am dying with curiosity.

Lis. Alas, fortune and love have conspired to make me wretched! This morning, my father very cautiously gave me to understand that he had heard of my passion. I, imprudent as I was, paying little attention to his sage warning, went out this evening; he followed me, and I was taken.

Cel. Banish so wild a thought, Signora. Is it possible that a man of your father's prudence could have known this, and, instead of preventing you from continuing the intrigue, have taken the means to publish his own and your disgrace? No, Signora; my only fear was that he should have discovered us before we reached home; but, now we are safe at home, my fears are over. He, no doubt, came thither in search of some lady, and took you to be her.

Lis. You speak without thinking. Did he not say he felt a *father's* concern for the honor of the lady? Did he not dissemble his anger? Did he not forbid me to unveil? These precautions could not have been taken for a stranger! It is in vain to argue; he certainly knew me.

Cel. And what do you mean to do?

Lis. To throw myself at his feet, the moment he returns; for, let it come to the worst, a father will not kill his child; and to tell him I went to that garden for recreation.

SCENE IV.—*Enter* FLORIDA.

Flor. I am glad you are returned, Signora.

Lis. (*aside*) I will not trust her: I am not sufficiently acquainted with her disposition. (*aloud*) I have been to visit a friend.

SCENE V.

Enter the GOVERNOR, *and* FELIX, *who keeps in the Back-ground.*

Gov. Return immediately to Naples, and tell your master that his daughter, Florida, is my guest; and that her lover is a prisoner in the fortress.

Fel. Good, my lord; but there is one objection: I did not follow your lordship into the garden, and the lady who came out was veiled, so that I cannot be certain it was my young lady. It is not possible, under that disguise, to distinguish one person from another, and I might be mistaken.

Gov. Your precaution is just: come forward, and speak to her.

Fel. It will be better that she should not see me, because she will look upon me as a spy, and a mischief-maker; and, though a servant must obey his master, there is no reason he should make himself odious to the rest of the family. If I can see her without her seeing *me*, I shall run no such risk.

Gov. Well, come with me. Yonder is my daughter.

Fel. And the lady on her left hand is Donna Florida! That is sufficient, my lord.

Gov. Yes, it is her, beyond a doubt; for the other women are my daughter's attendants.

Fel. I return to Naples contented. My lord, I am your humble servant. [*Exit.*

SCENE VI.—*The* GOVERNOR *advances toward the Ladies.*

Cel. Here is my lord!

Flor. (*to* Lisarda) If this opportunity be favorable, dear lady, speak to him of me, and ask his permission to receive me in your house.

Lis. I will.

Flor. Exert all your influence.

Lis. Retire to the window. (Florida *retires.*)

Gov. Well, Lisarda, are you not delighted with the new friend I sent you? You are silent!

Lis. (*aside*) I shall expire!—My lord, if your child is not totally unworthy to petition for——

Gov. Do not tease me with your importunities; it cannot be.

Lis. Surely, my lord, so venial a fault may be forgiven?

Gov. It is not so venial as you think.

Flor. (*aside*) How earnestly she pleads! Her father's eye is continually on me.

Lis. Was it then a crime to go incognito to a public garden?

Gov. A crime! A father's honor ought to be held sacred.

Lis. Your just reproof penetrates my soul. My lord, on my knees I implore your forgiveness.

Gov. Do you think I am angry with you, because I deny your request? Believe me, child, it is only from necessity.

Lis. I will not rise till you are moved by my sorrow.

Flor. How much I owe her!

Gov. My dear Lisarda, I cannot comply. No door shall be unlocked, till the church has made all secure.

Lis. I will not so much as look through the lattice, only make me happy in your affection.

Gov. Nothing is more easy, my child. That you may be convinced how dear you are to me, listen to the reception I shall give your friend. (*to* Florida) You are welcome, young lady, to my house, which I beg you will consider as your own. I am not a severe censor of the follies of love; neither am I surprised at the accidents which have befallen you, as they are frequent in such adventures. Here you will be safe and happy,

for you shall not quit my house, till you are honorably mar‑
ried. If my respect for yourself were even less, the earnest
entreaties of my daughter, whom I tenderly love, would induce
me to protect you with my life.

Lis.   Heavens! What is it I hear?

Cel. (*aside to* Lisarda) You see, Signora, how mistaken
you were, in supposing that your father knew you; since he
thinks she was the prisoner!

Lis. (*to* Celia) Fortune, most unexpectedly, has turned
evil into good! Oh that she may not change!

Flor. (*aside*) Lisarda has related my history, to induce
her father the more readily to grant me an asylum. Excellent
idea! I am spared the shame of telling it myself. (*aloud*)
My lord!

Cel. (*aside*) Would she were silent! She will spoil all, I
fear.

Flor.   The virtuous and noble are ever the protectors of
helpless woman!   Behold one at your feet: since you are in‑
formed of my unhappy story, take pity on a distressed
stranger, and preserve her honor.

Lis. (*to her women*) Nisa, Celia, what is this? By what
lucky accident is evil thus converted into good?

Flor. (*to* Lisarda) To you, beauteous Lisarda, my obliga‑
tions are infinite. You not only have received me with kind‑
ness, but have exerted your influence with your honored father
in my behalf. I owe you my life.

Lis. (*aside*) Her words are ambiguous! I will favor the
mistake. (*aloud*) The obligation is mine, not yours, my dear
friend. All the influence I possess is at your command.

Gov.   You shall find it is great: I will do all I can.

[*Exeunt* Florida *and* Nisa.

SCENE VII.

Lis.   As we ought to proceed cautiously, in this affair, pray
tell me, dear Sir, who this lady is?

Gov.   Her birth and family are noble; she eloped with
a Cavalier. You see, by her example, to what dangers indis‑
cretion may expose your sex.

Lis. (*aside*) Alas! I tremble yet.

SCENE VIII.—*Enter a* Servant.

Serv.   My lord, a Cavalier, booted and spurred, asks to see
you.

Gov.   It is Don Juan.

Lis. (*aside*) Here is a new torment.

SCENE IX.—*Enter* DON JUAN, *booted and spurred.*

Don J. I am most happy, my lord, that you esteemed me worthy of the honor I now enjoy, in being permitted to kiss your hand. However fortune may have given me cause of complaint, in delaying my happiness so long, the pleasure I now receive fully compensates for her cruelty.

Gov. You are most welcome, Don Juan. We have been for some days in impatient expectation of your arrival: you have given us much anxiety.

Don J. Being happily arrived, I will not consume the time in vain regret.

Gov. How gallantly you look the soldier! But you do not speak to Lisarda?

Don J. I am mute with admiration! My senses are entranced! Her eyes are brilliant suns! (*to* Lisarda, *taking her hand*) Beautiful Lisarda, if it be not too much presumption, let me take this fair hand; the quiver in which Love stores his keenest arrows, since it rivals the virgin snow, not melted by the rays of Phœbus! Report had taught me to expect you were lovely; but I find you beyond all praise! You alone car accuse Fame of speaking in modest terms. Yet, no; your beauty is acknowledged to be incomparable. If I am confused, you must impute it to your matchless perfections.

Lis. I have often heard that Love, whom the poets feign blind, was the son of Mars and Venus: I now can believe it, since a soldier can flatter. Others have affirmed that Adonis was the father of Love: nor can I deny it, since, with the valour of Mars, you combine the graces of Adonis.

Gov. A truce to compliments: the palm is due to Lisarda.

Don J. Who can stand in competition with her? How lovely is her person! How charming are her manners!

Gov. I will show you to your apartment: you must be weary. I will not apologize for the plain accommodation you will find; you are a soldier, and will excuse it.

Don J. Excuse! Am I not in the sanctuary of a divinity?

[*Exeunt* Don Juan *and* Governor.

SCENE X.

Lis. Since we are left a moment free, tell me, Celia, what you think of my adventure?

Cel. Your fears and danger are now happily past. But how came your father to suppose the strange lady his prisoner?

Lis. Seeing a stranger here, it was natural enough he should draw that inference.

Cel. I saw your fears were vain.

Lis. 'Tis most extraordinary! Though totally ignorant of the lady's history, my answers were applicable.

Cel. Affairs of love are so alike!

Lis. I've now another fear.

Cel. Since you have escaped the worst, and your bride-groom is arrived, ought you to think of any thing but joy?

Lis. How littel, Celia, do you know the force of love! Difficulties, in a thousand instances, do but increase its violence. I cannot endure that a gentleman, to whose generosity I am so much indebted, should languish in confinement: neither will I, should he, as I fear, prove to be the Cavalier of Laura, cherish an improper love. I will clear up this cruel doubt. You shall carry him a note from me, inviting him to come and see me to-morrow night, if he can bribe or elude the vigilance of his guards. I will continue the deception and receive him, not in my own character, but as the lady, whom he supposes to be a prisoner.

Cel. Dear lady, be advised!

Lis. Expostulation is in vain.

Cel. Reflect——

Lis. I am resolved.

Cel. For once, be persuaded.

Lis. Would you see me die?

Cel. Consider——

Lis. Be silent.

Cel. The danger——

Lis. I see it.

Cel. Your life——

Lis. Is indifferent to me.

Cel. Your honor——

Lis. My honor? Ridiculous fear!

Cel. I am anxious——

Lis. For what?

Cel. Your good. I fear——

Lis. What is it you fear?

Cel. Your ruin!

Lis. You intend then to make a solitary pilgrimage to the Holy Land?

Cel. How so?

Lis. As the only chambermaid, who was vexed to see her mistress in love.   [*Exeunt.*

SCENE XI.—*Changes to the Fortress.* Don Cesar; Camacho.

Cam. Your gallantry, Sir, has brought us into an enviable situation!

Don C. Did you see her? The sight of such a face cannot be too dearly bought.

Cam. St. Jago defend me from her face! It were better she had been ugly; you would not then have been gallant, and we should not be here. But her malicious eyes have set the spells of justice upon us.

Don C. Blasphemer!

Cam. Nay, Signor, if you are angry, it ought to be with that angel of malice! It was not accident that introduced her to us; she came with mischief in her heart, and a plausible tale at her tongue's end, of danger and death to entrap you, Sir, a loyal knight, and me, a faithful squire. You believe in the authenticity of her nobility? Think no more of it, Signor: we are not in fairy land, where fell magicians, captive princesses, enchanted forests, and adventurous knights, are met with at every step.

Don C. If she were not a person of consequence, why should the Governor detain her a prisoner?

Cam. To get a clear riddance of her.

Don. C. No, Camacho; I have a different suspicion: she most probably is a woman of rank, who has been unfortunate: for merit and beauty are no guard against the malice of fortune. The secrecy she observes, and the pursuit of the Governor, confirm me in this opinion. The latter, no doubt, was informed of her being at the garden, at the same time that he discovered my retreat. How touching was her distress, when she implored my protection! How unwillingly she made the discovery of her rank!

Cam. You are eloquent, Sir. By this circumlocution, no doubt, you mean to say that Donna Florida, and her faithful affection, are forgotten?

Don C. Forgotten? Oh, no! Never, never can the first attachment of my heart change! The painter, about to begin a portrait, can easily sketch an outline, if the canvass be untouched. But, if outlines have already been traced, he cannot proceed, till they are obliterated. The divine image of my adorable Florida is engraven on my heart; and, till it is erased, no other can make any lasting impression.

Cam. Oh, I'll answer for that, if we should again be visited by this veiled sorceress. Something assures me, we have not yet done with the agents of darkness.

SCENE XII.—*Enter* CELIA, *veiled.*

Cel. Signor Fabio?

Don C. You come timely, to bring life and consolation to a wretch almost exhausted.

Cel. Here is a note from the lady, who was taken prisoner with you, and who languishes in sorrow.

Don C. Take this diamond *, and let it grace the hand which brings me so fair a gift.

---

* A part of this speech, in the Spanish, is so far-fetched that it is unintelligible: it is, literally, " son of the sun, which would be a wandering star if, like a gilded ornament, it should be seen placed in the eighth zenith."

Cam.   Will you show me its colour!

Cel.   No!

Cam.   I have a diamond the twin to that; let me see your face and it shall be yours.

Cel.   No.

Cam.   Oh! Then your face is——.

Cel.   Ugly, do you think?

Cam.   Why, if it were handsome, you would not hide it.

Cel.   Look, then! Is it so very disagreeable.

Cam.   I don't wish to see it. (*turns away his head.*)

Cel.   Impertinence!

Cam.   You are unwilling to show, and I to be shown.

Cel.   You shall have the diamond, if you will look.

Cam.   I am inexorable.

Don C.   (*to* Celia) My lovely prisoner shall be obeyed.

Cel.   Fare you well.   [*Exit.*

Cam.   Adieu, my Infanta! Tell your mistress the pitcher that goes so often to the well is at last broken. (*to* Don Cesar) Well, Signor, what says the note? Any new mischief in cogitation?

Don C.   She tells me to visit her this night, and that she has bribed the women of Donna Lisarda to introduce me into the Governor's house; to which she adds a thousand unnecessary cautions, such as to come alone, and to be secret.

Cam.   And you freely promised to go, having no doubt the keys of this prison in your pocket?

Don C.   What should prevent me?

Cam.   The guards.

Don C.   A bribe will set the most vigilant to sleep.

SCENE XIII.—*Enter* Don Juan.

Don J.   I come, Don Cesar, to condole with you; while you have to congratulate me. According to naturalists, there are two poisons, which, when mixed, are not only harmless but nutritive. Now good and ill fortune are both poisons, which, taken separately, may be fatal. You are weighed down by sorrow; I am oppressed with joy: let us then join stock, and make a fair equilibrium.

Don C.   You are content then, Don Juan?

Don J.   Oh, my good fortune exceeds all that imagination had conceived; and love has presented me with the master-piece of nature. When I had provided myself with jewels and suitable apparel, I left my friend the Alcaide, and hiring post horses hastened to the Governor's palace; or rather the temple of the sun, by whose glorious rays all other splendor was thrown into shade. There I beheld heaven reduced to one sphere, spring to a single flower, the zephyr to a breath, the riches of Aurora to a pearl, and the sun to one glorious beam : for, in Lisarda, these miracles of nature are concentrated ; and I am most fortunate in being the possessor of beauty and merit so incomparable.

Don C. And I am most unfortunate ; for I am involved in an intrigue in despite of myself, which seems only to promise vexations. As you justly observed, Don Juan, my misfortunes will be an antidote to your glory. Suppose yourself questioned as a casuist, be the subject love, and answer accordingly. Picture to yourself an alabaster forehead, eyes that are living suns, cheeks that shame the carnation ! I have beheld Flora, Queen of May, rivalled in all her fragrant charms. But ask me not who this angel is, for of that I am ignorant myself. I can only tell you that she invites me, by this note, to visit her tonight, if I can elude the vigilance of my guards. I promised to go, rashly depending on your influence with the Alcaide.

Don J. Do not torment yourself with useless fears, Don Cesar: I have no doubt of his compliance. Camacho, tell the Alcaide I want to speak with him. (*Exit* Camacho) He is my intimate friend, and will readily suffer you to quit the fortress, in my company.

Don C. Ask him to let me accompany you, when Night has spread her raven wing.

SCENE XIV.—*Enter* Alcaide *and* CAMACHO.

Alc. What are your commands, Don Juan.

Don J. You see I am once more your guest ; for where Don Cesar is I must be.

Alc. The obligations I owe you are sufficient to command my services.

Don J. Suffer my friend this night to go with me, if I deserve this act of friendship.

Alc. Reason and law would argue against compliance, but I cannot refuse you : only give me your word that your friend shall return before morning.

Don C. Ere the rosy dawn dispels the shades of night, I shall again be your prisoner.

Alc. Till then, may you prosper ! [*Exit* Alcaide.

SCENE XV.

Don J. Now, my friend, I'll attend you: wherever you lead, my sword and arm are at your service.

Don C. You cannot with propriety stay so long from the Governor, and your bride. Pray return to the palace.

Don J. It is not just that I should lead you into danger, and there leave you.

Don C. I entreat !

Don J. I will not be refused.

Don C. (*aside*)   How vexatious ! To carry him to the governor's house, and to expose the friend to whose generosity **I**
am so much indebted, would be cowardly and base.

Don J.   Why do you hesitate?

Don C.   You think me ungrateful, for concealing my
foolish intrigue from you.   Thank Heaven, the friendship
which subsisted between Pilades and Orestes, or Euryalus and
Nisus, has not been unexampled : in you I have a perfect
friend ; do not think I am insensible to your zeal, but forgive
me if I request you to leave me.   I am ignorant who the lady
is, and I was required to be alone.

Don J.   It were in vain to combat such obstinacy ; farewell.
(*aside*) Ill timed mystery ! Impertinent love !   [*Exit.*

SCENE XVI.

Don C.   Camacho!

Cam.   Signor?

Don C.   Give me my pocket pistol.

Cam.   Here it is, Signor : but is it properly charged ?   You
must not go ill provided.

Don C.   It is as it ought to be.

Cam.   Am I to remain here?

Don C.   Yes.   [*Exit,*

Cam.   Your worships will bear witness that here I am *.

SCENE XVII.—*Changes to the Governor's House.*

Enter Lisarda *and* Nisa *with a Light.*

Lis.   Nisa.

Nisa.   Signora?

Lis.   Is my father retired to his chamber ?

Nisa.   He is.

Lis.   And Don Juan?

Nisa.   Yes, Signora.

Lis.   Where is Laura?

Nisa.   In her room, weeping as usual.   Night and day, she
mourns her cruel destiny.

Lis.   Her tears, I fear, are the confirmation of my misfortune.   Where is Celia?

Nisa.   She is waiting at the garden gate, for the Cavalier.

Lis.   When he comes, treat me without ceremony, and
dissemble my real quality; because he is to suppose me the
lady whom my father took prisoner, and in whose name I have
made this appointment.

Nisa.   I hear gentle footsteps.

Lis.   It is he, no doubt.

---

* This is addressed to the audience.

SCENE XVIII.—*Enter* CELIA *followed by* DON CESAR.

Don C. Gloom and the silence of night are favorable to love.

Cel. Tread softly, for the Lady Lisarda is not yet in bed, and the Governor sleeps hard by.

Don C. Cupid, lend me thy wings!

Lis. You are welcome, Signor.

Don C. In those fair eyes I view the light of heaven.

Lis. Celia, watch at the door, which leads to your master's chamber: do you, friend Nisa, take care that your lady does not surprise us.

Nisa. I tremble.

Lis. Why so?

Nisa. Because my lady is so nigh.

Lis. Keep on the watch, and fear nothing.

Nisa. I have cause enough to fear, for my lady is a dragon of virtue: if she knew such interviews were carried on in her house, her fury would exceed all bounds.

Don C. How anxious I was, Signora, to find an opportunity of speaking with you! I am in a labyrinth of doubt, and am at a loss to account for your imprisonment.

Lis. Nay, that is easily done. I was mistaken for a lady, whom it seems you have carried off, and in search of whom the Governor came.

Don C. I carried off a lady! You are jesting.

Lis. I am serious.

Don C. This is an ingenious artifice, to evade satisfying my suspicions. Am I so contemptible that I cannot excite jealousy? Do you think that, if a lady had been concealed with me, I should have been so regardless of her feelings as to have seen and conversed with you? Were not your terror, and the desire you showed that I should protect you, sufficient proof you were afraid of being discovered? If the Governor had been mistaken in the person, you would now be free. I am persuaded some slighted lover has taken this unmanly revenge on you.

Lis. Do you think that a lover of mine could be guilty of so contemptible an action? Am I so very insignificant? You may be assured, I am a woman of rank; and, being such, the adventure is not at all improbable.

Don C. I believe you, Signora; but I wish to hear more.

Lis. Sit down.

> [*As they are going to sit, the pistol of* Don Cesar *goes off.*

Don C. Heaven defend us!

Lis. What will become of me?

Cel.   I am half dead!

Nisa.   Unfortunate accident!

Gov.   (*within*)   What is that?   Who goes there?

Lis.   Answer!   Wretched me!

Nisa.   I cannot speak!

Cel.   I am breathless!

Don C.   Who can provide against unforeseen accidents?

Cel.   I hear my lord in his chamber ; he is certainly rising.

Lis.   I believe my end is nigh.

Don C.   What is to be done?

Lis.   You must jump through the window into the court, which leads to the vestibule, where you may escape by the door.   I am too adventurous!   The victim of my own imprudence!   I give you my word, you shall know who I am, and the destiny of her in whom you are deceived, and whom you love.

Don C.   My life is at your devotion. (*jumps through the window.*)

SCENE XIX.

Enter the GOVERNOR *in his Shirt and Doublet, with a Sword and Buckler**.

Gov.   Who went out?

Lis.   Nobody, Signor. (*aside*)   Wretched me!

Gov.   What ails you?   Why are you thus disturbed?

Lis.   The pistol that went off frightened me.

[*A noise within.*

Gov.   What is that?

Lis.   I don't know.   How I tremble!

Gov.   Give me the light ; I will search the house, though, if my honor be lost, I cannot hope to recover it.   [*Exit.*

[*Scene changes to the Vestibule of the Palace: total darkness.*

Don C. (*groping*)   I am in a pretty dilemma: in seeking the door, I have got I know not whither, and am quite bewildered.   Why did I come here?   Gracious Heaven!   How shall I satisfy my suspicions?   How extricate myself from difficulties?   All is dark!   What shall I do?   I cannot find the door, yet this is certainly the vestibule, for here is the porter's chair, which fortunately is empty.   I will conceal myself behind it, and trust to chance for my deliverance.

[Don Cesar *conceals himself behind a porter's chair: and the* Governor *enters on one side, with a light and his sword drawn:* Don Juan *on the other, with his naked sword.*

---

* The reader must remember that Calderon wrote at the beginning of the 17th century.

Gov. The noise proceeded from this place. Who goes there?

Don J. Hearing your voice, my lord, I left my chamber.

Gov. (*aside*) To increase my perplexity.

Don J. What means all this noise?

Gov. Nothing! Nothing! (*aside*) My honor forces me to dissemble. (*aloud*) I thought I heard a noise near my apartment, and I rose and searched the house, but found nobody, except my daughter, who had been disturbed by my rising. It was no doubt imaginary.

Don J. You were not deceived, my lord, in thinking somebody was in the house; for I heard a noise like jumping out of a window.

Gov. (*aside*) It is in vain to endeavour to conceal my dishonor. (*aloud*) I have searched the house, and am satisfied: if you are not, take the light and search further.

Don J. (*taking the candle*) Look to the door, my lord, that no one may escape. I will search the vestibule.

Gov. There is nobody thus far.

Don J. But here is a porter's chair; a man may easily conceal himself behind it.

Gov. Examine.

> [Don Juan *looks behind the chair and perceives*
> Don Cesar, *who makes signs to him not to*
> *betray him.*

Don J. (*aside*) Merciful God! What is it I see?

Gov. Have you discovered any one?

Don J. No, my lord. (*aside*) Would to Heaven I had not!

Gov. I have searched every other place.

Don J. It is evident—my lord—that—that I was mistaken. The wind might cause the clapping of a door, or—— You had better retire, Signor.

Gov. Return to your chamber, Don Juan, in peace; for, be assured, nobody was in the house.

Don J. Good night, my lord; I, as well as you, have been deceived. [*Exit* Governor.

SCENE XX.

Don J. We mutually seek by evasion to hide our dishonor, and conceal our misfortunes. Great God! How shall I act? Cesar concealed here! Cesar steal into this house at the very moment when I would have protected him with my life? Am I the author of my own dishonor! He might well say he could not tell me the lady's name, since, oh God! it was Lisarda. My friendship and confidence are betrayed, no less than my honor; and each, individually, calls for revenge. I could easily kill him, but how could I then fulfil my word, and bring him back to prison? Have I not promised to defend his life?

And shall I take that life? Heavenly Powers! What am I to do? Must one arm protect, the other kill? Yet die he must? When honor is in question, all other considerations must vanish. Don Cesar!

Don C. (*advancing from behind the chair, and kneeling to* Don Juan) Behold me at your feet.

Don J. Follow me, Don Cesar, and leave vain apologies.

Don C. What is your intention?

Don J. To be revenged on a traitor.

Don C. Your honor and your love, Don Juan, are not injured. I am not a coward, but I would not have you commit an action of which you would afterward repent, without having the power to remedy the mischief.

Don J. How?

Don C. Listen to me, and your doubts shall be satisfactorily answered.

Don J. Is it possible?

Don C. It is.

Don J. Would to Heaven it were!

Don C. First, hear me; then, if you still doubt, seek revenge.

Don J. What excuse can justify your violation of honor, confidence, and friendship? Honor, in breaking into this house; friendship, in seducing the affections of my mistress; and confidence, in making me the accomplice of my infamy? Have I not reason to complain, when my friend is false, treacherous, and dishonorable?

Don C. I may, perhaps, have slightly sinned against confidence and friendship: but the honor of my friend is a sacred altar, at which I would, if necessary, sacrifice my life. I came here to visit a lady, who is a prisoner, and who was taken with me: this is a sufficient reason for me to pay her the attention of a gentleman, and a courtier. You must not be offended at my concealing her abode from you, since it was out of delicacy and respect to your mistress, under whose roof she lives. If you think I have dishonored a family, to which you are so highly indebted, my life is at your service, and I shall die the victim of your unjust suspicions. This honest confession ought to satisfy your honor, banish your suspicions, and restore me to your confidence: since the only wrong you suffer is in doubting my honor, my friendship, and my sincerity.

Don J. These excuses seem good, but they are insufficient: give me till to-morrow, I then will answer you.

Don C. With all my heart. I will return to prison.

Don J. Expect me there.

Don C. Adieu, till to-morrow.

Don J. Adieu.   [*Exeunt.*

ACT III.

SCENE I.

The Vestibule in the Governor's Palace. DON JUAN.

Don Juan.

EVER since the rosy dawn first awoke the god of day, my anxious fears have chained me to this spot. I will know my fate. The fair prisoner shall receive neither letter nor message, till I have spoken with her. By taking her unprepared, I shall either be confirmed in my misery, or relieved from the load which oppresses me. Oh, I would give my life to find myself mistaken! If only to imagine my suspicions are just wounds like the arrow of death, how shall I support the reality? I have accused my friend! My misfortune is unequalled, since the remedy will kill no less than the disease. Yonder is Celia—Celia?

SCENE II.—*Enter* CELIA.

Cel. What risen already, Signor?

Don J. Is your lady awake?

Cel. She is getting up.

Don J. Then Aurora a second time shall hail adoring mortals.

Cel. I am now going to my lady; have you any message, Signor?

Don J. Tell her, I am wafting my sighs to her window.

[*Exit* Celia.

SCENE III.

Don J. Oh, what torments the jealous suffer! This strange lady is late this morning: I will however wait; for, as the proverb says, bad news travels post, while the good walks on crutches. This tardiness may be a lucky omen. Oh, how I shall repent my rashness, if my suspicions prove false!

SCENE IV.—*Enter* GOVERNOR.

Gov. Don Juan?

Don J. My lord!

Gov. So early a riser? I fancy the same wish mutually brought us here.

Don J. Very likely.

Gov. You seem to seek me; and I came to find you.

Don J. What is your pleasure, my lord?

Gov. That you may know how highly I esteem you, I will
no longer defer your happiness. I well know that love is impatient of delay. This night you shall be the fortunate husband of Lisarda.

Don J. (*aside*) New fears assail me!

Gov. (*aside*) His hesitation confirms my suspicions.

Don J. My lord, since it was your intention to have deferred
this favor for a few days, pray do not regard me; I can wait.

Gov. I only waited to make the necessary preparations,
which are now finished.

Don J. (*aside*) Cruel perplexity!

Gov. (*aside*) It wears a gloomy aspect. I too plainly
perceive that Don Juan, as well as myself, discovered the infamy of last night—If you refuse your consent to-day, Don
Juan, to-morrow it will be my turn.   [*Exit.*

SCENE V.

Don J. What a cruel dilemma! But here comes the lady I
seek. Oh, jealousy, death alone can set thee at defiance!

SCENE VI.—*Enter* FLORIDA.

Flor. You are here early, Signor.

Don J. Yes, and solely to speak with you, Signora.

Flor. Pray let me hear.

Don J. Will you trust to my honor, and truly answer the
questions I may ask?

Flor. I will.

Don J. You safely may, for you are deeply interested in
them. Speak freely: do you know Don Cesar Ursino?

Flor. Yes, Signor. Would to Heaven I never had known
him! He is the cause of my being here; for his sake, I have
endured woes unspeakable; and have sacrificed my reputation
to the love I bear him.

Don J. (*aside*) This is a favorable beginning—Did you
meet him by night?

Flor. Often have I met him at the risk of my life.

Don J. (*aside*) Take courage my heart! (*aloud*) Tell me,
without reserve, did you meet him in the garden?

Flor. Spare me, Signor! A garden was the scene of my
disgrace! and its fragrant flowers bore silent testimony of my
cruel fortune.

Don J. This is sufficient! You have given me new life.
(*aside*) Oh, honorable friend, pardon my unjust suspicions! I
am undeceived—Adieu, Signora: accept my grateful acknow-
ledgments, and do not mention what has passed between us to
Lisarda.

Flor. Stay, Signor—Whither in such haste?

Don J. Since my doubts are satisfied, it is but just that I should fly to my friend Don Cesar, who expects me in his prison : I wish to hear no more—Adieu ! [*Exit.*

SCENE VII.

Flor. Fly to Don Cesar ? What does he mean ? His inquiries, his knowledge of my lover's imprisonment, and his eagerness to see him, fill me with new doubts. Yet, most probably, he questioned me that he might bring my lover intelligence of my abode. He plainly gave me to understand, by telling me he was going to see him, that he had been desired by Don Cesar to inform me of his imprisonment—Shall I not fly to console him ?

SCENE VIII.—*Enter* LISARDA *and* CELIA. FLORIDA *going.*

Lis. Why do you hurry away ?

Flor. Not being ignorant, little as my deserts are, that my felicity will be yours, I must inform you my lover is a prisoner here. I have just now received the intelligence, and he has been told that I am in your house. Oh, how fortunate was my coming hither ! He cannot accuse me of having been a despised vagrant, in his absence ! I am wild with joy ! To-day, I shall see my beloved Cesar ! [*Exit.*

SCENE IX.

Lis. Vexation on vexation !

Cel. What vexation ?

Lis. Are you blind to the tender fear which lurks in every pang, and which shrinks from conviction as from death ? Am I not most wretched ? Is not the malice of fortune unconquerable ?

Cel. In what ?

Lis. Do I not too plainly discover that the Cavalier, whom, alas, I find I love, is betrothed to this lady, whom I protect. Yes, events all rush on " from bad to worse * !"

Cel. Supposing there only to be one duellist in the world, Signora, your fears would be reasonable ; but not when three persons out of four † commit the same fault. Banish these gloomy illusions ! If Jealousy be an astrologer, and draws this black horoscope, for that very reason you ought not to believe a syllable of it.

---

* Lisarda has a very long speech, with poetical quotations, repeating the incidents already known. Calderon appears to have doubted either of the memory or the understanding of his audience.

† This proves the dangerous excess of duelling, at that time, in Spain.

SCENE X.—*Enter* CAMACHO.

Cam. (*to himself*) I am embarked in this blessed adventure, with the risk of being turned neck and shoulders out of doors. However, I will break the enchantment!

Cel. Here is the servant of Signor Fabio.

Lis. (*to* Celia) His servant! It was he, no doubt, who informed Laura that his master was in prison. I will know the truth. He has never seen my face; we must dissemble.

Cel. (*to* Camacho) What brings you here, friend, with so little ceremony?

Cam. My legs brought me; and, if you, ladies, are offended, they shall carry me back again to the same time and tune. I cannot brag much of my agility in dancing, for my right foot cannot beat measure with my left; but they can beat a quick retreat.

Lis. Say, good soldier, who are you?

Cam. I would tell you, if I could; but verily it is more than I know myself, for I belong to a master, God mend him, who keeps me in a continual state of jeopardy. He, like a knight possessed, is galloping through the labyrinth of love in search of a sun in eclipse; or, to speak plainer, of a lady enveloped, from the sole of her foot to the crown of her head, in a veil. Oh, rare invention; the most convenient in the world! If either of you are a prisoner, say so for love of God; for I, a stranger here, am come solely to find such a lady, and if I return unsuccessful, I may expect a broken head. Suffer me then to pay my most sovereign homage to her beauty, and have the goodness to point her out.

Cel. (*to* Lisarda) Did not I tell you, Signora, that the astrologer lied?

Lis. He may come to seek the lady who is a prisoner, unknown to herself.

Cel. How skilful the imagination is in tormenting itself!

Lis. (*aside*) While jealousy dissembles, love speaks the truth. (*to* Camacho) Is your master so partial to this lady?

Cam. Yes, Signora.

Lis. Is it for her beauty, or her wit?

Cam. Oh, for both.

Lis. Does he praise her much?

Cam. Oh, he praises her inordinately.

Lis. He loves her then?

Cam. Oh, no; there is a first love to be effaced. My master only amuses himself; because, you know, one face obliterates another in painting.

Lis. Obliterates! Painting! What do you mean?

Cam. That is more than I know. But I think you are the lady that is to obliterate the other: pray tell me if I guess right?

Lis. (*aside*) I shall expire!—No, insolent audacious intruder, I am not. I am the Governor's daughter, and will not suffer such intrigues to be carried on before my face. The woman you seek is under my protection, for this house is the sanctuary of honor. Dare again to enter these doors, and four lackeys shall toss you out of the window.

Cam. Four! Weigh me, and you will find that three are sufficient. Three! Nay, two will execute the task. Why do I say two? One is quite enough. One! A half, a quarter, an arm, a hand, nay, a finger would master me: so, before they make their appearance, I shall beat a march—Adieu, Signora! [*Exit.*

SCENE XI.

Lis. My ill fortune pursues me in every trifle.

Cel. You listen too much to your fears.

Lis. I will end this cruel suspense. I will let him know that, if he can bribe his guards, I will elude the vigilance of mine; and that I will meet him wherever he likes.

Cel. Good!

Lis. Should he name a place of rendezvous, I will take this lady with me; and, if he prove to be her Cavalier (preserve me, Love, from so cruel a disappointment) I will renounce my hopes: but, if I am fortunately mistaken, my love shall conquer all difficulties.

Cel. But, supposing him to be a man of strict honor, your consenting to meet him, on such terms, will give him an ill opinion of you.

Lis. Never fear. I shall find a remedy for all inconveniencies.

SCENE XII.—*Enter* FLORIDA, *veiled.*

Lis. Where are you going, Laura?

Flor. With your permission, lady, to a prison, which contains my soul!

Lis. (*aside*) Wretched me! Say rather going to take my life! Shall I suffer her to leave me distracted with suspense?—Is my house so little worthy of respect, Signora, that you take your veil and go when and where you please?

Flor. My fortunes are now so low it little matters, since they have brought me from Naples to this place, that I should go from hence to a prison.

Lis. Have you no recollection of the interest we have shown for your honor? What will my father say, should he find you gone?

Flor. I will return before he comes; it is not very late.

Lis. You must accompany me on a visit, this evening.

Flor. Can you expect that I shall delay seeing my betrothed husband?

Lis. I want you.

Flor. I will return instantly : I only wish to see him.

Lis. But I wish you to stay.

Flor. I shall then be at your service.

Lis. It is in vain to argue ; you cannot go.

Flor. Indeed, Signora, I must.

SCENE XIII.—*Enter* GOVERNOR.

Gov. How ? Wrangling !

Lis. The lady is angry, because I wish her well. She would fain have gone out and not asked your permission.

Gov. Was that all ?

Flor. I own, my lord, I should have consulted you ; but surely it is no crime to visit a man whom I adore, to whom I am betrothed, and who is in a prison !

Gov. Very true ; but you are detained a prisoner, that you may not see him.

Flor. A prisoner, my lord !

Gov. Are you so forgetful ? Do not you remember the garden ?

Flor. Oh, yes ! Too well !

Gov. Came you not a prisoner from thence ?

Lis. (*aside*) The mistake will be discovered.

Flor. A prisoner ? No, my lord.

Gov. Did not I find you there ?

Flor. I came here voluntarily.

Gov. Did I not send you hither under an escort ?

Flor. (*to* Lisarda) For the love of God, Signora, explain this.

Lis. Did I not find you concealed in my house ? How should I have known your story, but from yourself.

Flor. What strange misunderstanding is this ?

Gov. You still persist in denying it ? I shall leave you together : for Heaven's sake, recollect yourself, lady ! You will drive me mad !   [*Exit* Governor.

SCENE XIV.

Flor. I sent here a prisoner !

Lis. No.

Flor. Then, why did you so cruelly mortify me ?

Lis. Pardon me, Laura * ; I acted from necessity. Come with me this evening ; you shall then know all, and your anxiety shall cease.

Flor. Patience, I follow thy steps !   [*Exeunt.*

SCENE XV.—*Changes to the Fortress :* DON JUAN, DON CESAR.

Don J. I am ashamed of having doubted your friendship ! But Love, whom the poets describe as blind, and to whom the

---

* The name Florida assumes to Lisarda.

gods have allotted Jealousy as a guide, must plead my excuse.
Nor think it an idle invention that Love is the slave of Jealousy, and must implicitly follow her dictates. My suspicions
are now removed, my doubts cleared, and I am perfectly satisfied: if you are not, cut my throat.

Don C. Though I might justly complain, dear Juan, of
your incredulity, I will be silent. I love you too well not to
overlook the first cause you ever gave me of dissatisfaction. I
confess that appearances were against me, and that your generosity in sparing my life was great; but I must likewise own
that I would not admit the apology of any man, but yourself,
who had doubted my honor. How were you undeceived?

Don J. It pains me to recollect that I wronged you: let us
consign this disagreeable affair to oblivion. My eyes and lips
will bear witness that your mistress is handsome.

Don C. Rather say beautiful.

Don J. But Lisarda is incomparably more lovely. Her
beauty is a sun, to which all beauties are satellites! A boundless ocean, in which the noblest rivers are lost!

Don C. Her beauty may be less; but, in wit and understanding, my prisoner cannot be inferior. Suffer me to read
you a billet I have just received; for, since Love has dropped
the mask, secrecy would be absurd.

Don J. It will give me pleasure.

Don C. You will find I have not exaggerated her merit.

SCENE XVI.—*Enter* CAMACHO.

Cam. Thank Heaven, I have escaped! I can scarcely move
one foot before the other.

Don J. What is the matter?

Don C. Why are you so frightened?

Cam. Oh, I have windows, balconies, and lackeys at my
heels! (*to* Don Cesar) I went, Signor, to catch a glimpse at
your lady prisoner, to see if she were as handsome and as
witty as you said; but I stumbled upon a she-dragon, who
called herself Lisarda, and who fell into a desperate fury, on
hearing the business I came about, and threatened to have me
tossed out of the window, if ever I set foot in her doors again.

Don J. I believe you. Lisarda is no less prudent than she
is beautiful. But let us hear the billet, Don Cesar, that we
may admire the wit of the fair writer.

Don C. (*reads aloud*) "If you can bribe your guards, as
I have bribed mine, I will see you this evening; but on
three conditions. First, that you send a sedan chair to the
door of the great church; secondly, that you find a place
where we may safely converse; and, thirdly, that you leave
your pistols at home."

Don J. The style is courteous and tierce; but the attempt appears to me a rash one.

Cam. Signors, listen to a tale which I shall have the honor to recount. A country boor, loaded with a cord, a pole, a goat, a fowl, an onion, and a saucepan, came trudging from market: a strapping lass, on the same road, called out and desired he would stop to speak with her. " Wounds!" exclaimed the clown, " don't you see I'm loaded? Would you have me lose my purchases?"—" You are a ninny," said she : " cannot you stick the pole in the ground, tie your goat to it by the leg with the cord, cover your fowl with your saucepan, and put the onion in your mouth?" When a woman is bent on doing a thing, no human obstacle can prevent her.

Don J. (*to* Cesar) What is your plan?

Don C. If you could again prevail on the Alcaide to let me out, as the day is declining, I would immediately seek a lodging and meet the lady.

Cam. Your lordship is laden as heavily as the countryman; nay more so.

Don J. I will answer for the permission of the Alcaide, and I can offer you my apartments with safety ; for that side of the palace has a private door, which leads into a back street. You can go there, in a coach, and receive your mistress.

Cam. The thought is excellent! You certainly, Signor, have taken a lesson of the country lass.

Don J. Go, Camacho; hire a chair. Here is the key of my apartments; put every thing in order, and then fetch the lady. Make haste.

Cam. So! I am like a cook, who prepares the most dainty dishes, without being permitted to taste one of them! I must be content with looking on and admiring!   [*Exit* Camacho.

SCENE XVII.

Don C. How can I acknowledge your kindness?

Don J. Let it atone for my injustice, yesterday.

Don C. Will you indeed procure my freedom, and leave me your apartments for to-night?

Don J. It will be better that you should go now, than wait till night. But here comes the Governor.

Don C. His coming hither is strange!

SCENE XVIII.—*Enter* Governor.

Gov. You here, Don Juan!

Don J. I too am a prisoner, my lord.

Gov. A prisoner!

Don J. Yes; since my friend is in prison.

Gov. You speak well : but, if this argument holds good, we are all prisoners; for we are all the friends of Don Cesar.

Don C. Language can feebly express how deeply I feel your kindness! May your days be long, and happy!

Gov. Don Juan, do me the honor to leave me with your friend : we have much to say to each other.

Don J. I obey your commands.

Don C. *(aside)* Vexatious interruption ! What an opportunity have I lost ! I shall never be so fortunate again. *(whispers* Don Juan) You see my situation, Don Juan ; if the lady should be arrived at your apartments, since cruel fortune will not allow me to keep my appointment, see her yourself (she will, no doubt, be disguised as before) and tell her I am distracted that I am prevented from meeting her : but do not, for your life, let her perceive that you know her.

Don J. You may depend on me.

Don C. Once more, remember, she must not in the least suspect that you know her.

Don J. She shall not. [*Exit.*

SCENE XIX.

Gov. Let us be seated, Don Cesar. *(they sit.)*

Don C. I am entirely at your devotion.

Gov. First, it is necessary to inform you that Don Alonzo Colona is the friend of my youth ; the just regard I have for his honor, and happiness, urges me to interest myself in your concerns. Do not consider me as a stern judge : it is true, I wish to serve my friend ; but with moderation and wisdom. Violence can do no good ; therefore, it will be virtue to forgive the past, and to settle the affair amicably. I have obtained your pardon, which is confirmed in this letter, on condition that you make an honorable reparation to the young lady. In short, if you consent to marry his daughter and return home, Don Alonzo will receive you with open arms,

Don C. My lord, you are noble, and bind me your eternal debtor. It was the ungovernable rage of jealousy which impelled me to commit the violence of which Don Alonzo justly complains. I now am convinced that my jealousy was unfounded, and I am ready to marry the lovely Florida, whenever you please.

Gov. You shall be married this night.

Don C. But can the marriage take place so soon?

Gov. Why not? You are here, and the lady you know is at my house.

Don C. Of that I was ignorant.

Gov. Was she not in your company when I made you my prisoner?

Don C. What mistake is this? My lord, if you imagined

the lady whom you took with me was my charming Florida, you were mistaken.

Gov. But how could her father's servant, who likewise saw and knew her, be mistaken?

Don C. Have you not any other lady a prisoner in your house?

Gov. No. Is not the lady I found with you Donna Florida?

Don C. My lord, once more I assure you, it is not her.

Gov. I shall lose all patience! Did she not herself, with the most touching confusion, acknowledge her love, and the imprudence she had committed?

Don C. This acknowledgment may be applicable to any other lady.

Gov. Granted. But if her domestic followed, and recognized her, what can you further allege?

Don C. That he did not speak the truth.

Gov, You will drive me mad!

Don C. Take me to the lady, and, if she affirm to my face that she is the daughter of Don Alonzo, I will marry her instantly.

Gov. You speak fairly. Come.

Don. C. Deliver me, oh Heavens, from this labyrinth of doubt!

Gov. Holy Virgin, unravel this strange entanglement!

Don C. (*to* Governor) It is her, you say, whom you found in the garden?

Gov. Yes.

Don C. Then, on my honor, it is not Florida.

Gov. The affair is more perplexed than ever!

[*Exeunt* Governor *and* Don Cesar.

SCENE XX.

Changes to the Apartments of Don Juan, *in the Governor's Palace.* Lisarda *and* Florida, *concealed in their Veils, followed by* Camacho.

Cam. This is the house, ladies. I took a long circuit to avoid being followed; (*aside*) and that you might not know where you were.

Lis. We have been so long veiled in the dark, that I have not the least idea where we are.

Cam. My orders were to bring you here, and then to make the outside door fast. Remain where you are! These are the apartments of a young gentleman; you will find enough to amuse you. Adieu, ladies. [*Exit* Camacho.

SCENE XXI.

Flor. (*aside*) I have been silent all the way, that Camacho might not discover me. Don Cesar must certainly be in this city. But why is Lisarda here in disguise? Is he unfaithful? Must I witness his infidelity? Heavens grant this adventure may end well!

Lis. We may now breathe a little more freely, Laura; for nobody is here to see us. (*unveiling, and recognizing the place*) Great God!

Flor. Why do you look so frightened, Signora?

Lis. Do not ask me; Laura: I am dead!

Flor. What is the matter?

Lis. Matter enough, alas! I brought you with me to meet a gentleman, for reasons which you shall hereafter be told, and thought we were in a strange house; instead of which, I find myself at home. These apartments are those of Don Juan: *you* have not seen them before, but I know them too well. The door opens into another street; and I, coming thus without either guide, caution, or light, like a bewildered sparrow, fell into the net. My ruin, alas, is certain! And who can I blame, but myself? Let me examine whether it be reality, or an illusion! Who could have thought that circumstances, on which life and death depend, could so deceive me! These chairs, this writing desk, that looking glass, that tapestry, are the same! There is nothing to hope! I am in my own house. Heavens! how could this happen? But I will not weakly despair; if I have so often frustrated the malice of fortune, why should I now fall her victim? The door here, in the wainscot, communicates with my apartments: if any person were within, it might be opened. If we could but escape, we might easily find an excuse to satisfy the person who expects us. But supposing that out of our power, the mischief would be trifling. Let us listen at the key-hole.

Flor. Yonder is Celia, working at your chamber window, which looks into the garden.

Lis. Let us call. (*calls*) Celia! You do not know who calls, because you cannot see us. Come to the wainscot door.

Celia. (*at the door*) Who is there? Who wants me?

Lis. It is I, Celia. Open this door, and you shall know all.

Cel. My lord left the key on his writing desk, this morning: I'll run and fetch it.

Lis. Oh that your speed could equal my impatience!

Flor. We have no chance of escaping.

Lis. How so?

Flor. I hear the door, and a man's step.

Lis. It must be Don Juan. What shall I do? Good Angels protect me! I must have recourse to art. Throw this veil over you, Laura, and conceal your face while he unlocks the door.

SCENE XXII.—*Enter* DON JUAN.

Don J. The lady is not in the anti-chamber. I must search this. (*seeing* Lisarda) *You* here, Signora! What does this mean?

Lis. Why it means, Signor Don Juan, that I, knowing a lady was waiting for you, am courteous enough to keep her company. Fearing she should find the time hang heavy on her hands, I left my room, and came through the little door in the wainscot to show her the way out. You are really a courtly gentleman, a faithful lover, and a very honorable bridegroom!

Don J. Signora!

Lis. Do not aggravate your guilt, by making false excuses.

Don J. Oh, no!

Lis. You are a discourteous cavalier! a faithless and ungrateful lover!

Don J. Do you know this lady?

Lis. Would you have me, like yourself, give offence to those who have not offended me?

Don J. Only listen, and you shall be convinced.

Lis. My heart is not so deeply interested in the affair, Don Juan, as to make any explanation necessary. It is not jealousy I feel, but a proper feeling of the offence you commit against decorum, and your contempt of my person. Is it possible? Bring a lady secretly into my house before my face! Convey her hither in a chair, with a footman at her heels, who is guarding the outward door like a bull-dog, and who may be one of my domestics, to whom you have given this honorable commission! I know all!

Don J. Pray, listen.

Lis. I will hear nothing.

Don J. Be convinced.

Lis. You cannot justify yourself.

Don J. A friend——

Lis. Oh, this will not do. You would have me believe that a friend borrowed your apartment, to receive his mistress: a thing frequently done by young men. The excuse is frivolous.

Don J. Hear me, I conjure you, Signora.

Lis. Those who listen wish to be convinced; I am totally indifferent. Give me the key then——

Don J. You must not leave me, till you know——

Lis. I do not want to know. Let me be gone. (*to* Florida) Go, Signora, and think yourself fortunate that you have met with a person who owes herself too much respect to treat you as you deserve. (*aside to her*) Pardon, my dear Laura! Cruel necessity is to blame.

Don J. (*aside*) Oh, friendship, how severe are thy laws!—Indeed, Signora, you must not go, till you have heard my justification.

Lis. If I do not wish to hear it, to what purpose is your speaking?

Don J. Oh, lady, you ought to know me better! Do not think so meanly of your lover; and must I implore you to think more highly of yourself?

Lis. You *will* speak? Oh, what a weak defence you make!

SCENE XXIII.—*Enter* CELIA *through the Wainscot Door.*

Cel. (*privately to* Lisarda) Signora?

Lis. What do you want?

Cel. The door is open.

Lis. You were very slow: but no matter.

Cel. What does all this mean?

Lis. (*aside*) Go, softly, and bring some refreshments into my room; this poor lady is in need of them: then see if the outside door is open.

Don J. Why will you refuse to listen to the truth? I hear footsteps! Heavens, it is your father! Let me conjure you to be silent.

Lis. (*aside*) Indeed, I shall be the first to speak. If I can find a good excuse to refuse his hand, why should I not take this opportunity of recovering my freedom?

SCENE XXIV.

Enter GOVERNOR, DON CESAR, *and* CAMACHO.

Gov. What is the matter? Hearing a confusion of voices as I entered the house, I came hither to learn. You here, Lisarda?

Lis. I came hither——

Gov. For what?

Lis. To visit a lady.

Gov. A lady here! Who can it be?

Lis. That lady in a veil, who came to visit Don Juan.

Gov. You have little cause to treat my house with such levity and disrespect, Signor.

Don J. Since you, my lord, think me culpable, my friend must pardon my revealing the truth: for the laws of friendship are not so rigorous as to require a man to lose his honor, which I now am in danger of losing, when I hoped the most enviable felicity. This lady cannot be injured by my confession; for she is the fair choice of Don Cesar, and the same whom your lordship took a prisoner. He has before seen and conversed with her; and she came this evening to meet him. If aiding my friend be an unpardonable offence, I plead guilty.

Flor. (*aside*) I converse with Cesar! I see him!

Don C. (*aside*) If the lady, who is unveiled, be the same to whom I spoke, who can the other be?

Gov. Unveil, Signora, since you are known. There is no great impropriety in your appointing to meet your bridegroom. I wish beside to convince him that you are Florida; for he affirms the contrary.

Flor. (*unveiling*) Yes, I am Florida, my lord; for no other woman can be so unfortunate.

Don C. Heavens! What do I see!

Gov. Tell me now, Don Cesar, is it Florida?

Don C. Yes, my lord.

Gov. You surely had a plot upon my wits, when you persisted in denying the truth, at the very time you intended to visit your mistress?

Lis. (*aside*) Since Fortune has now done her worst, I am consoled. I have lost my lover, but my honor may yet be preserved. (*aloud*) If you all wish to have the solution of these enigmas, which have given you so much uneasiness, know that I have, from the first, been the confident of the lovely Florida, and wished to monopolize the glory of restoring her to happiness and honor. I quarrelled with Don Juan, to punish him for so lightly weighing the respect due to this house, and his bride.

Flor. Since my honor is recovered, why need I inquire any further? (*to* Cesar) I am yours.

Don C. I thankfully accept the blessing, (*to* Lisarda) if you are content.

Lis. (*to* Cesar) The pleasure of doing good restores me to serenity and joy.

Gov. Since Love has joined one couple, let Reason unite a second. Don Juan, take Lisarda's hand.

Don J. (*to* Lisarda) My faith and heart are yours!

Cam. (*to the audience*) Since our adventures are terminated by a double marriage, I may with propriety deny the proverb, "from bad to worse," and inform you that the comedy is finished.

Don C. (*to the audience*) And you, noble senate, kindly excuse the faults of the author, who throws himself on your mercy.   [*Exeunt Omnes.*

THE END.

REMARKS.

THIS Comedy is an excellent specimen of that species of dramatic composition in which Spain appears most to have delighted, and her authors to have attained the greatest excellence. Instead of keeping the attention alive by character, and humor, or such events as produce a rational pathos, the efforts of the poet were on the continual stretch, to discover how lovers should be brought on the brink of destruction, and delivered by some unforeseen incident, or fortunate stratagem, suggested at the moment. The more entangled these incidents were, the greater the danger they produced, and the more extraordinary the miracle by which it was eluded, the higher was the delight that auditor and author received. The pursuits, which the nation thought proper to dignify by the titles *love* and *honor*, were those by which it was particularly characterized : but, as there was a large mixture of alloy to debase that which was in some respects so noble, the poet had not often the art to purify, and separate the bad from the good. In the preceding comedy, various of the characters, in other respects highly honorable, yield either to direct falsehood, or that evasion, which does not appear conscious of being criminal. Evasion and falsehood cannot, perhaps, be banished from the stage, while the follies and vices of men are there exhibited ; but they should appear in their native colours, and lead, as they do in real life, to those consequences by which their authors are always either despised or punished. Rules so rigid, it is true, are much more easily written than observed; but the difficulties will be less, as the taste and morality of spectators improve. In the Spanish, authors did not generally divide their pieces into acts, but *jornadas*, or days, of which there were usually three ; and, so little did they regard the unities of time and place, their three days appear to have been taken at such intervals as might suit their story. Neither are the scenes themselves, nor the places to which they change, generally marked in the old Spanish comedies : they are obliged to be divined by the text, as in the present instance.

To the unity of action, however, they often adhere more closely than those rival nations who have superciliously affected to hold them in contempt; for, though two or more love intrigues are involved in the plot, it is from the mistakes of them all that intricacies and difficulties arise, so as to influence each other and form a single fable. The comedy of FROM BAD TO WORSE [*Peor está que estaba*] only requires judicious alterations to ensure success on the stage. Its figurative and often inflated style is but an example of what was supposed to be the true sublime and beautiful, among the poets of Spain.

DRAMATIC BIOGRAPHY.

CALDERON DE LA BARCA*.

To the edition of this poet's dramatic works, printed at Madrid in 1726, a life of him, by *Don Juan de Vera Tassis y Villarroel*, is prefixed, from which most of the following particulars are taken. Like many or rather most other Spanish works, the style in which this life is written is ridiculously inflated, and bombastic: but, as it appears to have been composed by a contemporary and friend of Calderon de la Barca, the desire to give a sufficiently high degree of praise might increase such a defect. The facts, however, apparently, have been carefully collected, from public records and from the sister of the poet, Dorotea, a nun in the royal convent of Santa Clara, at Toledo.

" Calderon de la Barca was born in 1601, on the day of the holy circumcision, of honorable parents, under whom he began his education. He was afterward sent to the university of Salamanca, where he is said to have studied mathematics, philosophy, geography, chronology, history, sacred and profane, and law, civil and canonical. During his studies he began to discover the perfect poet, and to illustrate the theatres of Spain with his ingenious comedies.

---

* A beautifully embellished head (by H. Thompson, R. A.) of this poet will be given, in the next Number.

" At the age of nineteen, he left Salamanca ; and at twenty-five he served the king at Milan, and afterward in Flanders; being no less excellent in arms than in letters. We find him continue thus doubly to be employed, particularly in writing pieces for the celebration of royal festivals, for which he received many honors and rewards from his majesty. As a poet, his facility and fecundity were astonishing : he appears to have written a hundred and twenty pieces, each of three jornadas, or acts, equal in length to dramas of five acts ; eight or more of one act each ; and about a hundred of *Autos Sacramentales,* which are a kind of religious mysteries. All these seem to have appeared in print, as most libraries are in possession of his three act pieces ; and there is a catalogue of the others at the beginning of this common edition of his works.

" The *Autos Sacramentales* were annually written, to celebrate religious festivals at the cities of Madrid, Toledo, Seville, and Grenada.

" At the age of fifty-one, he became a churchman ; at sixty-three, he was received into the venerable and noble congregation of Saint Peter; at sixty-six, he was elected *Capellan Mayor,* or chief; and he died at the advanced age of eighty-one.

" The living images that he left of his wonderful genius, and the strong pictures which his elegant writings contain of his copious and incomparable understanding, are almost incredible. His mental vigor, in early youth and old age, was equally displayed. At little more than thirteen, he nobly began his career with a piece entitled *El Carro del Cielo ;* and concluded, at eighty-one, with *La Gran Comedia,* Hado y Divisa. In this interim (beside a great number of manuscript pieces, as we find from catalogues) he produced two hundred *Loas;* [Prologues] a hundred *Saynetes;* [Interludes] a Book on the Public Entry of the Queen-mother ; a long Discourse on Death, Judgment, Heaven, and Hell, in a poetical stanza of eight lines ; a Treatise in defence of the Dignity of Painting ; another on Comedy ; beside Songs, Sonnets, Romances, and innumerable compositions, which gained the prizes in learned academies, and was honored by the invariable applause of the best judges. His works are preserved, with veneration, in the library of the college *Mayor de Oviedo* at Salamanca, as among the most select of Spain. Our catholic monarchs acknowledged his *Autos*, as jewels worthy of royal capacity; and sent them, with commentaries, as presents to the Emperor of Germany and King of France. He was the honored and rewarded Cavalier of three monarchs: Philip III. the Pious, Philip IV. the Great, and Charles II. the Beloved; whom God preserve."

Much more might be selected from his Spanish biographer, and from other documents printed at the beginning of each volume of his Comedies; but an abstract only is or can be given here. It may however amuse the critic, the scholar, and the philosopher, to turn to the article Calderon, in *Le Nouveau Dictionnaire Historique* *; where he will find a meagre account of this great man, and the following remarks:

" The rules of the dramatic art are violated, in almost all
" his works. In his tragedies, we find the dignity, the mean-
" ness, and the irregularity, of Shakspeare; traits of genius
" no less powerful; humor equally out of place; inflation no
" less capricious; and a similar jumble of action and incident.
" He knew neither truth, probability, nor nature. His come-
" dies were a little better; but, in his tragedies, the most con-
" temptible ignorance of history is seen."

Was the contemptible ignorance, here so dogmatically pronounced, due to Calderon, or to the author of this article? The praise given to Calderon by his biographer, Don Juan, may have been too great: yet, when we recollect all the thoughts, all the imagery, all the invention, of a poet so extraordinary, we may doubt if any praise can at all equal the truth. And what will an English reader think, when he sees Calderon and Shakspeare coupled, as examples of the most defective and, speaking generally, the most contemptible of poets? There is scarcely any thing that can fall from the pen of man more degrading than the trash of such loquacious, such

---

* A French work of biography, in many volumes.

presumptuous, such ignorant critics. Shakspeare had great faults; Calderon might have still greater; but Voltaire, after whose dictates these pretended critics prate, had not sufficiently studied them, so as well to understand either their beauties or their defects: for, if he had, he himself deserves the contempt with which he endeavoured to load their memory. Of such wilful injustice, let us hope, so great a man could not be guilty.

NEW PIECE

FIRST PERFORMED IN MARCH, 1805,

CALLED

OUT OF PLACE.

THOUGH this is the period of the season generally the most productive of new pieces, the attention of the town has been so astonishingly attracted by the performances of Master Betty that, except himself, all novelty is prohibited, because unnecessary, at the theatre where he acts. The pleasure of admiration is paradoxically sympathetic: it spreads from breast to breast, increasing till it becomes rapture, without any individual knowing why or how it began. A man of fashion publicly said, of Master Betty, *he must have been sent from heaven; and he should not be in the least surprised if he were to see him some night ascend from the stage!* The admiration that at present has seized upon the minds of men, with such absolute dominion, is a phenomenon that well deserves the inquiry and development of the philosopher: but it must be at some distant period; for the voice of truth is too feeble to be heard till the wild freaks of insanity shall subside.

One of the most fallacious of principles is that which pretends to found itself upon unanimous consent: unanimous meaning an undoubted majority of opinions. It was that undoubted majority which for so many ages continued to maintain the supremacy of the pope; and that still, in numberless instances, continues to maintain errors, physical, moral, and religious, so as to be destructive both of body and mind, among the people where they are to be found. And who are

the people among whom they are not to be found? The multitude must always prevail. A madman only would pretend to
show his skill in swimming by endeavours to stem and turn a
roaring torrent. That man has a pitiful ambition, who seeks
the honors of martyrdom on a trifling or a contemptible occasion: the grandeur of the cause only can render such honors
glorious. A rabbit-woman, a bottle-conjurer, or a Cock-lane
ghost: no matter what! Whatever folly is in fashion, reign it
must: and, as for disputing, it is not yet decided whether the
devil has or has not horns. *It's a Mad World, my Masters,* is
the title of an old comedy.

Such reflections will intrude: the times give birth to them;
and would do to many more, were they indulged.

The only new piece at present to be noticed is a two act
opera, by Mr. Reynolds, entitled OUT OF PLACE, or THE LAKE
OF LAUSANNE. Such performances only pretend to afford
amusement for an hour, and seldom to instruct or to inform.
Many well-meaning moralists inconsiderately laugh at the supposition that the theatre is a place where information may be
obtained, not remembering that moral conduct depends upon
the consequences of human actions being well understood;
and that he who best develops those consequences is the best of
moral instructors. To afford innocent amusement, however, is
a desirable and happy talent. In writing this piece, little care
has been taken to form a plan, and give probability to incidents,
or consistency to character. At what era the action is supposed to have happened it is impossible to discover: the costume is that of two or three centuries past: the praises of Wil-
liam Tell are sung, who is well known to have been the
deliverer of his country; yet a Governor, who is one of the
principal characters in the piece, capriciously and at pleasure
gives his orders to imprison, put to death, or release, whoever
he pleases. Such violent authority could only have existed
since the French revolution. Pleasantry, and to afford an opportunity for favorite singers to be heard, were what Mr. Reynolds had in view, and these he has effected. Mr. Fawcett
does great justice to the whimsical effrontery of the servant
out of place; and the person who for the first time goes to this

performance must be very cynical, if he does not sometimes laugh. He to whom the singing likewise does not afford plea-sure must be difficult to please.

THE ART OF ACTING.

In the last number of this work, room was wanting to con-tinue the subject on the Art of Acting; and in the present num-ber the third chapter of that continuation will be again omitted, not because so valuable a subject is thought to be uninteresting to theatrical inquiry, or to the pleasure and benefit of society; far, far the reverse; but to make room for the following long extract, in which that art is incidentally treated of by exam-ple; and in which M. Marmontel, the author of it, does but describe a vicious mode of acting, common perhaps to all na-tions, for it is every where a subject of complaint. This ex-tract was sent me by a friend, at Paris, where the Memoirs of Marmontel (a posthumous work, by that author, lately pub-lished) are at present read with avidity.

'I had long been in the habit of disputing with Mademoiselle Clairon, concerning the manner of declaiming tragic verses. I blamed her for too much violence and impetuosity, too little sup-pleness and variety in her performance, and especially for her loud and continued exertions, which were rather a-kin to rant than to sensibility. This I modestly endeavoured to make her understand. "You have," said I, " all the means of excelling in your art; and, great as you are, it would be easy for you still to rise above yourself, by managing more carefully the powers of which you are so prodigal. You tell me of your uncommon success, and of the advantages I [as an author] have gained by them: you oppose me by the opinion of the town, the suffrages of your friends, nay by the authority of M. de Voltaire, who himself recites his verses with emphasis, and who pretends that tragic verses require, in declamation, the same pomp as in the style. I can only answer, I have an irresistible feeling, which convinces me that declamation, like style, may be noble, majes-

tic, and tragic, with simplicity; and that expression, profoundly
to penetrate, requires gradations, shades, and those unforeseen and sudden traits, of which it cannot admit, while it is
forced and violent." To this she used to reply, sometimes with
impatience, that I should never let her rest, till she had assumed a familiar and comic tone in tragedy. "Ah! no, Mademoiselle," said I, "that you will never have; nature has
forbidden it; you even have it not, while you are speaking to
me; the sound of your voice, the air of your countenance,
your pronunciation, your gestures, and your attitudes, are all
naturally noble. Dare only to confide in this charming native talent, and I dare warrant you will be the more tragic."

' Other counsels than mine prevailed, and, tired of being
importunate without utility, I had yielded, when I saw the actress suddenly and voluntarily come over to my opinion. She
was to play *Roxane*, at the little theatre at Versailles. Visiting her there at her toilette, for the first time, I found her
dressed in the habit of a sultana, without a hoop, her arms
half naked, and in the true oriental costume. I congratulated
her. "You will presently be delighted with me," said she.
" I have just been on a journey to Bourdeaux; I found there
but a very small theatre, to which I was obliged to accom-
modate myself. The thought struck me of reducing my action to it, and of making trial of that simple declamation you
have so often required of me, and it had the greatest imagi-
nable success. I am about to try it again here, on this little
theatre. Go and hear me. If it succeed as well, farewel to
my old declamation."

' The event surpassed her expectations and mine. It was no
longer the actress, it was Roxana herself, whom the audience
saw and heard. The astonishment, the illusion, the enchantment, were extreme. All inquired, where are we? They
had heard nothing like it.

' I saw her after the play; and was about to congratulate her
on her success. "Ah!" said she, " don't you perceive that
it ruins me? In all my characters, the costume must now be
observed; the truth of declamation requires that of dress; all

my rich stage wardrobe is from this moment rejected; I lose twelve hundred pounds worth of dresses! But the sacrifice is made. You shall see me here within a week, playing *Electre* naturally; in short, as I have done Roxana."

'It was the *Electre* of Crebillon. Instead of the ridiculous hoop, and the ample mourning robe, in which we had been accustomed to see her in this character, she appeared in the simple habit of a slave, her hair dishevelled, and her arms loaded with chains. She was admirable in it; and some time afterward she was still more sublime in the *Electre* of Voltaire. This part, which Voltaire had caused her to declaim with a continued and monotonous lamentation, acquired, when spoken naturally, a beauty unknown to himself; for, on seeing her play it on his theatre at Ferney, where she went to visit him, he exclaimed, bathed in tears and transported with admiration, "*It is not I who wrote the part; 'tis she: it is a new creation!*" And, indeed, by the infinite shades she introduced, and by the expression she gave to the passions with which this character abounds, it was perhaps that of all others in which she was most astonishing.

'Paris, as well as Versailles, recognized in these changes the true tragic accent; as well as the new degree of probability which a strict observance of costume gave to theatrical action. Thus, from that time, all actors were obliged to abandon their fringed gloves, their voluminous wigs, their feathered hats, and all the fantastic costume that had so long shocked the sight of men of taste. Lekain himself followed the example of Mademoiselle Clairon; and, from that moment, their talents excited mutual emulation, and they became worthy rivals of each other.'

The above relation, as given by Marmontel, so perfectly coincides with the views in which this Journal is begun, and will be continued, that a thorough perusal of it, till a perfect comprehension of the practice which it blames, and the true and natural manner it admires, are understood, is most seriously recommended. Why was Garrick so wonderfully great? It was because he had a like strong conviction, or rather feeling, of the true and the false manner. To avoid all possible song, or whine, to deliver the words in the tone and manner of men discoursing with each other under the influence of passion, and to understand all the various and distinct feelings, which the successive words of a sentence must have in the minds of persons who speak such words, were the indefatigable studies of his life. How glorious was the reward!

The inveteracy of habit is such that, even when it is good, it is to be feared. But what is it when bad? It appears as if it could only be eradicated by an indefinite lapse of ages. There is so strong a propensity in the human ear to adopt lengthened sound, to imitate without discrimination, and to be proudly self-satisfied when supported by the authority of numbers, that extraordinary and continual efforts are necessary, to bring it back to recollection and reason. Endless repetitions are necessary to a child, before it can remember the alphabet; but the child is much more easily taught than such persons; for it has no self-satisfaction, no conceit, no false prejudices to conquer. It has much to remember, but it has nothing to forget. Mrs. Siddons is a noble actress! In her impassioned scenes, the man who can listen without frequent surprise and ecstasy must have no discrimination, no feeling, nor any sense of the true dignity of excellence. Mr. J. P. Kemble is too often cold, and declamatory: but he has his inspired moments, which give, perhaps, the greater delight by bursting upon the audience when they are least expected. Both brother and sister, however, are the practical patrons of this hateful recitative, and are therefore theoretically its defenders. Mr. Kemble contends that blank verse demands a recitation peculiar to itself. Can passionate or unimpassioned discourse ever require tones in which it is never heard, except by children repeating the catechism, or their imitators? As a tragedian, Mr. Cooke has the proud honor of being nearly free from this sing-song defect; this puerile school-boy habit of whining out a lesson.

ESSAY ON DRAMATIC COMPOSITION.

(*Continued from No. III. p. 216.*)

====

UNLESS the facts that have been stated, concerning the moral tendency of the drama, can be disproved, it must be admitted that of all the human efforts and known means, by which the most useful, essential, and dignified moral effects may be produced, the drama affords the best and least doubtful. Of this truth churchmen every where seem to have had an imperfect perception. Through all Christendom, there has been a strong conviction of the moral consequences of dramatic exhibitions, since there is not perhaps a story, in the Old or New Testament, which has not been dramatized. That the imaginations of men in darker ages, who have treated such subjects, were not sufficiently chastised; that they often made a very improper and incoherent jumble, in which buffoonery no less immoral than gross and disgusting largely participated; that they pretended to discourse of things concerning which it were perhaps better never to discourse; that they embodied the mystical, gave form and figure to the occult, and alarmed the theologian and the statesman, is only a proof that such subjects were not well understood, or properly treated.

In Spain, the *Autos Sacramentales* were the delight of church and state.

In Italy, likewise, not only the Old and New Testaments, but the Legends of Saints, have afforded almost innumerable subjects for their *Rappresentazioni Sacre*.

In France and England, Mysteries, Moralities, and holy Interludes, were alike frequent : nor is it to be presumed that sacred dramas would ever have been prohibited, but for the strange abuses that were committed, by companies who formed themselves in all the various christian states; where they were guilty of such wanton indecencies and daring outrage against church ceremonies and dignitaries as became insufferable, even in those rude ages.

The tragedy of *Athalie* is still, by many, supposed to be the *chef d'œuvre* of Racine. The story of *Esther* afforded him another dramatic subject. *Le Jugement de Salomon*, three years ago, was a highly popular piece at one of the theatres on the Boulevards, at Paris; and was so affecting that it was translated, with some faint disguise by an alteration of names, and performed at the Little Theatre in the Haymarket. Our present Oratorios are the shadowy remains of sacred dramas. When good sense and good taste shall have made so much progress as to relieve the public from their prejudices, and restrain authors within the limits of common sense, the Scriptures may again afford many most interesting subjects for dramatic composition. This is an opinion which will cause some men to be angry, some to smile, and some to soberly consider. Could the abuse of things prove their destructive tendency, there would be nothing which would not be destructive; for the best of things are daily abused.

Desirous that wise and good men should seriously reflect on the subject, the moral tendency of the drama has been insisted upon, with the hope that the numbers of those who are already inclined to this opinion may be increased, and their conviction strengthened.

Of the art of dramatic composition men have spoken with such authority, from their books, and with such little inquiry or rational self-conviction, concerning the certainty of the rules that ought to be observed, that, it will be deemed a presumptuous audacity to call these rules in question. In this age, the benefit that results from free inquiry will scarcely be doubted: to *search into all things* was an apostolic maxim; and that *knowledge puffeth up* was another. To take rules for granted is easy; to understand them is difficult.

Time, place, and action, are what criticism has called the three indispensable unities. We will begin with time.

It is alleged that the illusion of the scene should be perfect, and that consequently the time of a dramatic performance should be confined to twelve hours. It appears rather surprising that criticism should speak of dramatic illusion as being *capable of perfection.* If we reflect on the operations of mind, when strongly excited, they will be found to be multifarious, mingled, and rapid, beyond its own recollection. It cannot itself distinguish the minuteness of the interval of time, in which it can suppose itself at Rome, hearing Marc Antony harangue over the dead body of Cesar, be called to recollection by the noise or elbow of a neighbouring spectator, and again be back at Rome, listening, and connecting the past and the present. Unless there be some uncommon disturbance, or event, its operations are not perceptibly impeded: it is attentive to the tale it hears, the passion of the scene, and the suspense in which it is held. If it be not in an artificial state, perverted by some previous *cold examination,* and influenced by some preconceived rules, from which it has drawn conclusions which, if not just, are no less ridiculous than prejudicial, mind in itself is entirely plastic. When unfettered, it is led implicitly by the narrative, and even delights so to be led; yes, delights in what unimpassioned criticism has so sagagiously discovered to be absurd. It can contemplate a child in the arms of a woman, imagine that woman to be a court lady, and the child the daughter of a king and queen; can suppose it to be exposed in a desert, saved by a shepherd, grown up to the age of puberty, in reality a princess, but in appearance a shepherd's daughter; and can readily believe so beautiful a creature is beloved by a prince, and at last restored to the arms of a jealous king, who was called Leontes. Such is the nature of mind that, even while reading what is here so briefly written, all this has been supposed. These facts are not to be denied: nor the pleasure the imagination takes in thus indulging its flights. Why should these pleasures be restricted or entirely destroyed by rules which, pretending to correct absurdity, are themselves absurd? If twelve hours are allowed to be necessary to the fable, in the general composition of a play, why should twelve years be denied? The time of performance is two hours and a half. To the mind in such a state, minutes and years are words, that are only so far important as they lead the mind to perfectly understand the story: to every thing else, if unprejudiced, it is totally indifferent. But the spectator, who has been gravely informed, with an assumption of dogmatical superiority, that a child cannot grow up to the state of woman in two hours' time, is struck with so important a truth, and goes to the theatre highly self-satisfied at the acquisition of such essential knowledge.

It is to be regretted that the critics, who made this miraculous discovery, though Aristotle, alas, be at their head, had not with equal phlegm more maturely considered the nature and the powers of imagination.

All dramatic compositions are an appeal to the mind, which they are solely intended to occupy. The actors, or persons supposed, are but shadows, seen by it *as in a glass*. Time and space are entirely relative words. Time is but the instant of consciousness, and space the limits of sight. On the associations, the recollections, of mind the dramatic art is founded. Since it can combine and multiply them so rapidly, since it can be affected by them with such supreme pleasure, or pain, is it wisdom, nay is it not absurd and destructive to the dramatic art, to exclude the poet from the use of the means which these pretended unities would destroy, and which are among the most necessary to the truth and passion of the scene?

So redoubtable has been the voice of long-received criticism that men, the most capable, have not ventured to probe the subject. The late Doctor Johnson, whose name in elegant and sound criticism deserves to be revered, has slightly touched the question, in his preface to the works of Shakspeare; but he honestly avows his timidity, at only daring to doubt of rules, which have so long been received and applauded. It will be easy to show that they never were, and never could be, obeyed; and men, who are more willing to endure the opprobrium of not being orthodox critics, will venture to be more rash. There is no great danger, perhaps, in the present case; for the high priests of prejudice are daily less numerous, and the victims sacrificed to the fanaticism of former ages are few.

(To be continued.)

SOME ACCOUNT

OF THE RISE AND PROGRESS OF THE GERMAN STAGE.

(*Continued from No.* III. *p.* 218.)

COMIC operas first made their appearance, in 1752, in Germany, where they have been highly successful. Originals, translations, imitations, good and bad, are now all of them abundant. The first opera performed by the company of Koch was an imitation of *The Devil to Pay*, from the English. Weisse was the German author, who, beside the honors he acquired of this kind, is regarded as one of the best dramatic poets in the language. The opera was universally applauded, and is still a favorite, notwithstanding the clamors of Gottsched and his cabal, by whom the piece and comic operas in general were cried down.

Madame Seyler, who now (1782) is reputed to be one of the first actresses of Germany, first appeared in 1755 : tragedy and serious comedy were the parts she chose. *Miss Sarah Sampson**, by Lessing, one of the best pieces on the German stage, appeared in the same year. This style of writing became more in favor than heroic tragedy.

The miserable war, which desolated Germany from the year 1756 to the peace, impeded the progress of the theatre. Banished and disdained by most of the provinces, the Muses found no asylum but in the Free Imperial city of Hamburg.

In 1758, the authors of *La Bibliothéque des Belles Lettres* bestowed the laurel on Codrus, a tragedy in verse, by *M. Von Cronegk*, a gentleman of Franconia. The great talent there displayed, as well as in his Olinthis and Sophronia, gave hopes to Germany that this hopeful poet, of 26, would soon reach the summit of fame ; but he died, of the small-pox, the following year. He had travelled through a part of Europe, and had passed the year 1753 at Paris, where he allowed he had received

---

* A tragedy, in the style of Lillo.

much benefit from the great actors and masterly works of the
French.   He left several comedies imperfect, and a volume of
charming fugitive poems.   It might have been said, at this
time, that some evil genius had sworn destruction to the German stage.   *Schlegel*, from whom so much was hoped, also
died in the flower of his age : and a youth of genius, perhaps
superior to both the above poets, was carried off at twenty.   This
was *M. Von Brawe*, who, in a piece entitled *The Free Thinker* *,
has left a proof of noble talent.

In the course of the year 1759, five volumes of the dramatic
works of Weisse, successively appeared, were well received,
and secured to their author an honorable place among the
favorite poets of the nation, and the creators of good taste.
Beside the plan and regularity to be admired in his tragedies,
we there find strong situations, scenes well conducted, and
characters accurately designed.   His style is noble, neither
inflated nor vulgar ; and his comedies abound in traits of excellent humor.   In the latter are found faithful pictures of German manners ; and their construction announces a perfect
knowledge of the world, and of the theatre.

In 1764 an actress appeared on the same stage, who afterward became its highest ornament : her name was *Brandes*,
who is now (1782) the delight of Germany.

DRAMATIC ANECDOTES.

BARRY the actor, who died at the beginning of 1779, and
whose name well deserves to be preserved, was perhaps in no
part so excellent as in that of Romeo ; for which he was particularly fitted, by a superiority of demeanor, an uncommonly
handsome and commanding person, and a silver-toned voice.
At the time that he attracted the town to Covent Garden, by
his excellent performance of this part, Garrick found it abso-

---

* L'Esprit Fort: the author does not give the German title.

lutely necessary to divide the attention of the public, by performing himself at Drury Lane. He wanted the natural advantages of Barry, and, great as he was, would perhaps have
willingly avoided such a contention. This at least seems to
have been a prevailing opinion; for, in the garden scene,
when Juliet in soliloquy exclaims—

" Oh, Romeo, Romeo, wherefore art thou Romeo ?"

an auditor archly replied aloud—*Because Barry is gone to the
other house.*

Many anecdotes have been told of persons wholly absorbed
and lost in the illusion of the scene. A woman in the gallery,
when the tragedy of Essex was acted, knowing from the story
that Essex must die since the Countess of Nottingham would
not give the ring which the woman had seen the countess
hide, exclaimed in an agony—*She has got it in her bosom !*

When the School for Scandal was first performed, the
behaviour of some well dressed farmers in the pit was very
remarkable. During the progress of the skreen scene, their
emotions were so strong they could not stand still; and,
when Sir Peter was left alone with Charles, they kept whispering and elbowing each other—" He'll have t'other peep !"
—' No he won't.'—" The youngster will find her out! He's
going ! There ! Now !"—and when the skreen was thrown down,
they hallooed, stamped, and jumped with pleasure.

Mademoiselle Dumesnil, an actress at Paris about the middle of the last century, was performing the part of Cleopatra.
In the fifth act, her imprecations are almost horrible : among
others she exclaims, in the excess of rage,

Je maudirais les Dieux, sils me rendoient le jour.
I'd curse the Gods, were they to give me life.

" Get to the devil, vile hussey !" exclaimed an old officer,
sitting on the front seat of the stage box, and at the same time

giving her a push on the back. For a while, this act of delirium interrupted the performance. When the noise ceased, Mademoiselle turned and thanked the officer for having given her the most flattering mark of applause she had ever received.

———

At present, while it is so decidedly the fashion to seek admiration and excellence in a state of immaturity, the following anecdote may be aptly repeated.

In the time of Queen Elizabeth, plays were performed by the children of the Chapel Royal, and one boy (Sal. Pavy) *who died in his thirteenth year*, was so admirable an actor of *old men*, that Ben Jonson wrote the following epitaph on him :

EPITAPH ON S. P. a CHILD OF Q. EL. CHAPPEL.

Weepe with me, all you that read
 This little storie :
And know, for whom a teare you shed,
 Death's self is sorry.
'Twas a child that so did thrive,
 In grace and feature,
As *Heaven* and *Nature* seem'd to strive
 Which own'd the creature.
Yeeres he numbred scarce thirteene
 When *Fates* turn'd cruell,
Yet three fill'd Zodiackes had he beene
 The stages jewell;
And did act (what now we mone)
 Old men so duely
As, sooth, the *Parcæ* thought him one,
 He plai'd so truely.
So, by error, to his fate
 They all consented ;
But viewing him since (alas too late)
 They have repented.
And have sought (to give new birth)
 In bathes to steepe him ;
But, being so much too good for earth,
 Heaven vowes to keepe him.

This celebrated child was an original performer in Jonson's *Cynthia's Revels*, and *Poetaster*, in the years 1600 and 1601.

———

In the reign of Lewis XIV. an Italian actor, who named himself Scaramouch, was so popular that he saved money enough to buy an estate, and asked leave to return to his own country. Finding himself ill-treated there, he petitioned and was permitted to return. At this, though he was publicly blamed, the public rejoiced, and for more than six months crowded to see Scaramouch again. Molière and his excellent company fell into neglect, the comedians murmured and reproached Molière, on whom they depended as author and manager. " Why don't you write for our support? Must impotence and buffoonery carry all before them? Is there no way to rouse the public to common sense?" Weary of such like reproaches, Molière told them they must retire, like Scaramouch, till the town should wish for their return ; but that for his own part he should suffer things to take their natural course : the public would not always be Scaramouch mad; they would be tired with bad things as well as with good. Molière had sagacity, and was a true prophet: the very next comedy he wrote the concourse was drawn to his house, and popularity once again was the friend of merit.

———

Though a man of so much wit, Molière's deportment was serious, his manners grave, and his taciturnity remarkable; yet on the stage he performed many of the most farcical parts. One evening, being to personate Sancho Pancha, and enter riding on an ass, he mounted behind the scenes, waiting for his cue : but the ass, not understanding the prompter, would not wait; nor could Molière hinder him from making his entrance: in vain did the distressed Sancho tug the halter ; in vain he called to his favorite Baron, and his servant maid La Forest, to come to his assistance. Seeing her master on the crupper pulling with all his might, the girl laughed so heartily that she had not the power to move ; and Molière was at last obliged to hold by the side scenes, and let the ass slip from under him, go forward, and act as he should please.

———

During the run of the comic opera of Cymon, when Mr. Vernon was in pursuit of his supposed mistress Silvia, and came on singing

Torn from me, torn from me, which way did they take her?

A wag in the pit replied in time and tune

They're gone to Long Acre! They're gone to Long Acre.

The house was in a roar of laughter; and Vernon with great presence of mind, as soon as there was silence, sang

Oh, ho, are they so; I shall soon overtake her.

———

MISCELLANIES.

———

Provincial Theatres of Wolverhampton, Stafford, and Kidderminster, from the Letter of a Correspondent.

THE theatre at Wolverhampton, though there is much insipidity and want of talent, is yet well supplied, considering its distance from the metropolis. It witnessed the early attempts of a *Siddons,* and a *Kemble,* who have there declaimed, in barns and town-halls, with more than Roman eloquence, to " some quantity of barren spectators :" ready and thundering applause was often the stimulant to exertion, and perhaps the sweetest reward of their labours. The theatre closed on the 7th of March, under the management of *Mr. Hoy.* At the beginning of the season, *Mr. Quick* afforded a prominent relief to dulness; his Scrub, Miser, and Sir Benjamin Dove, are the genuine emanations of rich and irresistible comedy. Our ladies have the rage of appearing in breeches: *Mrs. Aikin in Hamlet, Mrs. Bonville in Douglas,* and a *female Roscius,* eleven years of age, *in Achment.* This custom is subversive of the design, and destructive of the interest, of the stage. The pretended Roscius, *falsely and ignorantly so called,* afforded us nothing but half-studied shrieks, shrugs, and starts, ill-timed and unnatural.

Cymbeline was performed here; and the king, discovering his children, exclaimed, with ignorance and false emphasis,

" What, am I *mother* to the birth of three ?"

And the audience burst into a loud and convulsive laugh. The king and royal family were wholly out of countenance; but, after a pause, his majesty stepped forward, and assured the ladies and gentlemen, he had spoken nothing but the author. The laugh was then repeated, and continued, till another performer came forward and kindly informed us it was a *metaphor !!!* This gave birth to much merriment, and some dispute; for the performers pretended they were accurate: but, had Shakspeare himself been alive and present, hearing the passage so pronounced, he must have laughed. Some of our heroes, when they die, have such a lively method, there is scarcely room for them, on our small stage.

Since *Mrs. Harlowe* left this theatre, Mrs. Aikin is our best performer. Her comedy is preferred: in her tragedy, there is too much studied artifice; nor has she sufficient variety, and modulation.

Mrs. Bonville is a great favorite with us: she played Hob in the Well, at her benefit, in a style so natural, spirited, and characteristic, that it might have done credit to any theatre in the kingdom.

We have few other performers that deserve to be mentioned, *Mr. Shuter* and *Mr. Archer* perhaps excepted. The first is young, and, with an assiduous cultivation of his talents, may expect fame in his profession. Mr. Archer, though not correct, is deserving of notice.

The young Roscius is to perform at this place in July.

STAFFORD.

Mr. Steven Kemble performed Falstaff here, a few nights, in the Christmas holidays. *Captain Stanton* is the manager; but the claims of his company, on the score of merit, are few;

and, most probably, its members are not ambitious of being particularized for their bad qualities. Vulgarity of physiognomy is rather too common among them, and often so striking and uncontrolled as to be that which

" No wig can soften and no rouge disguise."

KIDDERMINSTER.

Though less respectable in its circuit than the former, this company possesses much more ability. *Mr. Crisp*, the manager, is almost universal; but his chief excellence consists in countrymen, boldly delineated, yet natural, and heightened by just and characteristic humor. *Mr. Watkinson* and *Mrs. Egerton* have both considerable merit, and deserve better situations. It is a relief, however, to reflect that the energies of mind are never, perhaps, wholly exercised in vain. Some solitary individual,

" By chance directed, or by fancy led,"

may feel enjoyment, and induce others to enjoy. The provincial Theatres are less an amusement than a pleasant lounge, where the mind may in lassitude indulge, and, like a gentle sea, be moved but not ruffled by the flux and reflux of thought.

A respectable friend has put a tragedy, called *Henry and Almeria*, into the hands of the Editor, of the author of which he relates some interesting anecdotes. This author's name is *Andrew Birrell:* he is an engraver, of some merit in his profession; but is infirm, oppressed by marriage, and pining in poverty. It is true, the tragedy abounds in faults; but it has sufficient pathos and knowledge of the human heart to prove that the talents of the author only require that cultivation which reading and books might bestow, in order to render him well worthy of public support. To inform the world where indigent genius languishes, for protection, is a melancholy duty. The tragedy is sold by Longman and Co.

The Editor presumes he may likewise safely recommend a comedy, in three acts, which has never been performed, but which is published, and entitled *Custom's Fallacy*. He is acquainted with the author's name ; but, as it does not appear in the title page, imagines it is intended to be withheld at present from the public. The piece has its faults, but it has sufficient comic merit to afford very great hope that the author's name may hereafter be known to advantage.

In the performance of Romeo and Juliet, it would be unjust not to notice the uncommon merit of Mrs. H. Johnston. A perfect performance of this youthful, sweet, impassioned, and poetical character will perhaps never be seen : for, even in an actress of the high powers of Mrs. Siddons, before the mind can be so matured as to well comprehend the part of Juliet, the pristine freshness of youth is flown. Mrs. Johnston, however, makes a noble advance to excellence : her voice is so engaging, her manners so playful, her transitions so natural, and the impassioned parts in many places are so truly felt, that she deserves the notice of the managers; for by the public she is already greatly noticed.

It is highly to be regretted that there is no complete edition of the works of that dramatic poet, Mr. Foote, who so long shone the luminary of the period at which he lived, and of whom so little has been said after his death. Since the time of Shakspeare, perhaps no Englishman, *as actor and poet*, has received such great and such frequent applause as the late Samuel Foote : he was indeed the Molière of his age. His theatre was upon a small scale, and it was rather his delight to give an exquisite sketch than a complete comedy : yet many of his pieces show how perfectly he was qualified for that difficult task, but that the nature of circumstances, and perhaps his love of pleasant society, of which he was the soul, enured him to negligent habits. There is an edition, in two volumes, of his works; but few of his very early pieces are there to be found. The following is preserved in the London

Magazine of 1767. Like every thing the author wrote, it abounds with satirical strokes at the times, and especially at the state of the theatres, when pantomimes and coronation processions were so attractive as to make it difficult for genuine comedy to be heard *.

Extract from the Occasional Prologue *in Prose, at the Opening of the Theatre Royal in the Haymarket. Written by* S. Foote, *Esq.*

Enter Scaffold, *(the Builder.)*

Foote. Well, Master Scaffold, what's the best news with you?

Scaff. Sarvent, Master, I hope things are as they should be?

F. Perfectly.

S. *Conwenent* and *greable,* and quite *a propoz.*

F. If the public, whose servant I am, are but satisfied, you are sure of my voice.

S. Why, I don't see any fault they can find; the *Orchester* indeed is rather too small.

P. No, pretty well.

S. Ay, at present; but if in the winter you should chance to have Oratoris, you will scarce have room for the *Hapsichol.*

F. Oh! that may be easily altered.

S. True. Well, Master Foote, let us now talk a little of business.

F. Oh! the deuce!

S. A pretty long account——here it is.　　[*Shews the bill.*

F. Very well; but why do you bring it to me?

S. To you! to be paid, to be sure.

F. I pay you!

S. Without doubt.

F. No, there you are mistaken, my good Master Scaffold, you are much better off; it is these ladies and gentlemen who are to be your paymasters.

* If any correspondent can indicate sources of information concerning the life or early writings of this poet, the editor, and perhaps the public, will be highly gratified.

S. What, the gentlefolks above and below?

F. Ay, the whole public; for, if they don't, I am sure it is out of my power.

S. Why, I can't say, but my security is mended; that is if so be as how they be willing—but—ah!—this is one of your skits, you will never leave off;—but come, Master Foote, you should not be long winde, consider what expedition we have made; all this work here in three months, a tight job, Master Foote.

F. And you, Master Scaffold, claim much merit from that?

S. To be sure.

F. Look into the pit.

S. Well, I do.

F. I will undertake that less than half that number of hands shall undo more work in an hour, than you can complete in a year.

S. May be so; I see there is amongst them some tight likely lads: but come, Master, let us now be *serus* a little.

F. Upon my word, I am serious: I consider myself as a trustee for the public, and what their generosity bestows upon me I will most justly assign over to you.

S. Ay, why then, since that is the case, let us hear a little of how and about it: well now, and what scheme, what plan have you got, to give a jog to the generous?

F. Why, I have some things they have lik'd, and others that I hope they will like.

S. What, I suppose men and women, and talking stuff, that you take out of play-books?

F. Of that kind.

S. Ah! pox! that will ne'er do; could you not give 'em a christening, or funeral? or hey! or, ay, that is the best of 'em all; zooks, let 'em have a *crownation*.

F. No.

S. No, why not? why then we shall have 'em crowd hither in shoals.

F. No, no, no, Scaffold:

No long processions crowd my narrow scenes,
Lamp-lighting peers, and mantua-making queens.

S. Why, as you say, that work is little better than *scandalous magnation:* Hey, gad, I have a thought! give 'em a *pantomime:* I likes to see that little patch-coated feller slap one, and kick t'other, and then pop he is out of the window.

F. Nor shall great Philip's son, thro' our crime,
Sully his triumph by a pantomime.

S. Philip! pshaw, I'd never mind Philip, nor any of the family: what harm can they do you? Come do, and I'll bate of my bill;—do, for the carpenter's credit.

F. Your credit!

S. Ay, and to punish the prigmatical poets, for in that kind of work you will have no occasion for them.—There, you know, our trade takes the lead.

F. Well, well, we'll feel a little for the taste of the town; and if no other method can be found of paying your bill—— for we, Mr. Scaffold, may assume what airs of reforming we please; the stage is at best but an echo of the public voice; a mere rainbow; all its gaudy colours arise from reflection; or, as a modern bard more happily says,

" The drama's laws, the drama's patrons give;
" For we that live to please, must please to live."

S. Why then, after all, I find I am in a hobble.

F. May be not; come, hope for the best. Prompter!

Prompt. Sir.

F. Are the actors ready to open?

Prompt. Immediately.

F. Stay, and see the result of this evening:
Consult with care each countenance around,
Not one malignant aspect can be found,
To check the Royal Hand that rais'd me from the ground.

―――

COSTUME.

Though it has not been pretended to give likenesses of the performers, of whom we have given the stage dresses, the likeness in every instance, perhaps, has been as great as when such things *have* been pretended, in monthly journals. The figure and appearance of Master Betty, with a profile view of his face, though far from perfect, are yet as similar as most of the prints that have been multiplied upon the town. The sketch, taken while seeing him in character, was intended to convey an idea of his dress, demeanor, and person; and this end has been obtained.

Of the Indian costumes, those of the Soodder, the Sic, and the Sudsopê, are given in the present number. The Soodder, according to the religion of the Hindoos, is prescribed to serve the other classes, in handicraft and menial offices: the print represents him as a servant to a priest.

The Sic is in his family dress. An account of this curious tribe, given of them by Mr. Wilkins, is inserted in the first volume of the Transactions of the Asiatic Society. In the back ground they are here seen armed as soldiers.

The Sudsopê is represented as in the employment of a Godown, or warehouse Sircar.

TO CORRESPONDENTS.

The Editor acknowledges the satisfaction he receives to find that J. C. T. and the Subscribers in general, as far as he can collect their opinions, are satisfied with the plan, and execution, of The Theatrical Recorder.

He is particularly indebted to the Gentleman who has furnished this Number with an Account of the Theatres of Wolverhampton, Stafford, *and* Kidderminster.

MONTHLY LIST, FOR MARCH, 1805.

DRURY-LANE.

FEB.

28. Lovers' Vows (Young Roscius) - The Wedding Day.

MARCH

2. Douglas (Young Roscius) - - - The Devil to Pay.
4. Romeo and Juliet (Young Roscius) The Irishman in London.
5. The Honey Moon (by Command) The Lady of the Rock.
7. Romeo and Juliet (Young Roscius) The Devil to Pay.
9. Douglas (Young Roscius) - - - - Of Age To-morrow.
11. Barbarossa (Young Roscius) - - The Anatomist.
12. The Honey Moon - - - - - - - The Lady of the Rock.
14. Hamlet (Benefit of Roscius) - - The Wedding Day.
16. Ditto - - - - - - - - - - - - - The Lying Valet.
18. Ditto - - - - - - - - - - - - - Two Strings to your Bow.
19. The Honey Moon (by Command) Matrimony.
21. Douglas (Young Roscius) - - - The Citizen.
23. Hamlet (Young Roscius) - - - - Who's the Dupe?
25. Romeo and Juliet (Young Roscius) United Britons, and the Virgin Unmask'd.
26. The Beaux Stratagem - - - - - The Lady of the Rock.
28. Douglas (Young Roscius) ✓ - - - United Britons, and the Devil to Pay.

COVENT-GARDEN.

FEB.

28. To Marry, or Not to Marry - - Out of Place, or the Lake of Lausanne.

MARCH.

2. Ditto - - - - - - - - - - - - - Ditto.
4. Ditto - - - - - - - - - - - - - Ditto.
5. Ditto - - - - - - - - - - - - - Ditto.
7. Ditto - - - - - - - - - - - - - Ditto.
9. The School of Reform - - - - - Ditto.
11. To Marry, or Not to Marry - - Ditto.
12. Ditto (by Command) - - - - - - Ditto.
14. Ditto - - - - - - - - - - - - - Ditto.
16. The School of Reform - - - - - Ditto.
18. To Marry, or Not to Marry - - Ditto.
19. The Blind Bargain - - - - - - - Ditto.
21. The Cabinet - - - - - - - - - - Raising the Wind.
23. The School of Reform - - - - - Out of Place.
25. Richard III. - - - - - - - - - Ditto, *changed to* The Review.
26. To Marry, or Not to Marry (by Command) - - - - - - - - Love à la Mode.
28. The English Fleet - - - - - - - Honest Thieves.

THE

THEATRICAL RECORDER:

BY

THOMAS HOLCROFT.

Contents of Number V.

London:

Printed by C. Mercier and Co. No. 6, Northumberland-court,

Where the Work may be procured:

And at all the Booksellers;

And published for the Author, by H. D. Symonds, Paternoster-row.

1805.

THE SAGE AND HIS FATHER:

A COMEDY,

IN ONE ACT,

TRANSLATED FROM

THE FRENCH OF M. HOFFMAN.

DRAMATIS PERSONÆ.

MERVAL.

CLITON.

FRONTIN.

ELIZA.

ROSETTA.

THE SAGE AND HIS FATHER:

A COMEDY, IN ONE ACT.

~~~~~~

SCENE I.—CLITON, *alone, in a Morning Gown, Velvet Cap, and seated at a Library Table, covered with Folios; his Demeanor grave and scholastic.*

Cliton.

A GREAT author hath sagaciously said, life is but the mirror of affliction. Scarcely are we acquainted with ourselves ere we become a prey to inquietude. I, who only delight in my philosophic studies, am continually overwhelmed by domestic cares. My father——It is lamentable to have to complain of a father—My father disturbs my repose, and afflicts my heart, by conduct of which a youth might be ashamed. But, however I may grieve, I must never forget he is my father. Heaven grant I may not hear of more of his thoughtless tricks! (*rings.*)

SCENE II.—*Enter* FRONTIN.

Clit. What time did my father come home last night?
Front. Sir—I—he—forbad me to tell.
Clit. I must know.
Front. Nay, Sir.
Clit. (*grave severity*) Will you speak?
Front. If I must I must! It was five in the morning.
Clit. Five! Is not his health impaired?
Front. Lord, Sir, you are too careful by half: you need not be afraid. Your father came in this morning as frolicsome as ever: singing, dancing, chucking my wife under the chin——Scarcely any young man I know would have looked so fresh and gay.
Clit. Your account, Sir, displeases me. I request you will answer to what you are asked, and nothing more.
Front. Sir——
Clit. Go! But by no means inform my father how much his conduct makes me suffer. [*Exit* Frontin *laughing.*

SCENE III.—CLITON.

Clit. 'Tis even so! My father ruined past recovery, unless I seriously interfere. My counsels, my remonstrances have had no effect: Ah! Were I but older, he then perhaps would listen; but he is as much a boy as ever. When I was born, his habits were quite confirmed. Wretched effects of a neglected education! Oh, age! Oh, manners! How are you changed! Lost, confounded! Morality extinct, philosophy a child, old age a coxcomb. Amusements the most frivolous, a joke, a pun, a riddle, any thing to get rid of time. What were our grey beards, when they were boys? Ah, were my father but my son, I should hope in time that sage advice might reform his character, but as it is——Ah me!

SCENE IV.

MERVAL, his Father, is heard singing at a Distance.

Clit. What warbling is that? Surely it cannot be my father?

Merv. (*singing as he enters*) Good morrow, my dear boy; good morrow.

Clit. (*coldly*) Good morrow, Sir.

Merv. How sad you look!

Clit. I do indeed. I wish you could give me your superfluity of mirth.

Merv. Sblood, I have not enough for myself! I have not a single agreeable quality to spare.

Clit. So early dressed and powdered like a stripling.

Merv. If you will not preach, I'll tell you why.

Clit. (*significantly*) I can guess.

Merv. Can you?

Clit. May I ask how you passed the night?

Merv. Oh, not a moment lost. I did not sleep a quarter of an hour! Charming women, a delicious supper, songs, repartees, pleasures on pleasures, and projects for the morrow! Was that passing my night ill?

Clit. And how long do you suppose this can continue?

Merv. Just as long as I live. What can I ask more?

Clit. (*sighing*) Ah, my father, could you——

Merv. Ah, my brethren, the sermon is beginning. You young dog, would you preach to your father? Pshaw! You are a lunatic, and what is worse yours is melancholy madness.

Clit. If so, my father, you suppose yourself a sage?

Merv. To be sure! He that enjoys life is wise; while he that grieves is a madman, spreading infection, and of whose bite we should beware.

Clit. Heavenly powers!

Merv. Ay ; sigh, groan, and write a folio on human folly.

Clit. (*bows*) Which I will dedicate to my father.

Merv. Ah, ah ! sarcastic ! So much the better : at least, there is pleasantry in that. Write epigrams on me with all my heart ! Wit of any kind, quibbles, puns, jokes, what you will, any thing but a lecture.

Clit. (*deeply sighing*) Oh, my father ! The more I hear, the more I am convinced some serious measures must be taken, to snatch you from the precipice on which you stand.

Merv. The son regenerate the father ! Quite in nature, I confess : only be kind enough to tell me which way.

Clit. One which prudence prescribes : marriage.

Merv. Marry me ! With all my heart. I like the scheme. You are right, boy : 'tis time the account should be closed. And will you, my young Mentor, have the goodness to find me a wife ?

Clit. No doubt. Should I suffer you to choose for yourself, all my labor might be lost.

Merv. An excellent, a friendly fellow ! Shake hands, my boy ! Bring her quickly, and let her be just what I should like. You shall find your father most obedient and submissive to filial authority.

Clit. I have been forming this project ever since Madam Eliza and her niece have returned from the country.

Merv. Better and better ! The niece is charming, and the aunt is not to be despised.

Clit. I have been told that, during the life of my honored mother, you were much more prudent than at present.

Merv. True, very true. An adorable woman, and nothing can better prove my attachment to her than the means I daily take to make me forget her loss. But, while taking the pains to find a wife for your father, you should follow the good example you so solemnly recommend, and find one for yourself.

Clit. In that, my father, you are not so far from reason as your smiling might seem to suppose. Nature and society equally require man to submit to domestic duties. The state demands a fresh supply of citizens, and I have little esteem for him who refuses to fulfil that social obligation. On this subject I have a plan, which I will communicate to my father, when the time shall come. Why do you laugh ?

Merv. Me ? I am all admiration ! Your wisdom is astonishing ; and, should it continue to increase, bless me, how wise will you be when you are old !

Clit. Might I not reply, Sir, your follies are astonishing ; and, should they increase, what indeed will they be at last ?

Merv. You are very pleasant.

Clit. Rather, deeply grieved.

Merv. Take comfort.

Clit. You give me none.

Merv. (*laughing*) You will always find me submissive to the laws of a son whom I so profoundly revere.

Clit. Take my advice; marriage is necessary. (*aside*) A fop at fifty is an error in nature.

Merv. (*aside*) A grave philosopher at twenty-one wants—— he even wants a beard! Ha, ha, ha!

Clit. Change your manners, I conjure you, Sir.

Merv. Fear nothing: I will have pity on your paternal grief.

SCENE V.—*Enter* FRONTIN.

Front. The ladies desire to know if you are at leisure?

Merv. Certainly. I am impatient to pay them my respects.
[*Exit* Frontin.

SCENE VI.

Merv. Well, son, but I hope you do not intend to appear before the ladies in that cap and gown?

Clit. By no means, Sir. I love propriety; but I can never hope my dress should equal the elegance of yours.   [*Exit.*

Merv. Go, silly pedant; the time will come when two fine eyes will be worse than book-worms to your philosophy. It has been truly said that nature finds an equilibrium: if one has too much, another has too little, and a just balance is kept. My son is ridiculous from too much prudence, of which excess nobody can accuse me. But here comes the amiable aunt.

SCENE VII.—*Enter* ELIZA.

Merv. Good morrow, my charming Eliza! Where is your lovely niece?

Eliza. Oh, at her toilet, consulting her glass. Young girls never think themselves handsome enough: dressing is never done.

Merv. They have their little plans.

Eliza. Yes, yes. It has a meaning. When in the country, nothing but negligence and indifference: scattered hair, pins ill placed, the gown carelessly thrown over the shoulders; but, should the shadow of a man be seen, the brain and the hands are as busy! Ribands, feathers, flowers, trinkets of every kind.

Merv. So much the better: the women ought to think of us.

Eliza. Yes, yes, Sir, we know you.

Merv. Nay, but were not you the same?

Eliza. Much like others.

Merv. Well, this marriage project?

Eliza. What do you mean?

Merv. Between my son and your niece.

Eliza. I find, on reflection, it must not take place.

Merv. Nay, but why?

Eliza. Your son is a pedant, proper only to torment a wo-man. I would secure happiness and pleasure for my niece.

Merv. His character will change.

Eliza. As yours has done.

Merv. (*aside*) A little malice in that remark.

Eliza. A formal starched husband, for ever preaching phi-losophy, old at one and twenty! What will he be at fifty? Always dreaming, and never letting a word escape. Phleg-matic, inflated, cold as marble, a grumbler, a sermonizer, who would insist that his wife should chop logic, and never let her amuse herself with any book but the Encyclopedia; me-lancholy by day, in a lethargy all night, and as to tenderness and affection, oh, not one word! Wisdom to be sure is good, but not in excess.

Merv. Your portrait is far too hard featured.

Eliza. To own the truth, I would rather have such a thoughtless creature as yourself for a husband.

Merv. Then pray take me. I am quite at your service. What do you say?

Eliza. Nay, nay; that's another matter. That would in-deed require some courage.

Merv. I have enough for both.

Eliz. A fine argument!

Merv. Come, come; say the match is made.

Eliza. It is as it may happen.

Merv. And for the young people likewise?

Eliza. Oh, no, by no means.

Merv. But supposing your niece to be willing?

Eliza. Which she is not.

Merv. If she is, will you consent?

Eliza. Yes: but she is not.

Merv. So you say. Here she comes.

Eliza. And the philosopher with her; quite a propos.

SCENE VIII.—*Enter* ROSETTA *and* CLITON, *at opposite Doors. CLITON in an old-fashioned Dress, clean, neat, and formal; em-broidered Waistcoat, black Velvet Breeches, white Silk Stock-ings, a round Wig, his Hat under his Arm, and a Gold-headed Cane. He salutes the Aunt* ELIZA *gravely; and smiles at com-paring his Father and himself.*

Merv. Why really, son, you may well expect to please the ladies; for you seem to have taken no little pains for that purpose.

Eliza. Yes, the young gentleman has quite a gallant air. Is not that your opinion, niece?

Ros. I have no fault to find. Outward appearances have

little to do with the heart: where that is good, the rest is indifferent.

Merv. (*whispering* Eliza) You hear! She will not?

Clit. Attend to this charming young lady, my father, and acknowledge that the young are destined to be your instructors.

Merv. Your little impertinences, my good youth, deserve to be punished; therefore be pleased, Mr. Philosopher, to sing us a song.

Clit. I sing, Sir!

Merv. A song! Immediately, no delay!

Eliza. Charming! I shall delight to hear wisdom sing.

Clit. What, make me a ridiculous——

Merv. No evasion! Sing you must. You would not be so rude as to refuse this charming young lady, who is going to ask you.

Ros. I have no right to make such a request, but I own it would give me pleasure.

Clit. Who can refuse youth and innocence? You, lovely lady, must be obeyed. I'll sing you the only song I ever learned in my life.

Eliza. It will be something very pleasant, I warrant.

SONG.

Of wit or beauty which to choose
Some hold it difficult, I grant:
But which will turn to better use?
The one a flower; th' other a plant:
That falls to quick decay;
This weathers many a wintry day:
That fades, and strews the ground;
This mounts the skies, and lives renown'd!
Ah! brief is beauty, apt to fly,
If it live but in the eye:
But you have it many a year,
When you hold it by the ear.

Merv. Ha, ha, ha! (*they all laugh heartily*) I shall never recover! Hold beauty by the ear is excellent! Ha, ha, ha! Where did you pick up these fine rhetorical figures?

Clit. In authors, Sir, that you seldom read.

Eliza. The young gentleman is happy at complimenting beauty.

Ros. The song is full of meaning, and teaches a profitable lesson.

Merv. Ha, ha, ha! Beauty held by the ear! Well, well, I will give you a song of less philosophy, but more good sense.

SONG.

Like butterfly, I lightly wing
    From tree to tree;
There sip the dewy sweets and sing,
    Like honey bee.
Pink, violet, or rose,
To me their pearls disclose!
    I love to range,
    To taste and change,
    For pleasure flies,
    And he that's wise,
    From Time's diurnal wing,
Brushes, fresh, fair, and young, the sweet delights that spring.

'Tis surely time enough to think,
When we can neither love nor drink;
Nor will I sigh, and cease to live,
While I can taste the fruits the Gods so freely give.

Clit. But, Sir, the loss of time is irreparable: ought it to be employed in singing? 'Tis singular, I own, but you have for once consented to a serious and reasonable plan, and duty bids me seize the present opportunity, to put it in execution. (*to* Eliza) Will you, Madam, kindly permit me the honor of a private conversation with this young lady, that I may clearly explain myself?

Eliza. In private with my niece?

Ros. With me, Sir?

Merv. Oh, don't be alarmed; there is no danger in being alone with my son.

Eliza. I doubt if your son will say as much for you.

Merv. I would scarcely say it for myself.

Eliza. (*to* Merval) Why any mystery?

Merv. (*to* Eliza) You know what you promised me?

Eliza. Well?

Merv. Now for the proof. Will she or will she not refuse?

Clit. Are you agreed? May I put my interrogations?

Merv. Patience, good, Sir, we will retire: preach as long as you please, only preach to the purpose.

Eliza. And pray, niece, listen with profit. (*aside*) Oh for a corner! that I might overhear this charming conversation.

Merv. Come, come: the conference shall not be disturbed.

        [*Exeunt* Merval *and* Eliza *laughing.*

SCENE IX.

CLITON *seats himself in a large Arm Chair, and with grave Polite-*
ness points to another, for Rosetta *to sit by his Side.*

Clit. Be pleased, young lady, to place yourself there.

Ros. Sir !

Clit. Fear nothing. (Rosetta *smiles and sits down*) First permit me to say, my child, that I feel a lively interest in your happiness ; and, be assured, I speak with sincerity.

Ros. (*smiling*) I believe you, Sir.

Clit. (*very gravely*) This principle established, you will listen to me with that confidence which you would place in a tender, affectionate, and reasonable father.

Ros. I own, Sir, these are the sentiments you inspire.

Clit. Good ! a very proper reply. Now to the second item : do you feel any inclination to the marriage state?

Ros. Why——

Clit. No evasion, I request. Answer plainly ; yes or no.

Ros. (*smiling*) Since you love precision, I must confess I have no aversion to marriage.

Clit. Perfectly well : no answer can be more clear. My third question is, have you made a choice?

Ros. Your questions are very pressing.

Clit. By no means ; for, if your choice be made, I have nothing more to say.

Ros. (*imitating his slow gravity*) My—choice—is—not—made.

Clit. Good. Have you confidence enough in me to accept the party I shall propose?

Ros. I have already had the honor to tell you my confidence in your prudence is unlimited.

Clit. (*aside*) A charming young person, upon my word ! (*aloud*) I return you thanks. These points all explained, I have only to name your spouse ; a man who will find happiness in such a wife. You alone are capable of restoring him to reason : your charms only can make the bonds of marriage the permanent limits of felicity.

Ros. Such is the husband I certainly desire.

Clit. (*rising with great satisfaction*) Then, sweet young lady, 'tis now concluded : to-morrow you shall marry my father.

Ros. (*astonished*) Sir ! I do not understand you.

Clit. Nothing could be more clearly explained ! I engaged to find my father a wife, and you a husband.

Ros. (*aside, with great vexation*) This is insufferable !

Clit. (*aside*) She ruminates, and should not be disturbed. I must own, she is truly amiable ! and I feel how great is the sacrifice I make to my father. (*aloud*) Well, my child?— why not speak? Do you reject my proposal?

Ros. (*affecting to smile*) By no means, Sir : it is so very rational ! You wish to find a wife for your father, and have honored me with your preference : but you will permit me to add a single condition.

Clit. What is it, young lady ?

Ros. I also wish to find a husband for my aunt, and give you the preference.

Clit. (*calmly*) I will think on the subject. This interchange is founded on reason: my father is too wild, and dissipated; and nothing less than merit like yours could exclusively gain his affection. I am not so imprudent, and therefore your aunt may be a proper match for me.

Ros. (*aside, after listening with astonishment*) Better and better!

Clit. Well, my dear, may I have the happiness to announce your consent to my father?

Ros. (*curtseying*) Please to tell him, Sir, I rely on his discretion.

Clit. (*with transport*) You are an adorable young lady; nor can I longer forbear to salute you.

Ros. (*retiring*) Be not too hasty, Sir: when I have the honor to be your mother-in-law, and you my uncle, why, then——

Clit. At your own discretion, sweet innocent. I will write to the notary, that he may draw the contracts of marriage.

[*Exit, after taking his hat and cane.*

SCENE X.

Ros. Is it possible? Can there be such a youth! With every gift of nature, all that could make him amiable; how has he found the secret to be so far the reverse! He must be mad; and I still more so, since I felt a wish to gain a heart of such insensibility. Was it all a mistake, or is it a dream? Have I misunderstood him? Would he try me? Would he make me a jest? My thoughts are all confused. So young! So formed to please! Can he be thus cold? Oh, love, love, finish thy work! Either erase his image from my heart, or give him all the sensibility I feel! His father! My aunt! Impossible! Ridiculous!

SCENE XI.—*Enter* ELIZA.

Eliza. Well, is your dialogue ended?

Ros. It was but short.

Eliza. And is your conversation a secret?

Ros. You can never guess the subject.

Eliza. Guessing is unnecessary; I know it.

Ros. Surely not!

Eliza. It's no mystery: the sage has been proposing marriage to you.

Ros. And do you know who he means to make his own wife.

Eliza. Certainly: 'tis you.

Ros. There, aunt, you are mistaken.

Eliza. Who then?

Ros. (*laughing extravagantly*) It is you!

Eliza. How! Me?

Ros. (*continuing to laugh*) You, you, you!

Eliza. (*surprised and pleased*) Would he marry me?

Ros. I tell you again, yes: marry you! *my* aunt!

Eliza. (*affronted*) Well, Miss, and what is there to laugh at? Is there any thing so very ridiculous in this proposal?

Ros. Nay, surely aunt, you must think him mad?

Eliza. (*with volubility and passion*) How mad? Impertinence is worse than folly! To prefer a woman of the age of reason to a thoughtless chit, like yourself, is to be mad! No, no; that is, not his defect. This young man has been wronged! Mocked, laughed at, when he abounds in reason and good sense! I myself supposed his philosophy only affected. I am sorry I did him so much injustice. Do not deceive yourself, Miss; he is a very extraordinary youth.

Ros. (*laughing*) He is indeed; very extraordinary.

Eliza. No more of your insults, if you please, Miss: be gone, and do not tax those with folly who have more understanding than you will ever possess.

Ros. I shall obey my aunt.

Eliza. As you ought.

Ros. (*going*) This surpasses every thing!   [*Exit.*

SCENE XII.

Eliza. And does he wish indeed to marry me. Dear youth! How much discernment! And so young! I must take care in future, not to speak ill of people, before I know them better. Here comes his father, of whom one may indeed say any thing without the least danger of doing him wrong.

SCENE XIII.—*Enter* MERVAL.

Merv. Well, they have settled the business, no doubt.

Eliza. To admiration!

Merv. I told you so; and we must think of our marriage?

Eliza. What marriage, may it please you?

Merv. Ours, ours!

Eliza. Ours indeed! I do not understand you, Sir.

Merv. Nay, I don't speak Greek!

Eliza. Humph! I suppose you do, Sir, for 'tis past my comprehension.

Merv. Hey day! What now? You are joking?

Eliza. No, Sir, it is no joke.

Merv. Why, did not you agree to marry me, provided——

Eliza. I marry you!

Merv. And why not? Did you not give your promise?

Eliza. Could you not see, I was but laughing at you?

Marry you indeed! An old rake, who thinks of nothing but
pleasures, and follies; destitute of reason and good sense;
racking his brain to appear an Adonis; running after balls, and
pastimes, and neglecting nothing but his wife! No, Sir, my
husband must be prudent, reserved, serious, and sage, as becomes a man. Regular in his affairs, just in his decisions, and
one who prefers the useful to the frivolous. I have much
friendship for you, Mr. Merval; that I own; and, *as a friend*,
will see you as often as you please: but, with respect to marriage, I am your humble servant. [*Exit*.

SCENE XIV.—MERVAL.

Merv. If she is not fit for Bedlam, why——I am. This
morning, she wished to marry such a cheerful good humoured
fellow as myself; and now, forsooth, he must be prudent,
reasonable, serious, and sage! What time of the moon is it?
Weather cocks and women! Really, ladies, you are charming
creatures! Nothing less than love and adoration, this minute,
and the next, you are the most incoherent, crazy, capricious,
fantastic cameleons that nature knows.

SCENE XV.—*Enter* CLITON.

Clit. All is settled, dear Sir; all is settled: she consents,
and you may marry her to-morrow.

Merv. Who?

Clit. The charming, the lovely niece.

Merv. What the devil are you talking of?

Clit. Your admiration is natural. I kept my project a secret, that you might have the pleasure of surprise. It was to
marry you to this beautiful young lady, to whom I made an
offer of your hand, which she has accepted.

Mer. Accepted! Me!

Clit. Once more, I tell you yes. I own, I spoke rather
flatteringly in your favor; but I obtained her consent. I have
written to the notary, and to-morrow shall have the pleasure to
confirm your happiness.

Merv. Are we all lunatics alike?

Clit. How, Sir! Do I deserve no thanks for procuring you
the hand of so sweet a lady?

Merv. Oh, do not fear I should complain of that.
Sblood! The delicious niece, instead of the strange coquettish
aunt! Why, you are too good, my boy! If these are the
only kind of tricks you would play me, we shall be the
dearest friends on earth.

Clit. I would not wish to make a merit of such a sacrifice,
but, while I resolutely spoke in your favor, I was far from
insensible to the power of that sweet young lady's eyes.

Merv. Oh, oh, my young sage! What, you have found out that she has eyes, have you! Hark you, my boy! I would neither deceive you, nor have you deceive yourself. How can the lovely Rosetta really consent to marry me, since I know she is in love with you.

Clit. In love with me!

Merv. Beyond all doubt.

Clit. How do you know?

Merv. I know because——because she told me so.

Clit. Oh, Sir, if she be in love with me, you must be sensible——that——will——quite derange my plan. Justice requires that no constraint should be put upon the inclinations.

Merv. (*laughing*) A notable discovery, and made just in proper time. Reflect further on it, pay your court to the young beauty, speak for yourself, show your repentance, ask her hand of the aunt, and, for once in your life, make yourself agreeable. (*laughing*) If, after all, I must absolutely marry the niece myself, Heaven help me, but I submit! for, to speak the truth, any day that you shall please, I will exchange ten aunts for one niece! (*aside*) He has it!   [*Exit.*

SCENE XVI.

Clit. She loves *me*! That is very singular! Had I but known it! Why did not she tell me so? She is a sweet creature!—— I saw that plain enough. Then she is so graceful, has such an ingenuous countenance——Hey day! I fear I am in danger of resembling my father——It's all over! I must retract, and speak to the aunt.

SCENE XVII.—*Enter* Eliza *after first speaking behind.*

Eliza. Where is he? Where can I find him?

Clit. Here she comes.

Eliza. I have been seeking you every where.

Clit. And I am enchanted to meet you.

Eliza. Enchanted! But, are you indeed? Charming youth! Well, speak, speak!

Clit. I wish to inform you of a project——

Eliza. I know it! I know it!

Clit. I rather think——

Eliza. I tell you, I know the whole!

Clit. If so, I wish to ask your consent to——

Eliza. You have my consent: it's yours to-day, to-morrow, for ever.

Clit. Are you willing to grant——

Eliza. Every thing so prudent and charming a youth can ask.

Clit. Nay, but, do not deceive yourself concerning——

Eliza. Dear, dear! don't I tell you I know the whole? You are too amiable to be refused!

Clit. Will you then fix the time for this happy union?

Eliza. To-morrow, to-day, whenever you please.

Clit. Since there is no difficulty, permit me to explain myself to your lovely niece.

Eliza. Nay, I do not want the consent of my niece.

Clit. You are too just and good to have her married against her own consent.

Eliza. How married? Who do you mean to marry?

Clit. Your niece, as I hope.

Eliza. (*astonished*) And have you been talking of my niece all this while?

Clit. Certainly.

Eliza. Is it her you wish to marry?

Clit. I do.

Eliza. (*confused and vexed*) Why, as to my niece, I—'tis a different affair—and I must tell you (*aside*) The blockhead! (*aloud*) My niece has a very particular taste: she has no opinion of a young man, little better than a boy, who is serious, melancholy, dismal, absent, pedantic, and who affects the importance of philosophy: beside which, I must inform you, Sir, my niece will not marry without her aunt's consent. Your very humble servant. (*aside, and going*) The pedagogue! Who would have him for a husband! [*Exit.*

SCENE XVIII.

Clit. What vertigo is this? She is little better than crazy, yet I was willing to marry her! That was wrong. I must be candid and own my error; it was very wrong. Yes, yes, there is a visible difference between the aunt and the niece! The one inconsistent, ridiculous, disagreeable, and the other with such candor; so fresh and fair, such sweetness in her smiles, so charmingly graceful—Hold, hold, young man—Beware! Yet what is there to fear? The heart of man is formed for love—I hear her coming, and now, I know not why I have I know not what foolish fears. Come, come, let me recollect myself.

SCENE XIX.—*Enter* ROSETTA.

Ros. What have you said to my aunt, Sir? I never saw her so angry, and she looked at me quite—quite terribly.

Clit. I am sorry, young lady, but I—I only asked your hand in marriage.

Ros. You mean for your father, no doubt?

Clit. Oh, no; for myself.

Ros. How so? You told me differently.

Clit. I own it. Wishing to see my father happy, I could not have made a better choice: but—since—you love me, you must own that I ought to marry you myself.

Ros. I love you, Sir?

Clit. Certainly you do, for you told my father so; (*with joyful gravity*) and I am sure you are incapable of falsehood!

Ros. (*hesitating, confused*) Your father might not understand the sense in which I spoke.

Clit. (*very seriously*) Nay, Miss, you need have no fears; for I do assure you the confession gave me no offence.

Ros. (*smiling*) No, indeed! How am I to be certain of that?

Clit. (*solemnly*) Young lady, I never tell a lie.

Ros. Your father might have pitied my indiscretion.

Clit. (*arguing*) Indeed you depart from the question. Come to the point: do you love me (*sighing*), or do you not?

Ros. You are very singular.

Clit. Then, you do not?

Ros. I did not say that.

Clit. Why then you do?

Ros. I am quite surprised to—— But supposing I did like you, must we therefore be married?

Clit. No doubt. If you prefer me to my father, and I love you better than your aunt, duty requires their consent and ours.

Ros. Your language was very different just now; and how can I be convinced that your sentiments are so far changed?

Clit. Charming young lady, look at me—a little fuller in the face.

Ros. Well, Sir?

Clit. Beholding such beauty, who could forbear to love; and especially the man that is beloved by you?

Ros. Your arguments are all your own.

Clit. They are sincere, and therefore must convince you. We love each other, and to marry is our mutual duty.

Ros. You set out late, but you travel fast.

Clit. What proof of affection can I give? (*kneels.*)

Ros. Sir! Sir! Philosophy!

Clit. Is at your feet.

SCENE XX.—*Enter* MERVAL.

Merv. Go on.

Clit. and *Ros.* Heavens!

Merv. Go on, I tell you! If that be not wisdom, I am a fool.

Clit. My father——

Merv. You mean your rival. So, so! This is your college philosophy! Do you mean, young lady, to complete his education?

Ros. Do not judge too severely!

Merv. Not judge! I am in such a passion! Before my face! I, who am severity itself! I, who am your husband elect! Your aunt must know this proof of your love of wisdom.

Ros. If you speak, I am ruined!

Clit. You would not be so malicious, Sir?

Merv. Well, on certain conditions, I am silent.

Ros. Pray name them!

Merv. You are in such a hurry!

Clit. I am all obedience.

Merv. The first is, my rival must either fight me or shake me heartily by the hand.

Clit. (*pressing and kissing his hand*) The duel is soon over.

Merv. The second will be something of a more difficult point.

Ros. Speak.

Merv. You, young lady, must salute the philosopher.

Ros. I, Sir!

Merv. I know it is very shocking, but it must be done.

Clit. Let me pay the penalty? (*offering to kiss her.*)

Merv. No, no; that will not do. Come, resolve! I must have my revenge.

Ros. Do not look then!

Merv. Me! Oh, I am blind! (Rosetta *kisses* Cliton.)

SCENE XXI.—*Enter* ELIZA.

Eliza. So! So! Go on! Once more!

Clit. and *Ros.* Ah!

Merv. I am glad you are come: you are wanted.

Eliza. Was there ever such a——

Ros. My dear aunt!

Eliza. Aunt, indeed! It is very becoming to——

Merv. (*laughing*) Becoming? Yes, to be sure! She was only studying philosophy.

Eliza. Raillery is very proper! Hypocrisy deserves encouragement!

Merv. Don't be angry. He loves a person of a ripe age: pleasure and beauty must be held by the ears, and you were his choice! Ha, ha, ha!

Eliza. Oh, I was willing to amuse myself, and so—pretended to believe it all.—He was caught in the trap.

Merv. Oh, it was a trap, then?

Eliza. Certainly! What could you suppose?

Merv. Very true; and from a reasonable woman like yourself! We therefore return to our treaty: youth to youth, and age to age.

Eliza. Pray speak for yourself.

Clit. Ah, Madam!

Ros. My dear, dear aunt!

Merv. Don't you hear? It was but a trap!

Eliza. Well, well; the shortest follies——

Merv. Are the best.

Eliza. But is that, young gentleman, to be your wedding suit?

Merv. Oh, we have only to change clothes, and all will be right.

Eliza. Agreed.

Clit. Most willingly; and while we pardon the mistakes of each other, let us hope that our defects will be pardoned by all.

[*Exeunt Omnes.*

REMARKS.

THE foregoing truly pleasant little comedy is rather founded on the manners of our neighbours, the French, than on our own; but it may be reconcileable to either, though not precisely as it is written in the original. In that, the son is supposed to be only sixteen; and he assumes one of the customary paternal duties, in France: that of providing a wife, asking the parties if they are agreed, and superintending the marriage of a relation.

The humor lies in the son, a youth, or as he would be esteemed in England a boy, taking upon himself to perform all these duties, reverse the order of things, and provide a wife for his father, a *Parisian Anacreon.* These family matches, which for reasons of convenience unite the young and the old, are perhaps more frequent in France than other countries; for it is there tacitly understood that the young will not suffer greatly under any abstinence of affection or constraint of virtue. Young or old, the husband there will generally have his *petite maitresse,* and Madame her *bon ami:* in their opinion, things are then as they should be; nobody suffers any inconvenience: wit, wealth, and beauty, are each made the most of for the present, to the entire satisfaction of the parties. This they vauntingly style the *Savoir vivre:* a knowledge of life, which they presume they almost exclusively possess. The songs are here several of them turned into prose, for they do not singly present any poetic subject, but rather tell the story. The author appears to have not, *poetically,* supposed characters to sing: for, though Cliton had sung before and sings afterward, he makes him preface the song that good manners oblige him to sing by affirming it is the only one he ever learned. I know nothing of the author, M. Hoffman, except that he is still living, as I believe, has written many dramatic and other poetical works, and is held in very deserved esteem for his talents.

THE MOTHERS:

A COMEDY,

IN ONE ACT,

AS PERFORMED

AT THE THEATRE LOUVOIS AT PARIS,

TRANSLATED FROM

THE FRENCH OF C. G. ETIENNE, AND GAUGINAN-
NANTEUIL.

DRAMATIS PERSONÆ.

M. GERARD, a Citizen of Paris . . M. Picard.

FREMONVILLE, Merchant of Bordeaux M. Dorsan.

M. DE LIEGE, an Amateur of Dancing M. Clozei.

AMADEUS FREMONVILLE . . Mlle. Suzanne.

VICTOR GERARD, a Boy Ten years of

    Age . . . . . . Mlle. Adelé.

A VALET . . . . . . M. Thiphaine.

SOPHIA, Wife of M. Gerard . . Mad. Sara Lescot.

MAD. DE FREMONVILLE . . Mad. De Lille.

The SCENE Paris—in a Hall common to the Apartments of
M. Gérard and Mad. De Frémonville.

THE MOTHERS:

A COMEDY, IN ONE ACT.

SCENE I.—SOPHIA *alone, at Work.*

Sophia.

SO! My two waistcoats are now embroidered. It is a holiday to-day, and I will go to my son, at school, and take him a little present. Neither shall the other poor boy be forgotten. I have placed him with my Victor at the same school, without mentioning it to any body. Sweet fellow! To be abandoned at so tender an age. Yet, I must mention it to my husband. His heart is good, but his humors are very singular. (*considers*) Perhaps, the best way will be to bring them both here. Ah! I am quite perplexed; for I have another request to make. Madame Frémonville has not lately heard from her husband. Accustomed as she is to live expensively, for some time past, she has had recourse to me. We have been friends from childhood, and I am happy to be able to oblige her. (*looks to the door*) Here comes my husband.

SCENE II.—*Enter* M. GERARD, *in a Domino.*

Ger. Well, my dear.

Soph. In masquerade!

Ger. Have you passed a pleasant night?

Soph. Exceedingly. I do not ask how it has been passed by you.

Ger. (*throwing off his domino*) I flatter myself I have pleased and puzzled many a female. Perhaps you would not think it, my dear, but I am a charming fellow—in masquerade.

Soph. I am only fearful for your health, love. At your age——

Ger. My age! I am not fifty, and far from being as old as many a young rake. I have never been guilty of excess—always prudent, at bed and board, as you know, my dear.

Soph. What pleasure can you find in these unmeaning masquerades?

Ger. Can you ask? Women personating men, and men women; age mimicking childhood, and childhood age; old boys, and young drivellers; the rich in rags, the poor in brocade, the servant turned master, and the master servant; dancing, chattering, singing, bawling, nobody heard, nobody minded; seeking for those we cannot find, and finding those we do not seek; all in motion; coming, going, elbowing, scarcely room to breathe! Don't you think all that charming? Oh it is divine!

Soph. Really, you ought, my dear, to have more good sense.

Ger. I'm a philosopher, and consider things like one. I don't blame *you.* Each to his taste. Fifty though I am, I delight in pleasure; and you, though young and handsome, love your children. We neither of us seek to follow the fashion, but do just what we like.

Soph. True: but I have a favor to ask.

Ger. Speak, my dear; I can refuse you nothing—except money.

Soph. Nay but—that's it. I want a hundred louis.

Ger. Sblood! a hundred louis! Within these two months, I have given you three hundred and more.

Soph. They are all gone.

Ger. The devil! Which way? You keep no company.

Soph. I have yours.

Ger. Take no pleasure.

Soph. There is house-keeping.

Ger. Have no jewels.

Soph. Oh, yes; my children.

Ger. Dress as simply as any tradesman's wife in town; yet a lady of fashion could not be more expensive! Were you to live like our neighbour here, Madame Frémonville—Oh, she's a charming woman! What luxury! What elegance! What exquisite taste! Her husband is absent, but not disgraced by her, for she lives in style. As I live, here she comes.

SCENE III.—*Enter* Madame Fremonville.

M. Frem. My sweet friend, I am happy to see you.

Ger. We were just speaking of you, dear Madam.

M. Frem. And I have good news for you, Sir.

Ger. Have you, my angel?

M. Frem. You are invited this evening to the foreigner's ball *, where you will meet the first dancers of Paris.

Soph. (*laughs*) Among whom my husband certainly ought to be.

---

* *Au Bal des Etrangers:* this was a place where the company was supposed to be very select.

Ger. Why, in that respect, I rather flatter myself—Hey?

M. Frem. Hear the proscript. (*reads a note*) Do not fail to bring with you the young Cavalier, whose manner of dancing is so entertaining.

Ger. Oh, very true. I am gaiety itself. Not perhaps quite in the modern style; but, when I happen to hit the *pas de basque*, or the *pas de bourré*—ha, ha! Then you should see the clean cuts I give!

Soph. So you have a mind to steal my husband?

Ger. It is your own fault, my dear Madame Gérard! Why not come with us to the ball? Just as you came in, Madam, I was blaming my wife; and you shall hear whether I had not cause.

M. Frem. Oh, fie! Blame your wife! That is so like a tradesman! Will you never become fashionable?

Ger. Nay, but hear. Day and night, she is always employed about her children. Not that I find much fault on that account: it may be all very well: but why the plague be quite a slave? You are a mother yourself, yet all goes smoothly, and one hears and knows nothing of the matter.

M. Frem. (*confused*) Sir——

Soph. Say no more, my dear.

Ger. I have never so much as seen your son: with us, on the contrary, there is such an eternal racket! Laughing, crying, kissing, teaching, papa here, mamma there! She will bring her brats all up herself, and I have not a moment's peace. Look you, my dear; you will at last force me to keep my own room.

M. Frem. You appealed to me, Sir?

Ger. I did, Madam. Speak, pronounce, judge the cause.

M. Frem. Then I pronounce you are in the wrong: but, to soften the rigor of my sentence, I must tell you *De Liége* is quite satisfied with you.

Ger. What! The charming dancer? The Zephyr* of Toulouse! He gave me a lesson: showed me the step *à jetté-battu*. He tells me, my feet have too much of the libertine; my legs quite—— Hey? As you see; and that I perform a gavotte almost to perfection. He is to give a lesson for the cursed *jetté-battu*. Damned difficult! It is not yet got quite down to my feet, but I have it in my head; it will descend gradually. Good by, my dear. I don't bid you adieu, my angel! [*Exit.*

SCENE IV.

Soph. He is crazy. I wish you would speak to him a little of his eccentricities.

---

* Monsieur Des Hayes, supposed to be next in merit to Vestris, if I do not mistake, was and is still called the Zephyr at Paris.

M. Frem. But why complain ? He is always good humored, and I wish every husband were the same.

Soph. Have you written an answer to M. de Frémonville ?

M. Frem. Not yet. I began my letter above two months ago, but I am always interrupted; scarcely can finish a line: the milliner, the mantua-maker, the jeweller; now a jaunt in the country, then a tea party; one day preparing for the ball, another for the opera. Really, it is quite cruel living in Paris. Oh! 'tis impossible there to write a letter.

Soph. Far off as your husband is, thinking of you in the West Indies, he'll not be pleased at such indifference.

M. Frem. Oh, very true. I am quite angry with myself: at least I should be, if I had time to think ; but that you know one can never find. Beside, he will be home before my letter could reach him.

Soph. Well, but do me a favor : stay at home and deny yourself to-day. I have such a charming project !

M. Frem. (*eagerly*) What ! A party of pleasure ?

Soph. Oh, so delicious !

M. Frem. A ball, a concert, a——

Soph. A thousand times better. I am going to fetch my son from school : my carriage is ready. Now do you profit by the opportunity, go round in it with me for your son, and we shall pass the most charming day.

M. Frem. Why—yes—very charming : but, I am engaged. I have promised *De Liége*.

Soph. Is it an affair of importance ?

M. Frem. Oh dear! yes quite. First, we are to see my new curricle ; and then, in the evening, there's the new opera. One duet, I am told, is quite exquisite! ravishing! Oh dear, I should die !

Soph. A duet! Can that equal the pleasure of embracing your boy ? I dare say, you have never seen him since he has been at Paris; for neither I nor my husband have ever met him here.

M. Frem. Nay, now, my dear, don't scold me : he is at one of our best boarding-schools. *De Liége* assures me his master treats him like a father.

Soph. Ah, my dear fathers find no substitutes.

M. Frem. I am quite vexed to refuse you, but you see it would be quite impossible. Wait only a few days and then— beside, *De Liége* has promised this very day to go to the school, and bring me news of my son.

Soph. Well, since you are so determined not to enjoy the sweetest of pleasures, I shall say no more. I only wish yours may equal mine. Good morrow.

M. Frem. Nay, but, a word—Have you thought——

Soph. Yes.

M. Frem. I am really ashamed, but, when my husband returns——

Soph. I have asked Mr. Gérard for the money, and for the first time am refused.

M. Frem. Cross ill-natured wretch!

Soph. You called him good humored : but fear nothing ; we shall succeed. You are right not to stay at home, since you do not like the cheerful sports of youth ; for I shall not only bring my boy but one of his playfellows, in whom I take an interest. Here comes *M. De Liége,* and I shall leave you together. [*Exit.*

SCENE V.—*Enter* DE LIEGE.

De L. Madam, the humblest of your humble servants.

M. Frem. Good morrow, my dear *De Liége.* Well, what news from school?

De L. (*aside*) How the devil shall I tell her.

M. Frem. What's the matter? How you look.

De L. Your alarm is kind ; but the liberal arts, of which you know dancing is one, so absorb the faculties of mind that at last the body is affected. At present I come——

M. Frem. To speak of my son.

De L. I really don't know——boys have tricks.

M. Frem. Tricks! How? What has happened?

De L. Don't be alarmed. A trifle.

M. Frem. Go on.

De L. A mere trifle. A week ago, he—ran away.

M. Frem. Heavens!

De L. They have not yet heard where.

M. Frem. Wretched woman!

De L. I find they could make nothing of him. In the first place, he had a sort of negative propensity for dancing—It seems, beside, you sometimes forgot to pay ; and masters then are such negligent kind of fellows——

M. Frem. I am ruined! Search must be instantly made.

De L. Gently, Madam, gently! Don't be alarmed.

M. Frem. Have you any consolation for me?

De L. Um—not precisely : but I hope this letter, which the porter gave me at the gate, may bring news.

M. Frem. Give it me. (*reads*) Bordeaux— (*struck*) My husband is returned.

De L. (*aside*) More bad news. I'm out of luck to-day.

M. Frem. (*after having read*) And will this very day be here! Dreadful situation!

De L. And what is mine?

M. Frem. I dare not meet him.

De L. Ah, you don't know all yet. I have worse news. Your coach-maker will not send the curricle, till he has received five and twenty louis on account.

M. Frem. Spare me, Sir : respect the feelings of a mother.

SCENE VI.—*Enter* M. GERARD.

Ger.   Oh, are you here! Is it thus you keep your promise?

De L.   I should have been punctual, but here is my excuse.

M. Frem.   (*aside*)   How shall I act? What will become of me?

Ger.   A sufficient one, I grant. Beside, you danced so well, at the last ball, that I must forgive you.

De L.   Had you a good seat?

Ger.   I was not there; but I read your praise in the morning paper.

M. Frem.   My dear De Liége *, we must all go in search of my child: every means must be taken. M. Gérard knows Paris, if we could but prevail on him to join us.

De L.   Ask him.

M. Frem.   I dare not.

De L.   Then I will.

Ger.   Hark ye, De Liége, if Madam will permit me, I wish you would let me repeat my lesson. Hem! the *jetté-battu.*

M. Frem.   I am in trouble, at present; pray spare me.

Ger.   (*to* De Liége)   What's the matter? A cloud seems to darken those angel eyes!

De L.   You shall hear. (*aside*)   I'll tell him of the curricle, but she must not hear; she may be too delicate. (*whispering* M. Gérard)   She is in deep affliction, and you can help her.

Ger.   Can I? That would make me the happiest man on earth!

De L.   Procession-day, to *Long-Champ*, will soon be here, and the workmen——

Ger.   I comprehend. I am at her service.

De L.   A hundred louis might——

Ger.   (*to* M. Frémonville)   Madam, I shall be happy to serve you.

M. Frem.   The trouble may be too great?

Ger.   Poh! 'Tis done in a moment: nothing so easy.

De L.   (*to* M. Gérard)   Be discreet.

M. Frem.   You may relieve me from the most cruel torment.

Ger.   Pray say no more: you may command my services. (*to* De Liége)   How charmingly she looks! I could worship her! I am in a delirium! I will go for the money. (*aside, going*)   How lucky it was that I did not give it to my wife!

[*Exit.*

SCENE VII.

De L.   While M. Gérard is gone, I, on my part, will hasten to find the runaway; and I shall be much deceived, dear

---

* *Mon ami*, in such intercourse, at Paris, means quite as much as *my dear.*

Ma'am, if you have not this day both your curricle and your
son; till then your most obedient.   [*Exit.*

SCENE VIII.—Madame Fremonville, *alone.*

M. Frem. What an inconsistent creature! How can I place
the least confidence in one so thoughtless! M. Gérard is no
better. Ah, Sophy, had I but followed your example! Poor
boy! Perhaps at this very moment——— I tremble to think———
What shall I say to my husband? This is all lost time: I ought
to depend only on myself. I must hasten to the school; I may
there hear more. (*calls*) *Lapierre! Picard!* My coach.

SCENE IX.—*Enter* Footman *and* M. DE FREMONVILLE.

Footm. My master, Madam.

M. Frem. I am ruined!

Frem. (*affectionately kissing her*) At length, my love, I am
come back, and we once more meet. How tedious has my
absence been! I thought, at landing, to have found you at our
house in Bordeaux; but how was I surprised to hear you had
been living so long at Paris!

M. Frem. I—had my reasons.

Frem. Which I think I can divine: the education of our
dear boy?

M. Frem. (*aside*) I shall sink.

Frem. How is the charming fellow?

M. Frem. Nay, how are you?

Frem. Oh, that I had him in my arms!

M. Frem. You tell me nothing of your affairs?

Frem. Ah, they are bad enough! But my boy.

M. Frem. Have you had losses?

Frem. Is he at home?

M. Frem. (*aside*) What shall I say? (*aloud*) No, love, at
a boarding-school.

Frem. Let us go and see him instantly.

M. Frem. (*aside*) Heaven deliver me! (*aloud*) After so
long a journey, you must have need of rest.

Frem. Can I feel fatigue, when I once again meet all that
I love on earth? Come, come; away!

M. Frem. (*aside*) I am at my wit's end. (*aloud*) This
is a holiday, and perhaps———

Frem. He may be taking a walk; scouring the fields.
Well, well, it cannot be helped: but I am the more eager to
go because I wish to examine the school, to which you have
sent him.

M. Frem. How examine? None but gentlemen's sons are
received there.

Frem. Ah, love, I am sorry, but we must take him away:
my correspondents have deceived me.

M. Frem. And your immense fortune lost!

Frem. Some feeble remnants excepted. Education of a high kind is excellent, for the children of the wealthy and the great; but ours must be taught the useful: it will be the only, and perhaps the best, inheritance we can leave him.

M. Frem. Alas! What do I hear? In consequence of your letters, I have myself incurred expences far beyond our means.

SCENE X.—*Enter* M. GERARD.

Ger. Madam, your business is done.

M. Frem. Hush!

Ger. You see the means were soon found.

M. Frem. Found! Is he?—But be silent, or I am ruined.

Frem. Who is that gentleman, Madam?

M. Frem. M. Gérard: the husband of the friend of whom you have heard me speak so often.

Ger. (*aside*) One of her creditors, I suppose; and she'll not receive the money, lest he should see it. (*whispering*) Do you owe him much?

M. Frem. Oh, certainly; but he is——

Ger. A creditor!

M. Frem. No.

Ger. Not a creditor? In that case, Madam, here are the hundred louis. Could I lay my fortune at your feet, it would delight me.

M. Frem. What do you mean?

Frem. Gently, Sir. A wife, who acts with propriety, cannot accept presents from any person but her husband.

Ger. Oh! her husband is nobody knows where.

M. Frem. You are deceived, Sir; this is my husband.

Ger. (*aside*) Oh, the devil! Here is a blunder! (*aloud*) Sir, nothing could delight me more than your acquaintance! Quite enchanted! How well you look! In excellent health, I warrant.

M. Frem. You quite astonish me, Mr. Gérard; and I beg you will explain yourself immediately.

Ger. How, Madam! Did not yourself tell me you were in the utmost distress?

M. Frem. 'Tis too true; but I said nothing of money.

Ger. In that case, I ask a thousand pardons. De Liége spoke to me, and, as I suppose, has ill explained himself, or I am a fool; for I imagined it was for you. Upon my soul, Madam, I am the most confused of your humble servants.

Frem. I am satisfied, Madam; let us retire.

Ger. I hope, Sir, this unfortunate misunderstanding will not deprive us of your friendship. I and my wife will take a plea-sure to——

Frem. Sir, I shall not fail to show my respect to the bosom friend of Madame Frémonville.   [*Exit with his wife.*

SCENE XI.—M. Gerard.

Ger. A cursed cross husband-kind of look. I like his wife much better. So! Here comes mine.

SCENE XII.—*Enter* Sophia, Amadeus, *and* Victor.

Vict. Good morrow, papa.

Ger. Good morrow, child; good morrow.

Amad. I hope you are very well, Sir?

Ger. Who is this little fellow?

Soph. A playfellow of Victor's.

Ger. Ay, ay! Why did not you bring the whole school home? Apropos: the husband of your friend is arrived.

Soph. Ah! I am glad of that.

Vict. Shall I repeat my task to you, papa?

Amad. Shall I show you my drawings, Sir?

Ger. No, no! Here is a crown apiece for you; only, my good boys, let me be at quiet. (*cuts a caper*) I must go and take a lesson myself. [*Exit.*

SCENE XIII.

Soph. Well, Amadeus, do you like the school of your playfellow?

Amad. Yes, Ma'am: but I have done nothing there yet; I begin to-morrow.

Soph. Were you taught any Latin at your other school?

Amad. Latin indeed!

Vict. Is it not a grammar-school *?

Amad. I cannot tell.

Vict. What did you learn?

Amad. The useful arts, I believe they call them.

Vict. I have a master for the Latin.

Amad. I was under a professor of dancing.

Vict. I study French grammar too.

Amad. I know nothing of that? I can only write poetry.

Soph. Poetry, my dear?

Amad. Yes, Madam: so I wrote a satire against my masters, for which they used me ill. Beside, my mamma did not pay my pension.

Soph. I wish to know who you are? What is the name of your mamma?

Amad. It is long since I saw her, and I never called her any thing but mamma.

Soph. And what your papa?

Amad. Oh, he has been gone a great great while.

---

* There is a distinction in the original between a college and a boarding-school, which would not be intelligible to an English reader.

Soph. Your mamma came sometimes to see you?

Amad. Oh, not for more than these five years. I only know that, when I saw her last, she was so fine! Her dress was more shewy than yours. But she did not love children when we were at Bordeaux——

Soph. Do you come from Bordeaux?

Amad. Yes——She always left me in the nursery, because, when I came into the drawing-room, she said I used to break and spoil the things: and indeed I see well enough, now I'm grown up, that children are very naughty.

Vict. Yes; I see that too.

Soph. And how did you come to Paris?

Amad. I did not come till four years after my mamma; and then my nurse brought me to the boarding-school. They used me so ill! Beat me, did not give me enough to eat, and vexed me——till one day, finding the door open, I ran away as fast I could. I lost myself, and they took me to a man in black, who put me into the newspapers.

Soph. Why did you not name the school you came from?

Amad. Yes, indeed! And so be taken back.

Soph. Well, but I hope you dare trust *me?* Tell me your master's name!

Amad. Why, it was *M. Frivolet,* near Tivoli-gardens: but I beg and pray you won't take me there again.

Soph. By no means, my dear. I only wish to find out your poor distressed mother.

Amad. Oh, Madam, she cares little about me.

Soph. Poor boy! Well then, shall I be your mother?

Amad. Oh, that you shall, with all my heart.

Vict. Then we shall be brothers: I am glad of that.

Soph. My dear children! (*they run to her arms and kiss her affectionately.*)

SCENE XIV.—*Enter* FREMONVILLE.

Frem. Oh, charming picture! A mother in the arms of her children! I, unhappy father, have lost a son! Pardon me, Madam, for interrupting such enjoyment.

Soph. (*kindly*) I suppose you are M. Frémonville.

Frem. I am, Madam.

Soph. Once more united to your spouse, and once more supremely happy.

Frem. (*aside*) Heigho!

Amad. You look quite sorrowful, Sir.

Frem. (*attentively regarding* Amadeus) Permit me, Madam, to kiss your boys. (*takes* Amadeus *in his arms.*)

Soph. But here is another, Sir.

Frem. What a charming little fellow!

Soph. Nay, but *this!*——Victor.

Frem. He is the youngest. The eldest I think is as fine a boy as I ever saw. (*again pressing him to his bosom.*)

Soph. (*vexed, and affectionately kissing her son*) I do not think he is a finer boy than Victor, Sir.

Frem. Pray, pardon me: like a good mother, you love them both alike. Oh, my poor lost Amadeus!

Amad. That is my name, Sir.

Frem. I have a boy so called.

Soph. Have you seen him yet, Sir?

Frem. Surely you know my misfortune?

Soph. What?

Frem. I hastened to his school, the moment of my arrival, and he is lost.

Soph. Indeed! Good Heavens! Lost say you?

Frem. Above a week.

Soph. You live at——

Frem. Bordeaux.

Soph. And your son is called——

Frem. Amadeus.

Soph. In a boarding-school at Tivoli?

Frem. Certainly.

Soph. 'Tis he! 'Tis he, beyond all doubt! Oh how happy am I! Take your son to your arms, Sir. There he stands. I found him.

Frem. My son! Is he indeed my son? Nature seemed to point him out.

Amad. My dear father! I am so glad! I loved you quite at first.

Frem. How has this happened! Pray speak.

Soph. Far from suspecting who he was, I adopted him, till his parents could be found. Here comes his mother: she was more thoughtless than guilty: let me entreat you to spare her.

Frem. I will; though I hope this incident will make her better feel a mother's duties. Let us send the boys away.

Soph. Go, my little friends, play in the garden.

Amad. Father, good by! (*kissing him.*)

Vict. Good by, mamma! (*embracing her.*)

SCENE XV.—*Enter* MAD. FREMONVILLE *and* DE LIEGE.

De L. Don't be alarmed: to be sure, it is a misfortune, and I will make all possible inquiries——after the ball.

Frem. What news, Madam?

M. Frem. Alas, none.

De L. No, none; absolutely none.

Frem. You, Sir, chose the school where he was placed?

De L. True, Sir; a master quite in the mode; one of my intimates; M. Frivolet.

Frem. The child was ill treated, was he not, Madam?

M. Frem. Oh, husband!

Frem. Yet, that could not be! You saw him often; questioned him, like a mother; inquired what progress he made; in fact, showed him a mother's love, which he tenderly returned.

De L. (*aside*) How husbands love to preach.

M. Frem. I sink with shame! Oh grant me but the power to confess my faults! The guilt is mine, and my neglect alone should be accused.

Soph. (*to* Frémonville) Do not prolong her sufferings.

Frem. Madam, I——The pain is too severe——Your son is found.

M. Frem. Found! Oh transport!

De L. I told you it was a trifle.

Frem. You are indebted to your friend for this, among the rest. While you forgot you *had* a child, this excellent mother gave shelter to a poor lost orphan!

M. Frem. Oh, Sophia!

Soph. Be comforted. I hear your boy: he comes running to your arms.

SCENE *the Last.*

Enter M. Gerard, Amadeus, *and* Victor.

Ger. Mighty well, Madam! I cannot be suffered to practise my steps in peace: these little dogs, with their hide and seek, disturb me even in the pavilion. Neither should I so much have minded, but this youth, this foundling, dances better than I do!

Frem. Go, my boy, and kiss your mother. (Amadeus, *instead of running to his mother, throws himself affectionately into the arms of* Sophia.)

M. Frem. Oh, wretched woman! I well deserve it!

Frem. What a lesson!

Ger. Nay, but gently! Gently!

De L. What is the matter?

Ger. Pray, how does it happen that my wife should be the mother of this boy, and you, Sir, his father? That I think requires some explanation, my dear.

De L. Not at all, my friend. Don't be alarmed.

Ger. Zounds, Sir, but I say I must know.

Soph. Come, come, have done joking, my dear: here is his mother.

Ger. In that case, all is very well. Let every man father his own children, and then many mistakes might be rectified.

Amad. (*in the arms of his mother*) So you are come back at last, mamma?

M. Frem. Can I ever hope you will forgive me ? Yet, after such a lesson, and such an example (*pointing to* Sophia) can I ever again be so guilty ?

De L. So you mean to mind your famHy ? Then adieu to dancing and balls.

Ger. How so ? However, if we do not dance, we may sing; and this is just the season.

VAUDEVILLE.

Sophia.

Too light, I grant, but lovely faiғ,
 By pleasure led astray,
Oh, take example from the tale,
 And profit while you may.
Of dancing, dressing, routs, and balls,
 Despise the wretched arts :
Or you may lose your children's love,
 Instead of gaining hearts.

De Liége.

Should my descendants e'er be born,
 I'll teach them all to dance;
Till, like myself, my children, fam'd,
 Shall be the pride of France.
The world shall wonder but to look
 How lightly they can tread !
For, when the heels have well been taught,
 No matter for the head.

Gérard.

The child we give the world, to-night,
 Has fathers more than one * ;
And such-like children some folks say
 Might quite as well have none.
The town has father'd many a child,
 Then be your favor shown;
The brat may grow a lusty boy,
 Should he become your own.

       [*Exeunt Omnes.*

---

* Vide title page.

REMARKS.

THIS excellent little piece has a peculiar interest in France, where mothers like Madame de Frémonville are, alas, too frequent. That such mothers *may be found* every where is true; but in England, happily, they are viewed like those monsters which, while we look, we scarcely can believe there are such things in nature. The easy manner also in which the husband is answered, and the hypocritical air of being satisfied that his wife has only been thoughtless, nothing more, though he finds her on his return surrounded by shameless fops and fools, his child abandoned, lost, his madam in debt, profuse, dissipated, and in the vortex of what just morality must call vice, that all this should pass off with a sigh and a shrug, is truly characteristic of the manners that prevail, in France, and that are supposed to possess all the charms of amenity; all the grace of being amiable, tractable; those of a person that will not be unhappy, nor cause unhappiness. The subject of the forogoing piece, in Paris, passes off gracefully in a light brief comedy: in London, probability would require it to be serious indeed; perhaps tragic. It appeared in 1802, at Paris, at the *Theatre Louvois*, and was received with much applause. Though they suffer their moral perversities, the people on such occasions shew they have a strong feeling of them. I know nothing of the authors

THE OPERA DANCER:

A DRAMATIC PROVERB,

IN ONE ACT,

TRANSLATED FROM

THE FRENCH OF M. CARMONTEL.

DRAMATIS PERSONÆ.

M. DU PAS.

LA FRANCE.

LE COMTE D'ORVILLE.

THE OPERA DANCER:

A DRAMATIC PROVERB.

~~~~

SCENE I.

M. Du Pas, *and* La France : Du Pas *in a Powdering Gown, taking off the Powder before the Chimney-glass.*

Du Pas.

LA France ! Has the tailor repaired my dancing dress ?

La F. Yes, Sir ; but he has no orders for the new breeches.

Du P. How, no orders ! What does he mean ? I spoke to him yesterday at the opera.

La F. I know it, Sir.

Du P. What more has he to say ?

La F. He talks of other people.

Du P. What people ?

La F. Why—Those that give orders.

Du P. How !

La F. They say, you have had already two pair of breeches, for that dress ; and as for three, it's too much.

Du P. They say all that, do they ?

La F. Yes, Sir.

Du P. Mighty well. It is Sunday to-morrow, and I shall not dance : I shall go into the country : tell them that.

La F. Yes, Sir.

Du P. Three pair too much ! I'll have a dozen. Order my carriage from the coach-maker's, do you hear ?

La F. Yes, Sir.

Du P. Ha, ha, two pair ! I'll give them a lesson—Somebody knocks ; see who it is—They shall repent.

SCENE II.—*Enter the* Count.

Count. Is M. Du Pas at home ?

La F. There he stands, Sir.

Du P. (*without turning*) Who is that ?

Count. I believe, Sir, you do not know me.

Du P. (*glancing*) Not I, Sir.

Count. I come to request you would give me your opinion on my manner of dancing, for I wish to dance in an opera.

Du P. (*disdainfully*) You!

Count. Yes.

Du P. (*without turning*) You are not tall enough.

Count. That is of no consequence. Will you see? (*dances.*)

Du P. (*with a side look*) Pshaw! Wretched!

Count. Yet, I have been told—— Look at this. (*dances again.*)

Du P. (*regarding him through the glass*) Pitiable!

Count. But, Sir——

Du P. Talking is in vain. You are not what we call a proper subject. I must likewise tell you, you have not a—a talent, a genius.

Count. But in this style, for example. (*dances.*)

Du P. That is all main strength. I'll not undertake to prepare you for the opera, not even as a *figurant*.

Count. I do not wish to dance at the opera, Sir. I would——

Du P. What, go on the stage at Lyons, or Bordeaux! A soaring ambition truly! Oh, fie!

Count. That is not what I mean. I speak of a private opera, in the country. I am the Count d'Orville.

Da P. (*astonished*) Sir! That is a different affair. Of the Count d'Orville I can only ask pardon. Did you know how I am persecuted—If one listens, to these kind of people, one can never get rid of them.

Count. That I can readily believe.

Du P. Let me see once more. (*to La France, after throwing off his powdering gown*) Take that away.

Count Let me have your sincere opinion. (*dances.*)

Du P. Upon my word! Go on! Vastly well! The head and shoulders quite at their ease! No constraint! All grace! Charming! Ay, ay; that is dancing!

Count. Are you really satisfied?

Du P. Oh, excellent! Excellent!

Count. I am glad of that. Do you approve my style in this? (*dances.*)

Du P. Go on! Amazing! Your ear good; your precision astonishing! Continue! Go on! That *entrechat* once more! Wonderful! Exactly as it should be!

Count. You think then I may venture?

Du P. Venture! I wish I had a dancer like you for the opera. I can't think what the devil possessed me, just now, when I talked so foolishly!

Count. You delight me, Sir. I love and admire your frankness!

Du P. But, as I told you, I am tormented about trifles. I am really in despair at not having paid you more attention.

Count. Well, well, but you are now satisfied. How do I carry my arms?

Du P. Admirably ! They are quite at ease.

Count. Yes, I think—Hey? And my head?

Du P. Cannot be better. Your ear accurate; each step firm ; every part sustained ; no constraint.

Count. The very qualities I admire ! I shall return and pay you my respects.

Du P. 'Twill give you too much trouble.

Count. Pardon me, Sir; I shall wish for your advice, at some other time, on a *pas de deux* that I have composed. It is quite charming! Greatly admired.

Du P. Whenever you please, *M. le Comte.* I shall always be at your commands. (*attends him as he goes out.*)

Count. Where are you going, Sir? No ceremony among us dancers.

Du P. I do but act as becomes me.

Count. The head and shoulders at ease, no constraint, all grace. I shall not forget !

Du P. Oh, there is no fear of that !

Count. Adieu.

Du P. M. le Comte, I am your very humble servant.

[*Exeunt Omnes.*

REMARKS.

Observations are here almost unnecessary, except it be to say that volumes of these small pieces are to be found in the French language ; that, for this species of writing, M. Carmontel is a celebrated author; that these Dramatic Proverbs, as they are called, chiefly consist of single incidents, with few scenes; that they excellently delineate national manners; and that frequent occasions will be taken to admit them into the Theatrical Recorder. The proverb which the author has here chosen to exemplify is—

Selon les Gens l'encens.

" Flattery according to rank."

DRAMATIC BIOGRAPHY.

RONSARD, A DRAMATIC AUTHOR, AND FAMOUS FRENCH POET, OF THE SIXTEENTH CENTURY.

IN the biographical department of this work, as it will not always be possible to confine myself to those authors only from whom translations are made, I may afford information and pleasure to many readers, by inserting the lives of authors now but little known, who once enjoyed the peculiar distinctions due to genius, and which distinctions the liberal, just, and feeling mind, takes a delight to see revived.

Peter *De Ronsard* was born in 1525, at the *Château de la Poissonière*, in the *Vendomois*. He was the son of Louis de Ronsard, knight and maître d'hôtel to the king: *Jeanne de Chaudrier*, his mother, was likewise of noble extraction. The day of his birth had nearly proved that of his death: *Le Pays* tells us that—" A damsel who carried him from the *Château de " la Poissonière*, where he was born, to the parish church, that " he might be baptized, carelessly let him fall. Fortunately it " was in a meadow, upon flowers, and all the harm that he " received was that of being thoroughly wet with rose-water, " which, according to custom, was taken for the baptism."

The father of *Ronsard* was a man of letters, and was said to have a talent for poetry. Under him our bard began his studies, and came at the age of nine to the college of Navarre at Paris, where, in six months, it is said, the excessive severity of his masters subdued his love of the Belles Lettres. Becoming afterward a page to the Duke of Orleans, who gave him to James Stuart, King of Scotland, married to *Magdelene* of France, *Ronsard* continued two years in Scotland, and, after his return, was employed by the duke in various negociations. During these travels he was overtaken by a tempest that endangered his life. It appears from dates that *Ronsard* was intrusted with secret negociations before he was sixteen, for

in 1540 he accompanied *Lazare de Baïf,* envoy from the king
to the diet held at Spires, and, on his return, followed *M. de
Langey* into Piedmont.   In these expeditions he acquired a
knowledge of history and languages, but brought back a beginning deafness, of which he was never cured.   Deafness at this
period, *Binet* observes, attacked the best French poets, *Ronsard,
Du Bellay, Dorat,* and others, as blindness had formerly the
greatest poets of Greece, Homer, Thamyris, Tiresias, and
Stersichorus. By this accident study to him became necessary ;
and his father, who was averse to these propensities, dying in
1544, *Ronsard* devoted himself to it entirely under the celebrated *Jean Dorat.   Ronsard* afterward studied under *Adrien
Turnebe* ; and at this time he translated the Plutus of Aristo-
phanes into French verse *.   The success of that work encouraged him ; he assiduously read and imitated the Greek poets ;
and, amid other successes, the prize of the Floral Games was
decreed to him, although he had not entered his name as a can-
didate.   Instead of a flower, the magistrates of *Toulouse* presented him with the figure of Minerva in massive silver ; and,
further to honor him, decreed him to be *Le Poëte François*
[the French poet.]   This Minerva he afterward presented to
Henry II. and the monarch appeared as much flattered by the
gift of the poet as the poet could have been had he received it
from the king.

Who shall arrive at the Temple of Fame, and as he travels
never tread on a serpent? *Ronsard* had his enemies: one of
them was the celebrated *Mellin de Saint-Gelais,* who, without doing justice to his beauties, was alive to his defects.
Saint-Gelais was himself a poet and a courtier, and, during
a time, seemed to balance the reputation of his rival ; but
the suffrage of the king at last was in favor of *Ronsard.*
This poet is conspicuous for the high opinion which he had
of his own genius: his works abound with praises on himself ;
and it is remarkable of him that, though he was the pride
and boast of the age in which he lived, his poems after-

---

* This appears to have been his only dramatic work.

ward fell into unmerited contempt : they had many faults, but they had many beauties : his introduction of Greek and Latin words, his style, and his thoughts, were frequently all vicious, far-fetched, studied, affected, and wanting that flow of passion which study should never interrupt. By efforts to enforce, to excel, and to attain the summit of excellence, the poet frequently falls into the extravagant and the obscure ; and these in particular were among the defects of *Ronsard*. He lived in the age of *Rabelais*, of whom, more than any other, he stood in awe. Triumphant over every rival, he seemed to live in fear of no one but *Rabelais*. He always carefully inquired, says a French biographer, where the jovial curate of *Meudon* went, that he might not be there. It is said that the conduct of Voltaire was the same with respect to Piron, whose sarcastic sallies and poignant jeers he dreaded. Ronsard had also a singular law-suit with *Joachim du Bellay*. He it was who first wrote what has been called Odes, after the manner of Pindar and Horace. *Bellay*, wishing to write in the same style, found means to procure the manuscript of *Ronsard* without his knowledge, wrote odes of the same nature, and, that he might be the first, hastened to have them published. This could not be calmly suffered by a man like *Ronsard*; he complained aloud, and, thinking Justice should raise her arm to punish a crime so flagrant, he instituted a process against *Bellay*, to recover his manuscript. It was returned, and, at the sight of such a treasure, his griefs appear to have been forgotten ; for, it is said, the rivals afterward lived in frank intercourse and good friendship. *Bellay* certainly did justice to *Ronsard*, for in his Art of Poetry he affirms, *Ronsard* first introduced the poem and the name of Ode into the French language.

Ronsard had another more troublesome affair to afflict him. He had a quarrel with the professors of religion, against whom, hurried away by the opinions of the age, and especially of the court, he hurled some darts, which were returned with so good an aim that his anger could scarcely be contained, though he pretended to feel nothing but contempt. He informs his antagonist he despises him too much to attempt refutation, but that he will *briefly reply to a few points*, and writes an epistle to him of six hundred lines. This epistle begins with *Quoi! Tu jappes Mastin?* [Cur, dost thou bark?] and continues and ends with similar amenity. In fact, this tedious epistle contains little more than two points: abuse of his adversary, and praise of himself. The thing most remarkable in it is his endeavour to repel the report of atheism against him, which had been publicly raised, and which, it is said, took rise from the following incident:

The tragedy of Cleopatra, by *Jodelle*, was performed with very great success before the court at *Hercueil*. Some days after, *Ronsard*, being at that village with a number of common friends, all poets, determined with them to celebrate *Jodelle* in a manner worthy of the season (it was then Carnival) by sacrificing a goat to him in imitation of the ancient Greeks. For this act of jovial thoughtless folly, people were either so stupid or so malicious as to seriously reproach him with having made an authentic profession of atheism. They might much more easily have convicted him of credulity, he having seriously reproached the nation for not putting faith in the prophecies of Nostradamus.

The old age of *Ronsard* was premature from his immoderate use of pleasures. Born robust, he was a gouty, infirm valetudinarian at fifty; after which he retired, sometimes to his priory of *Croix-Val*, and sometimes to that of *Saint-Cosme*, where he died in December, 1585. He preserved the gaiety of his mind, and almost with his parting breath dictated verses to his friends.

Ronsard was happy in his person, august, martial, and fine of figure; his limbs strong and proportionate; his countenance noble and liberal, with a light-coloured beard, chesnut hair, an aquiline nose, a mild yet serious eye, a serene brow, and his conversation familiar and attractive. The following short extract will show that whatever faults his works may have, he possessed the flow and feeling of a poet:

POUR LA FIN D'UNE COMEDIE.

Ici la Comédie apparoist un example,
Où chacun de son fait les actions contemple :
Le monde est le théâtre, et les hommes acteurs ;
La Fortune, qui est maitresse de la scéne,
Appreste les habits, et de la vie humaine
Les Cieux et les destins en sont les spectateurs.

En gestes différens, en différens langages ;
Rois, Princes et Bergers jouent leurs personnages
Devant les yeux de tous, sur l'échafaud commun :
Et quoique l'homme essaye à vouloir contrefaire
Sa nature et sa vie, il ne sçauroit tant faire
Qu'il ne soit, tel qu'il est, connu d'un chacun.

L'un vit comme un Pasteur, l'un est Roi des provinces ;
L'autre fait le marchand, l'autre s'égale aux Princes ;
L'autre se feint content, l'autre poursuit du bien :
Cependant le souci, de sa lime nous ronge,
Et fait que notre vie est seulement un songe,
Et que tous nos projets se finissent en rien.

La beauté regne au Ciel, la vertu, la justice :
En terre on ne voit rien que fraude, que malice :
Et bréf tout ce monde est un publique marché ;
L'un y vend, l'un dérobe, et l'autre achete et change ;
Un même fait produit le blasme et la louange,
Et ce qui est vertu, semble à l'autre pèché.

Il ne faut espérer estre parfait au monde,
Ce n'est que vent, fumée, une onde qui suit l'onde :
Ce qui etoit hier, ne se voit aujourd'hui.
Heureux, trois fois heureux qui au temps ne s'oblige,
Qui suit son naturel, et qui, sage, corrige
Ses fautes, en vivant, par les fautes d'autrui !

FOR THE END OF A COMEDY,

OR

EPILOGUE.

A mirror of mankind is Comedy ;
Where each may see his likeness.   All the world's
A stage : the men are actors.   Fortune does
But change the scene, and find the decorations :
Heav'n and the Fates but smile, and are spectators.
In different feats, languages, customs, kings,

Princes, peasants, all degrees, their parts
Perform, in sight of all, and on a common
Scaffold.   Whate'er disguise each mortal takes,
Each still is known ; for none can change themselves.
This man a shepherd is, and that a king.
One trades ; another deems himself a prince.
While one affects content, another's restless
Wishes are insatiate.   Our cares corrode
Us all ; and life's a dream with which our projects end.
Beauty, virtue, justice, are only found
In heav'n : on earth, malice and fraud are seen.
The world's a fair, in which we buy or sell,
Rob or exchange.   The thing which this man blames
The next commends ; and virtue is by some
Call'd sin.   Perfection can't be found below ;
Where all is smoke, wind, waves rolling o'er waves.
What is to-day to-morrow is no more.
Thrice happy he, whom times and seasons ne'er
Enslave ; who sagely and in freedom lives,
Deriving wisdom from the worlds' mistakes.

PIECES

FIRST PERFORMED IN APRIL, 1805.

WHO WANTS A GUINEA?

A COMEDY FIRST PERFORMED AT THE THEATRE ROYAL, COVENT GARDEN, APRIL 18.

AMONG the candidates for dramatic fame, Mr. Colman, the author of this comedy, holds a very distinguished rank ; and to attempt to deprive him of any part of that public applause, which has been justly, and nothing more than justly bestowed, would be nothing less than criminal. The poor rewards which genius obtains, when compared to its rank and worth, are so inadequate, that the smallest deduction is the most base, the most despicable, and the most ruinous species of robbery that man can commit on man.

The works of genius alone appear to be truly worthy of the assiduous inquiries of the liberal critic : though, perhaps, it but rarely happens that the critic can effectually instruct, and benefit, the man of genius. The first may remind the latter of defects, which in the ardor of creation necessarily escape; but, when the man of genius shall himself become cool and unbiassed, it is then generally himself who is the soundest critic, and best judge, of his own performances.

Criticism is necessary; but it is rather for the increase and development of public mind than for the improvement of the individuals to whom it first relates : but, when those individuals have a true sense of that in which the real worth and dignity of criticism consists, they rejoice at every opportunity in which they can contribute to its exertion, in a candid, manly, and instructive manner.

The faults of the comedy, here considered, are so radical that, unfortunately, they may be truly called the assassins of a multitude of beauties. But ought not these faults, grave as they are, to be treated with lenity? Ought the beauties, since they are so many, to be overlooked? Ought they not rather to. be dwelt upon with delight?

In the closet, yes is the ready and sure answer to these questions: but, on the stage, spectators being required to sit patiently for so long a space of time, and listen as well to the defects as to the beauties, when these defects inspire tedium, the task is too great. In such an assembly, there are too many of the thoughtless, the noisy, the conceited, the half instructed, puffed up with the little knowledge they have acquired, which because it is little they cannot contain within the limits of decency ; I say, there is too great and too mixed a multitude for any just balance between faults and beauties to be hoped.

When the public mind shall have attained that delicate sense of perceiving, of applauding, and of reproving that shall be just yet not violent, or if ever it burst into excess it must be excess of gratitude for mental pleasures received, authors will then acquire a dignity, which, now, were they at present to suffer it to be perceptible, they would be accused of the summit of arrogance and self-sufficiency.

In this comedy, the progress of the fable is nearly as follows :
Two neighbours, one possessed of rational benevolence, the

other rich but selfish in the extreme, discourse of a conflagration, which the night before had destroyed a great part of the
village in which they live. The good man, Mr. Hartly, further says it will give an opportunity to his friend Mr. Torrent,
(or Torrid) who has there just purchased an estate and manor,
to exercise his philanthropy upon the sufferers. One of these
sufferers, Solomon Gundy, enters, and, giving further particulars about the fire, says, he has saved an essential part of his
property ; which is the board under his arm ; for he can nail
it up against another wall, and begin the world again, since it
will announce his qualifications to the neighbourhood. This
villager is introduced, and made an agent in the piece, for the
sole purpose of interlarding his discourse with bad French, bad
English, bad pronunciation, bad any thing, that can make him
comical.

Mr. Colman is not blamed for this, but the bad taste of the
town. The town makes such wretched expedients absolutely
necessary, in order to supply broad laughter, for, instead of
wholesome food, it is insatiate after such garbage.

The scene changes to an inn, where Mr. Torrent, the new
lord of the manor, displays his quixote benevolence, and is
somewhat reproved for it by his friend, Mr. Hartly ; and
where Mr. Delamere, a poor officer and misanthropist, comes
to take shelter, after the fire, with all that is left him tied up
in a handkerchief.

Mr. Torrent eagerly offers him relief, which is proudly
rejected ; but Torrent furtively puts his bocket-book in the handkerchief of Delamere, saying, in a side speech, Delamere is
now a hundred and fifty pounds richer than he supposed. The
scene closes, after Mr. Torrent has hired Solomon Gundi as his
valet, informed Mr. Hartley that he had a young housekeeper
coming, not nineteen, of whom he knew nothing but from an
advertisement, which had described her as a most interesting
object of distress, and adding that he is the happiest man on
earth ; for a conflagration has most luckily happened, which
has ruined his tenants, and will give employment to riches
for which he has no use, by rebuilding the village in a proper

style, and setting all its inhabitants at their ease. Mr. Hartly reproves him for this rodomontade of benevolence, but to this Torrent is deaf.

We then become acquainted with an Irish baronet, who arrives at his friend's (a lord) country seat; my lord being absent, shows a letter from this friend to the steward, informs us that he was stripped a night or two before of his estate, by my lord himself, and that my lord has generously offered him this country seat, at the present, as an asylum from his creditors.

The servants at this country seat appear to be but three; the steward, the housekeeper, and the gamekeeper; and the baronet seems to be in full possession of all he wants, just at present, a female companion or pretty girl to toy with excepted.

We next become known to Mr. Oldskirt, and Fanny, on a heath, near the village; she going in search of her place of housekeeper to Mr. Torrent; and he accompanying her to see that all is right: she desirous he should wait at the adjoining village, till she has introduced herself to her master; and he taking offence, that she should wish to shake him off now she has got a place: she assuring him it is impossible she could be so ungrateful; and he consenting at last, and retiring, on condition that, it being dirty weather and he only five feet three inches high, if he should happen to sink over head and ears in the dirt, she would have him dug for.

By mistake, instead of the mansion-house, belonging to Torrent, Fanny goes to the country seat, where she finds the baronet; and he, wishing to have her company, makes her believe it is the house for which she asks.

Mr. Hartly informs Mr. Torrent that he has engaged a man of peculiar genius, and particularly worthy of protection and employment, to come down and lay out his grounds. Hartly retires, and Mr. Oldskirt comes from the village, intending to see that his darling Fanny is safely settled, and is mistaken by Mr. Torrent for the land surveyor. This Mr. Oldskirt is a remnant-broker, who had given protection to Fanny out of charity, and who, from the same motive, had told her on the heath that he had made his will, before he sat out on so very

perilous a journey (he is a cockney) and that there she is
named his executress, and chief legatee. By a succession of
very forced language and terms, Mr. Torrent and he beget and
continue an equivoque; he considering himself as Mr. Oldskirt, and Mr. Torrent thinking him the surveyor, the modest
man of genius; which supposition is further confirmed by Oldskirt requesting to dine in the housekeeper's room, instead of
consenting to keep company with Mr. Torrent.

Fanny, with the baronet, finds her virtue in some danger,
and becomes dreadfully alarmed; but more so than she had
cause to be: for, though a very dissipated fellow, the baronet
is not totally void of principle.

Meanwhile, Delamere, from the pocket-book, discovers the
name of Torrent, comes back to return the gift, which had
been clandestinely imposed upon him, and, at the same time, to
inform Torrent that his brother had been the bosom friend of
Delamere; one who had shared his fortune, seduced his wife,
and by jumping out of a carriage to give him gentlemanly satisfaction, had accidentally killed himself with his own sword,
at the very period when Delamere had become bound for his
debts, and by that means had ruined himself. He further adds
that his false wife had stolen away their infant daughter, and
that these combining misfortunes were the cause of his mi-
santhropy.

Torrent, deeply affected by the treachery of his deceased
brother, is eager to make reparation, which is refused: but
Delamere has likewise learned, from the pocket-book, that
Fanny, the housekeeper of Torrent, is his lost daughter, and
imperiously demands she shall be immediately delivered into
his power.

The mistake committed by Fanny, in going to the wrong
house, is now productive of the best scene in the comedy: at
least of the best acting scene: for Oldskirt enters, not being
able to find Fanny in the housekeeper's room, suspects some
foul play, and in the abundance of his affection for her, which,
by being real and heartfelt, becomes the more comic in such a
person, demands her restitution in so vehement and passionate

a manner that he naturally assumes the very deportment which has all the comic traits of bouncing and swaggering, combined with the delightful feelings of excellent intention.

Oldskirt is joined by Delamere, Torrent is overwhelmed by their clamour, Solomon Gundy is called in to assist in searching for Fanny, and a pursuit is immediately begun.

In this latter part of the play, Henry, a young sailor, makes his appearance, knocks at the selfish neighbour's house late at night, and the man (I believe he is called Potmore) holds a short dialogue with Henry, threatens to shoot him if he does not leave the premises, and surlily shuts his window.

Henry, fatigued and hungry, is dragging himself away, when Potmore's child, a boy of about seven years old, opens the window of the room in which he sleeps, invites Henry to come and take part of his bed, and reaches him a basket, left in that room by his mother, which contains refreshment. Henry, delighted with the child, gives him a boatswain's whistle, which he had snatched from the neck of the owner in a vain attempt to save him from drowning, and charges the child to wear it for ever, as a keep-sake.

This scene had a very good effect.

Different accidents, at last, are made to bring all the parties to the country seat, where the baronet has taken shelter; and, after various contentions, in which the characteristic propensity of the Irish to duelling is pourtrayed, Fanny is at length restored to her father and lover.

In this scene, it appears that the mother of Fanny died a lingering death of repentance, and testifying affection to her injured Delamere, but confiding her daughter to Henry, who, as a surgeon in a West India island, had contributed, both by his purse and skill, to save this deserted pair; and who, coming with Fanny to be married at London (does it appear why?) is there pressed as a sailor (how could that happen?) and, after having been made a prisoner by the French, is now escaped and returned in search of her.

Such are the principal incidents, as acted and related, in this comedy.

Of its defects, the most radical is want of plan; scarcely any interest is created; suspense is little felt; and it would be difficult for any one, who should see or read the piece, to declare what was the subject of it. Having little interest, it has no hero. Solomon Gundy might almost as truly contend for that honor as Delamere, Torrent, Henry, Oldskirt, or the Baronet. It is a jumble of characters, dramatically conceived, and in some parts executed with remarkable truth, but so unconnected as, when brought together, to have nothing to do: or, at least, nothing that forms a whole. It is evidently a work of haste, undigested and therefore inconsistent.

Of its beauties, as they are in detail and thus dispersed, it is not possible to give any adequate picture. But it is highly delightful to observe the general spirit of true philanthrophy, with which the sentiments abound. Had the author taken sufficient time, this spirit would not have so frequently worne the pitiful garb of a clap-trap; nor have so improperly and egregiously intruded itself where it was an impertinence, something which neither explained, coalesced with, nor promoted the plot, but induced us to yawn at what in itself was so excellent.

The characters also were sketched with a masterly hand, but not filled up; and, wanting a proper momentum, took every cross direction the circle could afford, instead of being impelled to the centre.

There was beside less of punning, and the quibbling despicable species of wit in which Mr. Colman has occasionally indulged, and which is so derogatory to the true standard of his genius.

Of the performers, since their established characters are well known, there can be no injustice in mentioning those first who were, on this occasion, the most prominent; and justice, therefore, requires the name of Mr. Simmonds here to take the lead. Not that his powers are equal, by any means, to those of some of his competitors; but they have been on many occasions most happily exerted, and this was one of them. Where his figure and manner happen to be well adapted to his part, there is perhaps no actor who produces a more highly comic effect.

Mr. Munden had that cast of character in which he both delights and excels, that of comic benevolence ; and the failure of the portrait was in the haste of the author.

Mr. Fawcet, at the beginning of his character, produced a very happy effect, in Solomon Gundy ; but this village pedant presently began to pall upon the ear.

Mr. Lewis, though considerably deficient in a good articulation of the brogue, gave so much of the true, dissipated, easy, fashionable rake, that we could scarcely wish to have seen the character pourtrayed in a different manner.

Mr. Emery, great as his merits are, had no good opportunity to make them appear : he could but act what was given him naturally, and in doing that he seldom fails.

Among the serious characters, Mr. Kemble takes the lead ; but it was impossible, on this occasion, that he should appear worthy of himself. The true misanthropist is a grand character, and requires masterly truth of drawing, with the finest chiaro oscuro of colouring.

Mr. Charles Kemble was very pleasing in Henry, and by no means wanted spirit. There is a propriety in his acting which is highly estimable ; time only is wanting to give him greater powers. He ought particularly to attend to the improvement of his voice, that he may acquire fulness of tone and perfect clearness of articulation ; in which, though far from deficient, he is far from the height of excellence.

Mr. Chapman and Mr. Waddy were respectable.

Mrs. Mattocks had so little to do that she could claim but a small part of the applause which she usually and justly receives. She delivered the latter part of the epilogue with a remarkably intelligent and feeling effect : she was too laboured in her endeavours to point out and pourtray the characters of the former part of the epilogue, especially as they had scarcely any features.

Mrs. Gibbs gave to Fanny an unaffected and engaging tenderness ; and Miss Waddy was pleasing in the little she had to say. The two children, one of them **Hercules, the baronet's** footboy, deserve encouragement.

———

A ballet pantomime entitled Aggression has appeared at Covent Garden, and continues to be acted : also a comic opera of two acts at Drury Lane, which will be noticed in the next number.

———

THE ART OF ACTING.

(*Continued from No.* II. *p.* 138.)

———

CHAP. III.

Of various Defects in Action, Walk, and Demeanor, common to inattentive Actors.

PREVIOUS to speaking of the more important parts of the art of acting, it may be beneficial to performers to remind them of various habitual defects, that have hitherto been frequent among them, and many of which imply a degree of folly, or of incapacity, that is highly degrading to their profession, which supposes, and indeed requires, extraordinary talents, industry, and discrimination.

An actor ought to be perfectly acquainted with the story, which he takes a part in relating : that is, with the plot, its progress, the intention of the author, in the whole and in every individual scene, the apartment or place in which every scene passes, and the deportment which the particular nature of that scene, and of the part he is to take in it, requires. He should remember, conscientiously, that every fault which he commits, in a new piece of which the public yet know nothing, is attributed to the author ; and that, by any inattention or mistake of his, he may bring ridicule and contempt on the piece, which are properly due to the actor. This is only urged, among other reasons, to remind and imprint, upon the memories of performers, the serious and the difficult nature of their duties.

Among performers, who are favorites with the public in particular, it is far from uncommon to see them so totally forget decency, the respect due to an audience, and the contempt which they bring upon themselves, as to look about them, into the boxes and the pit, in order either to discover who they know, or even, at some times, impudently to make slight nods, signs, or grins:—a fault so very insolent, and so totally forget-ful, not merely of public respect, but of the whole tenor of the business in which they are engaged, that it would be scarcely too severe a punishment if an audience were unanimously to rise, and insist on the performer, who thus transgresses, not daring to appear again for a month, and if they were, during that space of time, to lose their emoluments.

I say, this is a most audacious and insulting practice, and be-trays insensibility, consummate vanity, or rather effrontery, and great deficiency of intellect. The faults that follow are equally offensive to dramatic effect, but not to personal feeling.

Performers are not unfrequently seen to read a letter on the stage, and, perhaps from accident, perhaps from fright, or some passion which the scene is supposed to inspire, they will suffer the letter to drop, and never condescend to pick it up again.

It is needless to detail the many reasons that render such con-duct ridiculous, absurd, and unnatural. It is a fault for which no excuse can be offered.

Of the same nature is that of a stage hero, who, being about to tilt with another, puts himself into an attitude, but first care-fully, but with a flourish, throws away his hat; and after the battle, walks away bare-headed to cool himself: no doubt wish-ing it to be supposed he is either too important a person, or has too feverish a brain, at such a time, for him to walk with a hat on; and therefore the stage keepers are sent, in the face of the audience, to take it away.

Is this common sense? Does it not incur the sneers of every spectator who is attentive to the conduct of the scene?

Swords are frequently seen left, with the same unaccountable carelessness, when the owners hear their cues for leaving the stage.

In short, the neglectful and ridiculous incidents, of this nature, of which performers are very frequently guilty, do but denote a laxity of discipline, and prove, what we well know, that there is no person whose nightly duty it is to superintend the whole conduct of a piece, and exact a rigid but a just decorum. The want of such a censor, such a disciplinarian, is much greater than is imagined.

Going off at a wrong door, or rather where there is not supposed to be any door, nor any aperture, is another of these strange but still more familiar absurdities. It is true that, when a play is first put into rehearsal, great care is taken on this head; but the neglect, that nightly increases, becomes at length truly disgusting. The actors are not aware how much they offend common sense, and the people whose esteem they ought most carefully to court, when their slovenliness becomes so very reprehensible.

In the mode of entering and retiring from the stage, a judicious actor cannot too carefully consider what is the tone of feeling, which he himself is supposed to have in combination with that of other performers, or rather of the scene itself. Offence is sometimes given, to a discriminating judge, by the performer's neglect of this consideration, at entering; but more frequently at forgetting as it were to give intimation, either by a restless look, an attitude, an approach to the door, or some other mode of intending soon to depart. Unless in particular cases, departure should never appear to be unexpected, and abrupt; for then it is not only spiritless, but often improbable, and certainly unmeaning. To enter and retire perfectly in unison with the tone, or passion, of the scene, is what may be called a delicate branch of the art of acting; which, though it does not require deep study, demands great attention.

To tragedians and the performers of gentlemen, a short step is peculiarly destructive of dignity; while in characters of low breeding but of animation, it is no less a true mark of such persons. To step with measured affectation, like an opera dancer to a march, is no less laughable; it destroys reality: for a spectator cannot but imagine he sees a foolish actor, instead of the character he ought to personify.

The short step excites risibility at first, and at length contempt and weariness, when it is accompanied, as is seen in some actors, by a mechanical and uninterruptedly alternate habit of first stepping forward and then stepping back. Among country actors this is no uncommon fault; and in London it is seen, but, in a less glaring manner.

The action of the arms ought to be carefully modest and restrained. There are performers who, at the first sentence with their right hand, and the second with their left, continue an alternate through each speech. They must have taken peculiar pains to have acquired such a puppet-show mode of disposing of themselves.

There are many who have a seesaw eternally monotonous motion, which, were nothing else seen or heard, would soon lull every patient spectator to sleep.

There are others who continually shake a single finger; some two fingers; some the whole hand; but the shaking must continue, while they continue speaking.

A frequent clenching of the fist is a favorite mode, which several actors have, of endeavouring to make the audience believe how much they are in earnest; especially in the characters of tyrants.

The arms akimbo is also often thought the attitude of grandeur, instead of, as it really is, the certain sign of vulgar and inflated imbecility.

It is not possible to recollect, in the closet, all the various ill habits, and errors, into which performers fall, in their deportment. In comic actors, such mistakes are less noticed; but they are frequently quite as gross. " To suit the action to the word" is indeed a difficult task; for it is first highly necessary to inquire what words demand, or rather will endure, action. The arm that is always in motion is always unmeaning.

In all characters, where good breeding and education are supposed, ease is required; and violent action can never be proper, but to violent passion: the shades that lie between the two extremes are what require the studious discrimination of the performer.

Comic deportment should be as various as comic character: nay, indeed, there are personal varieties, which are indicated in the sketching and filling up of every comedy; so that two tradesmen, two fathers, nay two misers, or any other class of character, should be individualized, and have separate modes of behaviour.

One habitual error, very injurious to the piece and the performer, ought carefully to be noticed; which is, that there scarcely can be an occasion when an actor ought to speak with his profile, much less with half his back, turned to the audience; for then, not only his voice, but, his features, are without effect. Yet, there are many performers who will continue, through a whole scene, with the profile, a little more or a little less, toward the audience. This is an unpardonable fault. If possible, the face should front the stage, yet the eye remain totally unconscious of the presence of an audience; and, when the nature of the scene absolutely requires the actor to look directly at the person with whom he is speaking, he still should keep a three-quarter face to the audience.

(*To be continued.*)

ESSAY ON DRAMATIC COMPOSITION.

(*Continued from No. IV. p.* 278.)

IF, through the wide range of human events, one single story can be found, in which, without change of place, or prolongation of the time that actually was necessary for all the events that gave interest to the fable to have happened, if such a story can be found, the discovery has never yet been made: that is, supposing it to have variety, incident, and passion, sufficient at present for a dramatic composition of five acts.

Since therefore suppositions of some kind must be made, and since the mind is conscious that they must, it surely is but just to inquire what are the kind of suppositions that will produce the most delightful flights of imagination, will most favor a multiplicity of incidents, such as are now at least absolutely required on the stage, and will most enforce the passions in all their varieties?

From the age of Cardinal de Richlieu and Çorneille, which is nearly two centuries, the French have maintained, in all their critical codes, that the unities must be observed : and so firmly is this opinion established, even among the lowest smatterers of literature, and so far are they swayed by the firm conviction that to err against these rules is a dramatical mortal sin, that when a Frenchman happens to be present at a play in England, or elsewhere, and sees the scene change in the middle of an act, on all such occasions he is involuntarily shocked. From that moment, be the play good or bad, it stands condemned in his opinion ; and the nation itself is frequently stigmatized, by the epithet barbarians. Such is the force of prejudice : that is, of opinions, either not examined or very slightly, and impressed upon the mind as incontrovertible truths.

It would be an experiment worthy of those, who assert the necessity and possibility of preserving the unities to take any one of the performances that, during the space of two hundred years, the French poets, or indeed any others, have produced, and examine how far the unities have actually been preserved? what suppositions the writer, and consequently the audience, have been obliged to make? and afterward, with strict impartiality, to inquire whether their own rules, concerning probability and dramatic illusion, were not absurd? as likewise whether, by the restrictions which the poet laid upon himself while writing, he did not materially injure his own work ?

Such experiments might here be easily made; but they would be tedious, and any reader of intelligence can make them for himself. * A brief example, however, may show that nothing in the least has been advanced which facts will not justify.

---

* While I am writing on this subject, truth requires me to remark that I wrote the comedy of *Seduction* purposely to show that the observance of the unities was quite as much within the power of the English as of any other people. In that comedy, they are perhaps as strictly observed as in any other, in any language ; but, while writing it, I was well and often aware of

The *Tartuffe* is perhaps the masterpiece of Molière: but whether or not, the advocates of the unities scarcely can object that so excellent a comedy should be chosen.

No one, I suppose, will dispute that *the unity of action* should be as perfect as possible; and there are few comedies which, in this respect, are more admirable than the *Tartuffe*. Time and place therefore are only here to be considered.

It is necessary *to repeat* that, for probability and illusion to be perfect, the time ought not to exceed the time of action; the place should not be changed; and the mind should never encounter any thing, which is not immediately intelligible.

The scene is at Paris, at the house of Orgon; and, in the first scene, his mother, attended by Cleante, one of her sons, by Elmire the wife of Orgon, and by her grandchildren, is leaving the house, and tells them, with her characteristic rudeness, not to follow her out of ceremony. In fact, the whole first act *appears* to pass in the hall; for no directions, on this score, are given.

In the second act, it must have changed; at least *we must suppose so*, from the dialogue; for here we have a cabinet, or closet, that leads into the chamber where secrets are discoursed of.

In the third act, we have again a cabinet, to which Damis retires to listen.

In the fourth act, it is a furnished apartment, with tables and chairs, and Tartuffe is sent off into the next chamber, lest the discourse should be overheard.

In the fifth act the scene may pass any where in the house. But it is an utter improbability that one chamber should be the scene for the whole: though I see no reason why it should be removed out of the house. That Tartuffe should, *in the nature*

---

the unnecessary and prejudicial constraint that was imposed upon me, and of the many absurd, that is false, suppositions which I was obliged to adopt. The comedy was much applauded; but the force of habit, among English spectators, was such, that, I was repeatedly asked why I had not once given a change of scene? Preconceived opinions made the English weary of what the French would have approved.

of things, twice make love to the wife of his protector, and
that other scenes, in which the fear of being overheard is
clearly expressed, should pass in an apartment common to
comers and goers is totally incredible : and that the first act
does pass in such a place is certain.

Grant then that a change of scene is, perhaps, without excep-
tion, necessary to plays; and it then only depends on the poet
to make the spectator acquainted with such changes, and render
them intelligible; and this is in all cases required, could the unities or could they not be observed.

In this comedy however it is quite impossible *to suppose* the
unity of time observed.   In the nature of things, it would perhaps be extravagant to suppose all the events here recounted to
have passed in a week.   We first learn that Tartuffe is established in the house of Orgon, who has been from home two
days, inquires after the health of his family on his return, but
feels nothing for the illness of his wife, though much concerning Tartuffe.

His brother, Cleante, mentions the intended match, which
Orgon it seems had assented to, or projected, between Valére
and his daughter, Marianne ; but concerning which he now appears to be undetermined.

In the beginning of the second act, this indecision is entirely
vanished ; he is now resolved to marry his daughter to Tartuffe.
He surely had not taken this strange resolution in so short an
interval of time as that between the acts ! In the fourth scene
of the second act, Valére enters and has heard the report: now
time was surely necessary for such a report to be spread.

In the first scene of the third act, this intended marriage is
known to every body, and every body is enraged.   At the end
of the third act, Orgon first proposes to make a donation of all
his effects to Tartuffe, having first quarrelled with Damis, his
son.

Cleante returns, has heard of this family quarrel, declares it
to be publicly known, tells Tartuffe he is blamed by every
body, and the donation appears also to be in Tartuffe's possession.

In act the fourth, the marriage contract, between Tartuffe and Marianne, is brought on by Orgon; and there is no mode of averting his destructive obstinacy, but that, which his wife takes, of suffering Tartuffe to make love to her, while Orgon conceals himself under a table. This brings him to his senses, and he is in a dreadful alarm, not only for his wealth, of which he has made a donation, but for his personal safety; Tartuffe having at that moment retired.

The above is business that must have employed many hours; but who ever will carefully read act the fifth will find that several days, perhaps several weeks, are necessary for the events, there recounted, to have all passed with probability.

Tartuffe has applied to law, and persons are sent to seize the effects of Orgon. This is comparatively a trifle: the king has been informed, by Tartuffe, that Orgon had concealed the casket of a man, who had offended his majesty: nay, the king had detected Tartuffe to be a villain, formerly denounced, and had further heard the whole story of his plots upon Orgon, and the mischief he had committed. The king suffers Tartuffe to suppose he takes an officer with him to seize on Orgon, as a traitor; and this officer has received his full instructions, which are to seize Tartuffe, himself, in the presence of Orgon, and to declare his royal forgiveness and paternal care of this oppressed old fool.

No man will surely deny that the comedy is a most excellent one; but, after a fair examination, surely no man will pretend that it has the least claim to unity of time.

In the next number, it is my intention to give a similar abstract of the unities as they are observed in the *Phédre* of Racine, a tragedy by many supposed to be the masterpiece of the French stage. Should any other dramatic piece be pointed out to me, as more perfect in the preservation of the unities, and yet equally productive of that degree of intricacy, passion, and interest, which the frequency of dramatic exhibition has now rendered necessary, I shall be eagerly desirous to inquire into the fable and conduct of such a piece. It is strongly to be suspected that men have been flattering and inflating themselves with the discovery of rules, supposed to be perfect, but, dangerously erroneous, as well in their code for writing as for morality.

(To be continued.)

SOME ACCOUNT

OF THE RISE AND PROGRESS OF THE GERMAN STAGE.

(Continued from No. IV. *p.* 280.)

IN 1756, several merchants of Leipsic contributed to build a theatre there, with suitable decorations. This theatre was most remarkable for its painted curtain, of which however a description would be superfluous, except that, among its many other allegorical figures, Shakespear is there seen, having no imitator, and proceeding directly to truth.

In 1769, an undertaking was begun which, though not wholly successful, contributed greatly to national emulation, and the progress of the drama, and likewise to destroy that aversion, which most of the great entertained, for pieces written in the German language. The merchants of Hamburg combined to establish a theatre at that city, to which the best actors, from all parts, were invited; as likewise was one of the most able machinists of France. *Loewe* was chosen the director, and charged at the same time to give public lessons on the art of pantomime, and of theatrical action. Hence Hamburg soon became an academy for young actors; and that establishment would have been of great utility, had it not unfortunately been soon interrupted.

Lessing was invited to enrich this dramatic school, by new and original pieces. A considerable pension was proposed to him, but it could not determine him to take this charge upon himself. All that could be obtained of him was to instruct, both actors and spectators, by judicious criticism. With this view, he began the work called *Dramaturgie de Hambourg**; but the vanity of some actors was wounded, and he was soon obliged to be silent. Willing, however, to contribute toward raising the national and theatrical edifice, he laboured to cure the rage of German writers, in servilely imitating foreign works. He was particularly desirous they should truly feel how far the rules, given by the ancients, and especially by Aristotle, were practicable; which rules, by different parties, were too much and too little insisted on. It is to be regretted that the ill success of the theatre, at Hamburg, gave interruption to a work so precious, and so singular.

In the course of that and the preceding years, *Weisse* added to his fame, by a very happy imitation of *Ninette à la Cour*, and *La Partie de Chasse d'Henri IV.* of which he made comic operas, for the German theatre.

Some time after, one of the dramatic masterpieces of the same author appeared; which was Romeo and Juliet, imitated from *Shakespear:* but he avoided those irregularities, and numberless exaggerations, for which the first tragic writer of England is justly reproached †. *Madame Schultz* performed Juliet with so much truth and feeling that this part alone would have established her reputation.

In 1767, Lessing published, in two volumes, a new edition of his comedies; to which was added *Minna von Barnhelm*, written in 1763. This is the best comedy in the German language, and may not fear comparison with the best of foreign comedies ‡. It is impossible to judge of the original, by the translation, or rather imitation, which *M. Rochon de Chabannes* has given of it, in his *Amans généreux*; though this piece had great success, and has always been well received in France. The finest traits

---

* I have only the title in French before me.

† These common-place accusations of Shakespear scarcely deserve any other answer than a desire that the works of those, who pretend they have corrected his faults, should be compared, were it worth while, and a just estimate made of the different effects, which he and his improvers produce. He has great blemishes, but the true nature of them has not perhaps been well understood.

‡ This is a bold assertion, the truth of which deserves inquiry.

of the original have disappeared, in the French writer; the fable itself has taken a different direction, and every thing that marked the manners of Germany is suppressed. This is not meant as a reproach: the author's design was not to translate, but, having found a subject that pleased him, to produce such a piece as his nation should approve. Many German authors, of acknowledged merit, such as *Weisse, Bock, Meissner, Gotter, Weizel, Dyk,* and various others, have done just the same with respect to foreign productions, many of which they have not translated, but have imitated, and adapted to the German stage.

The enterprise of Hamburg dropped entirely, in 1668, and the company assembled there had no better fate than is common to German actors; that of wandering from town to town.

At this era, the ardor for dramatic writing was common through the empire, and theatrical pieces were every where produced: there was a deluge of them, but, except a small number which were decidedly good, they were generally the productions of mediocrity, immature, and tasteless. Criticism, dear to the German literati, began to speak aloud; sometimes well and sometimes ill, according to custom. Pieces, actors, nay companies, were condemned: not one performance escaped the scalping-knife, with which the critic was armed. The piece of the evening was dissected on the morrow; and collections of poetical pieces, epigrams, and anecdotes, relative to the theatre, were poured forth. The most useful and curious of these collections were those which have appeared since 1775, as published by *M. Reichard,* librarian at Gotha.

In 1772, *Emilie Galotti,* by Lessing, appeared; a tragedy which constitutes an epocha, in Germany. We shall here be silent, concerning all that Germany, all that the friends, all that the enemies, of Lessing have been able to say of that piece: but we are persuaded that those who shall read, or rather who shall study it, allowing for the difference of genius which pervades each nation, and the kind of drama which must necessarily result, will render justice to the poet, and will feel the truth, the precision, and the force of the characters, as they are maintained even in the minutest situations, the rapid and ani-

mated interest that pervades the plot, and, in a word, the numberless beauties that are dispersed through every scene*.

(*To be continued.*)

DRAMATIC ANECDOTES.

GARRICK, the *Roscius*, the *Æsopus*, the wonder of the dramatic art, began himself in the age of puerility to make trial of
acting: but he did not, though he was turned of eleven, begin
with Hamlet, Richard, and Romeo: the joyous little rogue
chose Serjeant Kite; and it is said the play was acted so far
beyond expectation that it was highly applauded. The ease,
vivacity, and humor, of this Liliputian Kite, were long remembered with pleasure, at Litchfield.

Soon after this, Garrick was sent to an uncle at Lisbon, a
wine-merchant, where he made himself particularly agreeable,
to the English, with whom he often dined. After dinner, they
usually diverted themselves by placing him on a table, and
hearing him deliver speeches from plays, and repeat verses,
highly to the satisfaction of the hearers.

Davies, who relates these anecdotes in his life of Garrick,
informs us that, when the latter acted at Covent Garden, from
September 1746 to the end of May 1749, the profits of the season amounted to eight thousand five hundred pounds; and
adds, by way of epigram, that Maddocks, the straw man, a few
years afterward, having exhibited at the same house, the net
profits were eleven thousand pounds. Whenever straw men,
or beings of straw, appear they are wonderfully inflammable,
and kindle a dangerous conflagration in the public mind. Elizabeth Canning, the Rabbit-woman, Fanny of Cock-lane,—stop
in time.

---

* A translation of this tragedy will appear, in the next number of The
Theatrical Recorder: it is indeed an excellent piece, though it may here
perhaps have been praised too much.

MISCELLANIES.

THEATRICAL people have recently found a topic of dispute, or amusement, as their different inclinations lead, in a recent incident. A contest arose, between Mr. Braham and the management, concerning songs that Mr. Braham wished to introduce, for Signora Storace's benefit, which privilege he was refused. This refusal he seems to have understood as a personal insult; and, after some altercation, gave up his engagement at the theatre. That Signora Storace might not suffer in her benefit, he once more appeared, on the first of April, in the opera called the Siege of Belgrade.

For some days preceding the performance, appearances seemed to denote that the disputants were each mustering their partisans; and, on the morning of the lady's benefit, it was whispered about town—" Won't you go to Covent Garden this evening? There will be warm work. Braham will be called to account, but he does not seem to be afraid." Accordingly, the house being very full, the moment he appeared, uproar became general.

On all such occasions, the spectators are so discordant, impatient, and vociferous, that, till they have exhausted themselves, it is difficult for any explanation to be heard. One wants one thing, another another. This man cries, Off! Off! Another, Go on! Go on! A third, Hear him! A fourth has a cat-call: a fifth is provided with a no less noisy ratan or cudgel. Among so great a number, there are many who, on all occasions, *speaking in their own phrase, encourage each other to keep it up, and enjoy the fun.*

Mr. Braham made various attempts to go on, to explain, to sing, or to do any thing that the circumstances suggested. When the audience were sufficiently wearied with their own noise, he was at last heard, and, as we are told, declared to the following effect:

" That, on former occasions, it had been customary to allow the privilege he had lately claimed; that he had exercised it himself, without opposition; had taken songs from what operas he pleased, to introduce in any piece that he pleased, for a benefit; and that, this established custom having been refused, by the managers, on the present occasion, he could only consider such a refusal as personal to himself."

The town replied by calling him to account for not having appeared on a former evening, when his name was in the play-bills of the day?

To this he answered that the fault did not lie with him; for he had several times previously sent word that he was determined to perform for the theatre no more; and, on the morning of that day, seeing his name advertised, he had written to Mr. Brandon, when there was sufficient time to have posted up different play-bills, that there might be no pretended ignorance of his resolution: so that, if the public were disappointed, it was totally the neglect or obstinacy of the management, and that he, Mr. Braham, ought not to be supposed the culprit.

This speech seemed entirely to turn the tide in his favor, and explanation from the other party was vehemently demanded. An apology was attempted; but Mr. Kemble, as acting manager, was violently called for; and Mr. Kemble was not in the house, nor was it known where he was to be found. This was insufficient: the audience insisted he must be sent for, and must appear.

Another delay occurred; but, at length, Mr. Kemble came, and, in reply to Mr. Braham's complaints, stated—

That he, Mr. Braham, might have been permitted to have taken whatever songs he pleased out of operas that were not now on the stock-list; but not from those that still brought money to the theatre.

To this it was answered, that no such proviso had before been made; and instances were cited in proof. However, at length, the audience, overcome by weariness, suffered the opera to proceed.

It was remarked that a multitude of Jews had flocked to the theatre, to support their favorite, Mr. Braham; and that one of them, in particular, a little man, in the pit, called, several times, Mr. Kemble! Mr. Kemble! and beckoned with his

finger, that he might have a particular hearing.   Mr. Kemble
advanced, bent forward over the orchestra, that he might hear
the better, and the little Israelite exclaimed——

"You had better beg pardon, at once, Mr. Kemble, and put
an end to it."

To this Mr. Kemble, raising himself with his accustomed
dignity, waved his hand and cried—

"Poh, poh, Sir, poh!"

As usual, on such occasions, some laugh, and some are angry ;
but it appears that Mr. Braham does not intend to perform
again at Covent Garden.   On the night when Mr. Braham was
advertised to appear, but did not, bills were distributed to the
auditors, and given at the door, as each person entered, to say
that Mr. Hill was to perform the part of Mr. Braham.   But to
this many replied, and with justice, you have brought us from
home, one, two, three, or perhaps four miles, and now inform
us at the door, that the performer, whom we came in particular
to hear, will not sing to-night; when you might and ought
to have told us this in the play-bills of the day, or of the
afternoon.

=====

The comedy of the Wheel of Fortune was performed on the
thirtieth of March, at Covent Garden ; and on the second of
April, by command, at Drury Lane.   One passage in it, where
General Tempest says—

Money I have none, for I did not understand the arts of government—

the audience of both houses applied the words to a high of-
ficial character, who at present stands reproved by parliament.
At Covent Garden, the spectators gave several rounds of loud
and general applause to the speech : and though his Majesty
was present at Drury Lane, and therefore the people were much
more respectful, they still testified their feelings by three times
distinctly giving applause.   It is not the intention of this work
to agitate or interfere in political questions, but to *record* all remarkable *theatrical facts.*

=====

When the Honey Moon also was performed on Saturday,
April 21, three distinct and vehement rounds of applause were

given, after the mock duke had declared that, "like other great men in office, he must make the most of his time, and retire with a good grace to avoid being turned out."

COSTUME:

The present number contains: 1. The elegant but simple dress of Miss Duncan in the Honey Moon: 2. A Byde or Physician, the offspring of a Bramuhn, and a woman of the Byce class: 3. A Causto of the writer cast in the service of a European: 4. A Dybuck, that is an astronomer, the offspring of a Rajpoot father and a Byce mother.

TO CORRESPONDENTS.

Several applications by letter have been made to publish the work on the Art of Acting separately, but for this the Editor is sorry he has not leisure. The youth who is persuaded he can rival our present Roscius, may not perhaps presume too far ; but he scarcely can expect that a work should be undertaken by which the interruption of the present plan of The Theatrical Recorder would be inevitable, in order that he may become so wonderful an actor.

Thanks are returned to Amicus, but a burlesque on Mrs. Siddons would be an injustice, that cannot be committed in The Theatrical Recorder ; for, though the highest praise is intended in this burlesque, it is given in such a questionable shape as could not but degrade a woman whose extraordinary talents demand the utmost respect.

To a Constant Reader the Editor is indebted for the information that a comedy called " The High Road to Marriage," by Mr. Skiffington, which was performed a few seasons ago for the benefit of Mrs. Glover, was taken from the same comedy, by Calderon de la Barca, as that from which the translation of " From Bad to Worse" which was given in No. IV. of this work.

A Correspondent from Coventry in desirous of a criticism on Master Betty, in Hamlet ; but he is surely not aware how invidious such a task would appear, at the present moment, were it performed with ability and honesty.

MONTHLY LIST, FOR APRIL, 1805.

DRURY-LANE.

MARCH
28. Douglas (Young Roscius) - - - United Britons, and The Devil to Pay.
30. Hamlet (Young Roscius) - - - - The Doctor and the Apothecary.

APRIL
1. Douglas (Young Roscius) - - - United Britons, and Bon Ton.
2. The Wheel of Fortune (by Com.) Of Age To-morrow.
4. Hamlet (Young Roscius) - - - - The Liar.
6. Barbarossa (Young Roscius) - - Richard Cœur de Lion.
15. Pizarro - - - - - - - - - - - - - United Britons, and The Irishman in London.
16. Hamlet (Young Roscius) - - - - The Spoiled Child.
17. The Honey Moon - - - - - - - Richard Cœur de Lion.
18. Douglas (Young Roscius) - - - - United Britons, and The Citizen.
19. She Stoops to Conquer - - - - - Ditto, and High Life Below Stairs.
20. The Honey Moon - - - - - - - Richard Cœur de Lion.
22. Douglas (Young Roscius) - - - - Of Age To-morrow, and Old Harlequin's Fire Side.
23. The Provoked Husband - - - - The Soldier's Return.
24. The Honey Moon - - - - - - - Ditto.
25. The Stranger - - - - - - - - - - Ditto.
26. The Venetian Outlaw - - - - - Matrimony.
27. The West Indian - - - - - - - - Richard Cœur de Lion.

COVENT-GARDEN.

MARCH
28. The English Fleet - - - - - - - Honest Thieves.
30. The Wheel of Fortune - - - - - The Lock and Key.

APRIL
1. The Siege of Belgrade (Benefit. Signora Storace) - - - - - - - Out of Place.
2. Douglas (Master Betty) - - - - The Birth Day.
4. The School of Reform - - - - - The Escapes.
6. Laugh when you Can (Benefit. Mr. Lewis) - - - - - - - - - - The Positive Man.
15. George Barnwell - - - - - - - - Aggression, or The Heroine of Yucatan.
16. The Wheel of Fortune - - - - - Ditto.
17. John Bull - - - - - - - - - - - Ditto.
18. Who wants a Guinea? - - - - - Marian.
19. Ditto - - - - - - - - - - - - - - Aggression.
20. Zara (Master Betty) - - - - - - The Padlock.
22. Who wants a Guinea? - - - - - Aggression.
23. Zara (Master Betty) - - - - - - The Poor Soldier.
24. Who Wants a Guinea? - - - - - Aggression.
25. Zara (Master Betty) - - - - - - Rosina.
26. Who Wants a Guinea? - - - - - Aggression.
27. Zara - - - - - - - - - - - - - - The Review.

THE

THEATRICAL RECORDER:

BY

THOMAS HOLCROFT.

CONTENTS OF NUMBER VI.

London:
Printed by C. Mercier and Co. No. 6, Northumberland-court,
Where the Work may be procured;
And at all the BOOKSELLERS;
And published for the Author, by H. D. Symonds, Paternoster-row.

1805.

EMILIA GALOTTI:

A TRAGEDY,

IN FIVE ACTS,

TRANSLATED FROM

THE GERMAN OF G. E. LESSING,

BY FANNY HOLCROFT.

DRAMATIS PERSONÆ.

HECTOR GANZA, Prince of Guastalla.

COUNT APPIANI, betrothed to EMILIA.

MARINELLI, Chamberlain to the PRINCE.

EDWARD GALOTTI, the Father of EMILIA.

CAMILLO ROTA, a Counsellor of State.

CONTI, a Painter.

ANGELO, a Bravo.

PIRRO,
BATTISTA, } Domestics.

VALETS, &c.

EMILIA GALOTTI.

CLAUDIA, her Mother.

THE COUNTESS ORSINA.

EMILIA GALOTTI:

A TRAGEDY.

~~~~~

ACT I.

SCENE I.

The Prince's *Cabinet. The* Prince *seated at a Table, and reading Papers.*

Prince.

UNGRATEFUL task, to read endless complaints! Petitions
that exceed the power of granting! Yet we are envied!
Could we give satisfaction to all, our lot indeed were enviable!
(*reading a signature*) Emilia? Ay, Bruneschi; not Galotti.
What does she ask? (*reads*) Unreasonable! Yet her name
shall gain her cause. (*signs it, and rings.*)

SCENE II.—*Enter* Valet.

Prince. Are any of the counsellors without?
Valet. None, your highness.
Prince. I have risen early: 'tis a lovely morn! I'll enjoy
the fresh breeze. Send for the Marquis, Marinelli. (*exit
Valet*) I can read no more. A name has thrown my thoughts
into confusion.

SCENE III.—*Re-enter* Valet, *bringing a Note.*

Valet. From the Countess Orsina, your highness.
Prince. The Countess? Put it down.
Valet. The courier waits.
Prince. I'll send an answer. Is she in town or country?
Valet. She arrived yesterday.
Prince. (*aside*) I'm sorry for it. (*aloud*) Dismiss the
messenger. (*exit* Valet) My dear Countess, I guess the
import. (*throwing the note scornfully on the table*) And yet,
I thought I loved her! How the heart deceives itself! Perhaps
I did. Oh, yes.

SCENE IV.—*Re-enter* VALET.

Valet. The painter, Conti——
Prince. Conti? Admit him. (*exit* Valet) He may turn
the channel of my thoughts. (*rising.*)

SCENE V.—*Enter* CONTI.

Prince. Good day, Conti. How thrive the arts?
Conti. But ill, your highness.
Prince. Indeed! I'd have them flourish in my domain.
Yet toil should not affright the artist.
Conti. It is his glory! But genius, if oppressed, may sink.
Prince. You misconceive: I mean his zeal should never
weary. What have you brought?
Conti. The portrait you commanded; and another, which—
Prince. I forget! Whose portrait did I command?
Conti. The Countess Orsina's.
Prince. True! (*coldly*) The commission is, methinks,
grown stale.
Conti. Fair ladies are allowed caprice: in three months the
Countess has granted me one sitting.
Prince. Where are the pictures?
Conti. In the antichamber, Prince.   [*Exit.*

SCENE VI.

Prince. Her portrait! I'm glad 'tis not herself. Perhaps it may
awaken feelings which she no longer can excite. Yet, no! The
spell is broken. Perhaps she bribed the painter thus to importune me? It were in vain. Another image, drawn in different
colours, on a finer canvass, must be obliterated from my bosom
ere she can regain my heart. I wish she could; for, when I
loved the Countess, all was frolic, mirth, and pleasure: now it
is the reverse. Yet no! Were I a thousand fold more gloomy,
I would not resume Orsina's degrading chains.

SCENE VII.

Re-enter CONTI, *with two Pictures, and places one against the
Wall; the other so as best to be seen.*

Conti. Prince, you must recollect the limits of our art: it
cannot catch the indefinite charm, which gives resistless grace
to beauty.
Prince. Excellent! Most excellent! Your pencil was inspired! But you have greatly flattered.
Conti. The Countess, Prince, is not of your opinion, nor
indeed am I. The artist must paint Nature as she would be
without the ravages of time, or imperfection of materials.

Prince. I love the man who studies the philosophy of his art. The Countess then capriciously——

Conti. Excuse me, Prince; I respect the Countess, and meant no censure.

Prince. As you please. What said Orsina?

Conti. She said, if that's my likeness, I am satisfied.

Prince. If! 'Tis quite in character.

Conti. And then the look she gave! You cannot trace it in this picture.

Prince. You speak my meaning: 'tis in that, Conti, you have so greatly flattered her. Oh, I well know that proud sarcastic look, which would disfigure grace itself. I will not deny the smile of irony sometimes becomes the coral lip; and scorn is an embellishment; but not excessive, as in the Countess. Their poignancy must be softened by eyes that captivate: those eyes are on the canvass, but Orsina has them not.

Conti. Prince, I am much concerned.

Prince. Why so? The Countess has large unmeaning eyes, and as the poets feign Medusa's; you have given them a sweetness, an expression, that does honor to your taste, yet merits blame. You own her true character cannot be read in this portrait: that is a fault. Pride here assumes the grace of dignity, the scornful sneer is changed to smiles, the gloom of discontent to soft melancholy.

Conti. (*chagrined*) Prince, is it the artist's fault if, when he has finished a portrait, ordered in the delirium of rapture, he finds the lover changed?

Prince. Why did not you bring it sooner, Conti? Put it aside. What is the other piece?

Conti. A female portrait.

Prince. I will not see it. I have a model here, or rather here, (*pointing to his head and heart*) which none can equal.—Let me have other subjects.

Conti. I may be surpassed in talent, but none can exceed this in beauty.

Prince. Conti, it is the painter's mistress! (Conti *shews the picture*) Heavens! Is it your work, or is it the creation of my fancy?

Conti. Prince, are you acquainted with the angel?

Prince. (*his eyes fixed on the picture*) By sight. Some weeks ago, I met her at an assembly with her mother; and since at mass, where it is unseemly to gaze. Her father is known to me, but is no friend: 'twas he opposed my claims on Sabionetta. He is a veteran, proud and unpolished, but honest and brave.

Conti. Such the father! Here is the daughter.

Prince. By Heaven, it seems to speak! Conti, 'tis the height of flattery to forget the artist in his works.

Conti. I'm far from satisfied, and yet dissatisfaction here

gives me pleasure. Oh that we could paint with our eyes.
How much is lost in the wide space between the eye and the
hand ! Yet I say the sense of my deficiency makes me proud :
ay, prouder than if I had executed all that my fancy has conceived. 'Tis this more than our works bespeaks the masterly
artist. Raphael still had been the sublime painter, though Nature had refused him hands?

Prince. What said you, Conti?

Conti. Nothing! Nothing ! Mere rhapsody : your soul is in
your eyes. How it delights me !

Prince. (*affecting coldness*) And so you rank Emilia with the
prettiest of our ladies?

Conti. Rank—the prettiest? Your highness jests.

Prince. Dear Conti, inexperience is easily deceived. Paint-
ers only can judge of beauty.

Conti. And must every feeling wait the cold decision of art?
Let those who from us would learn what beauty is inhabit cloisters. Yet, as a painter, I hold it as the most fortunate circumstance of my life that Emilia Galotti sat to me. This countenance, these lovely tresses, this neck of ivory, beauteous bosom,
slender waist, and fine proportioned form, are now the only
model from which I study female beauty. Her father has the
original, this is but a copy.

Prince. (*eagerly*) It is no doubt bespoke?

Conti. It is yours, Prince, if it please you.

Prince. Please? (*smiling*) You say you have made these
charms your study, Conti? Can I do better than make them
mine? Take back the other portrait for a frame.

Conti. Good.

Prince. Let it be magnificent : the picture shall adorn the
gallery.—A copy needs not such parade : it shall remain here, it
will be a pleasing study. Conti, I am your debtor. Thank
you, thank you ! The arts shall never languish while I have the
power to support them. Go to my treasurer, he will pay you
for the portraits ; you may name whatever sum you please.

Conti. I almost fear, my Prince, 'tis not my skill, but something else you would reward.

Prince. Oh, the jealous artist ! No, no ! Mark me : whatever sum you please.   [*Exit* Conti.

SCENE VIII.—*Manet the* PRINCE.

Prince. (*looking at the picture*) Millions would too cheaply
purchase such a gem ! Matchless work of art, do I indeed possess thee ! Oh that the original, Nature's sweet masterpiece,
were likewise mine ! Honorable matron, churlish father, give
me but her and all my treasures are your own. But, no ! I'll
win thee, charmer, from thyself. This eye of azure blue
beams modesty, and grace. This mouth, when from her coral

lips words sweet as honey flow, when smiles celestial dimple on her cheek, this mouth——Some one comes! My heart is jealous of thy mute beauties. (*turns the picture to the wall*) It is Marinelli. But that I sent for him, how exquisite a morning I had spent!

SCENE IX.—*Enter* MARINELLI.

Mar. Pardon, your highness, that I came not sooner.

Prince. The freshness of the morning invited me to walk; but, now, the day's too far advanced, and I have lost all inclination. Do you bring me news?

Mar. None of importance. The Countess Orsina arrived yesterday.

Prince. Here's her note, informing me—— Pshaw! I know not what. Has she spoken to you?

Mar. Am I not, alas, her confident? If I e'er again take such an office, Prince——

Prince. Make no rash vows, Marquis.

Mar. Indeed! May I retract? The Countess, perhaps, is not so much in fault?

Prince. Oh, yes; my nuptials with the Princess of Massa must interrupt at least all such connections.

Mar. If so, the Countess must be content.

Prince. My fate is harder far than hers; my heart is sacrificed to ambition: she has but to take back hers, while I, against my will, must part with mine.

Mar. But if a wife, whom policy presents, be all she asks, why take it back? A wife, so taken, cannot rob the mistress of her place: she fears some other rival.

Prince. Well, would you deem that a crime?

Mar. I, Prince! Oh, no! Confound me not with a weak woman, for whom I intercede in pure compassion. Yesterday, I own she greatly moved me: she waved all mention of your love, and wished to appear indifferent; but her cheek, now pale, now glowing, gave the lie to this affected calm, and showed the torture of her mind. She said the saddest things, and smiled and jested with the face of Niobe. She flies to books for refuge, and I fear they'll but distract her brain.

Prince. Weak is the mind which sinks under the first attack: her debility first gave me disgust; urge it not, in her behalf. She is weak by nature: enough! We'll change the theme. Affords the town no other novelty?

Mar. Little more. Count Appiani's marriage.

Prince. Appiani? Who is the lady? I knew it not.

Mar. Great secrecy has been observed: 'tis not a match to do him honor. You will but laugh, Prince, at these our sentimental fools: Love, soon or late, makes them his mockery. A girl, destitute of rank or fortune, has caught him in her net:

her bait a pompous show of virtue, feeling, wit, and such-like fooleries.

Prince. He who, unfettered by restraint, can yield his heart to innocence and beauty, is worthy envy, not compassion. Who is the happy virgin? I well know, Marinelli, you and the Count are foes; but he bears a gallant name, is handsome, rich, and honorable. I would win him to my service; it may yet be done.

Mar. 'Tis now too late. His plan is not to seek preferment, but to retire with his bride to Piedmont: there to chase the wild chamois, and see his cattle graze: what can he better? This match will shut the door of greatness on him.

Prince. What harm! He'll then be quit of ceremonious form, restraint, dulness, and not unoften pompous poverty. But who is she to whom he makes so great a sacrifice?

Mar. One Emily Galotti.

Prince. How, one——

Mar. Emilia Galotti.

Prince. Impossible!

Mar. Nothing more certain.

Prince. I say it is a mistake: the name is common; it may be a Galotti, but not Emilia.

Mar. Emilia—Emilia Galotti, Prince.

Prince. Then there are two Emilias: you said *one* Emilia Galotti. Fools would only so describe the first.

Mar. What means this sudden agitation, Prince? Know you the bride?

Prince. Question me not, but answer my inquiries: is it the daughter of that Galotti who so obstinately opposed me?

Mar. Even so!

Prince. Living here, at Guastalla, with her mother?

Mar. The same

Prince. Near the cathedral?

Mar. Even so.

Prince. In a word. (*showing the portrait*) There! Is it her you mean? Again drawl out your cursed phlegmatic " *even so,*" and stab me to the heart.

Mar. The very same!

Prince. Traitor!—And she will to-day——

Mar. Espouse the Count. (*the* Prince *snatches away the picture*) They are to be married privately this afternoon, at the father's country-house, at Sabionetta.

Prince. (*throwing himself on a seat in despair*) Wretched man! Life is a burden!

Mar. What thus moves you, Prince?

Prince. Moves? Traitor! (*springing on him*) I love the bride to madness. What avails me that you know it; that you all, long since, had knowledge of my passion, when you would eternally have had me wear the mad Orsina's chains! You,

Marquis, my *friend* to—— Oh! Princes never had, never can have, a friend! That *you* should treacherously conceal the danger which threatened my love, *you*—— May Heaven renounce me when I forgive the treason!

Mar. Amazement! My Prince love Emilia Galotti? May I be scorned of God and man if I had the slightest suspicion! Orsina's fears glanced a different way.

Prince. Forgive me, Marinelli, (*thowing himself in his arms*) and grant me your pity.

Mar. You see, my Prince, the fruits of your reserve. " Princes never had, never can have, a friend." The fault is theirs. This hour we are their confidents, the next we are strangers to them.

Prince. Ah, Marinelli, I scarcely knew my own heart.

Mar. Is Emilia aware of her power?

Prince. I tried in vain a second time to address her.

Mar. And the first—— ?

Prince. I was—— I cannot speak! You see me at the mercy of the waves, and ask how I came there! Save, if you can, then question me.

Mar. Are you then lost? If you have not, my Prince, confessed your passion to *Emilia Galotti,* you will declare yourself to the Countess Appiani: when virgin beauty lies beyond our reach, we wait to catch the wife, and frequently are gainers by the exchange.

Prince. Marinelli, change your tone, or——

Mar. The conquest may not afford so many charms, but——

Prince. Trifle no more!

Mar. But, I forgot, Appiani will retire from court: we must change our plan.

Prince. Oh, think, dear Marinelli, for me: were you in my place——

Mar. I would see trifles in their true light, and feel that my authority was not a *name.*

Prince. Tell me not of power which I cannot exert!— To-day is it?

Mar. To-day! In a few hours, advice will be of no avail. (*musing*) Am I at liberty to act? Will you consent——

Prince. To all! Only delay this fatal marriage.

Mar. Not a moment must be lost! Away, Prince, to your country seat: it lies on the road to Sabionetta. If I can remove the Count a while—— Yes, yes; he'll fall into the snare. You mean to send an ambassador to Massa? Nominate the Count on condition that he instantly depart.

Prince. Excellent! Bring him instantly to my villa.

[*Exit* Marinelli.

SCENE X.—*Manet the* PRINCE.

Prince. (*looking for the picture*) What! On the ground? Oh sacrilege! I'll gaze no more! Why cauterize the wound? Too long I've sighed in tender lethargy. Ah, should I lose her; should Marinelli fail!—Why trust to him alone? (*looking at his watch*) This is the hour in which Emilia pays her pure devotions in the adjoining church. What if I try to address her? But on such a day her heart will be too tenderly engaged to think of piety: yet who can tell? 'Tis but a step. (*he signs and hastily arranges the papers on his table.*)

SCENE XI.—*Enter* VALET.

Prince. Are any of the counsellors arrived?
Valet. Camillo Rota.
Prince. Show him in. (*exit* Valet.) I have but a moment for him: another time his conversation will be most welcome. (*taking a paper*) Ay, Emilia! If your protectress were——

SCENE XII.—*Enter* CAMILLO ROTA, *with Papers in his Hand.*

Prince. Approach, Camillo. (*gives him papers.*)
Rota. Good, your highness!
Prince. Here is a petition from one Emilia Gal— Bruneschi. I have signed 'tis true; but 'tis no trifle: put aside or dispatch it, as you please.
Rota. I have no will but yours, my Prince.
Prince. Have you brought me any thing to sign?
Rota. A sentence of death.
Prince. With all my heart. Quick, dispatch.
Rota. (*astonished, and looking stedfastly at the* Prince) I said, your highness, it was a sentence of death.
Prince. Will you dispatch? I am in haste.
Rota. (*looking after the papers*) I have it not: excuse me, Prince, to-morrow——
Prince. As you please: good day. I'll talk with you to-morrow.　　　　　　　　　　　　　　　　　　　　　　[*Exit.*
Rota. (*arranging the papers*) With all his heart? Sign a sentence of death *with all his heart?* He should not in this humor have signed, though the criminal had slain my only son. This atrocious speech has stabbed me to the soul!
　　　　　　　　　　　　　　　　　　　　　　　[*Exit* Camillo Rota.

ACT II.

SCENE I.—*A Hall in the House of* GALOTTI.   CLAUDIA, PIRRO,
coming from different Sides.

Claudia   (to Pirro.)

WHO dismounted?

Pirro.   My master, lady.

Claud.   Your master? Is it possible!

Pirro.   He is close behind.

Claud.   So unexpectedly! (*going to meet* Galotti) My love!

SCENE II.—*Enter* GALOTTI.

Gal.   Good morrow, dearest Claudia! Have I not surprised
thee?

Claud.   Most agreeably: if thy coming has no serious motive?

Gal.   Be at ease: the joy of to-day awoke me betimes;
the morning too so fine, the distance so short! So many things
to be remembered! In a word, I come to see that all is right,
and then I'm gone. Where is our child? No doubt engaged at
her toilet?

Claud.   In sweet converse with her soul! She is gone to mass.

Gal.   Alone?

Claud.   'Tis but a step.

Gal.   Accidents may happen at the threshold.

Claud.   Be not uneasy, my love; rest within while I bring
refreshment.

Gal.   I'll not deny thee; but 'twas wrong to let her go
alone.

Claud.   Remain here, Pirro; we are not at home to visitors.
[*Exeunt* Claudia *and* Galotti.

SCENE III.—PIRRO, *and soon after* ANGELO.

Pirro.   That is to the curious: how I have been questioned
these two long hours! But who comes yonder?

Ang.   (*half behind the scenes, in a short cloak, under which he
conceals his face, and slouched hat*) Pirro! Pirro!

Pirro.   One I know? (Angelo *comes forward, with his face
uncovered*) Heavens! Angelo? Is't thee?

Ang.   Myself. I long have watched an opportunity to
speak with thee.

Pirro.   Dar'st thou walk forth in open day? Has not a price
been set upon thy head, since thy last murder?

Ang. Thou art not inclined to win it?

Pirro. What brings thee here? Seek'st thou my destruction?

Ang. Blockhead! (*showing him a purse of gold*) Seest thou this purse? 'Tis thine.

Pirro. Mine!

Ang. Yes. Hast thou forgotten the German, thy late master——?

Pirro. Hush!

Ang. Betrayed to us by thee, on the road to *Pisa*——

Pirro. Lower your voice.

Ang. He kindly left, with other valuables, a diamond ring, (thou recollectest?) too costly to be immediately disposed of. It has been sold for a hundred pistoles: here is thy share. (*offering the purse.*)

Pirro. I dare not take it: keep the whole.

Ang. Nay, if thou wilt sell thy life dog-cheap, so be it. (*going to put up the purse.*)

Pirro. Give it. (*takes the purse*) Now speak thy errand, for I'll not believe that alone brought thee.

Ang. Indeed? Knave! Think'st thou we'd defraud a comrade? Such things may happen with your men of honor; but with us never. Fare thee well! (*pretends to go, then returns*) One question. What brings old Galotti hither, quite alone?

Pirro. Oh! A very trifle: his daughter is this day to be married, at his villa, to Count Appiani: he could not so long defer the joy of seeing her.

Ang. Will he soon be gone?

Pirro. So soon that if thou'rt not alert he'll find thee here. But what would'st thou with *him*? Take heed; he's not to be——

Ang. Don't I know him? Have I not served in his regiment? What could I gain by him? When do the bride and bridegroom follow?

Pirro. At noon.

Ang. With any company?

Pirro. Only the bride's mother: two friends at *Sabionetta* are to assist at the ceremony.

Ang. How many servants?

Pirro. Two beside myself. I ride before.

Ang. Good! Good! Whose equipage is it?

Pirro. The Count's.

Ang. That is unlucky: his people are brave; yet, if——

Pirro. Amazement! What is thy design? The few jewels the bride may wear cannot pay the risk.

Ang. No, but the bride herself is worth the venture.

Pirro. And thou would'st have me an accomplice in the rape?

Ang. Thou go'st before? Gallop full speed without turning thy head.

Pirro. No, I'll not do it.

Ang. How! Would'st thou act the farce of conscience? Rascal! I think thou know'st me. If a word escape thee, should I find any change of plan——?

Pirro. For Heaven's sake! Angelo!——

Ang. Be wise and yield! Resist at thy peril!

        [*Exit, with a menacing gesture.*

Pirro. Ha! Let the devil touch but a hair of thy head and thou art damned for ever! Wretched man!

SCENE IV.—*Re-enter* Galotti *and* Claudia.

Gal. I cannot stay.

Claud. A moment longer: she will be so grieved to have missed thee.

Gal. I must once more embrace the noble youth and call him son. How congenial are our tastes! How I rejoice that he will retire to his native vallies from the haunts of vice and folly!

Claud. And I grieve. Shall not we lose our darling Emilia?

Gal. Lose? We shall leave her in the arms of a tender and worthy husband: wilt thou repine at her felicity? Thou reviv'st my old suspicion that it was not the wish to educate her well, but the pleasures of the court, which induced thee to reside with her in town, away from a husband and a father who so fondly cherished you both.

Claud. Unkind Edward! For once let me defend this town and court which thy stern virtue so abhors: 'twas here alone love could have joined two hearts formed for each other.

Gal. Granted! But, dear Claudia, we have rather to thank fortune than thy prudence. 'Tis well this town education finished so well. Two persons have met whose hearts sympathize: let them seek the abodes of innocence and peace. What could our son do here? Bow, flatter, cringe, and become the worthy rival of a *Marinelli*, to gain riches he needs not, and pretended honors which to him are none.—Pirro!

Pirro. I am, here, Signor.

Gal. Lead my horse to the Count's door; I shall immediately follow. (*exit* Pirro) Why should Appiani serve *here*, when at home he gives the law? Beside, his union with our daughter will ruin his credit with the Prince, who hates me.

Claud. Less, perhaps, than thou believ'st.

Gal. I am indifferent.

Claud. Did I not tell thee his highness had seen our daughter?

Gal. The Prince? Where?

Claud. At the last assembly of the chancellor Grimaldi, which he honored with his presence: he was so gracious!

Gal. Gracious?

Claud. Conversed with her so long!

Gal. Conversed?

Claud. Was so enchanted with her gaiety and wit——

Gal. Enchanted?

Claud. Extolled her beauty in such flattering terms——

Gal. And thou speak'st in the tone of congratulation! Oh, vain, foolish mother!

Claud. Why?

Gal. Well, well! 'Tis now of little matter. Ha! If I imagined—— 'Tis there he could inflict a mortal wound—When libertines admire, they would seduce. I shudder but to think. Why not immediately acquaint me? I would not on this day let any thing unkind escape my lips. *(taking her hand)* Farewell! Heaven grant no ill come of this imprudence! [*Exit* Galotti.

SCENE V.—*Manet* CLAUDIA.

Claud. Oh, what a man! How stern his virtue! If indeed it merit the name! With him all is suspicious, and deserves reproach. If knowledge of mankind create distrust, who would not remain in ignorance? But Emilia returns not. What can have staid her?—The Prince loves not the father; does it follow then he would seduce the daughter?

SCENE VI.—*Enter* EMILIA, *in great Terror.*

Emil. Thank Heaven, I'm now in safety! Or has he pursued so far? *(throwing aside her veil)* Is he here, my mother, is he?—No, Heaven be praised!

Claud. What has befallen my Emily?

Emil. Nothing! Nothing!

Claud. And yet thy looks are wild, thy frame convulsed.

Emil. What have I been forced to hear! And in what a place!

Claud. I thought thee gone to mass——

Emil. Even there! What place is sacred to vice? Ah, my mother! *(throwing herself in* Claudia's *arms.)*

Claud. Speak, my child, ease my apprehensions: what ill can have befallen thee in so holy a place?

Emil. On such a day too, when my thoughts should have been intent on Heaven!

Claud. Our devotion, my dear Emilia, cannot at all times be equally fervent: it is sufficient we desire the grace of Heaven to obtain it.

Emil. And that we sin to be guilty.

Claud. Such, I'm sure, my child, was not thy wish.

Emil. Oh, no! But, against our will, we may be made the accomplice of vice.

Claud. Be calm! Collect thy thoughts and tell me, if thou canst, what has befallen thee.

Emil. I went late, and could not approach the altar: scarcely had I raised my vows to Heaven, when some one placed himself behind me so close that I could turn no way, however desirous, fearful of interrupting the devotions of others. Oh that my fears had met no greater cause! But soon I heard a deep sigh, and the name not of a saint—the name —mother, be not angry, of your daughter! Oh that a thunderbolt had saved me from the shame of hearing more! He spoke of beauty, love; complained that this day, destined to make me happy, brought misery to him; implored my pity. All this I was compelled to hear, but made as though I had not heard, nor once turned my head: all I could do was to pray that Heaven would strike me deaf, though it were for life! At length mass was over: I dreaded to behold the offender who dared to violate the sanctuary of Heaven: trembling I rose and saw——

Claud. Who, my dearest child?

Emil. Divine, my mother! I could have sunk into the earth; 'twas *himself*.

Claud. Nay, who?

Emil. The Prince.

Claud. The Prince! Oh blessed be the impatience of thy father, who would not await thy coming.

Emil. Has he been here, and gone without seeing me?

Claud. Hadst thou related thy adventure in the moment of confusion——

Emil. Surely my conduct merits not reproach?

Claud. As little, child, as mine; and yet—yet—Ah, thou know'st not thy father! In his passion he would have confounded innocence with guilt; and cast the blame on me, though I could not foresee, much less prevent, the mischief— But say, what followed, when thou recognized the Prince? I hope thy looks betrayed the contempt he deserved.

Emil. I had not the courage a second time to look: I fled—

Claud. And he followed?

Emil. I marked it not till, at the church portico, I felt my hand was seized—by *him*. The impropriety of drawing the attention of the people was the only reflection I was capable of making: he spoke and I answered him; but what he said, or I replied, has utterly escaped me. I know not how I disengaged myself from the Prince; I can only remember finding myself in the street, hearing him behind, and thinking I was followed into the house.

Claud. Fear, child, has neither sense nor sight. I never shall forget the alarm in which thou camest rushing in. No; he dared not so far urge the insult. Oh God, if thy father knew it! He was in wrath when I told him the Prince admired thee! Calm thyself, my Emily; think what has passed a dream

—th' impression will be less. This day will secure thee in future from impertinence.

Emil. But must not I, dear mother, tell the Count?

Claud. Not for the world! Why vex thyself and him for trifles? Nay, if he should not, for the moment, be disturbed, know, my child, that poison still is poison, though it work slowly: that which makes no impression on the lover is deeply felt by the *husband.* The lover may be flattered to dispute his conquest with a rival so high in rank; but when it is secured—Ah, child, he then too frequently assumes a different face! Preserve thee, Heaven, from the sad experience!

Emil. Your counsel, dear mother, will always be revered; but, should my Appiani learn the adventure from any but myself, would it not increase the uneasiness he might feel? To keep a secret from the Count would weigh upon my heart.

Claud. Romantic folly! Be silent! Let him not remark thou hast been disturbed.

Emil. I yield, dear mother, to your better judgment. Ah! (*with a deep sigh*) how light I feel! I am again myself! What a foolish, timid creature I am! Might I not have acted differently without wounding the laws of decorum?

Claud. I am glad my Emily's good sense suggests the remarks I was loath to make. I knew, thy terror past, thou would'st perceive its folly. The Prince is a courtier; thou art unaccustomed to the sentimental cant of gallantry, where nothing seems to imply too much; and all, in fact, means nothing. A compliment thou hast construed a wish; a wish a declaration: thus, my child, thy ignorant simplicity made thee mistake the Prince's meaning.

Emil. Oh, my mother! I blush to think how simply I behaved! No; I will not tease my good Appiani with my silly terrors: he might think me vain. Ha! I hear his step.

SCENE VII.—*Enter* Count Appiani. *He does not perceive* Emilia *till she accosts him.*

App. Ah, dearest Emily! I thought not to find you here!

Emil. I hope, my lord, you will be cheerful even when I am absent. Why so serious? Is not this day worth a smile?

App. 'Tis worth my life! Th' excess of happiness perhaps makes me serious. (*seeing* Claudia) Ah, dear Madam, *you* here too! I long to call you by a name more tender.

Claud. It will be my pride! How fortunate thou art, my Emily! Ah! why would not thy father share the pleasure of this meeting?

App. I have torn myself, this moment, from his arms; or rather he from mine! Oh, what a man, my Emily, your father is! In him you recognize each lofty virtue. How my heart expands, in his presence! Never is my soul so fortified in good

and resolute to steer a noble course! Without such thoughts,
indeed, I were not worthy such a father, nor to be the husband of his Emily.

Emil. Ah, why would he not wait till I returned?

App. Because for so short a visit his emotions might have
been too strong.

Claud. He thought to find thee making preparation for the
approaching happy ceremony, and heard——

App. What raised my tenderest admiration, my excellent
Emilia! I shall then have a wife, who, with simplicity, ful-
fils a sacred duty, nor makes of piety a pompous farce.

Claud. Time is precious, children. Go, Emily, to your
toilet.

App. Why, honored Madam?

Claud. You would not lead her, thus attired, to the altar?

App. Who can look at Emilia, and think of dress? Why
change her apparel?

Emil. No, my dear lord! Some trifling alteration is necessary, but simplicity shall be preserved. One moment's patience, and I am ready: the only ornament I mean to wear
shall be the last you presented me: were it not *your* gift I
should almost dislike it, for I thrice have dreamed——

Claud. Dreamed? What, my child?

Emil. That on my head the diamonds changed to pearls——
Pearls, dearest mother, are the emblem of tears!

Claud. Child, thy interpretation is wilder than the dream.
Pearls are thy favorite ornament.

Emil. True, dear mother, true!

App. (*thoughtful and melancholy*) " Pearls are the emblem
of tears."

Emil. How! Are you, my lord, affected at a dream?

App. I am ashamed to own it: but when the imagination
takes a gloomy tint all objects catch the hue.

Emil. And why should you be sad? Do you recollect how
I was attired when first, my lord, I had the happiness to meet
you?

App. I see you ever thus: absent or present.

Emil. Such is my bridal dress: a robe the same, flowing
and easy.

App. Excellent!

Emil. My hair——

App. Waving in ringlets down thy neck.

Emil. I'll not forget the rose! A little patience and you
shall see me as you wish. [*Exit* Emilia.

SCENE VIII.

App. " Pearls are the emblem of tears!"—A little patience——yes, if time could be defied! If minutes were not
ages!

Claud. Emily's remark, my lord, was that of a child. Why thus moved? You are nearly arrived at the goal of your wishes: do you repent?

App. (*taking her hand*) My mother, can you harbour such a thought? Unusual sadness, it is true, preys upon my heart: the space between the cup and the lip, though little, often is unattainable. My thoughts, my feelings, nay my dreams, these two last days, confirm this truth. A gloomy chain of images pass through my mind—I know not what thus agitates and——

Claud. Count, you alarm me!

App. I am angry with my friends, myself——

Claud. Why?

App. They require I should acquaint the Prince ere I espouse your daughter; and I have weakly yielded to their entreaties. I must now perform this painful task, and seek his highness.

Claud. (*struck*) How! The Prince?

SCENE IX.

Enter PIRRO, *who is immediately followed by* MARINELLI.

Pirro. Madam, the Marquis Marinelli asks to speak with the Count.

App. With *me?*

Pirro. Here he is (*opens the door and retires.*)

Mar. Excuse the intrusion, Signora——My lord, I have sought you at your house, and learned that you were here. A matter of importance brings me hither. (*to* Claudia) Signora, may I trespass on your goodness? My business with the Count——

Claud. I'll leave you, gentlemen!——

[*Exit* Claudia *curtseying*

SCENE X.

App. Now, Marquis!

Mar. I come from the Prince.

App. What is his pleasure?

Mar. I am proud to be the bearer of news so good: and if Count Appiani will not wilfully misunderstand a friend devoted to his interest——

App. A truce, I beg, to compliments.

Mar. I have done. His highness means to send an embassy to settle his approaching nuptials with the Princess of *Massa:* he was long perplexed on whom to fix his choice; at last it fell upon you, Count.

App. On me?

Mar. Which choice, if friendship may boast of trifles, was at *my* instigation.

App. I am at a loss for thanks. I long had renounced the hope of being noticed by his highness.

Mar. I knew, my Lord, he only waited a proper occasion to prove the high esteem in which he holds you. If Count Appiani be not worthy of such honor, my friendship deceives me.

App. Friendship! The word has thrice escaped your lips. With whom am I conversing? I never dreamed of *friendship* from the Marquis Marinelli!

Mar. I served you, Count, nor waited your permission: the fault, I own, was great, unpardonable! But the honors which await you are equally glorious; I doubt not you will eagerly embrace them.

App. (*after reflecting*) I will.

Mar. Then follow me.

App. Where?

Mar. To the Prince who is at *Dosalo.* All is prepared; you must depart this day.

App. This day?

Mar. This hour, perhaps; the business is important.

App. Indeed! I am sorry then I must decline the intended honor.

Mar. How?

App. I cannot go now, to-morrow, nor the next day.

Mar. You jest, my Lord!

App. With *you?*

Mar. Ha! Very pleasant! Then the jest regards the Prince?——Better still!——You cannot go?

App. I hope his highness will find my reason for declining his favor good.

Mar. I would fain hear it.

App. Oh, a trifle! In a few hours I'm to be married.

Mar. Indeed! What then?

App. What then? The question is mockery!

Mar. Your marriage will not be the first that has been deferred: not, I believe, agreeably to the wish of the bride and bridegroom; but, when the master commands, Count, methinks——

App. The *master!* Those who volunteer their services are not *slaves.* *You* owe the Prince boundless submission; but I do not: I came uncalled for to his court; I sought to honorably serve him, not to be his slave. I am only dependent on a higher power.

Mar. High or not, a master is a master.

App. I'll not discuss the question: inform the Prince it grieves me to decline his favors, but I am this day to lead a lovely bride to the altar.

Mar. May I presume to ask her name?

App. Emilia Galotti.

Mar. The daughter of Galotti?

App. The same.

Mar. Humph!

App. What say you, Signor?

Mar. If *she* is the bride, you may with little difficulty defer the ceremony till your return.

App. *Defer the ceremony?*

Mar. The good folks will not be over nice.

App. *Good folks?*

Mar. Emilia will still be yours.

App. *Still be mine!* Impertinent ape!

Mar. Count, *that* to me?

App. Why not?

Mar. Heaven and hell! You shall repent this language!

App. Pshaw! Apes I know are malicious, but——

Mar. Death and damnation! You must give me satisfaction.

App. That is understood.

Mar. I would immediately call you to account, only I would not disturb the joys of so *tender* a lover, on such a day.

App. Kind considerate soul! (*his hand to his sword*) I cannot, it is true, go to *Massa*, but I have leisure to take a walk with you. Come, Sir! Come!

Mar. A little patience, Count.   [*Exit suddenly.*

SCENE XI —Appiani, Claudia, Galotti.

App. Worthless wretch! Ha! This has brought me to myself! I am a different man! My pulse beats high: my blood again circulates.

Claud. (*anxiously*) Heavens, Count! I heard your voices loud, and angry! Your cheek glows: what is the matter?

App. Nothing, honored Madam: the chamberlain has done me service; he spares me the trouble of seeing the Prince.

Claud. Indeed?

App. We now may set off the earlier; I'll give the necessary orders to my people, and be with you in a moment.

Claud. May I be easy, Count?

App. Perfectly so, dear Madam.
                    [*Exit through different doors.*

ACT III.

SCENE I.—*A Hall in the Country House of the* Prince.

The Prince, Marinelli.

Marinelli.

IT was all in vain; the Count with scorn refused the proffered honor.

Prince. Emilia will then be his.

Mar. Such are the probabilities.

Prince. My hopes were raised so high! You must have failed in skill: thus it is, when fools by chance conceive a happy plan, if the execution be not given to a man of sense.

Mar. So! This is my reward!

Prince. Reward for what?

Mar. For having hazarded my life in your service. When I found that neither raillery nor reason would induce the Count to sacrifice his love to honor, I drove him to extremities, which made him forget himself. He broke into invective, and I demanded immediate satisfaction. My reflection was that one of us must die. If Appiani fall, the day will be our own; if I am killed, he will be forced to fly, and time will thus be gained.

Prince. How! Did you that, Marinelli?

Mar. I ought to have known the gratitude of princes.

Prince. What said the Count? According to report, he is not a man to whom a challenge need be repeated?

Mar. No doubt, in ordinary cases—Who could blame him? He replied, he had something more important on his hands, this day, than to fight, and postponed the duel till a week after his nuptials.

Prince. With Emilia Galotti! Oh, the thought is frenzy! These are your boasted efforts, your mighty sacrifice!

Mar. What could I more, my Prince?

Prince. More! Say, what have you done?

Mar. Tell me, Prince, what was the result of your conference in the cathedral this morning?

Prince. (*ironically*) How kind is this curiosity! Forsooth, I must satisfy you—All passed to my heart's content. Concern yourself no more, my *serviceable* friend: she half-way met my wishes; nay, I might have taken her with me. (*cold and commanding*) Now, Sir, you know all: leave me!

Mar. Ay, ay! This is the burden of the song, and would have been had I attempted impossibilities. Impossibilities, said I! Not so; but a bold step: Emilia once in our power, I'll answer for it the nuptials take not place.

Prince. This man would talk one into the paradise of fools. I have but to give him a detachment of my guards, he will attack a single carriage, and triumphantly seize on a *woman!*

Mar. Prince, women have been carried off without the appearance of violence.

Prince. If you knew that, you should have acted; not have trifled away the time in idle boastings.

Mar. But one ought not to be made responsible, Prince, for unforeseen accidents, through which the plan might fail.

Prince. Is it my practice, Marquis, to blame people for evils they cannot foresee?

Mar. Then, Prince—(*the report of a pistol is heard*) Ah!

what was that? Heard I rightly? Was it not the report of a pistol, my Prince?

Prince. Explain!

Mar. What would you say, my Prince, if I had been more active than you think?

Prince. More active? To the point!

Mar. Suppose all I promised were fulfilled.

Prince. Is it possible?

Mar. Do not, Prince, forget I had your consent.

Prince. But the execution——

Mar. Is intrusted to persons on whom I can depend. The park lies close to the road-side; the carriage, as it passes, will be attacked by feigned banditti; my people, from the park, run to the assistance of the attacked : one of them, in the confusion of the affray, will seize the bride, as if to save her, and conduct her hither. Such, Prince, is my plan : what say you now?

Prince. That I am greatly surprised : I fear too, Marquis—— (Marinelli *goes to the window*) For what are you looking?

Mar. It must be over! Right! A mask springs through the outward gate; no doubt he brings me intelligence : retire, my Prince.

Prince. Ah, Marinelli!

Mar. Before I did *too little;* now I have done *too much :* is it not so?

Prince. No; but I see not whither all this tends.

Mar. Tends?—To make you happy. Quick, Prince, retire : you must not be seen.   [*Exit* Prince.

SCENE II.—Marinelli; *soon after* Angelo.

Mar. (*again going to the window*) The carriage slowly returns to town : so slow? A servant at each portico? I fear the project has but half succeeded; that the Count is only wounded! The mask enters the house : 'tis he, 'tis Angelo : fool-hardy villain! But he knows the windings of this place : he nods to me; he must be certain of his man. Ha, Count, you would not go to Massa; you must take a longer journey— Who taught you so well to know the nature of apes? Yes, they are malicious!—Now, Angelo?

Ang. (*taking off his mask*) Prepare, Signor Marquis, she will instantly be here.

Mar. The plot has succeeded?

Ang. It has.

Mar. And the Count?

Ang. So, so! But he must have had his suspicions, for he was on his guard.

Mar. Quick to the point : is he dead?

Ang. Poor gentleman!

Mar. Here! Let this ease thy *compassionate* heart. (*gives him a purse.*)

Ang. My poor Nicolo! His death bought victory dear.

Mar. What was the loss on both sides?

Ang. I could have wept over the brave youth, though I gain by his death, for I am his heir: 'twas I revenged him: such is our law; as good a one as faith and friendship could impose. Signor, this Nicolo——

Mar. No more of him. The Count, the Count——

Ang. Furies! He aimed justly at Nicolo's heart; but my aim, in return, was no less sure. He fell, and if he still breathed when they replaced him in the carriage, I'll answer for it he'll not come out alive.

Mar. If that is certain, Angelo!——

Ang. Withdraw your practice if I am a false prophet. Have you further commands, Signor Marquis? Time is precious; we must this day cross the frontiers.

Mar. Then be gone.

Ang. Should you want me again, Signor Marquis, you know where to inquire: I am secret, skilful, and more reasonable than my comrades.   [*Exit.*

Mar. Good! Good! Yet no: it might have been better—. Fie, Angelo! You are a bungler! A second shot at once had done the business. The Count, poor man, perhaps may linger. Fie, Angelo! That is exercising your trade with cruelty; like a blockhead. The Prince must not learn Appiani's death till he perceives the advantage he may derive from it. Oh, that I were but sure he is dead!

SCENE III.—*The* PRINCE, MARINELLI.

Prince. She is hastening down the alley with the domestic: terror has lent her wings: she must not yet suspect the truth; she thinks she has escaped from thieves: but how long will she continue in this belief?

Mar. At least we have her here.

Prince. Will not her mother and the Count seek her? Can I refuse them admission?

Mar. I cannot at this moment answer you; but we shall see: have patience, my Prince; the first step is already taken.

Prince. To what effect, if I must part with her?

Mar. Perhaps—a thousand things may turn to our advantage, Prince, and you forget the principal.

Prince. The principal? What is it you mean?

Mar. That seductive and winning eloquence which can never fail to serve the enamoured Prince.

Prince. Except when most he needs it; as I this day have cruelly experienced. In vain I tried the force of flattery and elo-

quence of love: I could not obtain a single word. Trembling
and mute she stood; her eyes cast down, as 'twere a culprit
before the awful judge. Her fears were catching. I trembled, and stammered an apology. I scarce dare trust myself to
speak with her again; at least I cannot yet meet her eye.
You must receive her, Marinelli. I'll wait in the adjoining
room till I am more calm.   [*Exit* Prince.

SCENE IV.

MARINELLI: *soon after* BATTISTA *his Servant, leading in* EMILIA.

Mar. . She could not see him fall; she fled too quick. Ah,
here she comes!/ I too had better retire a moment. (*retires to
the back ground.*)
Batt. This way, young lady.
Emil. (*out of breath*) Ah! Ah! Thank you, friend!
Thank you! But Heavens! Where am I? Quite alone? Where
is my mother? The Count? Are they behind?
Batt. Most probably.
Emil. Are you not sure? Have you not seen them? Did
not the ruffians fire?
Batt. Perhaps they did.
Emil. Oh, there is no doubt! The Count, perhaps, or my
mother, may have been wounded.
Batt. I'll go immediately and seek them.
Emil. Not without me: I will, I must go with you. Come,
friend!
Mar. (*stepping forward*) Ah! What misfortune, or rather
what lucky accident, young lady, has procured us this honor?
Emil. (*surprised*) You here, Signor? Is this your house?
Excuse me, Signor Chamberlain, we have been attacked by
banditti: people came to our assistance, and this worthy man
took me from the carriage and brought me here: but I shudder to find myself only in safety; my mother perhaps is yet
in danger! The robbers fired as I escaped! She may be dead,
and do I live?—Excuse me; I must fly to seek the friends I
ought not to have left.
Mar. Be calm, dear young lady! All is well: the friends
for whom you feel such tender anxiety will soon be here. Battista, fly and seek them; perhaps they are in search of the
young lady: bring them here.   [*Exit* Battista.
Emil. Indeed! Are they all safe? Have they escaped un-
hurt? Ah, this day has been to me a day of terror! But I
should not wait their arrival; I'll seek them.
Mar. Why, Signorina? You are breathless and exhausted:
rather compose yourself, and suffer me to show you to a less
public apartment. The Prince, no doubt, is gone to meet
your respected mother, and will bring her to you.
Emil. Who, said you?

Mar. Our gracious Prince.

Emil. (*struck*) The Prince!

Mar. On the first intelligence of your disaster, he flew to your assistance: he is furious that such daring outrage should be committed, as it were, at his threshold: he has ordered the offenders to be pursued; and, if they are caught, their punishment will be exemplary.

Emil. The Prince? Where am I then?

Mar. At *Dosalo;* his country seat.

Emil. Heavens! And you think he'll soon be here?

Mar. He comes.

SCENE V.—*Enter the* PRINCE.

Prince. Where is she? Where? We have been seeking you, Signorina, in vain. You are not ill? Then all is well! The Count, your mother——

Emil. Ah, Prince, where are they? Where is my mother?

Prince. Not far off.

Emil. Oh, God, in what a state shall I find one or both! I see, your highness knows more than you will say.

Prince. Not so, dear young lady; deign to accept my arm and be consoled. (*offering to lead her away.*)

Emil. (*irresolute*) But, if my fears deceive me, why are they not with your highness?

Prince. Come, Signorina, and divert the gloomy images which prey upon your mind.

Emil. What shall I do? (*wringing her hands.*)

Prince. How, Signorina, can you suspect me?

Emil. (*falling at his feet*) At your feet, Prince——

Prince. (*raising her*) I am cruelly abashed! Yes, Emilia, I deserve this mute reproach: my conduct cannot be justified, but love is my excuse. Forgive my weakness; I ought not to have troubled you with a confession which was unavailing. Your speechless terror sufficiently punished me: this accident, which once more procures me the happiness of speaking to you ere my hopes receive a mortal stab, perhaps forebodes me good, since I again may implore your pity—Nay tremble not, sweet Emily—my fate is in your hands. No word or look shall give your purity alarm: but wound me not by unjust suspicions. Doubt not a moment of your power! You need no other advocate, Emilia, than yourself! Come and receive that homage which you perhaps will learn to justly estimate. (*forcing her away*) Follow us, Marinelli!

[*Exeunt the* Prince *and* Emilia.

Mar. Follow us! Humph! That means stay where you are! Why should I follow? He may try how far he can proceed in this *tête-à-tête.* My business is to see they are not interrupted: the Count is safe enough, but the mother may break

upon them : I am much deceived if she quietly return to town
and leave her daughter in our power : Battista ! How now ?

SCENE VI.—*Enter* BATTISTA.

Batt. (*hastily*) The mother, Signor Chamberlain.
Mar. Ha! As I thought ! Where is she?
Batt. If you do not prevent her she will instantly be here.
I did not, as you may suppose, hasten to seek her, but I heard
her cries at a distance. She flies in search of her daughter,
followed by the few inhabitants this solitary place affords, who
willingly conduct her through the park. I know not whether
she has learned the Prince is here : what must be done ?
Mar. Let me consider ! (*musing*) To refuse her admittance
when she knows that Emilia is here would be impolitic. 'Tis
true she will not look pleased when she finds her daughter in
the wolf's grasp : no matter for her looks, but Heaven spare our
ears. What then ? The strongest lungs may be exhausted ;
even a woman's : and, if I judge the sex fairly, most of them
would covet the title of *step-mother* to a Prince.
Batt. I hear her, Signor !
Claud. (*within*) Emilia ! My child ! Where art thou ?
Mar. Go, Battista ; and dismiss the inquisitive persons who
conducted her.

SCENE VII.

Enter CLAUDIA, GALOTTI ; *meeting* BATTISTA *at the Door.*

Claud. Ha ! The very man who helped her out of the carriage, and led her away. Wretch, I know thee ! Where is my
daughter ?
Batt. Are these my thanks ?
Claud. Oh, if you deserve my gratitude, (*in a milder tone*)
forgive me, worthy man ! Where is she ? Oh, keep me not on
the rack ! Where is she ?
Batt. She could not, Signora, be better in paradise. Here
is my master, who will conduct you to her. (*to people who press
forward*) Back, good people.

SCENE VIII.—*Enter* MARINELLI.

Claud. Your master ? (*sees* Marinelli *and* starts) Is that
your master ?—*You* here, Signor ? and my daughter ? *You*
conduct me to her.
Mar. Most willingly, Madonna.
Claud. Hold !—Are you not the gentleman who visited
the Count at my house, this morning ? and with whom he had
high words ?
Mar. High words ? That was more than I knew : a trifling
difference of opinion——

Claud. Is not your name Marinelli?

Mar. The Marquis Marinelli.

Claud. Good! Hark you, Signor Marquis, the name of Marinelli followed by a curse—No, do not let me calumniate the noble deceased; the curse is in my thoughts! *Marinelli* was the last word of the dying Count.

Mar. Of the dying Count? Count Appiani? Your discourse, Signora, is no less enigmatical than singular: of the dying Count? I do not understand you.

Claud. (*slow and bitter*) Marinelli was the last word of the dying Count! Do you understand me *now?* I, like you, at the moment did not understand, though it was said in a tone, a tone! I hear it still! What must have been my agitation not to have immediately understood!

Mar. Well, Madonna? I was the Count's friend, his intimate friend; and if he named me in his dying moments——

Claud. Oh, in a tone! I cannot imitate, I cannot describe it; but such a tone implies all. How? attacked by banditti? No: they were assassins! Hired assassins!—And Marinelli was the last word of the dying Count: pronounced in a tone!

Mar. In a tone!—Is the voice of agony in a moment of terror sufficient to implicate an honorable man?

Claud. Oh, could I but imitate that voice before the tribunal of justice!—Yet wretched me! I forget my daughter. Where is she? How? Dead?—Was it her fault that Appiani was your enemy?

Mar. I pardon the injustice of an afflicted mother. Come, Madonna, your daughter is here, in yonder chamber; her terrors are no doubt appeased: the Prince himself is soothing her with the tenderest pity.

Claud. Who?—Who, said you?

Mar. The Prince.

Claud. The Prince! *Our* Prince.

Mar. Who else?

Claud. Oh, wretched Claudia! My daughter—and her tender father! He will curse the hour of her birth, curse her unfortunate mother!

Mar. For Heaven's sake, Madonna, wherefore these terrors?

Claud. Oh, it is too evident! This morning, in the sanctuary of heaven, at the shrine of holiness, in the presence, as it were, of the Eternal, the villainy began; the horrid project was conceived! (*to* Marinelli) Ha! Murderer! Base murderer! Too cowardly to stab with thy own hand, but wicked enough to be the vile accomplice of another's crime, the infamous caterer to his passions; thou art the vilest of assassins, the scorn of the vicious. Thou! Thou! Oh that I could annihilate thee with a look!

Mar. My good lady, you know not what you say; moderate your violence, and recollect where you are.

Claud. Where I am? Recollect? Does the lioness, robbed of her young, roar less fearfully in the royal forest?

Emil. (*within*) Ah, my mother! I hear my mother!

Claud. It is her voice! 'Tis my Emily! She hears me; and shall I be silent? Where art thou, my child: I come! I come! (*she rushes into the chamber:* Marinelli *follows her.*)

ACT IV.

The Scene continues.

SCENE I.—*The* PRINCE *meeting* MARINELLI.

Prince.

MARINELLI, I must be collected, and obtain some light on this affair.

Mar. Oh brave maternal rage! Ha, ha, ha!

Prince. Can you laugh?

Mar. Had your highness witnessed her fury, which vented itself in loud cries, then how instantaneously your presence calmed her violence! Ha, ha, ha! I well knew that no mother would treat a prince contemptuously, because he finds her daughter handsome.

Prince. You are a light observer, Marinelli. Emilia fell senseless in her mother's arms, and the good lady forgot her rage in her affection: it was to spare her daughter, not the *Prince,* that she only hinted at what she otherwise had proclaimed aloud; and which I shudder to have heard and understood.

Mar. What means your highness?

Prince. Why dissemble? Speak out! Is it true or not?

Mar. Suppose it were!

Prince. Suppose? Then it is. He is dead? Dead! (*threatening*) Marinelli! Marinelli!

Mar. Well?

Prince. By the Almighty God I am innocent of his blood! Had you informed me it would have cost Appiani his life, I would not have consented, though my own had fallen the sacrifice.

Mar. Informed? As if I had calculated on the Count's death! I charged Angelo to let no person be hurt. There would have been no blood shed, had not the Count first offered violence: he shot one of the men through the heart.

Prince. Indeed! (*sarcastically*) He should have quietly suffered the joke !

Mar. That Angelo should be provoked to revenge the death of his companion——

Prince. (*in the same tone*) Oh, very natural !

Mar. I have reproved him.

Prince. Reproved ? How friendly !—Warn him to quit my territories, *my* reproofs might not be so gentle.

Mar. Just as I foresaw ! I and Angelo are one : a concerted plan and chance the same. Your highness promised I should not be blamed for any unforeseen accident which might happen.

Prince. Might happen, say you ? or *must ?*

Mar. Better and better ! Yet, Prince, permit one observation before you plainly tell me I am a villain. The Count's death is *nothing less* than indifferent to me. I challenged him : he owed me satisfaction; he is now dead, and my honor is wounded. Granting your suspicions, under other circumstances, might have been just: does not this clear me from such an imputation? (*with increasing heat*) Is it possible your highness can so wrong me !

Prince. (*yielding*) Well, well——

Mar. Oh that he still lived ! I would give all I possess; (*bitterly*) nay, the favor of my Prince ; that inestimable jewel, so difficult to retain !

Prince. I understand ! Well, so be it. His death was accident, *mere accident !* You assure me so, and I'll take your word. But will Emilia, her mother, or the world, be so complaisant ?

Mar. (*coldly*) Scarcely.

Prince. Then what will they think ? Your shrug is significant—That Angelo is a hired ruffian, and I am an assassin !

Mar. (*still more coldly*) Nothing more likely.

Prince. I ! Your Prince !—Or I must from this moment resign all thoughts of Emilia.

Mar. (*totally indifferent*) As you must have done had the Count lived.

Prince. (*at first violent, but immediately recovering his temper*) Marinelli !—But no ; you will not drive me to extremities. I will speak in your own language. The Count's death is a for-, tunate event ; the only one that could bring my love to a happy issue ; and, as such, we will not inquire how it happened. What is a Count more or less in the world ? Shall not we reason thus ? Agreed ! When it is my interest to wink at a crime of little moment, I am not more scrupulous than others ; but the crime must be secret, and the advantage great : in our case it is neither secret nor advantageous. A career is opened it is true, but we are stopped at the first step. The Count's death will be imputed to us: was that in your *wise* calculations, of which you promised wonders ?

Mar. If your highness will permit me——

Prince. Well? What can you urge in their defence? Explain yourself.

Mar. I am accused of blunders which are not mine.

Prince. Be explicit, I command you.

Mar. I shall, Prince. What error in my calculations has given rise to these injurious suspicions? None; the fault lies in the master stroke which your highness so graciously put to my plans.

Prince. I?

Mar. Allow me to remark the step your highness took this morning in the cathedral, no matter for its grace, or propriety, was not in the figure of the ballet *.

Prince. What has it discomposed?

Mar. Not the time, but the measure of the dance.

Prince. Humph! Do I understand you?

Mar. To speak more intelligibly : was not Emilia unacquainted with the passion of your highness when I undertook the affair! Was not her mother equally ignorant? If I built upon these circumstances, and the Prince undermined the foundation I had laid——

Prince. (*striking his forehead*) Fool! fool!

Mar. If he betrayed himself?

Prince. Cursed interference!

Mar. Had he been silent, how could my plans have excited the slightest suspicion against him, in the mother or daughter?

Prince. Why must you be in the right?

Mar. Truly I am to blame! Forgive me, Prince.

SCENE II.—*Enter* BATTISTA *in haste.*

Batt. The Countess, your highness.

Prince. The Countess? What Countess?

Batt. Orsina.

Prince. Orsina?—Marinelli—Orsina?—Marinelli?

Mar. I am no less surprised than your highness.

Prince. Run, Battista, she must not alight. I am not here. I will not see her. Let her instantly return. Go! Run! (*Exit* Battista) Silly woman! What can she want? How came she to know we were here? Has she heard any thing? Does she come a spy upon my actions? Ah, Marinelli, speak! Advise me! Will the man who called himself my friend resent? Will he abandon me for a trifling altercation? Must I ask his pardon?

Mar. Ah, my Prince, you are again yourself, and my life is at your devotion. Orsina's arrival is no less perplexing to me than to your highness. She will not, I fear, be denied. What can be done?

Prince. I will not see her : I'll retire.

---

* It is Lessing who puns.

Mar. Then lose not a moment. I will receive the Countess.

Prince. Only to dismiss her; waste no time in idle conference, we have more important affairs on hand.

Mar. All is arranged, my Prince. Take courage: the day will yet be ours—But I hear her coming. Retire, Prince, into that cabinet: (*exit* Prince *into the cabinet*) I fear the Countess will give us some trouble.

SCENE III.—*Enter the Countess* ORSINA.

Countess. (*not perceiving* Marinelli) What can this mean? Nobody to receive me but an insolent valet, who would scarcely suffer me to alight? Am I at *Dosalo?* That *Dosalo* where all were eager to pay me homage? Where love and rapture flew to welcome me? These walls are the same, but—— Ah, Marinelli! I am glad the Prince has brought you: yet no, the affairs that bring me hither require I should have private conference with his highness. Where is he?

Mar. The Prince, fair Countess?

Countess. Who else?

Mar. You then expected to find him here? *Your* visit at least is unexpected.

Countess. How so? Did he not receive my letter this morning?

Mar. Your letter? Oh, yes; I recollect he mentioned it.

Countess. Well? Did I not request an interview here today? It is true he sent no answer, but I learned he actually set off for *Dosalo* an hour afterward; *that* I thought was sufficient, and I came.

Mar. A singular coincidence!

Countess. Coincidence? Do not I tell you it was an appointment? How you look, Signor Marquis! What is there to perplex your mighty sagacity? Where is the wonder?

Mar. Yesterday you were resolved never to see his highness more.

Countess. The night is a good counsellor. Where is he? In the chamber from which sighs and complaints issued as I passed? I would have entered, but the impertinent valet prevented me.

Mar. My dear Countess——

Countess. The voice was female: what does this mean? Oh, tell me! If I am your *dear* Countess, tell me! Curses on these court sycophants! Every word is a falsehood. But what matters it whether you tell me or not? I will see myself. (*going.*)

Mar. (*stopping her*) Whither go you in such haste?

Countess. Where I should have been long ago. Think you it becomes me to hold a paltry altercation with you in the antichamber, when the Prince is expecting me in his apartment?

Mar. You are mistaken, fair Countess: the Prince expects you not: his highness cannot, will not see you.

Countess. Yet he is here? Here in consequence of my letter.

Mar. You are mistaken.

Countess. You said it had been received ?

Mar. Received : but not read.

Countess. (*with violence*) Not read? (*less violent*) Not **read !** (*mournfully, the tears in her eyes*) Not once read ?

Mar. Owing doubtless to forgetfulness, not *contempt.*

Countess. (*proudly*) Contempt? Is that a thought for me! Why speak the degrading word ? Marinelli, your consolation is impertinent. Contempt! Contempt and Orsina! (*she gradually softens her tone till it is that of melancholy*) He no longer loves me : cruel certainty ; and another sentiment must replace that of love ; such is the law of nature : but why contempt? Is it not indifference ? Is it not, Marinelli ?

Mar. Certainly ! Certainly !

Countess. (*ironically*) Certainly ? Oh the wise oracle that says what it is bid ! Indifference! Indifference replace love ? That is replacing something with nothing : for learn, thou court echo, from a woman, that indifference is a mere sound, an empty name which means nothing. The soul can only be indifferent to what does not occupy it, to that which has no existence : and to be indifferent to things which do not exist is to annihilate nonentity. Is that reasoning beyond thee, man ?

Mar. (*to himself*) Oh how prophetic were my fears!

Countess. What is it you mutter ?

Mar. Pure admiration! Who is ignorant, charming Countess, that you are a philospher.

Countess. Indeed? Yes, yes, I am. But have I now betrayed myself, or has the secret before escaped me ? Shame on my folly! Is it strange the Prince should despise me ? How can a man love a thing who dares, in his defiance, have ideas ? To think as little becomes woman as a painted face does man. The pretty puppets should only laugh to keep the lord of the creation in good humor. Shall I not laugh, Marinelli ? Ah, at what ? The pleasant accident of which we were speaking. I wrote to appoint a meeting with the Prince at *Dosalo,* and he came hither without having read my letter. Ha, ha, ha! A singular occurrence! Very pleasant and natural! Why do not you laugh, Marinelli ? The dread lord of the creation may *laugh* with us, though we, poor creatures, dare not *think* with him. (*serious and commanding*) Laugh, I say !

Mar. Instantly, charming Countess ! Instantly.

Countess. . Automaton ! The moment is passed. No, no, do not laugh : for look you, Marinelli, (*musing : then with emotion*) that which excites my laughter, has its serious side like every human occurrence. Chance ? Is it by chance that the Prince, contrary to his intentions, will see me here ? By chance ? Believe me, Marinelli, the word is blasphemy. Nothing under the sun is owing to chance ; and *that* least of all which is clearly design. Almighty, all merciful Providence, forgive me that I have joined this foolish sinner in calling *that* accident which is evidently thy immediate work. (*hastily to* Marinelli) Dare again lead me into such a crime!

Mar. (*to himself*) This proceeds too far. (*aloud*) But Countess—

Countess. Silence to your *buts,* they demand reflection, and my head! My head! (*holding her hand to her forehead*) Marinelli, conduct me quickly to the Prince, or I shall be unfit to see him. We must have a conference.

SCENE IV.—*Enter the* PRINCE *from the Cabinet.*

Prince. (*as he enters*) I must come to his aid.

Countess. (*perceiving the* Prince *yet irresolute whether or no to accost him*) Ha! There he is!

Prince. (*speaking as he crosses the saloon without stopping, and passes the* Countess) Bless me! Our charming Countess! I am grieved, Signora, that I cannot avail myself of the hónor of your visit. I am engaged. I am not alone. Another time, my dear Countess! Another time! To-day you will return immediately. Immediately! Marinelli, I shall want you. [*Exit* Prince.

SCENE V.

Mar. Well, Countess, you have heard it from himself. Am I worthy of belief?

Countess. (*stupified*) Heard? From himself?

Mar. From himself?

Countess. (*with emotion*) " I am engaged——I am not alone." Is an excuse given to every importunate intruder the respect which is my due? Could he not gild the bitter pill?—" Engaged?" with whom?—" Not alone?" Who is with him? Marinelli, dear Marinelli, take pity on me; invent a falsehood to soothe my anguish; it will cost you so little! How is he engaged? Who is with him? Say any thing, no matter what, and I will be gone.

Mar. (*to himself*) On that condition I may tell you a part of the truth.

Countess. Well, speak, Marinelli. The Prince said " another time, my dear Countess," was it not so? That he may keep his word, that he may have no pretence again to disappoint me, quick, Marinelli, your excuse, and I will depart.

Mar. The Prince, Countess, is actually engaged : there are persons with him whom he can by no means quit! Persons who have escaped a great danger. Count Appiani——

Countess. Is with him? 'Tis a pity you are caught, at the first word, in a falsehood. Quick, another. Count Appiani, if you do not know it, has been shot by banditti. I met his carriage returning with the corpse. Is it true, or was it a dream?

Mar. Alas, it was no dream! But the persons with him, his bride, whom he was conducting to *Sabionetta,* and her mother, were fortunately saved and brought hither.

Countess. And these are the persons with whom the Prince is engaged? Is the bride handsome?

Mar. His highness is deeply concerned at her misfortune.

Countess. That I will hope he would be, even were she *plain.* Her fate is horrible! Poor child! Thou hast lost him for ever, at the moment he was to have been thy partner for life! Who is the bride? I have so long been absent from town, that I know nothing.

Mar. Emilia Galotti is the young lady.

Countess. Who? Emilia Galotti? Emilia Galotti? Marinelli! Beware lest I take this falsehood for truth!

Mar. Why so?

Countess. Emilia Galotti?

Mar. Of whom you scarcely can have any knowledge.

Countess. Yes, yes; though it were but of a day! Seriously, Marinelli, is it Emilia Galotti? Was *she* the unhappy bride whom the Prince consoles?

Mar. (aside) Have I said too much?

Countess. Was Count Appiani her bridegroom? The deceased Count?

Mar. The same.

Countess. Excellent! Excellent! Most excellent! *(clapping her hands.)*

Mar. What do you mean?

Countess. And I could embrace the fiend that has instigated him to the act.

Mar. Who? Instigated? To what?

Countess. Yes, embrace! though *Marinelli* were that fiend!

Mar. Countess!

Countess. Come hither! Look at me! Stedfastly.

Mar. Well?

Countess. Do you divine my thoughts?

Mar. How should I?

Countess. Are you not a party concerned?

Mar. In what?

Countess. Swear! No, do not swear; you will have another sin to answer for. Yet what is a crime the more to a soul already damned? Are you innocent?

Mar. You terrify me, Countess.

Countess. Indeed! Is your *pure* heart free from suspicion?

Mar. Of what?

Countess. Well, then, I will tell you a secret that will make you shudder. But you are too near the door; we might be overheard. Approach, and listen. *(laying her finger on her lips)* But remember it is a secret! *(approaching her mouth to his ear as if she would whisper, but speaking very loud)* The Prince is an assassin.

Mar. Countess! Countess! Are you frantic?

Countess. Frantic? Ha, ha, ha! (*laughing aloud*) Intellect was never more clear. The Prince, Marinelli—(*softly*) but the secret must go no further—the Prince is certainly an assassin. Appiani fell not by the hand of banditti, but was killed by hired ruffians.

Mar. How can a suspicion, so horrible, escape your lips, or enter your thoughts?

Countess. How? Very naturally. This Emilia Galotti, who is now with the Prince, whose bridegroom was so hastily thrust out of the world, was this morning accosted by his highness in the cathedral after mass: he had a long and interesting conversation with her. Of that I am certain; my courier, who saw them together, brought me the intelligence. Now, *most worthy* Marquis, am I frantic? Can I not discriminate? or will you tell me, *this* too is chance? If so, Sir, you as little understand the vices of men, as the wisdom of Providence.

Mar. Countess, you will bring disgrace on yourself——

Countess. If I speak the truth aloud? So be it! I will proclaim it in the public squares; and he who contradicts me is the assassin's accomplice. Farewell! (*going, is stopped by Galotti, who hastily passes her.*)

SCENE VI.—*Enter* GALOTTI.

Gal. Excuse me, lady——

Countess. I have nothing to excuse: for I have nothing *here* to take amiss. Address yourself to that gentleman. (*showing him* Marinelli.)

Mar. (*aside, looking at* Galotti) The father is come to complete our embarrassment.

Gal. Forgive an anxious father, Signor, for coming unannounced.

Countess. Father? (*again returning*) Emilia's no doubt! Ha! his arrival is fortunate.

Gal. A domestic came breathless to inform me that my family was attacked by banditti in this neighbourhood; I flew to their rescue, and heard that Count Appiani had been conveyed wounded to town, but that my wife and daughter had taken refuge here. Where are they, Signor, where are they?

Mar. Be calm, brave officer; your wife and daughter received no injury, save that of terror: they are both well; the Prince is with them. I will immediately announce you.

Gal. Why announce?

Mar. For reasons you cannot but approve. You know, Colonel, you are not on friendly terms with his highness. If he has kindly received your wife and daughter, it is in consideration of their sex. *Your* unexpected appearance might offend him.

Gal. You are right, Signor.

Mar. But first allow me the honor, fair Countess, of seeing you to your carriage.

Countess. I am in no hurry.

Mar. (*taking her hand*) Nay, it is my duty.

Countess. (*disengaging herself*) Softly so please you! I will excuse your attendance, Signor Marquis. Thus it is with courtiers! They make politeness an obligation that they may neglect essential duties. Go and announce this worthy gentleman; *that* is your province.

Mar. Do you forget the Prince's desire?

Countess. Let him come and repeat it. I fear him not!

Mar. (*aside to* Galotti, *whom he takes apart*) Signor, I must leave you with a lady who—who—whose intellects are—you understand me. I give you this caution that you may affix no importance to the frequent wildness of her discourse: you had better not accost her.

Gal. Very well. Pray announce me, Signor. [*Exit* Marinelli.

SCENE VII.—*The* COUNTESS *looking at* GALOTTI *with compassion; he slightly glances at her.*

Countess. (*after a pause*) So the Marquis whispered to you! Unfortunate man——

Gal. (*half aloud*) Unfortunate?

Countess. He spoke not truth; and least of all the truths which await your ear.

Gal. Await? Know I not enough? Lady!—But speak, speak!

Countess. You know nothing.

Gal. Nothing?

Countess. Tender and excellent father! Oh, that you were mine! Forgive me! The unfortunate should be one family! Your rage should be mine, and no less would I share your affliction.

Gal. Rage? Affliction? Lady! But I forget. Continue.

Countess. If it were your only daughter, your only child! Nay, were she not—The child whom calamity overtakes is ever the dearest.

Gal. Calamity? Madam! Why do I question her? Yet, by Heaven, this is not the language of insanity.

Countess. Insanity? Was *that* the secret he had to impart? Well well; it was not perhaps the worst of his impostures. I feel he might in that be right, and believe me, Signor, he whose understanding can unshaken support *certain things*, has none to lose.

Gal. What am I to think?

Countess. That I merit your esteem! You, worthy man, have understanding; it is written on your respectable and determined brow. Yet if I say but a word it is lost.

Gal. Madam! Madam! Speak to the point at once, or I
shall have none to lose. Keep me not on the rack, or I will not
allow you are of that class of the deranged who deserve our
pity and esteem. Speak, or I shall cease to respect you.

Countess. Then listen. You have been informed that Appiani is wounded : only wounded ? The Count is dead !

Gal. Dead ? Dead ? Ah, Madam—This is too much ! You
threatened to rob me of my understanding, and you break my
heart.

Countess. This is not all. The bridegroom is dead ; and the
bride, your daughter, worse than dead !

Gal. Worse than dead ? Oh say she is dead ! for I know
but *one* thing worse than death.

Countess. No, good father, not dead ! She lives, she lives !
She now breathes a new existence : pleasures, rapture, and adoration, while they last, will make life one scene of varied delights.

Gal. Madam, speak at once the fatal word ! Make me
frantic : distil not your poison drop by drop into my soul :
speak !

Countess. This morning the Prince addressed your daughter
in the cathedral : this afternoon she is at his country seat.
Combine the facts.

Gal. The Prince addressed my daughter ?

Countess. With ardor and familiarity ! They had not a
little to say. If he gained her consent, if no violence was used,
it is fortunate : in that case no rape has been committed—only
a trifling assassination.

Gal. Calumny, atrocious calumny ! I know my daughter :
if murder has been committed, violence must have been used.
(*looks wildly round and stamps*) Now, Claudia ! Now, fond
mother ! Are we not much indebted to his princely courtesy ?
Gracious Prince ! Enviable distinctions !

Countess. Does it work, good father, does it work ?

Gal. I am in the tiger's den. (*shaking his cloak, and finding
himself without any weapon*) No steel ! (*searching his pockets*)
Nothing ! Nothing ! Still I have hands !

Countess. Ha! I understand! I can relieve your difficulties.
(*drawing out a dagger*) Take it quick ere we are surprised. I
have another resource left: poison ! But that is a woman's
weapon. (*presenting the dagger*) Take it ! Take it !

Gal. Thanks! Thanks! Dear lady, this arm shall chastise
whoever dares impeach your understanding.

Countess. Lose no time ! Hide the dagger. The opportunity of using it is denied me : *you* will be more fortunate, and
seize the first occasion that offers ; for *you* are a man. I am
but a woman, yet my resolution was fixed. Our confidence
may be mutual, for we are both injured, both insulted, by the

same bland monster. Oh, if you knew the cruel, the unspeak-ble, wrongs he has inflicted, nay still inflicts on me, you would orget your own. Do you know me? I am Orsina, the de-eived, abandoned Orsina. Abandoned, it is true, perhaps, to make way for your daughter: but is it her fault? She will soon be succeeded by another and another. Ha! (*in rhapsody*) What a heavenly idea! If we all (*we* the innumerable victims whom he has abandoned) could be changed into Bacchantes, into Furies, if we could fall upon the seducer and tear him piece-meal, till we had found that heart which the traitor promised to all but gave to none, how delicious were the banquet of revenge!

SCENE VIII.—*Enter* CLAUDIA.

Claud. (*looking round her, perceives and flies to her husband*) I was not mistaken! Ah, our protector, our saviour! Art thou come, Edward? So I supposed from the whispers and looks they interchanged. What shall I say, if thou art in ignorance? What if thou know'st the worse?—But we are innocent. I am innocent; thy daughter is innocent! In every respect innocent!

Gal. (*endeavouring to calm his agitation*) Good! Good! Only be calm and answer me. (*to the* Countess) Not that I have any doubts, Madam——Is the Count dead?

Claud. Alas, he is!

Gal. Did the Prince speak, this morning, to Emilia in the cathedral?

Claud. He did: but if thou hadst seen her terror, the agitation in which she returned——

Countess. Have I deceived you?

Gal. (*with a bitter smile*) I would not for worlds that you had.

Countess. Am I in my proper senses?

Gal. (*walking to and fro in violent agitation*) Oh!—I have not yet lost mine!

Claud. Thou bad'st me be tranquil, dearest husband: let me, in turn, conjure thee——

Gal. Tranquil? Am I not calm? Can man be calmer? (*restraining his feelings*) Knows Emilia that Appiani is dead?

Claud. She cannot know it; but I fear his absence gives her suspicion of the melancholy truth.

Gal. She weeps and complains?——

Claud. No, that is past: thou know'st she is at once the most timid and courageous of her sex: she is not mistress of the first emotion; but, that over, nothing can shake her fortitude. She holds the Prince at a distance, speaks to him in a tone!——Come, Edward, let us depart!

Gal. I came on horseback: what is to be done? (*to the*

Countess) Your carriage waits, Madam, to conduct you to town?

Countess. It does.

Gal. Would you permit my wife to be your companion?

Countess. Why not? Most willingly.

Gal. Claudia! (*presenting her to the* Countess) The Countess Orsina: a lady of excellent sense, my friend and benefactress. Thou wilt accompany her to town and send the carriage here: Emilia must not return to Guastalla, but go with me.

Claud. But—if—I am loath to part from the child.

Gal. Does not her father remain? They cannot refuse me access to her. No objections! Your hand, Countess! (*aside to her*) You shall hear from me! (*aloud*) Come, Claudia!

[*Exeunt.*

ACT V.

The Scene continues.

SCENE I.—MARINELLI, *the* PRINCE.

Marinelli.

YOUR highness may see him from this window walking to and fro under the arcades—he stoops to enter. No; he again turns back. He is not yet himself, but he is much calmer, at least he affects to be, which to us is the same. It is not probable he will dare express the suspicions those women have raised. His wife, as Battista heard, is to send him the carriage; for he came on horseback. Be assured, Prince, when he appears in your presence, he will humbly thank your highness for the gracious succour his family has received on this melancholy occasion, recommend his daughter to your future favor, quietly return with her to *Guastalla,* and there wait in submissive expectation of the consolation your highness may give his dear unhappy Emilia.

Prince. Should he not prove so tractable? And I very much question he will: I know him too well; granting he conceal his suspicions and stifle his resentment, if he take his daughter to *Sabionetta,* instead of returning to the city; keep her with him, or immure her in a convent, out of my territories; how shall I overcome that difficulty?

Mar. The fears of love are extravagant: he will do no such thing.

Prince. But if he should, how will the death of the unhappy Count benefit us?

Mar. Why this gloomy retrospection? The victor boldly advances, nor looks who falls, be it friend or foe. If the old

churl should prove untractable, what have you to fear, Prince?
(*reflecting*) Good! I have hit it! He shall not remove her further than we like: mark me, Prince: *shall not!* But we must
not lose sight of him. (*goes to the window*) He had almost
taken us by surprise; he comes: let him give free vent to his
anger; in the mean while, Prince, you shall hear how we may
elude the evil you dread.

Prince. (*threatening*) Marinelli!

Mar. Oh, in the most innocent manner possible. [*Exeunt.*

SCENE II.—*Enter* GALOTTI.

Gal. Nobody here? Good! I shall have time to cool! Nothing is more contemptible than a greybeard with the rash
impetuosity of youth; my reason tells me this daily, yet
I yield to the blind impulse of rage: and by whom was it excited? A woman whose jealousy has disordered her intellect.
What affinity have the injuries of insulted virtue to the revenge
of vice?—But I must save her! And thy cause, my son! (I never could weep, nor will I learn to-day) Thy cause I will trust
to Heaven. I am content that thy assassin enjoy not the fruits
of his crime: this will inflict greater torments than his conscience. When he roves in search of happiness from pleasure
to pleasure, the recollection of this untasted joy will embitter
every delight; in his dreams the bleeding bridegroom shall
lead his bride to the couch; then, if he stretch his voluptuous
arm toward her, he'll laugh in mockery, and the murderer
shuddering awake.

SCENE III.—*Enter* MARINELLI.

Mar. Signor Galotti, where are you?

Gal. Has my daughter been here?

Mar. No; but the Prince has been seeking you.

Gal. His highness will excuse me. I conducted the Countess
to her carriage.

Mar. Well?

Gal. Good lady!

Mar. And your wife?

Gal. Is returned with the Countess to send the carriage for
her daughter. The Prince will permit us so long to intrude?

Mar. Why this ceremony? His highness proposed to have
conducted the ladies to town in his own carriage.

Gal. My daughter must, at least, have declined the honor.

Mar. How so?

Gal. She must return to *Guastalla* no more.

Mar. No more? Nay, why?

Gal. The Count is dead.

Mar. Which is a stronger reason for her——

Gal. To go with me.

Mar. With you?

Gal. With me. The Count, I repeat, Signor, is dead. *Guastalla* is no place for her: she shall go with me.

Mar. Certainly the future abode of the daughter will depend on the father; but first——

Gal. What?

Mar. You must suffer her to be brought to *Guastalla*.

Gal. My daughter? To *Guastalla*? Brought? And why?

Mar. Why? Pray reflect——

Gal. (*passionately*) Reflect? I reflect that nothing here needs reflection. She shall, she must, go with me.

Mar. Signor, why so angry? I may be mistaken; that which I hold indispensable may be unnecessary. The Prince shall decide. I will bring him hither. [*Exit.*

SCENE IV.

Gal. How! Never! Give the law to me? Pretend to dispose of my daughter? Who dares so much? He who may dare all with impunity? Good, good! He shall see how much I too can dare when provoked. Short-sighted voluptuary! I fear thee not! The Prince, whom no law restrains, is odious as the despot who has no laws to restrain him; is that a truth thou hast to learn? Come! Come!—But whither does passion hurry me? Again I suffer my wrath to cloud my understanding. Before I act, I must know the extent of my injuries. The prating of a courtier is insignificant as himself: had I suffered him to continue, I might have learned under what pretence they would have her return to *Guastalla,* and have prepared an answer: but can I be ever at a loss? Peace, greybeard, peace!

SCENE V.—Marinelli, *the* Prince, Galotti.

Prince. Ah, my dear and estimable Galotti! Was such an accident necessary to bring you to your Prince? But I will spare reproaches.

Gal. In all cases, your highness, I hold it unbecoming a subject to approach his sovereign uncalled. I beg your highness will excuse the intrusion.

Prince. Oh, that others had your proud modesty! But now to the affair which brings you here. You wish to see your daughter? She is again afflicted at the sudden departure of her tender mother. Why separate them? I only waited till the amiable Emilia should be fully recovered to conduct them to *Guastalla:* you have in part deprived me of this triumph, but it shall not entirely be lost.

Gal. Your highness is too gracious! Suffer me, Prince, to spare my unhappy child the various mortifications which from friends and foes, pity and insulting joy, await her at *Guastalla*.

Prince. It were cruel to deprive her of the sweet condolence of friendship. I will take care, dear Galotti, the shafts of envy or malice shall not reach her.

Gal. Prince, paternal love is jealous of its tender duties. I am the best judge of that which now becomes my unhappy daughter: retirement for the moment, and a convent as soon as possible.

Prince. A convent?

Gal. Till then she shall remain under the care of her father.

Prince. Shall beauty so uncommon be immured in a convent? Shall a first disappointment render mankind hateful to us? Yet nobody can dispute a father's right: conduct your daughter, Galotti, where you please.

Gal. (*to* Marinelli) Now, Signor?

Mar. If you defy me!——

Gal. Oh, not in the least.

Prince. What is the subject of dispute?

Gal. Nothing, Prince, nothing. We only were contending who had judged your highness truly.

Prince. In what? Speak, Marinelli.

Mar. I am sorry to interfere with the condescension of my Prince, but the laws of friendship are sacred.

Prince. What friendship?

Mar. Your highness knows how highly I esteemed Count Appiani; the sympathy of our inclinations.

Gal. Heard you that, Prince? Sympathy! You are the only person that does.

Mar. Named by him his avenger——

Gal. You?

Mar. Ask your lady. Marinelli was the last word of the dying Count: and pronounced in a tone! A tone! May this terrific tone incessantly appal my soul if I do not take every means to discover and bring his assassins to justice.

Prince. You may rely on my support.

Gal. And my warmest wishes for your success. Good! Good! But to what does this lead?

Prince. Ay, Marinelli, be explicit.

Mar. People suspect that Appiani was not shot by banditti.

Gal. (*ironically*) Indeed?

Mar. But that he was sacrificed to make way for a rival.

Gal. (*bitterly*) Ha! A rival?

Mar. Even so.

Gal. May curses o'ertake the vile assassin!

Mar. A rival, nay a *favoured* rival.

Gal. How? Favoured? What say you?

Mar. Nothing but what rumor has whispered.

Gal. A rival? Favored by my daughter?

Mar. No: I would contradict her father were he to maintain such an opinion. (*to the* Prince) But in all cases, Prince, the most favorable presumptions have no balance in the scale of justice; and we cannot avoid interrogating the lovely and unfortunate Emilia.

Prince. Certainly not.

Mar. And where can this take place, if not at *Guastalla?*

Prince. You are right, Marinelli! You are right. Yes, yes; that alters the case, dear Galotti. Does it not? You must see——

Gal. Oh yes; I see!—I see what I see. God! Oh God!

Prince. What thus moves you? Why so angry with yourself?

Gal. That I did not sooner discover what I now so plainly see, nothing more. Well; she shall return to *Guastalla:* I will again take her to her mother, and, till the strictest examination have entirely absolved her, I will not quit the city. For who knows, (*with a bitter smile*) who knows that justice may not find it necessary to examine *me* too.

Mar. Very possibly! In such cases justice would rather exceed the mark than be negligent: for which reason I fear——

Prince. What?

Mar. That the mother and daughter will not be suffered to hold conference.

Gal. Not suffered?

Mar. And that it will be found necessary to separate them.

Gal. Separate the mother and daughter?

Mar. Mother, daughter, and father. The forms of an interrogation absolutely require this etiquette. I am extremely concerned, Prince, that I must enforce the necessity of Emilia's being at least conveyed to a place of security.

Gal. To a place of security? Prince! Prince!—Yes; certainly! Certainly! To a place of security! Is it not so, Prince? Is it not? Oh how scrupulous is justice! Excellent! (*suddenly feels in his pocket where he has the dagger.*)

Prince. (*flattering and approaching him*) Be calm, dear Galotti.

Gal. (*aside, withdrawing his hand empty*) There spoke his guardian angel!

Prince. You misunderstand the Marquis; you suppose he means a prison?

Gal. Let me think so, and I shall be at peace.

Prince. Not a word of imprisonment, Marinelli! It is easy to combine the forms of justice with the respect due to irreproachable virtue. If Emilia must be separated from her parents, the house of my chancellor is a proper asylum. No objections, Marinelli. I will conduct her thither myself, and consign her

to the care of his respectable consort : she will answer that the
young lady is safe. If you require more, Marinelli, you are
unreasonable. (*to* Galotti) You know the chancellor Grimaldi, and his lady ?

Gal. Certainly ; as well as the amiable daughters of the
noble pair : who does not ? (*to* Marinelli) No, Signor, do not
yield : if Emilia must be taken from us, let her be confined in
the deepest dungeon : insist upon this, I conjure you.—Fool
that I am with my request! Grey-headed fool ! Yes ; the good
sibyl was right : he whose reason can unshaken support *certain things*, has none to lose !

Prince. I understand you not, dear Galotti : what more can
I do ? Be calm, I conjure you. Yes, yes ; the house of my
chancellor shall receive her : I will be her conductor ; and, if
she is not treated with the respect she merits, my word is of no
weight : but fear nothing ; all will go well. You, Galotti,
will either follow us to *Guastalla*, or return to *Sabionetta*, as
you please : it were ridiculous to lay down the law to you.
Adieu, dear Galotti, till we meet again. Come, Marinelli ; it
grows late.

Gal. (*who has stood deep in thought*) How ? Shall I not
speak with my daughter ? Not even here ? I agree to all : the
contrivance is excellent ; the house of a chancellor, no doubt,
the temple of virtue. Take my daughter there, Prince, and
only there ; but let me first speak with her. She is ignorant
of the Count's death ; she will not conceive why she is separated from her parents : suffer me tenderly to acquaint her
with the calamities which have overtaken her. I must see
her, Prince, I must !

Prince. Then follow me.

Gal. Oh, a daughter may come to her father ! I must see
her alone ; our conversation will be short : pray send her to
me, Prince.

Prince. She shall come ! Oh, Galotti, that you would be
my friend, my guide, my father !

                    [*Exeunt the* Prince *and* Marinelli.

SCENE VI.

Gal. (*looking after the* Prince : *a pause*) Why not ? With all
my heart. Ha, ha, ha! (*looking wildly round*) Who laughs ?
By Heaven I believe 'twas myself ! Good ! 'Tis pleasant, very
pleasant!——It draws to an end, no matter what; but (*pause*)
if she participate the guilt ? If it were an every day intrigue ?
If she be unworthy of the sacrifice I would make ? (*pause*)
Make ? What sacrifice ? Have I the courage to own it to myself ? It is but a thought ! The thought of a moment. Horrible ! Avaunt ! Avaunt ! I will not wait for her. No ! (*raising
his eyes to heaven*) That Power which has plunged innocence in

this abyss, will snatch her from the precipice. Is my weak
arm required? Away! (*going, sees* Emilia) Too late! Ah!
Heaven demands my arm!

SCENE VII.—*Enter* Emilia.

Emil. How? You here, my father? Alone? Where is my
mother? Where is the Count? And wherefore are you thus
agitated?

Gal. And thou, my child, so calm?

Emil. Why not, my father? All is lost or nothing: tranquillity, whether forced or natural, has the same effects.

Gal. But what does thy heart forbode?

Emil. That all is lost——and yet, my father, we must be
tranquil.

Gal. Who art thou? A woman? And my daughter? Must
the man and the parent blush in thy presence? But say what
meanest thou?——That the Count is dead?

Emil. And the cause, the cause! Ah, my father, the horrible history, which I read in the wild and tearful eye of my mother, is then true? Where is she? Whither is she gone?

Gal. Home; if we could but follow her!

Emil. The sooner the better: for, if the Count be dead, if
his death had such a cause, why stay we here? Let us fly, my
father!

Gal. Fly? Ah, that flight were in our power! Thou art
in the ravisher's hands, and must there remain.

Emil. I remain in his power?

Gal. Alone; without thy mother, without me.

Emil. Alone? Never, my father! Never! Your daughter
torn from your protecting arms? Oh, fear it not! Who shall
dare detain me? Who force my will? Where is the man who
can force the will of another?

Gal. I thought, my child, thou wert tranquil.

Emil. I am, I am! But what is tranquillity? Basely suffering that which cannot, must not, be endured?

Gal. Ha! If such are thy thoughts, let me embrace thee,
my child. I always said Nature designed woman for her
masterpiece, but that her materials were too delicate: in all,
thy sex excels ours. Ah, if thy tranquillity has so noble a
basis, mine is again restored: let me take thee to my heart! Know,
then—under the pretence of interrogating thee before the tribunal of justice, oh infernal contrivance, they tear thee from
our arms to conduct thee to Grimaldi.

Emil. Tear me from your arms? Dare they propose this?
Have *we* no will, my father?

Gal. Burning with indignation, my hand was upon this
dagger (*drawing it out*) to stab one or both to the heart.

Emil. Forbid it Heaven! This life is all the wicked can expect. Give me the dagger, my father!

Gal. Child, it is no hair bodkin.

Emil. Nay, if it were, it still would perform the dagger's friendly part.

Gal. What? Is the case so desperate? Not yet; not yet. Remember thou hast only one life to lose.

Emil. And but one innocence!

Gal. Of which no force can rob thee.

Emil. But of which seduction may. Force? Who cannot resist it? Seduction is real violence. My feelings are youthful, and strong, as those of others: I have senses too. I am a weak creature who may be led astray. I know the house of Grimaldi; it is the temple of pleasure: a single hour spent in that society with my respectable mother raised a tumult in my soul which the strictest exercises of religion in a week scarcely could subdue. Of religion; and of what a religion! Thousands have sought refuge from dishonor in the overwhelming waves, and are sainted: the dagger! The dagger, my father!

Gal. If you knew what a dagger is!

Emil. A friend unknown is still a friend. Oh, give it! Give it me!

Gal. If I were to comply?—There. (*giving it.*)

Emil. And there! (*going to stab herself, is prevented by her father, who snatches the dagger.*)

Gal. Rash girl! No; it is not for thy hand.

Emil. True, a bodkin will serve. (*she searches for one in her hair, and feels the rose on her head*) Thou still there? Down, down, thou shouldst not deck the head of one——such as my father wishes me to be!

Gal. Oh, my daughter!

Emil. Oh, my father, if I understand you! Yet, no; you will not do't; or why so long have delayed? (*in a bitter tone, while she plucks the leaves of the rose*) In ancient times we're told a father to save his daughter from dishonor plunged the welcome dagger in her bosom, and gave her second life; but those were deeds of ancient times; such fathers have no existence now.

Gal. They have, my child, they have! (*stabbing her*) God! What have I done! (*catching her in his arms.*)

Emil. Plucked a rose ere it was rudely broken by the storm.

SCENE VIII.—*Enter the* PRINCE, MARINELLI.

Prince. (*entering*) How? Is not Emilia well?

Gal. Very well! Very well!

Prince. (*approaching*) What do I see? Oh, horror!

Mar. (*aside*) I am lost!

Prince. Cruel father, what have you done?

Gal. "Plucked a rose ere it was rudely broken by the storm:"——was it not so, my daughter?

Emil. Not you, my father!—I—I——

Gal. No, my child, not thee! Quit not the world with an untruth on thy lips. Not thee, my daughter ; thy father, thy wretched father!

Emil. Ah!——My father! (*she dies:* Galotti *lays her gently on the floor.*)

Gal. Thou art saved!—Well, Prince, does she still charm? Does this lifeless corpse, whose blood cries vengeance on your head, still excite desire?—(*after a pause*) But you wait for the finishing stroke : you expect, perhaps, I shall bury the dagger in my heart, like the cowardly hero of a wretched tragedy? You are mistaken. Here! (*throwing the dagger at his feet*) Here lies the bloody witness of my crime. I will deliver myself into the hands of justice : I go to meet you at her awful tribunal as my judge : then I shall expect you before the Judge of the universe! [*Exit.*

Prince. (*after a pause, during which he gazes on the corpse with horror and despair, to* Marinelli) Here! Take it up!—— How! you hesitate?——Wretch!——(*snatching the dagger from him*) Yet no, thy blood shall not mix with so pure a stream. Be gone, and never let me see thee more! Be gone, I say!—God! God!——Is it not sufficient, for the misery of their subjects, that princes are but men ; must they be surrounded by fiends who assume the mask of friendship?

The Curtain falls.

REMARKS.

THE chief defect in this Tragedy is that it is written in an explanatory, colloquial, and prosaic style : but this is what may be almost called the mortal sin of German literature ; it has never yet attained that laconic indication of the passions, which is best calculated to express their rapid, confused, and desperate course.

In other respects, Emilia Galotti is a masterpiece : the progress of the plot is truly dramatic, the contrast of the characters is finely imagined, and the feelings excited are among the noblest within the province of the tragic muse. This piece only requires a master hand to lop away its superfluities, preserve its beauties, and link them in a quick and poetical succession, to render it perhaps the finest modern tragedy known to the stage.

DRAMATIC BIOGRAPHY.

LESSING.

IT appears to be the prevailing doctrine, among the best critics in Germany, that Lessing is justly esteemed the greatest of their dramatic authors. Whether he has been lately rivalled by Goethe, Schiller, or Kotzebue, will be a subject more likely to be justly decided when those authors are no longer living. The name of Kotzebue, particularly, has, by the Germans themselves, been eminently treated with disrespect: while his works have been translated into all the languages of civilized Europe; and, in several instances, they have been every where, not merely well, but, rapturously received.

Whether the name of Lessing may be eclipsed, or not, it never can be far thrown into the back ground, among the present poets of Germany: nay, it will maintain a distinguished place, while true pictures of an imperfect state of morality shall continue to delight mankind.

It forms a part of the plan, of the Theatrical Recorder, to afford candid examples, as far as they can be afforded by translation, of the comparative merits of foreign dramatic authors. In the present number, therefore, the tragedy of *Emilia Galotti* is given; and this piece will hereafter be followed by one which is avowed to be the best of Lessing's comedies: *Minna von Barnhelm.*

Either the lives of men of literature have seldom that variety of incident, which is common to men of the world, or, such variety is seldom recorded. Bodily activity rather distinguishes the latter class, and mental the men who become famous in literature. They delight in the stillness of solitude, the seclusion of college walls, and the mute language of books. When they escape from these, it is but to associate with their prototypes; men of similar pursuits, propensities, and pleasures.

Gotthold Ephraim Lessing was a native of *Kamenz*, a small town in *Lausitz*, or Lusatia, where his father was a clergyman.

He was born in 1729, received the first part of his education from his father, who was a pious and learned man, and afterward from private teachers and the school of the place. From this, he went to the foundation school at *Meissen*, where he employed five years in studying ancient and modern languages, philosophy, and mathematics. The poets of antiquity were his delight : he entered into their spirit, translated, imitated, and from them produced poems of his own.

In 1746, he left Meissen, and went to the university of *Leipsic*, there to study theology, and the higher sciences : but he appears to have had no affection for the academical teachers there, J. A. Ernesti the philologist excepted, and rather chose to be his own master. His principal studies were philosophy, aesthetics*, mathematics, and natural history.

From his youth, Lessing had a strong propensity to dramatic poetry, and, while at Leipsic, cultivated the friendship of *Felix Weisse*, whose theatrical works are in such high estimation in Germany. He had also much intercourse with the players, who formed the company of *Madam Neuber*, and here wrote his first comic pieces : *Damon*, and *Die alte Jungfer*, which met with universal success.

Quitting Leipsic, Lessing joined his intimate friend, *Christlob Milius*, at Berlin, and here published his first collection of excellent poems, under the title *Kleinigkeiten*, or trifles, which, with some other writings, appeared in 1750.

He went thence to Wittenberg, where his younger brother, J. Gottlieb studied. Here he took the title of *Magister*, and, among other things, wrote a critic on the beginning of the Messiah, by Klopstock.

About two years afterward, he returned to Berlin ; where, in addition to a political journal, which was continued till the year 1756, he produced several learned works, began the *Theatralische Bibliotheque*, and made acquaintance and friendship with Friedrich Nikolai, Mendelsohn, Ramler, Sultzer, and others.

In 1756, he was appointed Hofmeister, at Leipsic, and was

---

* A word, in German literature, signifying principles of taste.

to accompany a young gentleman on his travels; but these travels were never begun, and Lessing remained at Leipsic till the year 1759, during which period he published various original works and translations.

He then once more returned to Berlin, and, in the following year, accompanied the Prussian general, *Tauenzien*, to *Breslaw*, as his secretary. This place he held till 1765, when he left Breslaw, visited his father at Kamenz, his friends at Leipsic, and once again came to Berlin, where he laboured at his *Laokoon* [Laocon].

Some wealthy friends of the dramatic art, at *Hamburg*, invited him to join them, in 1766, and aid in the improvement of the theatre, both as a poet and a critic. This office he undertook, but the theatre at Hamburg did not then succeed. The world however profited by the undertaking, for here Lessing wrote his *Dramaturgie*; a work full of acute and excellent criticism, on the dramatic art.

At this period, he also took part in the plan which *Bode*, of Hamburg, had formed, and, with the aid of men of letters, endeavoured to perfect; which was that of bringing German literature into better repute, by printing good editions of the best authors. *Klopstock, Von Gerstenberg, Zacharia*, and others, contributed their new works, in order to promote this undertaking. *Klopstock* made a journey to Vienna, in the hope that it would be supported by the emperor, Joseph, who appeared desirous to perform some eminent service to literature. Obstinate people however interfered, and the failure of the scheme so embittered Lessing that he proposed wholly to renounce the German muse, to retire to Italy, and there to write in Latin, for the learned world alone.

In 1770, we find him librarian at Wolfenbüttel, with the title of *Hofrath*, or court counsellor, to the duke of Brunswic. Here, in company with Prince Leopold of Brunswic, and to recreate his thoughts, he undertook a journey through Berlin and Vienna to Italy; and, at the end of eight months, again returned to Wolfenbüttel. In this library, his active mind was employed in the discovery and publication of its treasures, and he drew from it several. *Beiträge zu Geschichte und*

Litteratur *; he also committed to the press *Die Fragmente eines ungennante Deisten*†, which he there found. This terrible performance set the theological world in flames, excited a violent paper war, and drew on the editor many vexations; chiefly at the instigation of the pastor, Melchior Göz, of Hamburg. Our author, in 1778, then wrote Nathan, the Sage; which appeared the year following.

In the interim, he had married Madam König, a widow lady of Hamburg, who died in two years. From that period, he courted solitude ; his health declined, he fell into a lethargy, and expired at Brunswic, 1781, on the 15th of February.

The above account of the life of Lessing is chiefly extracted from an exceedingly useful work, before quoted ‡, entitled *Handbuch der poetischen Litteratur der Deutschen: von* C. F. R. Vetterlein : in which is given an account of the various editions of the works of Lessing. From these works it appears that Lessing spent a most indefatigable and honorable life, in those inquiries which he thought best could promote polite literature, and especially the dramatic art. Germany, in particular, is everlastingly indebted to his labors, which were unremitting, stimulated by the purest motives, and rewarded by the love and fame which he deserved. Active men of every class, who devote themselves to any useful purpose, deserve the reward and praise of the world: but men of literary and scientific research, perhaps, the most; for they promote that best and most necessary part of the accumulated knowledge of men, on which their social talents, moral virtues, and ultimate happiness depend.

---

* Aids to History and Literature.

† Fragment by an anonymous Deist.

‡ See life of Gellert: No. I. Theatrical Recorder, p. 51.

PIECES

FIRST PERFORMED IN APRIL AND MAY, 1805.

OF the new Pieces that have appeared, since the last number of this work, no other mention deserves to be made than that of simply recording insignificant facts: nor indeed has any appeared, but for the benefits of performers; and some of these are of so heterogeneous a kind that they are of no class, being chiefly extracts from old pieces.

The Soldier's Return, a comic opera of two acts, Drury-Lane, was barely mentioned in the last number, and merits nothing more in the present; except perhaps that it afforded Miss De Camp an opportunity to happily display her lively talents. The music, by Mr. Hooke, might have been worthy of a much better piece: the author of the words has not published his name. This piece appeared in April, previous to pieces for benefits.

The Venetian Outlaw was brought out by Mr. Elliston, for his benefit, and has been performed three times since. It is indeed an inefficient translation of a French piece, performed three years ago on the Boulevards, at Paris, and entitled *l'Homme a trois Visages.* I believe that the origin of this piece, and of our very admirable tragedy, Venice Preserved, strange to say, is the same, and derived from *La Conjuration de Venise,* by the Abbé Saint Réal. However, I do not state this as a fact, but as a conjecture.

The screaming and violence of Mrs. H. Johnson I have heard mentioned, by those who have seen this piece, with much disapprobation. If it be true, which I can neither deny nor affirm, I would be the first to warn her against and dissuade her from seeking applause by such means. In general, she has so much talent, and so natural and charming a manner of speaking, that it must truly grieve any true judge of theatrical merit to see these qualities debased, or in danger of change for the worse. If she can acquire a still more perfect articulation, and greater power of voice, with a still nicer discriminating feeling of the passions, she will bid fair to become one of the first performers on the stage.

For the benefit of Mr. Bannister, a translation of another French piece, of one act, was given, entitled, in the original, *Défiance et Malice;* and by the translator *Personation;* a word not much in use, and rather affected. It consists but of two characters, which were performed by Mr. Bannister and Miss De Camp; and the intrigue arises from the young lady sometimes disguising herself, and assuming the character of her *gouvernante*, and her lover pretending and appearing to be his own steward, while they alternately assume their natural characters. In the original, it has some wit and pleasantry : with the translation I am unacquainted.

THE ART OF ACTING.

(*Continued from No.* V. *p.* 349.)

CHAP. IV.

Of Propriety of Demeanor and of Action. The Class of Heroes.

AMONG the defects mentioned in the last chapter, I forgot one, which is very common : that of bowing and courtesying, at improper times, to an audience.

It appears strange that actors should have so little considered the nature of dramatic exhibition, as not to have it imprinted on their minds, that, when they are on the stage, they are supposed to be real and not fictitious persons; and that it is an injury, to scenic effect, whenever they are otherwise remembered than as the characters they represent.

In this respect, they should set the audience a good example : for audiences are composed of a large mixture of the illiterate, the inconsiderate, and persons educated among the vulgar; or only half informed, at best; with a select few, capable of distinguishing the merits of the excellent actor, and of bestowing well-deserved applause.

Performers, who are frequently seen in characters favorable to an actor, must be bad indeed, if they do not become the delight of the audience. When they appear, a social and pleasing gratitude bestows applause: but of this, whatever may be the feelings of the heart, the actor should appear to know nothing; for the applause is to the person, and to notice it is totally to forget the character, which is neither living nor present.

Scenic illusion is thus destroyed, and too often by that which betrays something like meanness of mind: for, surely, nothing can be more egotistical, or have a more pitiful humble air of begging approbation, than the manner in which performers, especially singers, will repeat their bows and courteseys, whenever they can find the slightest pretence. Like children watching for sugar-plums, they cry, Oh, how sweet! Pray let me have a little more!

At the beginning of a season, on a benefit night, or whenever a performer has personally to address an audience, are the chief if not the only times at which such reciprocal gratitude ought to be publicly expressed. Any of the injudicious acts of a mixed audience cannot authorize want of judgment, much less absurdity, in an actor.

I shall now proceed to consider that very essential branch, of the actor's art, which consists in characteristic demeanor.

To afford him assistance in this, since it will be impossible to specify the numberless characters that the drama includes, I shall endeavour to arrange the whole under different heads; and to divide them so as that they may all refer to one, or other, of these classes.

I cannot foresee the number of chapters that this may require. To note down all the varieties which would agree with and are indeed demanded in all the characters that have been drawn, or that may be imagined, would be an equally vain and puerile attempt: the best manner of developing the subject, perhaps, will be to choose characters familiar to the stage and to general observation, so as to classify action, and in part to discriminate, sometimes the shades and at others the strong differences, that ought generally to vary or contrast them in representation. I will begin with

HEROES.

The stage affords but few, if any, pure specimens of this class; for it generally requires other qualities to predominate, such as the lover or the ruler, and only to suffer those of the hero partially to be seen. I recollect none, in tragedy, in whom the heroic qualities appear more conspicuous than in Henry V. as drawn by Shakspeare.

The actor, who should be sufficiently attentive to the lessons given by our immortal bard, would generally find his principal characters so described, so marked, so individualized, that no man scarcely could err, concerning the manner in which these characters ought to appear. Henry V. is a hero; but he is also a king, and so pourtrayed, by the poet; with all that richness, yet true discrimination, that could at once dignify both king and hero. But the present inquiry must be confined to the heroic qualities of Henry.

Some may think that in the character of Hotspur the hero only is represented; and therefore that taste and judgment would rather select Hotspur, than Henry V. to exemplify the class of heroes. To this it may be answered, that Hotspur had many but not all of the heroic qualities; that his cognomen, Hotspur, did itself denote his deficiency; that his intemperance was such as, in a certain degree, to deprive him of his rank of hero; and that he sunk before the more perfect heroism of his rival, whom he too rashly despised.

Let the actor imagine Henry delivering the verbal challenge in his father's presence to Hotspur: let him observe the praise he bestows on his rival, and the modesty yet the firmness of his words, and figure to himself the deportment proper for such a scene.

> In both our armies, there is many a soul
> Shall pay full dearly for this encounter,
> If once they join in trial. Tell your nephew,
> The Prince of Wales doth join, with all the World,
> In praise of Henry Piercy: by my hopes—
> This present enterprise set off his head—

> I do not think a braver gentleman,
> More active-valiant, or more valiant-young,
> More daring, or more bold, is now alive,
> To grace this latter age with noble deeds.
> For my part, I may speak it to my shame,
> I have a truant been to chivalry;
> And so, I hear, he doth account me too :
> Yet—this before·my father's majesty—
> I am content that he shall take the odds
> Of his great name, and estimation,
> And will, to save the blood on either side,
> Try fortune with him in a single fight.

In this speech, the determined yet the cool hero is most admirably drawn.

In the next scene, not only his words but his manner of delivering them are thus charmingly described by Vernon.

> *Hot.*   Tell me, tell me,
> How show'd his tasking? Seem'd it in contempt.
> *Ver.* No, by my soul; I never in my life
> Did hear a challenge urg'd more modestly.
> . . . .
> He made a blushing cital of himself;
> And chid his truant youth with such a grace,
> As if he master'd there a double spirit,
> Of teaching and of learning, instantly.

The action is now to be considered.

Henry's words and deportment must have agreed ; they must both have been totally unassuming; yet, in them both, the most unshaken fortitude could not but have been apparent. The actor, therefore, should stand firm, and erect ; except that there should be no pride, not the slightest assuming air ; the body and the head should have an almost imperceptible inclination forward : every action should have a quickness approaching rapidity, to denote the ardor of his mind; yet so tempered, and restrained, as still more forcibly to suggest the fortitude and heroic continency of the hero.   When he comes to the line—

> Yet—this before my father's majesty—

the struggle with himself to contain the glorious daring, which almost shook his frame, should be apparent : there ought to

be a momentary swelling and stiffening of every limb; yet as
instantly once more to be tempered, by the apprehension of
being thought a boaster. He should then proceed with a distinct articulation, not a loud or threatening voice, and with
every corresponding firm majesty of gesture, to deliver
thoughts, publicly, which had been privately but thoroughly
examined, and concerning which his resolution was not to be
shaken. His action of arm should be seldom, but impressive.

This deportment, with those small variations that circumstances may demand, will be generally proper for heroes, when
speaking before persons whom they revere, but are fitted to
command: it must always contain a mixture of ease and amiable feelings, but a determination and cool fortitude that pictures the hero who speaks.

There cannot be a greater mistake than to imagine that the
heroic qualities of the soul ever appear in any exaggerated
manner. The superiority of man to man is then most decidedly pourtrayed, when the energy of action and of language are controlled, just so far as to convince the spectator
that, though that energy is mighty, it is held in due yet grand
subordination. The actor, who performs Henry V. should
never for a moment forget that he represents a monarch, of
whom Shakspeare makes the Archbishop of Canterbury say,
that, at the very moment when his father died—

> Consideration, like an angel, came,
> And whipp'd th' offending Adam out of him ;
> Leaving his body as a paradise,
> T' envelop and contain celestial spirits.

And afterward,

> List his discourse of war, and you shall hear
> A fearful battle render'd you in music.
>   When he speaks,
> The air, a charter'd libertine, is still ;
> And the mute wonder lurketh in men's ears,
> To steal his sweet and honied sentences.

These descriptions, separately and collectively, ought to be
studied by the actor, and so familiarized to his mind as to be

visible, as well in his whole deportment as in every individual gesture, step, and look : especially in his tone of utterance. He ought to be well aware that no man, who blusters, bullies, speaks loud, and appears to swell with his own importance, is capable of the general command of others: the foolish, the servile, and the self-interested, only, are so swayed. I do not, in this sense, speak of hereditary power; but of the command which superior genius acquires: and I grant it is difficult to personate superior genius.

The stamp of superior genius, throughout the play, is distinct and beautiful in the character of Henry V. as drawn by Shakspeare. Whenever he speaks, the purest philosophy flows from his lips. The cheerful serenity of his soul, his comprehensive yet undaunted view of the worst that can happen, and the glory, the everlasting fame, that will crown him, should he succeed in an enterprise so perilous, are delivered with such a temperate yet such a heroic flow of soul that, while we grant the difficulty of personating qualities so exalted, and so singular, we can scarcely, on the other hand, but imagine that they must inspire and seize on the soul of the performer.

It is for this reason, that is, because the contrast is so great, that a foolish actor, in any character thus divinely drawn, becomes so intolerable and painful to an intelligent spectator.

The difficulty of personating every character is that, not only of thoroughly comprehending the meaning of the author, but, of entering precisely into the feeling ; first of the scene, next of the particular speech, and lastly of the continual variations of feeling and intention, which every marking word in a sentence denotes.

This labor should be so complete, and familiar to the mind, that it ought not to have the least appearance of labor; and, were it indeed thus complete, it could not so appear, for it would no longer be labor: it would be perfect recollection, unshaken presence of mind, and, however impassioned, a delivery that would be delightfully natural. There would be neither sing-song, whining recitative, unmeaning rant, monotonous swinging of the arm, nor any of the common-place defects (I ought to say deformities) which are too frequent on the stage.

Perhaps a student of the art of acting may best remember if the rules, which he ought to observe, be contrasted in a negative and positive form.

Thus, *of the hero.*

1. He cannot roar : yet, not a single tone of his voice can be insignificant. I speak of him on the stage. No man strains and roars with his voice, who is not foolish, or confused : for confusion of mind, while it continues, denotes folly ; and a roaring voice denotes either, or both.

2. His delivery cannot be monotonous : for monotony denotes want of feeling ; and he discourses only of things of the greatest moment : or, if he ever have occasion to be familiar, there is discrimination and intention in all that he utters ; and monotony denotes vacancy of mind.

3. For the above reason, he cannot speak in recitative : for every approach to insipidity is the antipathy of heroism ; and the recitative of stage speaking is insipidity itself. It is a grown child repeating his lesson.

4. He cannot take short steps : for they are the marks of meanness, trifling, and indecision. The qualities of the hero are exactly the reverse.

5. He cannot swing his arm, or arms, in the air ; for that is monotony of action, and has all the vices that appertain to a monotonous delivery. His gestures, like his words, are decisive, dignified, and have a precise intention.

6. He cannot hold back his head : for that implies inflated self-sufficiency, and a desire of extorting slavish obedience. The hero has a consciousness that his power is acknowledged, and he only commands obedience when the want of it would be dangerous. He knows nothing of slavery ; except the obedience which reason exacts be so called. Tyrants only have slaves.

7. He cannot have a cringing and contracted deportment : for that denotes both mental and bodily debility, and the consciousness of superior power is never absent from the hero.

8. He cannot stiffen and endeavour to swell his limbs : for that, once more, depicts ostentation and imbecility.

9. He cannot either so act, or speak, as to denote confusion of mind : for ordinary minds only are confused. The heroic mind has frequent doubts; but it pauses, examines, and determines: for the thing which it most abhors is indecision. The hero vanishes, whenever indecision appears.

I pretend no more than to give these rules as warnings, to actors, against failings which are much too frequent. If they are true, he cannot but deduce from them, that, the deportment of a hero ought to be dignified, yet easy ; that of a perfect gentleman, yet disdainful of the gentility and mere ceremony of good breeding : immeasurably beyond them : while the varied tones of his voice, and each word that he utters, should make it evident that he fully comprehends every varied sense in which what he speaks can be understood. In brief: his presence of mind, unshaken fortitude, and especially his consummate intelligence, should approach perfection.

(*To be continued.*)

ESSAY ON DRAMATIC COMPOSITION,

(*Continued from No. V. p. 351.*)

THERE are three things which perhaps it is again necessary to repeat. First : if any suppositions are required of an audience, these suppositions destroy illusion, and are more or less liable to be improbable, or impossible : for example, to require the belief that two hours and a half are a day. Second : to the mind, one supposition is as easily made as another. And, lastly, the critics, who contend for the unities of time and place, require the time not to exceed twelve hours ; or, at most, a day and night; and that the scene ought not to change; or, if any indulgence be granted, that it should only change once, at the end of an act.

Well convinced of the impossibility of observing these rules, I have sedulously examined the comedies, and tragedies, of the authors by whom it is pretended they have been observed ; and I find that, with respect both to time and place, they have one general artifice, which, though founded in falsehood, blindfolds censure and extorts admiration.

This very simple trick is only that of being silent. They make no mention of time and place. Perhaps they will write, in the title page, the name of the place where they lay the scene, and the time in which they gratuitously suppose the action to pass.

They then begin their piece with a description of what they suppose the stage decorations ought to be ; and this is seldom any thing but a hall, with doors into different apartments, generally describing such halls as were never built, and such as, according to the practice of building, it is ridiculous to suppose. Why should these advocates for probability demand a style of architecture that, however well it might suit their purpose, which in fact it seldom does, is no where to be found?

In the *Phédre*, of Racine, nothing is said of time, or place, the following words excepted: *La Scene est à Trézene, ville du Péloponnese**. This indefinite method leaves the reader to suppose he is in a palace, a street, a market place, or where he shall please. The scene painter and the author will be equally desirous that the view, or the architecture, shall be grand.

In the first scene, we are informed that Theseus has been so long absent as for Hippolytus, his son, to despair of his return. We also learn that Hippolytus loves Aricia, and is hated by his mother-in-law, Phedra. Hippolytus however informs his convenient friend, Theramenus, that he determines to go in search of his father.

Œnone then enters, and very politely desires them to leave the place ; for the queen, Phedra, is coming, and adds that her illness and secret griefs are extreme. Can a spectator forbear to ask, why a sick and afflicted woman should wish to come

---

* The scene is Trezena, a town of Peloponnesus.

there, rather than any where else, and should send her maid, or confidant, on such a message?

Phedra sits down, and we must consequently suppose there are sofas, chairs, and furniture.   State requires more.

Having revealed her secret, Panopus enters, and informs her that Theseus is dead; that Hippolytus, whom we have just seen, is informed of his death; that Athens is divided, concerning the choice of a master; and gives further information of political intrigue.

How can all this have happened in less than ten minutes, when Hippolytus was on the stage, and knew nothing of such momentous affairs?

Œnone, however, the obliging confidant, tells Phedra that she may now love Hippolytus; since Theseus, his father and her husband, is dead. Phedra retires with this hope, and the act ends.

In the same place, the princess Aricia, and *her* confidant, Ismena, begin the second act, because Hippolytus has demanded to see her *there*, though he knew it to be the favorite place of Phedra, whom he would avoid.   After relating how much she loves him, and her dear Ismena giving her the sweet hope that her love is returned, Hippolytus enters, informs her that he means to depart, and secure Athens in her favor, declares his love, and is informed by his confident Theramenus, that Phedra is coming again, and is also in search of him.

Hippolytus sends Theramenus away, with orders that the signal for his departure be given, and Phedra enters.   He hears her avow her passion for him with horror, politely lends her his sword to kill herself, and her death only appears to be prevented by the return of Theramenus.

After expressing his surprise to see his master pale, speechless, and without a sword, he informs Hippolytus that the sails are set, for his departure, and that Athens had already declared, by a great majority, that the son of Phedra, who is the brother of Hippolytus, should reign.   A herald is arrived from Athens, and the youth is now king.   He adds that there is a report that Theseus is still alive, and has been seen in Epirus.

Will not the spectator imagine (not to mention the preparation of vessels, for the departure of Hippolytus) that the transactions at Athens, the intrigues of the contending parties, as well as the arrival and departure of messengers, on both sides, must require time? I should suppose, not one day, but, several weeks must be necessary for such intercourse; and we are now only at the end of the second act.

At the beginning of Act III. we are told that people (we must suppose them to be heralds, or rather deputies, from Athens) importune Phedra to be permitted to lay the honors of that city at her feet.

We next learn that Theseus is arrived. Theseus appears, and with him Hippolytus. The scene is still unvaried.

Theseus is the hero and monarch of many countries: can he come so suddenly, without any retinue, or precursors, thus at pleasure? Is not time necessary also for the arrival of these deputies; and, briefly, for all that must take place, whenever such-like events happen?

In Act IV. after the cruel debates produced by the supposed incestuous love of Hippolytus, Theseus retires, enraged, and intending to proceed to the altar of Neptune, and pray to this his protecting god for revenge. The sacrifices made by the Greeks to their gods, when they had favors to ask, were ceremonious, and required great preparation.

Act V. begins with Aricia and Hippolytus. Theseus afterward enters, and we find that he has already sacrificed to Neptune. Panopus enters to Theseus, and informs him that Œnone has thrown herself into the sea. Theseus then, in a passing way, begs Neptune not to be too hasty in his revenge.

It is not perhaps ten minutes, after Hippolytus goes off, before Theramenus enters, and unfolds the grand catastrophe of the tragedy. The terrible tale, which he then tells, with all its preparations for action, the incidents of that action, and its conclusion, are all out of probability to have happened in so short a space of time, as that which had passed since Hippolytus had left the stage.

If there be a person on earth who, after taking a candid view of this subject, can affirm that the unities, according to the rules prescribed by the French critics, are preserved, he is certainly a true believer in these critics, and sees with the eye of faith, not of the understanding.

However, I take every opportunity to repeat the assertion, that, if suppositions must be made by the spectator, one supposition is as easy to him as another; provided the discourse be of possible things, and that the poet be sufficiently clear and explicit.

With respect to place, it never happened in nature that a story, which must take twelve or twenty-four hours, or a longer time, in telling, should, with all its various incidents, be told in one open and public apartment, hall, street, portico, or place. The supposition is childish; and, if the spectator think at all, it must be a supposition. Surely, he can as easily suppose the action to pass in different places, since that would be not only probable but true, and by shifting the scene might pass as it were before his eyes? The more these unities are reflected on, the more mankind will be surprised at the credulity with which the pretended followers of Aristotle have been revered.

In the next number, an inquiry will be made into the poetic and dramatic evils, that arise from the observance, or rather the pretended observance, of time and place.

(To be continued.)

DRAMATIC ANECDOTES.

IN his Dramatic Miscellanies*, Davies says—" During this century, the public had not perhaps seen a proper outline of Iago, till Charles Macklin exhibited a faithful picture of this arch villain, 1744, in the Haymarket theatre, when *Foote was his Othello.*" Those, perhaps, who are only acquainted with this admirable comedian, and writer, in his own pieces, would scarcely have imagined Foote had ever performed Othello.

Cibber persisted so obstinately in acting tragedy, that he was at last fairly hissed off the stage. When the Sophonisba of Thomson appeared, Cibber, in the character of Scipio, was as much exploded as any bad actor could be, the two first nights. Wilkes gave the part to Williams, who, marching down the

---

* Vol. III. p. 470.

stage, was at first mistaken for Cibber, and was saluted with the music of catcalls and a repetition of hisses; but, as soon as the spectators were undeceived, their groans were converted to loud and long applause.

Verbruggen was so passionately fond of acting Alexander the Great, at that time the hero of the actors, that, instead of Verbruggen, in the dramatis personæ to many plays, he was called Mr. Alexander*. Verbruggen was so warm of temper that he had the temerity to strike an illegitimate son of Charles II. behind the scenes of Drury-lane. After so daring an insult, he was told, if he did not publicly ask the nobleman's pardon, he must act no more, in London. To this he consented, on condition that he might express himself in his own terms, and, coming on the stage dressed for the part of Oronooko, having first acknowledged that he had called the duke of Saint A. a son of a whore, added—*It is true, and I am sorry for it.*

Calderon de la Barca, in one of his pieces, called *La Scisma D'Inglaterra*, has taken the divorce of Henry VIII. as a subject, and, according to Davies†, has not ill sustained the characters of Henry, Wolsey, and Catherine. He paints the king as conscious of criminality, and Anna Bullen as proud, insolent, ungrateful, and lascivious. By a fiction of his own, he causes her to intrigue with the French ambassador, the king to overhear their discourse, send her to the Tower in a rage, and, she being there beheaded, her dead body is afterward brought upon the stage. Calderon pays as little respect to the unities of time and place as Shakspeare.

In the character of Gardiner ‡ (Shakspeare's Henry VIII.) Ben Jonson, the actor, preserved that decorum which becomes a bishop and privy counsellor. Hippisley, less chaste, added strokes of humor, that approached grimace; but Taswell's Gardiner degenerated into absolute trick and buffoonery, and, when he followed Cranmer off, he held his crutch over his head, that the ignorant and foolish might laugh. For this he sometimes paid dearly, by a well merited hiss from the judicious part of the audience.

When Theophilus Cibber was requested to contribute to the relief of Mrs. Willis §, once an excellent actress, but then old and poor, he urged that he had too large a family. " Dear, Sir! How can that be? you have neither wife nor child."— ' That may be; but I have a large family of vices.'

---

* Vol. III. p. 446.   † Vol. I. p. 434.   ‡ p. 427.   § p. 423.

MISCELLANIES.

Provincial Theatres: Rudgely; Stafford; Stourport; Wrexam; and Drayton: from a Letter by the Correspondent in No. IV.

THEATRE, RUDGELY, STAFFORDSHIRE.

*T*WO celebrated Rosciuses are performing, here, to about three pounds per night: Miss Swindall, who takes the whole of Master Betty's characters, and Master Marshall, who speaks prologues, and sings comic songs. Mr. Marshall, the father of this comic Orpheus, is the manager of the company, which consists of himself, three daughters, son, and son-in-law! Rolla himself, *here*, is polite enough occasionally to throw by his robes of state, and condescend to come and scrape in the orchestra, or settle the squabbles among boatmen, and colliers, in the pit. My attention was attracted, in one of the deep and most interesting scenes in *Jane Shore*, by a hoarse vulgar voice, crying out, from the gallery, "*Perish thy eyes, don't stay there, snivelling, but goa and send that* FUNNY MAN ON."

STAFFORD : AMATEUR THEATRICALS.

Several gentlemen of Stafford have been performing the tragedy of *Othello*, with the farce of *The Devil to Pay*, for the benefit of poor insolvent debtors, "who," agreeably to the words of their advertisement, "were virtually lost to the world, when a few pounds might restore them to their original value, and estimation, in society." The receipts of the house were eighty-five pounds eight shillings, by means of which several of the most deserving of these unfortunate prisoners will be restored to the blessing of freedom. This is a circumstance which does great credit to the city of Stafford, and furnishes a most worthy example to the lovers of theatricals, in other places. The different characters were respectably sustained. The prices were raised on the occasion, which was excused by a motto from Shakspeare :

Charity, like " mercy, is not strain'd ;
It droppeth, as the gentle rain from heaven,
Upon the place beneath."

* The spirited intelligence of this correspondent cannot but be kindly received, and gratefully, acknowledged.

THEATRE, STOURPORT, WORCESTERSHIRE.

Mr. Crisp's company have lately opened here, but with very indifferent success. Master Crisp, the most successful of the second Rosciuses, is a brother of the manager of this company, and has been introduced in his circuit. The relationship being known, the people suspected its being a run on their credulity, and, though he has played Master Betty's characters at most of the same theatres, with nearly an equal degree of success, he performed under his brother to silent four and five pound houses! So much for the discrimination of audiences. Stourport has not been accustomed to theatrical performances. Two boatmen, going into the pit one night, when there were few people in the house, after remaining a short time, returned and stood at the door; when, one of their brethren coming up, asked them if the play had begun. They replied, " No ;" and advised him not to go in at present, as there were two gentlemen just come in (meaning on the stage) who seemed to have some *private business with each other.* The principal fiddler in this company is occasionally an actor, and, when his parts are very short, he stands up and delivers his part of the dialogue in the orchestra.

THE WREXAM THEATRE has lately closed. Mrs. Bew, in this company, is an actress of considerable merit. Miss John-stone, though very young, is a handsome stage figure, and a pretty dancer.

THEATRE AT DRAYTON, SHROPSHIRE. This theatre opened on the 8th of May, under the management of Mr. Stanton. At the performance of Pizarro, a few years ago, at this place, when the high priests were addressing the sun, it unfortunately *took fire*, and the manager, who was officiating, first implored his deity—" Oh, power divine !"—then called out to the people behind—" D—n your e—s, put out the sun." The manager, alas, continued to swear, and the sun to blaze, to the no small amusement of the audience.

AN ESSAY ON STAGE COSTUME.

Of the enchanting effects produced by the dramatic art the public testify their great sensibility, by the delight with which they spend their time and money to procure for themselves such pleasures. To witness the working of the passions is the grand source of entertainment; but it has essential and seducing auxiliaries, among which the reality and the precision of decoration may justly rank, as the first. In proportion as the illusion is complete, the delight of the spectator is increased.

It is almost within the memory of man that the negligence, or rather total neglect, of costume was so great as for the most absurd and ridiculous errors to be nightly practised, on the stage. In France, Italy, and England, the heroes of Greece and Rome were every where though differently caricatured, in their external appearance. In one place, they had short hooped petticoats; in another, full-bottomed wigs; and in a third, cast court dresses, bought in Monmouth-street at London, and *La Fripperie* at Paris, or obtained by such means as were within the power of the players.

A more accurate investigation of this subject has every where lately begun to be encouraged. Numerous absurdities still prevail; but they are less violent, and daily diminishing. Mr. J. P. Kemble, and Mr. Johnson, machinist at Drury Lane, have judiciously and meritoriously contributed to their reform, which has been promoted also by many others.

A rational, and we may say almost exquisite part of the delight, which a spectator receives, is that of having his mind suddenly transported to all the appearances of time and place, which agree with the descriptions given by the poet.

If the scene be in Turkey, what coincidence, what immediately just associations, and what stealing pleasures come over the mind, at beholding mosques, minarets, flowing robes, turbans, and mustachios, with all the appurtenances that belong to them! It is no longer a playhouse, or a player, but reality itself: no fiction of the poet, but an action, that passes in sight and hearing, in which every thing so corresponds that the conviction of its existence cannot be resisted.

Another night, the scene lies in the age of chivalry, and the architecture, habits, and manners, of our famed ancestors rise in view: the solemn Gothic hall, lances, helmets, and armour; or, if these be not worn, the dresses of the age are seen.

Russians, Tartars, or nations of the East, perhaps rise to view; no matter from what quarter of the globe, be it Lapland, China, Peru, the woolly Negro, or the straight-haired Hindoo; and each country is more easily realized by appearances than by language. Their dress and colour scarcely can be mistaken; their idioms, sentiments, and passions, are difficult indeed to seize.

These being facts, it follows that one essential branch of the study of the drama, for stage representation, is costume; and, for this reason, considerable expence and trouble have been incurred, in the present work, to diffuse accurate knowledge on this subject. Those who imagine that the plates of costume have been given merely as pretty pictures, to invite purchasers, are greatly mistaken in the views with which the Theatrical Recorder is undertaken. As far as the author has the ability, it is intended to be a classical Repertory, for every thing appertaining to the drama; of which costume appears to be an essential part. If the scene be laid in India, among the Hindoos and converted Mahomedans, the plates that have been given, and that will appear, it is presumed, will furnish nearly complete examples of the different classes, or casts, which the poet may have occasion to introduce. The figures on this subject, are transcripts, done from engravings made and published in India. When this costume is complete, another will be given.

It would be less expensive and much more easy, to give pretended representations of this or that actor, in any favorite and impassioned character: but how few of these vaunted figures have had any the least resemblance to truth and nature? Of what value have they been? If we except a few masterly performances, by great artists, the residue are not worthy to be pasted on fire-screens.

If figures of costume have nothing else in their favor, they have at least the merit of being faithful, with respect to dress and picturesque effect; and have therefore a certain and invariable value.

It is not in the least intended to blame those who may think, or have thought, differently; but it is hoped they will coolly exercise their judgment, and examine the nature and the utility of the subject.

TO CORRESPONDENTS.

The Editor respectfully returns thanks to W. R. both for the friendly intention of his letter and the good opinion he is pleased to express. With respect to the subject of it, he takes the liberty to refer him to the above Essay on Costume, which he hopes will convince him and every reader that a collection of figures displaying the costume of the various nations of the earth will, if formed, become a useful source of instruction and amusement.

MONTHLY LIST, FOR APRIL AND MAY, 1805.

DRURY-LANE.

APRIL
29. The Country Girl (Benefit. Mr.
  Bannister) - - - - - - - - - Personation, and Comus.
30. The Honey Moon - - - - - - - The Soldier's Return.

MAY
1. The Wonder - - - - - - - - - - Ditto.
2. King Richard III. (Benefit. The
  Young Roscius) - - - - - - - - The Prize.
3. First Love - - - - - - - - - - - The Soldier's Return.
4. The Venetian Outlaw - - - - - Ditto.
6. Ditto - - - - - - - - - - - - - - Ditto.

7. The Belles' Stratagem - - - - - The Soldier's Return.
8. The Venetian Outlaw. - - - - - Sylvester Daggerwood, and Ditto.
9. First Love - - - - - - - - - - - Ditto.
10. The Honey Moon - - - - - - - The Devil to Pay.
11. The Beggar's Opera - - - - - - Bon Ton.
13. All in the Wrong (Benefit. Miss
          De Camp) - - - - - - - - - The Castle of Sorrento.
14. The Wheel of Fortune (by Com.) The Anatomist.
15. The Soldier's Daughter (Benefit.
          Mrs. Mountain) - - - - - - All for Fame, and The Poor Soldier.
16. The Country Girl - - - - - - The Soldier's Return.
17. Know your own Mind (Benefit.
          Miss Duncan) - - - - - - - The Scotch Ghost, and Rosina.
18. The Honey Moon - - - - - - - The Soldier's Return.
20. As You Like It (Benefit. Mrs.
          Jordan) - - - - - - - - - - Matrimony.
21. The Merry Wives of Windsor
          (Benefit. Mr. Palmer, Miss
          Mellon) - - - - - - - - - - True Lover's Knot, and The Castle of
                                      Sorrento.
22. The School for Scandal (Benefit.
          Miss Pope) - - - - - - - - Personation, and Comus.
23. The Wonder - - - - - - - - - The Soldier's Return.
24. Crazy Jane (Benefit. Mr. Kelly) Youth, Love, and Folly, and Blanche
                                      Queen of Castile.

COVENT-GARDEN.

APRIL
29. Hamlet (Master Betty) - - - - The Village Lawyer.
30. Who wants a Guinea? - - - - - Lock and Key.
MAY
1. Ditto - - - - - - - - - - - - - Harlequin Quicksilver.
2. Ditto - - - - - - - - - - - - - Ditto.
3. Ditto - - - - - - - - - - - - - The Review.
4. Douglas (Master Betty) - - - - Honest Thieves.
6. Tancred and Sigismunda - - - - The Prisoner at Large.
7. Who wants a Guinea? - - - - - Peeping Tom.
8. King Richard the Third - - - - The Miser.
9. Fontainbleau (Benefit. Mr. Incle-
          don) - - - - - - - - - - - - The Priest of the Parish, and Animal
                                      Magnetism.
10. Zara - - - - - - - - - - - - - The Priest of the Parish.
11. Douglas (Master Betty) - - - - Ditto.
13. Hamlet (Ditto) - - - - - - - - Ditto.
14. The School of Reform (Benefit.
          Mr. Munden) - - - - - - - Ramah-Droog.
15. Douglas (Master Betty) - - - - The Priest of the Parish.
16. The Surrender of Calais - - - - The Lake of Lausanne.
17. Barbarossa (Master Betty) - - - Marian.
18. Douglas (Ditto) - - - - - - - The Tale of Mystery.
20. Hamlet (Ditto) - - - - - - - - The Miser.
21. Douglas (Ditto) - - - - - - - - Rosina.
22. Othello (Ben. Mrs. Litchfield) - British Fortitude, and The Irish Widow.
23. Hamlet (Benefit. Master Betty) The Jew and the Doctor.
24. The Cabinet (Benefit. Mr. Hill) The Lake of Lausanne.

END OF THE FIRST VOLUME.

INDEX

TO

THE FIRST VOLUME.

———

1

DRAMATIC COMPOSITION, AN ESSAY ON - - 139

DRAMATIC TRANSLATIONS.

Comedies.

Tragedies.

NEW PIECES AND PERFORMERS.